OXFORD ENGLISH MEMOIRS AND TRAVELS

General Editor: James Kinsley

Anecdotes and Characters
of the Times

Alexander Carlyle in 1770 by David Martin

ALEXANDER CARLYLE

Anecdotes and Characters
of the Times

Edited with an Introduction by

James Kinsley

LONDON
OXFORD UNIVERSITY PRESS
NEW YORK   TORONTO
1973

Oxford University Press, Ely House, London W. 1

GLASGOW   NEW YORK   TORONTO   MELBOURNE   WELLINGTON
CAPE TOWN   IBADAN   NAIROBI   DAR ES SALAAM   LUSAKA   ADDIS ABABA
DELHI   BOMBAY   CALCUTTA   MADRAS   KARACHI   LAHORE   DACCA
KUALA LUMPUR   SINGAPORE   HONG KONG   TOKYO

ISBN 0 19 255414 X

Introduction, Notes, Chronology, and Index
© Oxford University Press 1973

Printed in Great Britain
by W & J Mackay Limited, Chatham

Contents

0355774

63536

Illustrations[1]

[1] See note on p. xxii

Introduction

FROM 1748 until his death in 1805 Alexander Carlyle was minister of
Inveresk, a pleasant lowland parish overlooking the sea near Edinburgh.
He wrote his *Anecdotes and Characters* during the last few years of his
life, in part from diaries and journals but mainly out of a remarkable
memory. The character which emerges from his papers is epitomized
with love, but without exaggeration, in the epitaph written for his tomb
by the philosopher Adam Ferguson:

Born on the 26th of January 1722. Deceased on the 25th of August 1805. Having thus
lived in a period of great lustre to the country, in arts and arms, in literature and
science, in freedom, religious and civil, he too was worthy of the times; learned and
eloquent, liberal and exemplary in his manners, faithful to his pastoral charge: not
ambitious of popular applause, but to the people a willing guide in the ways of
righteousness and truth. In his private connections, a kind relation, an assiduous
friend, and an agreeable companion; not immersed in speculation, but earnest in
action, to promote the merit he esteemed or the public cause he espoused; and, when
full of years, calmly prepared to die in peace.

It is proper to recall this record of a faithful ministry, for *Anecdotes and
Characters* is neither a manse journal nor a spiritual autobiography.
Carlyle's account even of the Kirk is political and social; his central
theme is not God, but men and manners. He neither prayed without
ceasing nor preached the gospel out of season. He was 'worthy of the
times' not merely because he moved with affectionate intimacy (and
often with effectual wisdom) amongst great men—Argyll, the third
Duke of Buccleugh (the agricultural 'improver'), Robert Adam the
architect, the actor Garrick, the philosophers David Hume, Ferguson,
and Adam Smith, Smollett the novelist, Robertson the historian,
Charles Townshend (whom Burke called 'the delight and ornament of
the House of Commons'), Lord Chancellor Wedderburn, the law lords of
Edinburgh—but because in this silver age of Scotland and the Kirk he
was an exemplar of liberal thinking, civilized living, and common sense.
   Carlyle's liberalism was exercised chiefly in the General Assembly of
the Kirk and in ecclesiastical society. 'There was a few of us', he says,

who besides the Levity of Youth and the Natural Freedom of our Manners, had an express Design to throw Contempt on that vile Species of Hypocrisy, which magnified an Indecorum into a Crime, and Gave an Air of false Sanctimony and Jesuitism to the Greatest part of the Clergy, and was thereby pernicious to Rational Religion. In this plan we Succeeded: For in the Midst of our Freedom, having preserv'd respect, and attain'd a Leading in the Church, we freed the Clergy from many unreasonable and Hypocritical restraints.[1]

Some of the scenes in which Carlyle and his friends had a liberal role are to us trivial or farcical—making it unnecessary for ministers to play cards behind locked doors, or, in the controversy over Home's tragedy of *Douglas*, establishing their right to attend the theatre. They can hardly have intended to create the climate in which the Assembly of 1784 had to meet on alternate days, when Mrs. Siddons was not appearing on the Edinburgh stage; but they did resist 'not merely . . . a Fanatical but an Illegal Exertion of Power, which would have stampd Disgrace on the Church of Scotland, kept the younger Clergy for half a Century Longer in the trammels of Bigotry or Hypocrisy, and Debar'd every Generous Spirit from entering into Orders.'[2]

They did more: they set a social standard for the clergy, both in discreet conviviality and in keeping polite company. Till this time, says Carlyle, Presbyterian ministers were 'Seldom admitted into Liberal Society'; 'a Clergyman was thought Prophane who affected the Manners of Gentlemen or was much Seen in their Company'. His friend Smollett heard with mortification that Carlyle was to be ordained to a 'Gothick Dilemma' in which he could neither improve his taste nor indulge his 'Spirit', but wondered whether 'there may be Douceurs in the Life of a Scottish Parson which I little dream of'. Carlyle had indeed his 'Douceurs'. He was admired by a servant at Pinkieburn for walking home, 'dacent man, as steady as a wall, after his ain share o' five bottles o' port', and the variety of his drink on the eve of the Battle of Prestonpans is worth remark—part of a bowl of whisky punch, a quarter share in a bottle of claret and four of burgundy, between two and five in the afternoon. But he knew where to draw a line, and deplored the 'Dissipation of manners' in Dr. Webster ('Dr. Bonum Magnum').[3] In an age of heroic self-indulgence—David Hume described himself as less gourmet than glutton[4]—Carlyle appreciated food of high quality and moderate

---

[1] p. 124.   [2] pp. 148, 163, 160.

[3] pp. 127, 67, 124; Smollett's *Letters*, ed. L. M. Knapp (1970), p. 4; J. H. Burton's edition of Carlyle (1910), pp. 250–1.

[4] 'Mrs. Baron Mure, who spoke a great deal but always to the purpose, looking out of a window when a knot of Scots authors were passing, and a friend bidding her observe the *literati*:– "You may rather call them the *Iterati* (Eaterati)", said she' (Henry McKenzie, *Anecdotes and Egotisms 1745–1831* (1927), p. 179).

cost. But eating and drinking were valued chiefly as stimulants of animated talk. Carlyle disapproved of 'Triffling . . . Tittle Tattle'—unlike even David Hume, whose 'capacious mind was fill'd with Infantine Anecdotes'; and everywhere in his memorials is a delight in convivial argument and wit. Carlyle was a member of the Select Society and the Poker Club, and says that 'free Conversation' at the 'Select' was more improving than the speeches: 'those Meetings . . . Rub'd off all Corners as we call it, by Collision'. He enjoyed 'Leading Minds', and his 'Neighbours and Companions of the first Rank in point of Mind and Erudition'.[5] But he moved as easily among the great as he did among the learned, making a 'prodigious impression among the courtiers' in London not only by his splendid appearance[6] but by 'the soundness of his sense, his honourable principles, and his social qualities'.[7] He was accused of being over-fond of high society; yet 'the aristocracy liked him; the two met half-way, and he . . . could hold his own with them'. His motive was neither selfish nor trivial. It seems, says Burton with little exaggeration,

to have been his one and peculiar ambition that he should dignify his calling by bringing it forth into the world, and making for it a place along with rank, and wealth, and distinction of every kind. This object he carried through with a high hand; and scarcely a primate of the proud Church of England could overtop in social position and influence the Presbyterian minister of Inveresk.[8]

During one of his excursions into polite society (at Buxton in 1778), Carlyle argued with Princess Dashkoff for 'the Superiority of Edinburgh as a Residence to most other Cities in Europe' (a common delusion with Edinburgh citizens): but she gave him 'the Precedency' in only one thing, 'that of all the Sensible Men I have met with in my Travels thro' Europe yours at Edinburgh are the most Sensible'.[9] Common sense was indeed the leading quality in these *literati* (despite their

[5] pp. 266, 150 note, 104.
[6] 'The grandest demi-god I ever saw,' Scott told Lockhart in 1818, 'was Dr. Carlyle . . . commonly called *Jupiter Carlyle*, from having sat more than once for the king of gods and men to Gavin Hamilton—and a shrewd, clever old carle was he, no doubt' (Lockhart, *Life of Sir Walter Scott*, 1914 edn., iii. 182).
[7] Chief Commissioner Adam, quoted in Burton, op. cit., p. 596. Cf. Lord Cockburn, *Memorials of his Time*, 1946 edn., p. 46: Carlyle's 'hold over his friends was derived from the charm of his private manners, which were graceful and kind. And he was one of the noblest looking old gentlemen I almost ever beheld.'
[8] op cit., pp. 569, 603. Cf. William Neil's essay on Carlyle in *Fathers of the Kirk* (1960), pp. 118–29: 'In his view the Church of Scotland must be identified with the whole life of the nation, and not merely with its devotional exercises . . . They would not perhaps have recognized the modern slogan "whole salvation not soul salvation", but in their own day that was what the Moderates stood for.'
[9] p. 215.

extravagant habit of describing one another as 'Men of Genius').[10] It marks the *Anecdotes* on almost every page. Thus Carlyle drily depreciates the cloistered appetite of the young Lord Selkirk for the classics: 'The Effect of [this] was, That with much Rectitude and Good Intention, and some Talents, he came into the World more fit to be a Professor than an Earl'. Carlyle displays political sense and tact in coping with Charles Townshend's foolish ambition, and a humorous prudence in dealing with the scruples of Robertson.[11] In all the complicated business of presbytery and Assembly, he has always a clear sight of the issues and a facility in argument and manoeuvre. The great Duke of Argyll, having once or twice given Carlyle his head in conversation and observed him from under his black sleeping-cap, resolved to nominate him Principal of Glasgow University, to 'manage That troublesome Society'.[12]

The Duke, however, probably saw something deeper than common sense and tact. Carlyle had (and knew it) what he calls 'Decernment . . . of characters'. David Hume lacked this, and so did Adam Smith, despite his readiness to 'Draw them'; Adam Ferguson's disparaged *History* is to be defended because it was 'more profound in Research into Characters, and Gave a more Just Delineation of them, than any Book now extant'. Carlyle relished this faculty of discernment in himself, and knew that it had grown out of his rich social experience: '. . . tho' I had been in London before . . . Yet I had not till then [1758] seen such a variety of Characters, nor had I acquird such a Talent for Observation, nor possess'd a Line for Sounding the Depths of the Human Character, Commensurate to that purpose as I now had.'[13] For him, human character and conduct were a source not only of instruction but of delight; in this he is akin to Smollett, and to Scott who took pleasure in the 'attitudes' of criminals in the courts. So the landlord at Yarmouth, where Carlyle stopped on his way to Holland in 1745, 'Entertain'd me much, for he had been several Years a Mate in the Mediteranean in his Youth, and was vain and Boastfull, and presumptuous, and Ignorant to my Great Delight'. Returning from London in 1769 with a 'Lad Being Fantastick and Vain, because he had an Uncle who was under Door Keeper to the House of Commons', Carlyle and John Home 'took him Stage about . . . To Enjoy him'. David Hume's 'Conversation was truly Irresistable, For while it was enlighten'd it was naive almost to puerility'.[14]

---

[10] Cf. David Hume, the only one whose title is beyond dispute: 'Really it is admirable how many Men of Genius this Country produces at present . . . the People most distinguish'd for Literature in Europe' (*Letters*, ed. J. Y. T. Greig, 1932, i. 255).

[11] pp. 43, 197–8, 242.   [12] pp. 194–5.

[13] pp. 140, 142, 144, 195.   [14] pp. 83, 267, 139.

Introduction

To Carlyle's humorous interest in people, his 'Decernment', sympathy, and profound sense, we owe invaluable portraits of Wilkes and Townshend in their student days at Leyden; one of John Home which explains his success at court and is, in concentration and phrase, almost a seventeenth-century 'character'—

he was very Handsome and had a fine person, about 5 F. 10½ Inches, and an agreable catching address. He had not much Wit and still less Humour, but he had so much Sprightlyness and Vivacity, and such an expression of Benevolence in his Manner, and such an unceasing Flattery of those he lik'd (and he never kept company with any Body else), the kind Commendations of a Lover, not the adulation of a Sycophant, That he was truly Irresistable, and his Entry to a Company was Rec'd, like letting in the Sun into a Dark Room;

one of Dr. Webster which, for its tone and judgment, might have been written by Bishop Burnet—

He could pass at once from the most unbounded Jollity to the most fervent Devotion; Yet I believe that his Hypocrisy was no more than Habit Grounded merely on Temper, and that his aptness to pray, was as Easy and Natural to him, as to Drink a Convivial Glass. His familiar Saying however, that it was his Lot to Drink with Gentlemen and to Vote with Fools, made too full a Discovery of the Laxity of his Mind. Indeed he liv'd too Long to preserve any Respect: For in his Latter Years his Sole Object seem'd to be where to find Means of Inebriety; which he at last too often Effected, for his Constitution having lost its vigour, he was sent home almost every evening, like other Drunkards who could not boast of Strength;

and informal, witty and affectionate sketches of Hume, Adam Smith, Robertson, and Blair.[15] (The carefully balanced 'Comparison' of Robertson and Blair 'After the Manner of Plutarch'[16] is biographically interesting, but has far less human appeal than the relaxed reminiscence of the *Anecdotes*.)

Like many of his friends Carlyle was an accomplished rhetorician. But there is little 'style' in the *Anecdotes*. What we savour in both narrative and 'characters' is the quality of shrewd, humorous, fully engaged *talk*, seasoned with dry wit (I suspect that the best passages had often been tried out over the claret before they were written down):

He Conversd none. . . I thought I might try to *Examine him*, and put a Question to him as we Enterd the Church Yard, which he Answer'd when we Got to the Far End of the Glebe. His Wife however made it well up. This with other Instances Convinc'd me that it would have been better if the Wives had Preach'd and their Husbands Spun.

. . . a Good Sensible Man, But with not many Words or Topicks of Conversation, for he was a Great Mathematician.

There arose much murmuring in the Parish against me as too Young, and too full of Levity . . . together with many Doubts about my Having the Grace of God, (an Occult Quality, which the People cannot Define).

Lindsay was . . . a first Rate at the Science of Defence in Raillery; he was too Goodnatur'd to attack. He had the Knack not only of pleasing fools with themselves, but of making them tolerable to the Company.[17]

Carlyle was a man of great generosity and sympathy. But these qualities are balanced, as they have to be in pastoral ministry, by hard, realistic detachment. A fine instance is his handling of the hypersensitive John Home, who lost a friend and a brother at the same time. Carlyle exhausts Home's stock of grief before he tells him the worst news; gets him 'taken up with [a] Suit of Mourning' the next day; and remarks:

there are very Superior Minds on which the Loss of Friends makes very little Impression. He was not Likely to feel more on any Future Occasion than on this: For as People Grow Older, not only Experience Hardens them to Such Events, but Growing Daily more Selfish, They feel less for other People.[18]

His charity can be delicate, as when he keeps silence after Robertson fails him over the Clerkship of the Assembly: 'I did not Chuse to put an old Friend to the Trial of Making his Fault Greater by a Lame Excuse.' There are rare moments when his spiritual strength comes through. He writes of his dead children, 'It was the Will of Heaven that I should lose them too Soon—But to Reflect on their Promising Qualities ever since, has been the Delight of Many a Watchfull Night and Melancholy Day. I Lost them Before they had Given me any Emotions but those of Joy and Hope:' a resourceful fortitude worthy to set beside that of the Covenanting professor, James Wodrow, who thanked God 'for the loan of my son Sandy for thirty years'.[19]

Carlyle wrote down 'Certain Facts . . . That may be Subservient to a Future Historian, if not to Embellish his Page, yet to keep him within the Bounds of Truth and Certainty'. To this category belong the sketches of Edinburgh's professional men, the academic and mercantile society of Glasgow, the Porteous riot and the Forty-Five, and the politics of the Kirk. But 'Facts' aside, the *Anecdotes* offers us a long series of moments vividly seen, acutely heard, and intensely felt: the escape of Robertson and the ensuing Porteous débâcle before the eyes of the lad from the country; the pathetic-comic picture of young Kinloch marching against the Highlanders, recalling Livy's *Gens Fabii* and being rebuked for discouraging the men; the circumstantial account of the prelude to the Battle of Prestonpans, through which Carlyle moves with busy irrelevance to his own ironic climax—the battle is over as he gets out of bed; the farce of Home's departure for London with the manuscript of *Douglas*; Carlyle and Home, on their way to golf with Garrick, accidentally

[17] pp. 49, 107, 134–5.   [18] p. 152.
[19] pp. 146, 271; H. G. Graham, *The Social Life of Scotland in the Eighteenth Century* (1950), p. 347.

reviewing the Coldstream Guards who 'Seeing our Clubs Gave us 3 cheers in Honour of a Diversion peculiar to Scotland'—sheer Boswell, this; the dramatic demise of the Revd. Dr. Jardine during the Assembly, at which Carlyle, 'anxious to know the Truth', learnt it and mendaciously reported 'hopes of his Recovery' in order that the vote might proceed....[20]

Behind these comic narratives, however, and behind the records of 'Triffling' conversation and intrigue, a lively reader will hear echoes of the other voice of 'Jupiter' Carlyle, who thus addressed the Assembly on clergy pay, to his own honour and that of his friends:

I must confess that I do not love to hear this Church called a poor Church, or the poorest Church in Christendom. . . . I dislike the language of whining and complaint. We are rich in the best goods a Church can have—the learning, the manners, and the character of its members. . . . Who have wrote the best histories, ancient and modern?—It has been clergymen of this Church. Who has wrote the clearest delineation of the human understanding and all its powers?—A clergyman of this Church. Who has written the best system of rhetoric, and exemplified it by his own orations?—A clergyman of this Church. Who wrote a tragedy that has been deemed perfect?—A clergyman of this Church. Who was the most profound mathematician of the age he lived in?—A clergyman of this Church. . . . Let us not complain of poverty, for it is a splendid poverty indeed! It is *paupertas fecunda virorum*.[21]

[20] pp. 17 ff., 60–1, 73, 152 ff., 174, 239.
[21] Burton, op. cit., p. 589.

Acknowledgements

MY main debt is to Mr. A. Carlyle Bell who, with a liberality worthy of his forbear of Inveresk, gave me permission to use the manuscript as copy-text, and allowed me unrestricted access to the Carlyle papers. I gratefully acknowledge information and advice given by my Nottingham colleagues, Professors J. T. Boulton, Kenneth Cameron, W. R. Fryer, Alastair Smart, and the Revd. Dr. William Neil (who first set Carlyle in the right cultural context); Professor William Beattie and the staff of the National Library of Scotland; Mr. J. M. Fewster of the Department of Paleography, University of Durham; Miss Ann Harrison, Librarian-Archivist at the Manx Museum; Mr. R. E. Hutchison, Keeper of the National Portrait Gallery of Scotland; my former schoolmaster, Dr. Alexander Law; the Revd. Professor James S. McEwen, Aberdeen; Prof. Dr. Frits Storms of the Katholieke Universiteit, Nijmegen; the editorial staff of Oxford University Press; and my wife, Helen Kinsley.

Note on the Text

THE autograph of *Anecdotes and Characters of the Times* (Carlyle's title, misleadingly altered to *Autobiography* by his first editor John Hill Burton in 1860) is now in the possession of Mr. A. Carlyle Bell. With his permission it has been used as copytext for this edition.

The Carlyle papers in the National Library of Scotland include:

1. A transcript of Carlyle's *Recollections*—a discursive account of events in his life 1723–37—with a supplement on 1738 written, according to Principal Lee of Edinburgh, in the summer of 1805; MS. 3463.

2. A transcript of *Anecdotes and Characters*, defective at the beginning, together with 'Paragraphs in the Original omitted in the Copy'; MS. 3462.

3. A transcript of *Anecdotes and Characters*, including the opening pages which are missing from MS. 3462, extracts from *Recollections*, and (ff. 404–44) the journal of Carlyle's tour of the North in 1765; MS. 3732.

4. Journals for the years 1771–1804, of the Highland tour, and of visits to London (1769) and Buxton (1778); sermons; speeches to the General Assembly; verse; correspondence (see Henry W. Meikle, *Times Literary Supplement*, 24 July 1943); the *Comparison* of Blair and Robertson, printed *infra*, pp. 277–82; a catalogue of Carlyle's library.

The autograph of *Anecdotes and Characters* is written in a series of seven notebooks:

1. An account of the 'Stipend of Inveresk as it was allocated in March 1781 Having Been Modify'd at £62—Money, Two Chalders of Wheat, Three Chalders of Barley, and Three Chalders of Oats. Communion Elements Included. The Grain to be paid at the Rate of the Highest Fiars of Midlothian', listing the heritors' contributions in cash and kind (pp. 1–19); 2 blank pages; the beginning of *Anecdotes*, dated Musselburgh 26 January 1800, and written on numbered rectos with supplementary notes, additions &c. on facing

versos (pages numbered 1–67, 53 omitted). The text tails off in the midst of an account of Professor Leechman (*infra*, p. 35). It is followed by a three-page list of fruit trees planted at Inveresk in 1786–90 and 1794.

2. A notebook 'got . . . on the 5ᵗʰ of Janʸ 1802', starting again with Carlyle's admission to the University of Glasgow in November 1743 and his 'character' of Leechman, the text again written on rectos (numbered 1–50) and facing versos. The narrative runs to 1745 (*infra*, p. 73).

3. The story continued without preamble, written on rectos with facing notes as before; continuing page numbering 51–96 (nos. 64, 65, 86 are repeated, no. 83 is omitted); and ending (at 1748) with the account of 'Lungs' Anderson at the top of a verso (*infra*, p. 115).

4. Continuing 'In Winter 1748 . . .'; headed 'Began July 1ˢᵗ 1803'; again written mainly on rectos, numbered 97–141 and running to the end of 1757 (*infra*, p. 167).

5. Beginning 'Early in the Year 1758 . . .'; rectos numbered 142–157 and (with no break in the text) 178–207; ending mid-1762 (*infra*, p. 217).

6. Continuing 'As we were to Go Round by Dumfries'; rectos numbered 208–225 and (again erroneously) 229–52 (nos. 211 and 216 repeated, 214 repeated after 215, 246 repeated); ending mid-1769 (*infra*, p. 270), 'the Manly System of the President'.

7. Rectos numbered 253–7; the final paragraphs in the hand of an amanuensis (*infra*, pp. 273–4).

Anecdotes and Characters, then, was written down slowly between the years 1800 and 1804 or 1805. Some of the narrative was based on diaries and journals (though Carlyle's diaries are mere memoranda, dates and names jotted down); and this probably accounts for his precise recollection of meals and their cost at a distance of half a century and more. But a great deal was set down from memory—a prodigious feat for a man of eighty: he confesses to remembering outward journeys far better than homeward ones (p. 248); he regrets not having 'Drawn a Journal' of his travels in 1758 (p. 191); he remembers sixteen of his fellow-students at Leyden in 1745 but forgets the names of a further half-dozen (p. 86). Sustained circumstantial narratives like those of the Porteous riot and the Forty-Five may have been written down soon after the event, and incorporated in *Anecdotes*. I think it likely, too, that the minister of Inveresk, accustomed to reminiscence among his friends and schooled (in the Scotch fashion) to preaching and public prayer without copy, shaped much of the Anecdotes in conversation before he took up his pen in 1800.

Except in a few places where Carlyle himself noticed some disorder, I have followed the sequence of the manuscript. One or two passages which Carlyle repeats in substance are given once only, and the repetitions are recorded in the notes. Hill Burton (1910) incorporated verso additions in the text; I have presented them as they appear in the manuscript, as supplementary notes. This arrangement would be merely distracting pedantry if these passages were in the main revisions and interpolations which Carlyle would have worked into his text had he lived to finish it in fair copy; but many of them are second thoughts, supplementary (and often tangential) information, and conscious digressions. I hope that my arrangement of this material will enable the reader to see more clearly both the shape of the manuscript and the way in which Carlyle's mind and memory worked.

The spellings of the manuscript have been preserved, except for obvious errors out of line with Carlyle's own practice. The long 's' and other scribal devices have been modernized. Most of Carlyle's numerous abbreviations have been expanded; I have retained those which, by their frequency and economy, cumulatively reduce the bulk of the text without baffling the reader. I have modified Carlyle's punctuation only where the text might otherwise be ambiguous or unintelligible. I have retained most of the original capitalization, since this often indicates emphasis; but I have ignored Carlyle's almost systematic initial capitals in 'He', 'Him', 'Her' &c., as I found this, in reading and re-reading, a persistent cause of false emphasis. (I should perhaps add in self-defence that it is often difficult to distinguish Carlyle's capitals and lower-case letters.)

Carlyle sat up all night to review Home's *Agis*, and 'was Oblig'd to Give it to the press Blotted and Interlin'd. But they are accustom'd to Decypher the Most Difficult hands' (p. 182). I hope I have not disappointed this expectation. His manuscript is in many places very difficult to read—and not only because of his awkward hand, his worn-out pens, and the effects of time, but also because of deletions and erasures by the author and over-writing and annotation by others. I have made guesses where these seemed safe enough in the context, and where guidelines survived in the manuscript; in a few places I have had to be content with a lacuna. Gaps left by Carlyle are so recorded; my uncertain readings, emendations, and interpolations are in square brackets.

Note on the Illustrations

MY frontispiece is a romantic portrait of Carlyle painted by Allan Ramsay's pupil David Martin (1737–98) in London in 1769–70 (by courtesy of A. Carlyle Bell, Esq!); 'it looks', said Carlyle, 'like a Cardinal . . . so gorgeously dressed . . . in a pink damask nightgown in a scarlet chair. Martin thinks it will do him more good than all the pictures he has done'. The portraits of Carlyle and his wife on p. [184] are also by Martin (again by courtesy of Mr. Carlyle Bell). The splendid picture of Carlyle in old age (p. [185]) was painted by Archibald Skirving (died 1819 at Inveresk); reproduced by courtesy of the Scottish National Portrait Gallery, Edinburgh.

The portraits of Carlyle's friends are: W. Millar's John Home (p. [72]; 1762; by courtesy of the Scottish National Portrait Gallery); Allan Ramsay's David Hume (p. [73]; 1754; by courtesy of H. I. T. Gunn, Esq!, W.S.); James Tassie's paste medallion of Adam Smith in 1787 (p. [88]; by courtesy of the Scottish National Portrait Gallery); Reynolds' William Robertson (p. [89]; exhibited at the Royal Academy in 1772; by courtesy of the Scottish National Portrait Gallery); Raeburn's Hugh Blair (p. [168]; by courtesy of the Revd. Dr. Ronald Selby Wright, Manse of the Canongate, Edinburgh); Allan Ramsay's third Duke of Argyll (p. [169]; 1749; by courtesy of Glasgow Art Gallery and Museum).

[Other representations of Alexander Carlyle include John Henning's paste medallion (1805; Scottish National Portrait Gallery); a portrait painted by Raeburn for Lord Haddington in 1796 and still in the possession of the Earl of Haddington; two miniatures, by George Sanders and D. M. Murphy, in the possession of Mr Carlyle Bell; Skirving's chalk drawing (Scottish National Portrait Gallery; owned by Inveresk Church); and caricatures in John Kay's *Original Portraits and Caricature Etchings* (1837–8).]

A Chronology of Alexander Carlyle

ALEXANDER CARLYLE

Anecdotes and Characters
of the Times

Having Observ'd how Carelessly and consequently how falsely History is written, I have long Resolv'd to note Down Certain Facts within my own Knowledge, under the Title of *Anecdotes and Characters of the times*, That may be Subservient to a Future Historian, if not to Embellish his Page, yet to keep him within the Bounds of Truth and Certainty.

I have been too late in Beginning this Work, as on this very Day I enter on the 79th Year of my Age; Which Circumstance, as it Renders it not Improbable that I may be Stopt Short in the middle of my Annals, so it will undoubtedly make it Difficult for me to Recall the Memory of many Past Transactions in my Long Life, with that precision, and clearness, which Such a Work Requires. But I will admitt of no more Excuses for Indolence or Procrastination, and Endeavour with Gods Blessing to Serve posterity, to the best of my Ability, with Such a Faithfull Picture of times and Characters, as came within my View in the Humble and Private Sphere of Life, in comparison with that of many others, in which I have always acted: Remembering however That in whatever Sphere of Life men act, The Agents and Instruments are still the same viz. The Faculties and Passions of Human Nature.

The First Characters which I could Discriminate were those of my own Family, which I was able to mark at a very Early Age. My Father was of a Moderate Understanding, of Ordinary Learning and accomplishments for the times, for He was Born in 1690; of a Warm, Open, and Benevolent Temper; most Faithfull and Diligent in the Duties of his Office, and an Orthodox and Popular Orator. He was Entirely Belov'd and much Caress'd by the Whole Parish. My Mother was a person of Superior Understanding, of a Calm and Firm Temper, of an Elegant and reflecting Mind. And considering that she was the Eldest of 7 Daughters and 3 Sons, of a Country Clergyman near Dumfries, and was Born in the [Year] 1700, had Rec'd an Education and Emprov'd by it, far beyond what could have been expected. Good Sense, however and Dignity of

3

Conduct were her chief Attributes. The effect of this, was that she was as much respected, as my Father was Beloved.

They were in very Narrow Circumstances, till the Stipend was largely Augmented in the Year 1732.[1] Two of the Judges, who were his Heritors,[2] L^ds Grange and Drumore, came down from the Bench, and pled his Cause. And the Estate of the Patron, then Morison of Prestongrange, Being under Sequestration, It was with little Difficulty, That a greater Augmentation than was usual at that Period was Obtain'd; For the Stipend was Rais'd by it from £70 to £140 p^r Ann.

[1729]

In the Year 1729 the Good People had a visit from London that prov'd expensive and troublesome. It was a Mrs Lyon, a Sister of my Fathers and her Son and Daughter. Her Deceast Husband was a Mr Lyon of Easter Ogill, a Branch of the Strathmore Family; Who had been in the Rebellion 1715, and having been pardon'd, had attempted to Carry on Business in London, But was ruin'd in the South Sea.[3] This Lady who came down on Business, after a few Weeks, went into Lodgings in Edin^r, where she lost her Daughter in the Smallpox, and Return'd soon after to my Fathers where she Remain'd for some Months; She was Young and Beautifull, and Vain; not so much of her Person, to which she had a Good Title, but of her Husband's Great Family, to which she annex'd her own, and by a little Stretch of Imagination, and a Search into Antiquity made it Great also. Her Son who was a year and an half Older than me, was very Handsome and Goodnatur'd tho' much Indulg'd. My Father was Partial to him, and I grew a little Jealous. But the excess of his Mothers Fondness soon Cur'd my Father of his: and as I was acknowledg'd to be the better Scholar of the two, I soon lost all uneasiness and came to Love my Cousin most sincerely, tho' He intercepted many of the Good things that I should have Got.

Not long after this another Sister of my Fathers Came Down from London, who was a Widow also But had no Children. She staid with us for a Year, for she Taught me to Read English, with the Just pronunciation, and a very tolerable accent, an accomplishment which in Those Days was very Rare.[4] Long before she came down, I had been taught to read, by an Old Woman, who kept a School, so perfectly, that at 6 Years Old, I had read a large Portion of the Bible to a Doz. of Old Women, who having been excluded the Church, by a Crowd, which had made me Leave it also, and whom I observ'd sitting on the Outside of a Door where they could not hear. Upon this I propos'd to read a Portion of Scripture to them, to which they agreed and Set me on a Tomb-Stone, from whence I read very audibly, to a Congregation which encreas'd to about a Score, the whole of the Song of Solomon. This would not Deserve to be noted but for the Effect it had afterwards.[1]

There Liv'd in the Town and Parish of Prestonpans at this time Several Respectable and Wealthy People. Such as the Mathie's, the Hog's, the Youngs, and the Sherriffs. There still remain'd some forreign Trade, Tho' their Shipping was reduc'd from 20 to half the Number since the Union,[2] which put an end to the Forreign Trade in the Ports of the Firth of Forth. There was a Customhouse Establish'd here, the superior officers of which with their Families, added to the Mercantile Class which still Remain'd, made a Respectable Society Enough.

The two Great Men of the Parish however were Morison of Preston-grange the Patron, and the Honourable James Erskine of Grange one of the Supreme Judges. The First was Elected Member of Parliament for East Lothian, in the 1ˢᵗ Parliament of Great Brittain, altho' The Celebrated Andrew Fletcher of Saltoun, was the other Candidate. But Government took Part with Morison, and Fletcher had only 9 Votes. Morison had been very Rich, but had suffer'd himself to be stript by the Famous Gambler of those times Coll! Charteris, whom I once saw with him in church, when I was 5 or 6 years of age, and being fully Impress'd with the Popular Opinion, that his Success at Play was by means of a Compact with the Devil, and that He was a Wizzard, who had a Fascinating Power, I never once took my Eye off him During the Whole Service, Believing that I should be a Dead Man, the Moment I Did. This Simple Gentleman's Estate soon went under Sequestration for the Payment of his Debts, Being one of many whom Coll! Charteris had Ruin'd.* He was so Imaginary and Credulous as to Believe, that close by his Creek of Morison's Haven, was the place where Sᵗ John wrote the Apocalypse, Because some Old Vaults had been Discover'd, in Digging a Mill Race, for a Mill that went by Sea Water. This had Probably been put into his Head, by the

---

* This Coll! Charteris, was of a very Antient Family in Dumfrieshire, The First of whom Being one of the Followers of Robert Bruce, had acquir'd a Great Estate, a small part of which is still in The Family. The Coll! had been otherwise well Connected, for he was Cousin German to Sir Francis Kinloch, and when a Boy was Educated with him at the Village School. Many stories were told of him, which would never have been heard of, Had he not afterwards been so much celebrated in the Annals of Infamy. He was a Great Proffligate No Doubt, But there have been as Bad Men, and Greater Plunderers than He was, who have Escap'd with little Publick Notice. But he was one of the Runners of Sir Robert Walpole, and Defended him in all places of Resort, which Drew the Wrath of the Tories upon, and particularly Sharpen'd the Pens of Pope and Arbuthnot against him. For had it not been for the Witty Epitaph of the Last,[3] Charteris might [have] escap'd in the Croud of Gamesters and Debauchees, who are only Raild at by their Pigeons and soon fall into total Oblivion.

5

Annual Meeting of the oldest Lodge of Operative Masons in Scotland, at that place, on St Johns Day.

My Lord Grange was the Leading Man in the Parish, had brought my Father to Prestonpans, from his Native Country Annandale, where he had been Settled for 4 Years, and where I was Born (at Cumbertrees). Lord Grange was Justice Clerk in the End of Queen Ann's Reign, But had been Dismiss'd from that Office, in the Beginning of Geo. 1.^{sts} Reign, when his Brother the Earl of Mar lost the Secretary of State's Office which he had held for some Years. After this, and During the Rebellion[1] Ld Grange kept close at his House of Preston, on an Estate which he had recently Bought from the Heirs of a Dr Oswald, But which had not long before been the Family Estate, of a very Antient Cadet of the Family of Hamilton. During the Rebellion and sometime after, Ld Grange amus'd himself, in Laying out and Planting a Fine Garden in the Stile of those times, full of close Walks and Labirynths and Wildernesses; which tho' it Did not occupy above 4 or 5 acres cost one at Least two hours to Perambulate. This Garden or pleasure Ground, was soon brought to perfection by his Defending it from the westerly and s. westerly winds, by Hedges of Common Elder, which in a few Years were above 16 Feet high, and Compleatly Shelter'd all the Interior Grounds. This Garden continued to be an Object of Curiosity down to the Year 1740, insomuch that Flocks of Company resorted to it from Edin.^r During the Summer, on Saturdays and Monday's, (for Sunday was not at that time a Day of Pleasure) and were highly Gratifyed by the Sight; There Being nothing at that time like them in Scotland, except at Aloa the Seat of the Earl of Mar, of which indeed they were a Copy in Miniature.

My Lady Grange was Rachel Chiesly, the Daughter of Chiesly of Dalry, the Person who shot President Lockhart in the Dark when standing within the Head of a Close in the Lawn Market,[2] because he had voted against him in a Cause Depending before the Court.* This Lady had been very Beautifull, but was of a Violent Temper. She had it was said been Debauch'd by her Husband before Marriage, and as he was postponing or evading the Performance of his Promise to Marry her, it was Believ'd that by Threatening his Life, she obtain'd the Fulfillment of it.

It was Lord Grange's Custom to go Frequently to London in the

---

* This man was the Son or Grandson, of a Chiesly who in Baillie's Letters is call'd man to the Famous Mr Alex.^r Henderson, That is to say Secretary, for he accompanied Mr Henderson on his Journey to London, and having met the Court somewhere on their way, Chiesley was Knighted by Char. 1.st—So that Being a New Family they must have few Relations, which added to the atrocious Deed of her Father, had made the Publick very Cool in the Interest of Lady Grange.

Spring, and tho' he seem'd Quiet and unactive here, it was suppos'd that he Resented his having been turn'd out of the J. clerks office in 1714, and might Secretly be Carrying on Plots when at London. Be that as it may, he had contracted such a violent aversion at Sir Robert Walpole, That having by Intrigue and Hypocrisy secur'd a Majority of the District of Burghs of which Stirling is the chief, he threw up his Seat as a Judge in the Court of Session, was Elected Member for that District, and went to London to attend Parliament, and to overturn Sir Rob.t W. not merely in his own opinion, but in the opinion of many who were Dupes to his Cunning, and his Pretensions to Abilities that he had not. But his first appearance in the House of Commons, undeceiv'd his Sanguine Friends and silenc'd him for ever.

He chose to make his Maiden Speech on the Witches Bill[1] as it was call'd, and Being Learn'd in Demonologia, with Books on which Subject his Library was fill'd, he made a Long Canting Speech, that set the House in a Titter of Laughter, and convinc'd Sir Robert That he had no Need of any extraordinary Armour against This Champion of the House of Mar. The Truth was that the Man neither had Learning nor Talents nor Ability. He was no Lawyer, He was a Bad Speaker. He had been rais'd on the Shoulders of his Brother the Earl of Mar in the End of the Q.s Reign, but had never Distinguish'd himself. In the Gen.l Assembly[2] itself, which many Gentlemen afterwards made a School of Popular Eloquence, and where he took the High Flying Side that he might annoy Government, his appearances were but rare, and unimpressive. But as he was understood to be a Great Plotter, he was suppos'd to Reserve himself for some Greater Occasions.

In M.r Erskine's annual visits to London he had attach'd himself to a Mistress, a Handsome Scots-woman Fanny Lindsay who kept a Coffee-House about the Bottom of the Hay Market. This had come to his Lady's Ears, which Did not tend to make her less Outragious. He had taken every method to Sooth her—as she Lov'd Command, he had made her Factor upon his Estate, and Gave her the whole Management of his affairs. When absent he wrote her the most Flattering Letters, and what was still more Flattering, he was said when present to have Imparted Secrets to her, which if Disclos'd might have Reach'd his Life. Still she was unquiet, and led him a miserable life. What was true is uncertain, for tho' her outward appearance was stormy and outrageous, Lord Grange not improbably exaggerated the Violence of her Behaviour to his Familiar Friends, as an Apology for what he afterwards Did. For he alleg'd to them that his Life was Hourly in Danger, and that she Slept with Lethal Weapons under her Pillow, and once Shew'd my Father a Razor that he had found conceald there.

Whatever might be the Truth he executed one of the Boldest and most violent Projects, that ever had been attempted, since the Nation was Govern'd by Laws. For he siez'd his Lady in his House in Edin: and by Main Force carried her off thro' Stirling to the Highlands; whence after several weeks, she was at Last Landed in S! Kilda a Desolate Isle in the Western Ocean, 60 Miles Distant from the Long Island. There she continued to Live to the end of her Days, which was not before the Year 17[45] in the most wretched Condition, in the Society of none but Savages and often with scanty provision of the Coarsest Fare, and but rarely Enjoying the Comfort of a Lib.[1] of Tea, which she Got from Ship Masters who accidentally Call'd. Lord Grange's accomplices in this atrocious act were Believ'd to be Lord Lovat, and the Laird of M?Leod, The first as Being the Most Famous Plotter in the Kingdom, and the 2ᵈ as equally unprincipled, and the Proprietor of the Island of S! Kilda. What was most Extraordinary, That except in Conversation for a Few Weeks only, This enormous Act committed in the Midst of the Metropolis of Scotland, by a Person who had been Lᵈ Justice Clerk, was not taken the Least Notice of by any of her own Family, or by the Kings Advocate or Sollicitor, or any of the Guardians of the Laws. Two of her Sons were grown up to Manhood, her Eldest Daughter was the Wife of the Earl of Kintore, who acquiesc'd in what they Consider'd as a necessary act of Justice for the preservation of their Fathers Life. Nay the 2ᵈ Son, was suppos'd to be one of the persons who Came Mask'd to the House, and carried her off in a Chair to the Place where she was set on Horseback. This artfull Man by Cant and Hypocrisy persuaded all his Intimate Friends, That this act was necessary for the preservation of her Life, as well as of his, and that it was only confining a Madwoman in a place of Safety where she was tenderly Car'd for; and for whom he profess'd not merely an affectionate Regard but the most passionate Love. It was many Years afterwards, before it was known that she had been sent to such a Horrid place as S! Kilda; and it was generally believ'd that she was, tho' kept in Confinement, yet comfortably, in some Castle in the Highlands, Belonging to Lovat or M?Leod. The Publick in General tho' Clamorous Enough, yet could take no step, seeing that the Family were not Displeas'd and supposing That Lᵈ Grange had satisfyed the Justice Cl. and other High Officers of the Law with the Propriety of his Conduct.

From what I could Learn at the time and afterwards came to Know, Lᵈ Grange was in one respect a character not unlike Cromwell, and some of his associates—a Real Enthusiast,[2] but at the same time Licentious in his Morals.

He had my Father very frequently with him in the Evenings, when he

8

kept him to very late Hours.* They were understood to pass much of their time in Prayer, and in settling the High Points of Calvinism, For their Creed was that of Geneva. Lord Grange was not unintertaining in Conversation, for he had a great many anecdotes which he Related agreably, and was Fair Complexion'd and Good Looking and Insinuating. After those meetings for private Prayer, however, in which they past Several Hours before Supper, Praying alternatly, They Did not part without Wine. For my Mother us'd to complain of their Late Hours, and suspected that the Claret had Flow'd Liberally. Notwithstanding this Intimacy, There were periods, of half a Year at a time when there was no Intercourse between them at all. My Fathers Conjecture was that at those times he was engag'd in a Course of Debauchery at Edin! and Interrupted his Religious Exercises. For in those Intervals he not only Neglected my Fathers Company, but absented from Church, and Did not attend the Sacrament, Religious exercises, which at other times he would not have Neglected for the World. Report however said, That he and his associates, of whom a M! Michael Menzies, a Brother of the Laird of St Germains, and Tho! Elliot W.S. the Father of Sir John Elliot Physician in London were two, past their time in alternate Scenes of the exercises of Religion and Debauchery.† Some Men are of Opinion that They Could not be Equally Sincere in both. I am apt to think they were, for Human Nature is Capable of wonderfull Freaks. There is no Doubt of their Proffligacy, and I have frequently seem them Drown'd in Tears, During the Whole of a Sacramental Sunday, when so far as my Observation could reach They could have no rational Object in Acting a Part. The Marquiss of Lothian of that Day, whom I have seen attending the Sacrament at Prestonpans with L! Grange, and whom no man Suspected of Plots or Hypocrisy, was much addicted to Debauchery. The Natural Casuistry of the Passions, Grants Dispensations, with more Facility than the Church of Rome.

About this time two or three other Remarkable Men came to Live in the Parish. The Celebrated Coll! Gardiner Bought the Estate of Bank-toun, where L! Drumore had Resided for a Year or two, before he Bought

---

* Those meetings might partly be Calculated to keep Grange free of his Wife's company, which was always stormy and outragious. I remember well that when I was Invited on Saturdays, to pass the afternoon with the two youngest Daughters, Jean and Rachel and their younger Brother John who was my Age then about 6 or 7, altho' they had a well fitted up closet for childrens play, we always kept alternate watches at the Door Lest my Lady should come suddenly upon us, which was needless as I observd to them, for her clamour was sufficiently loud as she came thro' the Rooms and passages.

† Passing the Day in Meetings for Prayers and pious Conversation, and their Nights in Lewdness and Revelling.

the Small Estate of Westpans, which he call'd Drummore, and where he resided till his Death in 1755.

The First Gardiner, who was afterwards kill'd in the Battle of Preston, was a noted Enthusiast—a very weak, Honest, and Brave Man who had once been a Great Rake, and was converted* (as is told in his Life written by Dr Doddridge) by his Reading a Book, call'd Gurnhalls Christian Armour, which his Mother had put in his Trunk many Years before. He had never lookt at it till one Day at Paris, where he was attending the Earl of Stair who was Embassador to that Court from the Year 1715 to the Regents Death, when having an Intrigue with a Surgeons Wife, and the Hour of appointment not being come, he thought he would pass the time in turning over the Leaves of the Book, to see what the Divine could say about Armour, which he Thought he understood as well as him. He was so much taken with this Book, That he allow'd his Hour of appointment to pass, never saw his Mistress more, and from That Day, Left off all his Rakish Habits, which Consisted in Swearing and Whoring (for he never was a Drinker) and the Contempt of Sacred Things, and became a serious Good Christian ever after. Dr Doddridge has marr'd this Story either thro' Mistake, or thro' a Desire to make Gardiners Conversion more Supernatural, For he says that his appointment was at midnight, and Introduces some sort of Meteor or Blaze of Light, that allarm'd the New Convert. But this was not the Case; for I have Heard Gardiner tell the story at least 3 or 4 times,† to Different Sets of People, for he was not Shy or Backward to Speak on the Subject, as many would have been. But it was at Midday, for the Appointment was at one a clock; and he told us the Reason of it, which was that the Surgeon or

---

* As he told my Father. The Leading Circumstances I have frequently heard him repeat when only my Father and I, and the Revd Mr John Glen his Son's Tutor were there. Tho, Dr Doddridge in his acc^t has varied the circumstances.

† and convers'd with my Father upon it after Doddridge Book was publishd, who always persisted in saying that his appointment was at one a clock for the Reason,[1] and that having changd his Lodging he found a Book when Rummaging an old Trunk to the Bottom, which my Father said was Gurnalls Christian Armour but to which Doddridge gives the Name of the Christian Soldier, or Heaven taken by Storm by Thos Watson. Doddridge in a Note says that his Edition of the story was confirm'd in a letter from a Revd Mr Spears, in which there was not the least Difference from the account he had taken down in writing the very night in which the Coll^l had told him the Story. This Mr Spears had been Ld Grange's chaplain, and I knew him to have no great regard to Truth when Deviating from it suited his purpose; at any Rate he was not a Man to Contradict Doddridge, who had most likely told him his Story. It is remarkable That tho' the D^r had wrote every thing down exactly and could take his oath, yet he had omitted to mark the Day of the Week, on which the Conversion happen'd, but if not mistaken, thinks it was Sabbath. This aggravates the Sin of the Appointment, and Hallows the Conversion.

Apothecary, had shown some Symptoms of Jealousy, and they chose a time of Day when he was necessarily Employ'd abroad in his Business. The Coll! who was truly an Honest well meaning Man, and a Pious Christian, was very Ostentatious; Tho' to Tell the Truth, he Boasted oftener of his Conversion than of the Dangerous Battles he had been in. As he told the Story however there was nothing Supernatural in it; For many a Rake of above 30 years of age has been Reclaim'd by some Circumstance that set him a Thinking, as the accidental Reading of this Book had done to Gardiner. He was a very Skillfull Horseman, which had Recommended him to Lord Stair, as a suitable part of his Train when he was Ambassador at Paris, and Liv'd in Great Splendour. Gardiner Married Lady Frances Erskine, one of the Daughters of the Earl of Buchan, a Lively little Deform'd Woman, very Religious and a Great Breeder. There Children were no way Distinguish'd, except the Eldest Daughter Fanny who was very Beautifull, and became the Wife of Sir [William] Baird.

Lord Drumore one of the Judges was a 2ᵈ or 3ᵈ Son of the President Sir Hew Dalrymple of N. Berwick, a Man very popular and agreable in his Manners, and an universal Favourite. He was a Great Friend of the Poor, not merely by giving Alms in which he was not slack, but by Encouraging Agriculture and Manufactures, and by Devoting his spare time in acting as a Justice of Peace, in the two parishes of Inveresk and Prestonpans where his Estate Lay; and Did Much to preserve the peace of the Neighbourhood, and to promote the Police[1] of the Country. It were happy for the Country if every Man of as much Knowledge and Authority as the Judges are suppos'd to have, would lay himself out, as this Good Man Did; By which they might prevent many a Lawsuit that Ends in the Ruin of the Parties. Lᵈ Drumore had many Children.

Mr Robert Keith of Craig, who was afterwards Embassador at Sundry Courts, and who was a Man of Ability and very agreable Manners, came also about this time to Live in the Parish. His Sons Sir Robert Murray Keith K.B. and Sir Basil Keith, were afterwards well known. There Liv'd at the same [time] there Colin Campbell Esq. a Brother of Sir James of Arbruchal, who was Collector of the Customs there, and when he was appointed a Commissioner of the Board of Customs Geo. Cheap Esqr. became his Successor, a Brother of the Laird of Rossie, all of whom had large Families of 7 or 8 Boys and Girls, which made up a Society of Genteel Young People, seldom to be met with in such a place.

When I was very Young I usually past the School Vacation first at Mr Menzies's of Sᵗ Germains and afterwards at Seaton House, when the Family came to Live there upon the Sale of their Estate. I was very often there, as I was a Great Favourite of the Lady's, one of the Sinclairs of

Stevenson, and of her two Daughters who were two or three Years older than I was. These excursions from home, open'd the Mind of a young person, who had some turn for Observation.

[1733]

The first Journey I made however was to Dumfries shire in the Summer 1733, when I was eleven years of age. There I not only became well acquainted with my Grand Father Mr A. Robison a very Respectable Clergyman, and with my Grand Mother Jean Graham and their then unmarried Daughters, But I became well acquainted with the Town of Dumfries, where I resided for several Weeks at Provost Bell's whose Wife was my Mothers Sister, two more of whom were settled in that Town, one of them the Wife of the Clergyman Mr Wight, and the other of the Sheriff Clerk. I was soon very Intimate with a Few Boys of this Town about my own Age, and became a Favourite by Teaching them some of our sports and plays in the Vicinity of the Capital that they had never heard of. At this time too I made a very agreable Tour round the Country with my Father and Mr Robt Jardine the Father of Dr Jardine afterwards Minister of Edin^r. Tho' they were very orthodox and Pious Clergymen, they had both of them a very great turn for Fun and Buffoonery, and wherever they went, made the Children quite Happy and set all the Maids on the Titter. That they might not want amusement, they took along with them for the first two Days a Mess[1] John Allan, a Minister who lay in their Route, with whom they could use every sort of Freedom, and who was their Constant But. As he had no resistance in him, and could only Laugh when they rallied him or play'd him Boyish Tricks, I thought it but very Dull Entertainment. Nor Did I much approve of their Turning the Backsides of their Wigs Foremost, and making Faces to Divert the Children in the midst of very Grave Discourse about the State of Religion in the Country, and the progress of the Gospel. Among the Places we visited was Bridekirk, the Seat of the Eldest Cadet of Ld Carlyle's Family, of which my Father was Descended. I saw likewise a small pendicle of the Estate, which had been assigned as the Portion of his Grand Father, and which he himself had tried to Recover by a Lawsuit, but was Defeated for want of a Principal Paper.[2] We Did not see the Laird who was from home. But we saw the Lady who was a much Greater Curiosity. She was a very Large and powerfull Virago about 40 years of age, and Rec'd us with much Kindness and Hospitality. For the Brandy Bottle, a Scotch pint,[3] made its appearance immediatly, and we were oblig'd to take our Morning, as they call'd it, which was indeed the Universal Fashion of the Country at that time. This Lady,* who I confess had not many Charms for me, was said to be able to empty one of those Large Bottles of Brandy, Smuggled from the Isle of Man, at a sitting. They had no Whisky at that time, There Being then No Distilleries in the South of Scotland. The Face of the Country was particularly Desolate, not having yet reap'd any Benefit from the Union of the Parliaments, nor was it Recover'd from the Effects of that Century of wretched Government which preceded the Revolution and commenc'd at the accession of James. The Border Wars and Depradations had happily Ceas'd; But the Borderers having lost what excited their activity, were in a Dormant State During the whole of the 17th Century unless it was During the time of the Grand Rebellion, and the Struggles between Episcopacy and Presbytery.

On this excursion we Din'd with Sir Wm. Douglas of Kelhead, whose Grandfather was a Son of the Family of Queensberry. When he met us in his Stable Yard, I took him for a Grieve[1] or Barn Man, for he wore a Blew Bonnet over his thin Gray Hairs, and a Hoddan Grey Coat.[2] But on a nearer view of him, he appear'd to be well Bred and Sensible, and was particularly Kind to my Father who I understood had been his Godson, having been Born in the Neighbourhood on a Farm his Father Rented from Sir William. His Mother who was Jean Jardine† a Daughter of the Family of Apilgirth had Died a week after his Birth in 1690. His Father lived till 1721.

In the Evening we went to visit an old Gentleman a Cousin of my Fathers James Carlyle of Brakenwhate, who had been an officer in James the 2ds time, and Threw up his Commission at the Revolution rather than take the Oaths. He was a little Fresh Looking old man of 86, very lively in Conversation and particularly fond of my Father. His House which was not much better than a Cottage, tho' there were two Rooms above Stairs, as well as Below, was full of Guns and Swords, and other warlike Instruments. He had been so Dissolute in his Youth, that his Nickname in the Country was Jamy Gae Loose. His Wife who appear'd to be older than himself tho' she was 7 Years younger was of a very Hospitable Disposition. This small House Being Easily fill'd, I went to bed in the Parlour while the Company were at Supper. But tird as I was, it was long before I fell asleep; for as my Father had Told me that I was to Sleep with my Cousin, I was in Great Fear, That it would be the

---

* a Daughter of Bell of Crowdenowe I believe.

† By this Lady he was Connected with the Family of Queensberry of which Sir Wm. was a Branch, For the Jardines had twice married Daughters of that House. My Father past much of his Youth at Jardine Hall, for his Mother Dying when he was an Infant, he resided there with an Aunt who kept House for Sir John Jardine.

Old Woman—weariness overcame my Fear however, and I Did not awake till the Tea Things were on the Table, and Did not know that it was the Old Gentleman who slept with me, Till my Father afterwards told me—which Reliev'd me from my anxious Curiosity. After Breakfast our old Friend would needs Give us a Convoy, and mounted his Horse a Gray Stallion of about 14½ Hands, as nimbly as if he had been 30 years old. Not long after he separated from us I took an opportunity of asking my Father what had been the Subject of a very Earnest Conversation he had had the evening before, when they were walking in the Garden. He told me that his Cousin had press'd him very much to accept of his Estate which he would Dispose to him, as his only Surviving Daughter had disstres'd him by her Marriage, and he had no liking to her Children. My Father had rejected his proposal, and taken much pains to convince the Old Gentleman, of the Injustice and Cruelty of his procedure, which had made him Loud and angry, and had Drawn my curious attention. He Died three Years after without a will, and the little Estate was soon Drown'd in Debt, and absorb'd into the great one, which made my Father say afterwards, That he believ'd he had been *Righteous overmuch*.[1]

This was the First Opportunity I had of Being well acquainted with my Grand Father Mr Alexr Robisone, who was a man very much respected for his Good Sense, and Steadiness and Moderation in Church Courts. He had been Minister at Tinwald since the Year 1697—was a Member of the Commission which sate During the Union Parliament. He was truly a man of a sound Head, and in the Mid'st of very warm times was Resorted to by his Neighbours both Laity and Clergy for Temperate and Sound Advice. He Liv'd to the [Year] 1761—and I pass'd Several Summers, and one Winter Entirely at his House when I was a Student; He had a Tolerably Good Collection of Books, was a Man of a Liberal Mind, and had more allowance to give to People of Different opinions, and more Indulgence to the Levities of Youth, than any Man I ever knew of Such Strict Principles and Conduct. His Wife Jean Graham, Connected with many of the Principal Families in Galloway, and Descended by her Mother from the Queensberry Family, as my Father was, at a Greater Distance by his Mother of the Jardine Hall Family; Gave the worthy people and their children an Air of Greater Consequence than their Neighbours of the same Rank, and tended to make them Deserve the Respect which was shewn them. When I look Back on the fullness of very Good Living to their Numerous Family, and to their cheerfull Hospitality to Strangers; When I recollect the Decent Education they Gave their Children, and how happily the Daughters were Settled in the World; and Recollect that they had not £70—pr ann. beside the £500 which was my Grand Mothers Portion, £100 of which was Remaining for

14

the 3 Eldest Daughters, as they were married off in their Turns, It appears quite surprising How it was possible for them to Live as they Did and keep their Credit. What I have Seen both at their House, and my Fathers on their Slender Incomes, Surpasses all belief. But it is wonderfull, what Moderation and a Strict Economy was able to do in those Days.*

In my Infancy I had witness'd the Greatest Trial they had ever Gone Through. Their Eldest Son a youth of 18 who had studied at Glasgow College, But was to go to the Divinity Hall at Edinr in winter 1724 to be near my Father then Remov'd to Prestonpans, went to Dumfries to Bid Farewell to his 2d Sister Mrs Bell; Left the Town in a clear Frosty Night in the beginning of Decr, But having miss'd the road about a Mile from Dumfries, Fell into a Peat-pot[1] as it is call'd and was Drown'd. He was impatiently expected at night and next morn. My next Brother and I had got some half pence to give him, to purchase some Sugar Plumbs for us, so that we were not the Least Impatient of the Family. What was our Dissappointment, when about Eleven a clock Information came that he had been Drown'd, and our Comfits Lost? This I mention merely to note at what an Early Age Interesting Events, make an Impression on Childrens Memories; For I was only then 2 years and ten months old, and to this Day I remember as well as any event of my Life.†

* On this Journey it was that I first witness'd an Execution. There was one Jock Johnstone, who had been Condemn'd for Robbery and Being accessory to Murder, and was to be executed at Dumfries. As there were no Soldiers in the Town and Neighbourhood, The Magistrates were alarm'd at a Report that was industriously propagated, That the Border Theives were to assemble in a Body, and Carry him off as he was Leading to Execution. This made them change the place of Execution, and instead of carrying him to the usual place, they Erected a Scaffold and a Gallows at the Door of the Prison, one Story above the Street, so that he might be executed in the Centre of the Town, and they arm'd about 100 of the Young Artizans, and plac'd them as a Guard Round the Gallows. Jock Johnstone was Young and Ignorant, Strong and Bold; and made a very Great Resistance. He struggled like a Wild Beast against 4 Town-officers, and was on the point of pulling down the Gallows and attempting to escape. At last the Magistrates bethought them of one man superior in strength to any three, a Master Mason or Carpenter, who prevail'd for the Honour of the Town to attempt the Business. He put by all the rest, and took Jock as if he had been a child in his arms and bound him fast, roaring like a subdu'd ox &c.

† We had a very Good Master at Prestonpans, an Alexr Hannan an old fellow College Student of my Fathers whom he brought there and who implicitly follow'd his Directions. He possess'd excellent translations of the Classics—

Here it may not be improper [to recall] an Extraordinary Incident, to shew how soon Boys are Capable of Deep Imposture. There was a Boy at School in the same class whose Name was Mathie—He was very Intimate with me, and was between Eleven and twelve years old, when all at once he produc'd more Money than any Body, Tho' his Mother was an Indigent Widow of [a] Shipmaster and Continued only to Deal in Hoops and Staves for the support of her Family. This Boy having at Different

[1735]

Two Years after this Journey into my Native Country, which had the Effect of attaching me very much to my Grand Father and his Family, and gave to him a great ascendant over my Mind, I was sent to the College of Edin! which I Enter'd on the 1ˢᵗ of Nov! 1735.—I had the Good Luck to be plac'd in a House where there was very Good Company, For John afterwards Coll! Maxwell and his Brother Alex! were Boarded, whose Tutor Being an Acquaintance of my Fathers took some charge of me. John Witherspoon The Celebrated Dr was also in the House, and Sir Harry Nisbet of Dean, and John Dalrymple now Sir John of Cranston, not being able to afford Tutors of their own and Being near Relations of the Maxwells, Came every afternoon to prepare their Lessons, under the care of our Tutor.

The Future Life and Publick Character of Dr Witherspoon is perfectly known; at the time I speak of he was a Good Scholar, far advanc'd for his Age; very Sensible and Shrewd, But of a Dissagreable Temper, which was Irritated by a Flat Voice, and aukward Manner, which prevented his making an Impression on his Companions of Either Sex, That was at all adequate to his ability. This Defect when he was a Lad, stuck to him when he grew up to Manhood, and so much rous'd his Envy and Jealousy, and made him take a Road to Distinction, very Different from that of his more Successfull Companions.

John Maxwell was Remarkably Tall and well made, and one of the Handsomest Youths of his Time. But of such Gentle Manners, and so Soft a Temper That nobody could then foresee, That he was to prove one of the Bravest Officers in the Allied Army under Prince Ferdinand in the Year 1759 &c.

Sir Harry Nisbet was a very amiable Youth, who took also to the Army, was a Distinguishd Officer and Remarkably Handsome, But Slain at an Early Age in the Battle of Val.[1] The character of Sir John Dalrymple whom I shall have occasion to mention afterwards is perfectly known. It is sufficient to say here, That the Blossom promis'd better Fruit.

I was Enter'd in Mr Kerr's class who was at that time Professor of Humanity and was very much Master of his Business. Like other School-

---

[Times] shewn more Money than I thought he had any right to have, I press'd him very close to tell me how he had got it. After many Shifts, he at last told me That his Grand Father had appear'd to him in an Evening, and Disclos'd a Hidden Treasure in the Garret of his Mother's House between the Floor and the Cieling—He pretended to shew me the Spot but would never open it to me. He made several appointments with me which I kept, to meet the Old Gentleman, but he never appear'd, and I tried every method to make him Confess his Imposture, but without Effect. After some time I heard that he had Rob'd his Mothers Drawers.

masters, he was very Partial to his Scholars of Rank, and having two Lords at his class viz. Lord Balgony and Lord Dalziel, he took Great Pains to make them (especially the 1ˢᵗ for the 2ᵈ was hardly ostensible) appear among the Best Scholars, which would not Do, and only serv'd to make him Ridiculous as well as his Young Lord. The Best by far at the Class, were Collⁱ Robert Hepburn of Keith, James Edgar Esqʳ afterwards a Comʳ of Customs, Alexʳ Tait Esqʳ Clerk of Session, and Alexʳ Bertram of the Nisbet Family who Died young. Wᵐ Wilkie the Poet and I came next in order, and he us'd to allege long after that we turn'd Latin into English better than they Did, tho' we could not so well turn English into Latine.* I mention those Circumstances, Because Those Gentlemen continued to keep the same Rank in Society when they grew up that they held when they were Boys. I was sent the same Year† to the First Class of Mathematicks, Taught by McLaurin, which cost me little Trouble as my Father had Carried me thro' the 1ˢᵗ Book [of] Euclid in the Summer. In this Branch I gain'd an ascendant over our Tutor Pat. Baillie, afterwards Minister of Borrowstownness, which he took Care never to forget. He was a very Good Latin Scholar and so expert in the Greek, that he Taught Drummond [the] Profʳˢ Class for a whole Winter, when he was ill; But he had no Matˢ nor much Science of any kind. One Night when I was Conning my Latin Lesson in the Room with him and his Pupils, he was going over a proposition of Euclid with John Maxwell, who had hitherto got no hold of the Science. He Blunder'd so excessively in Doing this That I could not help Laughing aloud. He was enrag'd at first but when Calm, he Bid me try if I could do it Better. I went thro' the proposition so readily That he committed John (afterwards Collⁱ) to my care in that Branch, which he was so Good natur'd as not to take amiss Tho' he was a Year Older than me. At the end of a week, he fell into the proper train of Thinking, and needed assistance no longer. Mʳ McLaurin was at this time a Favourite Professor, and no wonder as he was the clearest and most agreable Lecturer on that abstract Science that ever I heard. He made Matˢ a Fashionable Study, which was felt afterwards in the war that Follow'd in 1743, when nine Tenths of the Ingineers of the Army were Scottish officers. The Academy at Woolwich was not then Establishd.[1]

[1736]

I was witness to a very extraordinary Scene that happen'd in Edinʳ in

* which was Probably owing to their being taught better at the High School, than we were in the Country.

† This is not the Fact, for I Did not enter Mʳ McLaurin's Class till the year following.

the Month of Feb.ʳʸ or March 1736, which was the Escape of Robertson a Condemn'd Criminal from the Tolbooth Church in Edin.ʳ¹—In those Days it was usual to bring the Criminals who were Condemn'd to Death into that Church to attend Publick Worship every Sunday after their Condemnation, when the Clergyman, made some part of his Discourse and prayers to suit their Situation. Which among other Circumstances of Solemnity which then attended the State of Condemn'd Criminals had no Small Effect on the Publick Mind. Robertson and Wilson were Smuglers and had been condemn'd for Robbing a Customhouse, where some of their Goods had been Deposited. A crime which at that time Did not seem, in the Opinion of the Common People, to Deserve so Severe a Punishment. I was carried by an Acquaintance to that church to see the Prisoners, on the Sunday before the Day of Execution. We went soon into the church on purpose to see them come in, and were seated in a Pew below the Gallery in Front of the Pulpit. Soon after we went into the Church, by the Door from the Parliament Close, The Criminals were brought in by the Door next the Tolbooth, and plac'd in a long Pew not far from the Pulpit. Four Soldiers came in with them, and plac'd Robertson at the Head of the Pew, and Wilson below him, Two of themselves Sitting Below Wilson and two in a Pew behind him. The Bells were ringing, and the Doors were open while the People were coming into the Church. Robertson watch'd his Opportunity and suddenly springing up Got over the Pew into the Passage that Led into the Door in the Parliament Close, and no person offering to Lay hands on him made his escape in a moment. So much the Easier perhaps that every Body's attention was Drawn to Wilson who was a stronger Man and who attempting to follow Robertson was siez'd by the Soldiers, and Struggled so long with them, That the two who at last Follow'd Robertson were too late. It was reported that he had maintain'd his Struggle that he might let his Companion have time. That might be his 2.ᵈ Thought, but his First certainly was to escape himself, For I saw him set his Foot on the Seat to Leap over when the Soldiers pull'd him back. Wilson was Immediatly Carried out to the Tolbooth, and Robertson getting uninterrupted thro' Parliament Square down the Back Stair into the Cowgate, was heard of no more till he arriv'd in Holland. This was an Interesting Scene, and by Filling the Publick Mind, with Compassion for the unhappy person who Did not escape, who was the better character of the two, had probably some Influence in producing what follow'd. For when the Sentence against Wilson came to be Executed a few weeks thereafter, a very Strong Opinion prevail'd, That there was a Plot to Force the Town Guard, whose Duty it is to attend executions under the Order of a Civil Magistrate.

There was a Cap.ᵗ Porteous, who by his Good Behavior in the Army, had obtain'd a Subalterns Commission, and had afterwards when on half pay been prefer'd to the command of the Town Guard. This Man by his Skill in manly exercises, particularly the Golf, and by Gentlemany Behaviour, was admitted into the Company of his Superiors, which Elated his Mind, and added Insolence to his Native Roughness, so that he was much hated and Fear'd by the Mob of Edin: When the Day of Execution Came, The Rumour of a Deforcement at the Gallows strongly Prevaild; and the Provost and Magistrates, (not in their own Minds very strong) thought it a Good Measure to apply for 3 or 4 Companies of a Marching Reg: that Lay in the Cannongate, to be Drawn up in the Lawn Mercat, a Street Leading from the Tolbooth to the Grass Market S: the place of Execution, in order to overawe the Mob by their Being at hand. Porteous who it was said, had his Natural Courage increas'd to Rage, by any suspicion that he and his Guard could not execute the Law, and Being heated likewise with wine for he had Din'd as the Custom then was between one and two, became perfectly Furious when he pass'd by the three Companies Drawn up in the Street as he Marchd along with his Prisoner. M: Baillie had Taken Windows in [a] House on the N. side of the Grass Market for his Pupils and me in the 2: Floor about 70 or 80 Yards westward of the place of Execution, where we went in due time to see the Show. To which I had no Small Aversion, Having seen one at Dumfries* which Shock'd me very much. When we arriv'd at the House, some people who were looking from them were Displac'd, and [went] to a Window, in the common stair about 2 feet below the Level of ours. The Street is long and wide, and there was a very great Crowd assembled. The Execution went on with the usual Forms, and Wilson Behav'd in a manner very Becoming his Situation. There was not the least appearance of an attempt to Rescue. But soon after the Executioner had done his Duty, There was an attack made upon him as usual on such Occasions, by the Boys and Blackguards, Throwing of Stones and Dirt, in Testimony of their abhorrence of the Hangman. But there was no attempt to break thro' the Guard and Cut Down the Prisoner. It was generally said that there was very little if any more violence than had always happen'd on such Occasions. Porteous however, inflam'd with Wine and Jealousy, thought proper to order his Guard to Fire; Their Muskets Being Loaded with Slugs—and when the Soldiers shew'd Reluctance I saw him turn to them with threatning Gesture and an enflam'd Countenance. They obey'd and Fir'd; But wishing to Do as little harm as possible, many of them Elevated their pieces; The Effect of which was that some people were wounded in the Windows, and one unfortunate Lad whom we had Displac'd, was killd in the Stair Window by a Slug's entering his Head.

* The execution of Jock Johnstone—

19

His Name was Henry Black a Journyman Taylor, whose Bride was the Daughter of the House where we were; who fainted away, when he was brought into the House, speechless, where he only liv'd till 9 or 10 a clock. We had seen many people women and men fall on the Street and at first thought it was only thro' Fear, and by their Crowding on one another to escape. But when the Crowd Dispers'd we saw them Lying Dead or Wounded, and had no Longer any Doubt, of what had happen'd. The numbers were said to be 8 or 9 kill'd and Double the Number wounded. But this was never Exactly known. This unprovok'd Slaughter irritated the Commons to the last; and the state of Grief and Rage into which their Minds were thrown, was visible in the high Commotion that appear'd in the Multitude. Our Tutor was very anxious to have us all safe in our Lodgings, but Durst not venture out to see if it was practicable to go home. I offer'd to go a scout and soon return'd, offering to Conduct them Safe to our Lodgings which were only halfway down the Land Market[1] S^t, by what was call'd the Castle Wynd, which was just at hand to the west-ward. There we arriv'd safely, and were not allow'd to stir out any more that night, till about 9 a clock when the streets having [been] long quiet, we all grew anxious to Learn the Fate of Henry Black, and I was allow'd to go Back to the House. I took the Younger Maxwell with me and found that he had expir'd an hour before we arrivd. A single slug had Penetrated into the Side of his Head an Inch above the Ear. The Sequel of this was, That Porteous was tried and Condemn'd to be hang'd. But by the Intercession of some of the Judges themselves, who thought his Case Hard, he was Repriev'd by the Q. Regent. The Magistrates who on this Occasion, as on the former, acted weakly, Design'd to have Remov'd him to the Castle for Greater Security; But a Plot was laid, and conducted with the Greatest Secresy, policy and vigour, to prevent that Design, by Forcing the Prison the Night before, and Executing the Sentence on him themselves. Which to Effectuate, Cost them from 8 at night till two in the morning; and yet their Plot was manag'd so Dextrously, That they met with no Interruption, Tho' there were five Companies of a Marching Reg^t Lying in the Cannongate. This happen'd in the Month of Sepr 1736, 7th Day and so prepossess'd were the Minds of every person, that something extraordinary would take place That Day, That I at Prestonpans near 9 miles off Dreamt that I saw Capt Porteous hang'd in the Grass-Market. I Got up between Six and Seven, and went to my Fathers Servant who was Threshing in the Barn, which Lay on the Road side Leading to Aberlady and N. Berwick, who said that several Men on Horseback had pass'd about 5 in the Morn, whom having ask'd for News, Replied there was none, but that Capt Porteous had been Drag'd out of prison, and hang'd on a Dyers Tree[2] at 2 a clock, that Morning.

This Bold and Lawless Deed not only provok'd the Queen who was Regent at the time, but gave some uneasiness to Government. It was Represented as a Dangerous Plot, and was Ignorantly Connected with a Great Meeting of Zealous Covenanters, of which many still remain'd in Galloway and the West, which had been held in summer in Pentland Hills to Renew the Covenant. But this was a mistake for the murder of Porteous, had been Plan'd and Executed by a few of the Relations or Friends of those he had slain, who Being of a Rank Superior to mere Mob, had carried on their Design with so much Secresy Ability and Steadiness as made it be ascrib'd to a still higher Order who [were] political Enemies to Government. This Idea provok'd L.d Isla who then manag'd the affairs of Scotland under Sir R.t Walpole, to carry thro' an Act of Parl.t in next Session, for the Discovery of the Murderers of Cap.t Porteous, to be publish'd by reading it for twelve Months, Every Forenoon in all the Churches in Scotland Immediatly after Divine Service or rather in the Middle of it, for the Minister was ordain'd to Read it between the Lecture[1] and the Sermon, two Discourses usually given at that time. This Clause it was said, was Intended to purge the Church of Fanaticks, For as it was Believ'd that most Clergymen of that Description, would not Read the Act, They would become liable to the Penalty, which was Deposition. By Good Luck for the Clergy, There was another Party Distinction among them, besides that occasion'd by their Ecclesiastical Differences, viz. that of Argathelian and Squadrone;[2] of which Political Divisions, there were some both of the Highflying and Moderate Clergy.[3] Some very sensible Men of the latter class, having Discover'd the Design of the Act Either by Information or Sagacity, Conven'd Meetings of Clergy at Edin.r and form'd Resolutions, and carried on Correspondence thro' the Church to persuade as many as possible to Disobey the Act, That the Great Number of Offenders might Secure the Safety of the Whole. This was actually the Case, for as one half of the Clergy at Least Dissobey'd in one Shape or other, The Idea of Inflicting the Penalty was Dropt altogether. In the mean time, the Distress and Perplexity which this Act occasion'd in many Families of the Clergy, was of itself a Cruel Punishment for a Crime in which they had no hand. The Anxious Days and sleepless nights, which it occasion'd to such Ministers as had Families, and at the same time Scruples about the Lawfullness of reading the Act were such as no one could imagine who had not witness'd the same.* What seem'd

* The Part my Grand Father took was manly and Decided, for not thinking the Reading of the Act unlawfull, he pointedly obey'd. My Father was very Scrupulous, being Influenc'd by M.r Erskine of Grange, and other Enemies of Sir Robert Walpole. On the other Hand, the Good Sense of his Wife and the Consideration of 8 or 9 children which he then had, and who were endanger'd to be Turn'd out on the World,

extraordinary after all the anxiety of Government, and the violent Means they took to make a Discovery, Not one of those Murderers were ever found. Twenty Years afterwards, two or three persons Return'd from Different Parts of the World, who were suppos'd to be of the Number. But so far as I heard They never Disclos'd themselves.

In my 2ᵈ Year at the College (Novʳ 1736) Besides attenting MᶜLaurins 2ᵈ Class for Mathˢ and Ker's private class in which he Read Juvenal and Tacitus &c. and open'd up the Beauties and peculiarities of the Latin Tongue, I went to the Logick Class, Taught by Mʳ John Stevenson, who tho' he had no pretensions to Superiority, in Point of Learning and Genius, yet was the most popular of all the Professors on account of his Civility, and even Kindness to his Students, and at the same time the most usefull. For Being a Man of Sense and Industry he had made a Judicious Selection from the French and English Criticks, which he gave at the Morning Hour of 8, when he Read with us Aristotle's Poeticks, and Longinus on the Sublime. At Eleven he read Heneccius Logic, and an abridgement of Locke's Essay: and in the afternoon at 2, for such were the Hours of Attendance in those times, he Read to us a Compendious History of the Antient Philosophers, and their Tenets. On all which Branches, we were carefully Examin'd at Least 3 times a week. Whether or not it was owing to the time of Life at which we Enter'd this Class, Being all about 15 Years of Age or upwards when the Mind begins to open, or to the Excellence of the Lectures and the Nature of some of the Subjects, we could not then say, But all of us Rec'd the Same Impression, viz. That our Minds were more Enlarg'd, and that we Rec'd Greater Benefit from that Class than from any other. With a Due Regard to the Merit of the Professor, I must ascribe this Impression, Chiefly to the Natural Effect which the Subject of Criticism, and of Rational Logick has upon the opening Mind. Having Learn'd Greek pretty well at School, my Father thought fit to make me pass that class,* Especially as at that time it was Taught by an old Sickly Man, who could seldom attend, and Employ'd Substitutes.

---

pull'd him very hard on the Side of Obedience. A Letter from my Grand Father at last settled his Mind and he Read the Act.

    * which separated me from some of my Companions, and brought me acquainted with new ones. Sundry of my Class Fellows Remain'd another year with Ker, and Sir Gil. Elliott, John Home and many others went back to it that year. It was this Year that I attended the French Master one Ker, who for Leave given him to Teach in a College Room, Taught his Scholars the whole Session for a Guinea: which was then all that the Regents¹ could Demand for a Session of the College, from the 1ˢᵗ of Novʳ to the 1ˢᵗ of June. During that Course, we were sufficiently Masters of French to be able to Read any Book.—To Emprove our Pronunciation, he made us Get one of Molieres Plays by Heart, which we were to have Acted but never Did. It was the Medicin Malgré Lui, in which I had the Part of Sganarelle.

Besides the Young Gentlemen who had resided with us in the former Year, There came into the Lodging Below two Irish Students of Medicine, whose Names were Conway and Lesly, who were perfectly well bred and agreable, and with whom tho' a year or two Elder I was very Intimate. They were among the First Irish Students, whom the Fame of The First Monro, and our Medical Professors, had brought over and they were not Dissappointed. They were Sober and Studious, as well as well Bred, and had none of that restless and Turbulent Disposition, Dignified with the Name of Spirit and Fire, which has often time made the Youth of that Country, such Troublesome Members of Society. Mr Lesley was a Clergyman's Son of Scottish Extraction, and was acknowledg'd as a Distant Relation by some of the Eglinton Family. Conways Relations were all beyond the Channell. I was so much their Favourite both this Year and the Following when they Return'd and I liv'd so much with them That they had very nearly persuaded me to be of their profession.*

I was in use of Going to my Fathers on Saturdays once a Fortnight, and Returning on Monday. But this little Journey was less frequently perform'd this Winter, as Sir Harry Nisbets Mother Lady Nisbet, a Sister of Sir Robt Morton's, very frequently Invited me to accompany her Son and the Maxwells to the House of Dean within a Mile of Edinr where we past the Day in Hunting with the Grey Hounds, and generally return'd to Town in the Evening. Here I had an opportunity of seeing a new Set of Company, my Circle having been very Limited in Edinr, whose Manners were more worthy of Imitation, and whose Conversation had more the Tone of the World. Here I frequently met with Mr Baron Dalrymple, the Youngest Brother of the then Earl of Stair, and Grandfather of the Present Earl. He was held to be a Man of Wit and Humour, and in the Language and Manners of the Gentlemen of Scotland before the Union Exhibited a Specimen of Conversation, That was so free as to Border a Little on Licentiousness, Especially before the Ladies, but he never Fail'd to keep the Table in a Roar.

Having pass'd the Greek Class, I miss'd many of my most Intimate Companions who either Remain'd one Year Longer at the Latin Class, or attended the Greek; But I made new ones who were very agreable such as Sir Alexr Cockburn of Lan[g]ton who had been bred in England till now, and John Gibson the Son of Sir Alexr Gibson of Addison, both of whom Perish'd in the war that was approaching.

* At this Time the Medical School of Edinr was but Rising into Fame. There were not so many as 20 English and Irish Students this Year in the College. The Professors were Men of Eminence. Besides Monro the Proffr of Anatomy, There [were] Dr Sinclair   . As Edinr is the Capital of Scotland, the most Eminent Physicians will always Reside there and furnish a Succession of Learned Professors.

Early in the Summer I lost one of the Dearest Friends I ever had, who Died of a Fever. We had often settled it between us, that whoever should Die first, should appear to the other, and Tell him the Secrets of the Invisible World. I walk'd every Evening for Hours in the Fields and Links of Prestonpans, in Hopes of Meeting my Friend. But he never appear'd. This Dissappointment, together with the Knowledge I had acquird at the Logick Class, Cur'd me of many Prejudices about Ghosts and Hobgoblins and Witches, of which till that time I stood not a little in awe.

[1737]

In Summer 1737 I was at Prestonpans, and in July, two or three Days before my youngest Sister Jenny was Born, afterwards Mrs Bell, I met with an accident which confin'd me many weeks—which [was] a Shot in my Leg, occasion'd by the Virrall[1] of a Ramrod having fallen into a Musket, at a Review in Musselburgh Links, part of which Lodg'd in the outside of the Calf of my Leg, and could not be Extracted till after the place had been twice Laid open, when it came out with a Dressing, and was about the size of the Head of a Nail. This was the Reason why I made no excursion to Dumfriesshire this Summer.[2]

The next Session of the College in Novr 1737, I Lodg'd in the same House, and had the same Companions, as I had the two preceding Years. Besides Sir Robert Stewarts Natural Philosophy Class, which was very ill Taught, as he was worn out with Age and never had Excell'd, I attended McLaurin's 2d Class this Year, and Dr Pringle's Moral Philosophy, Besides two Hours at the Writing Masters to Improve my Hand, and a second attendance on Mr Kerr's private class. The Circle of my Acquaintance was but little Enlarg'd, and I Deriv'd more agreable amusement from the two Irish Students, who Return'd to their Former Habitation, than from any other Acquaintance except the Maxwells and their Friends. My Acquaintance with Dr Robertson began. I never was at the same Class with him, for tho' but a few months older, he was at the College one Session before me. One of the Years too he was siez'd with a Fever, which was Dangerous, and Confin'd him for the greatest part of the Winter. I went to see him sometimes when he was Recovering, when in his Conversation one could perceive the Opening Dawn of that Day which afterwards Shone so Bright. I became also acquainted with John Home this Year, tho' he was one year behind me at College, and 8 Months Younger, who was Gay and Talkative and a Great Favourite with his Companions. I was very fond of Dancing, in which I was a great pro-

ficient, having been Taught at two Different periods in the Country, tho'
the manners were then so strict that I was not allow'd to exercise my
Talent at penny weddings,[1] or any Balls but those of the Dancing School.
Even this would have been Denied me, as it was to Robertson, and
Witherspoon, and other Clergymen's Sons of that time, had it not been
for the Persuasion of those Aunts of mine who had been Bred in England,
and for some papers in the Spectator,[2] which were pointed out to my
Father, which seem'd to convince him, that Dancing would make me a
more accomplish'd Preacher if ever I had the Honour to mount the Pulpit. My Mother too, who Generally was Right, us'd her Sway in this article
of Education. But I had not the means of using my Talent, of which I was
not a little vain; when luckily I was Introduc'd to *Madame Violante* an
Italian Stage Dancer, who kept a much Frequented School for Young
Ladies, but admitted of no Boys above 7 or 8 years of Age, so that she
wish'd very much for Senior Lads, to Dance with her Grownup Misses
weekly at her Practisings. I became a Favourite of this Dancing Mistress,
and attended her very faithfully with two or three of my Companions,
and had my choice of Partners on all Occasions. Insomuch That I became
a great proficient in this Branch, at little or no Expence. It must be Confess'd however, that having nothing to Do at Stewarts Class, thro' the
Incapacity of the Master, and McLaurin's giving me no trouble as I had a
great promptitude in Learning Mathematicks, I had a Good Deal of spare
time this Session, which I spent as well as all the Money I got, at a Billiard
Table which unluckily was within 50 Yards of the College. I was so sensible of the Folly of this however, that next Year, I abandon'd it altogether.

Dr Pringle afterwards Sir John, was an agreable Lecturer tho' no
Great Master of the Science he taught. His Lectures were chiefly a Com-
pilation from Ld Bacons Works, and had it not been for Puffendorfs Small
Book which he made his Text, we should not have been instructed in the
Rudiments of the Science. Once a week however he gave us a Lecture in
Latin, in which Language he excell'd, and was even held Equal to Dr John
Sinclair Proff^r of the Theory of Medicine, the Most Eminent Latin
Scholar at that time, except the Great Grammarian Ruddiman. The
Celebrated Dr Hutchinson at Glasgow, who was the First who distin-
guish'd himself in that Important Branch of Literature, was now begin-
ning his Career, and had Drawn ample Stores from the Antients, which he
Emprov'd into System, and Embellish'd by the emotions of an Ardent
and Virtuous Mind. He was soon Follow'd by Smith who had been his
Scholar, and sate for some years in his Chair; by Ferguson at Edin^r; by
Reid, and Beattie, which last was more an Orator than a Philosopher,
Together with David Hume, whose Works, tho' Dangerous and Heretical,

illustrated the Science and call'd for the exertions of Men of Equal Genius and Sounder Principles.

[1738]

I Pass'd the greater part of this Summer at my Grand Fathers at Tinwald near Dumfries, who had a Tolerably Good Collection of Books, and where I read for many Hours of the Day. I contracted the greatest respect for my Grand Father and attachment to his Family: and Became well acquainted with the Young People of Dumfries, and afterwards held a Correspondence by Letters with one of them which was of use in forming my Epistolary Stile.

A New Family came this Year to Prestonpans, for Colin Campbell Esq.ʳ the Brother of Sir James of Arbruchal had fallen in arrears as Collector of the Customs, and was suspended. But his Wife Dying at that very time, an excellent woman of the Family of Sir James Holburn, and Leaving him 8 or 9 Children, his Situation drew compassion from his Friends, especially from Arch.ᵈ Earl of Isla and James Campbell of S.ᵗ Germains, who were his Securities, who had no chance of Being Reimburs'd for the Sum of £1000, or £800, of arrears into which he had fallen, But by his Preferment. He was soon made a Commissioner of the Board of Customs, an Office at that time of £1000 p̣ ann. This Depriv'd us of a very agreable Family, the Sons and Daughters of which were my Companions. Mʳ Campbell was Succeeded by Mʳ Geo. Cheap, of the Cheaps of Rossie in Fife whose Wife, an aunt of the L.ᵈ Chancellor Wedderburn was just Dead, and left a Family of 8 Children 2 of them Beautifull Girls of 16 and 18, and 6 Sons, the eldest of whom was a Year elder than me, but was an apprentice to a W.S.[1] at Edin.ʳ—This Family tho' less sociable than the former soon became intimate with ours; and one of them very Early made an Impression on me which had lasting Effects.[2]

In Nov.ʳ 1738 I again attended the College of Edin.ʳ and Besides a 2.ᵈ Year of the Moral Philosophy, I was a Third Year at M.ᶜLaurin's Class, who on account of the advanc'd age and incapacity of Sir Robert Stewart, not only Taught Astronomy, But gave us a Course of Experiments in Mechanicks, with many excellent Lectures on Natural Philosophy, which fully compensated the Defects of the other class. About this Time the choice of a profession became absolutely necessary. I had Thoughts of the Army and the Law, but was persuaded to Desist from any views on them, by my Fathers Being unable to carry on my Education for the Length of time necessary in the one, or to support me till he could procure a Commission for me, as he had no money to purchase, and by means of the long peace,

26

the Establishment of the Army was Low. Both these having Fail'd, by the Persuasion of Lesly and Conway my Irish Friends, I thought of Surgery, and had prevail'd so far that my Father went to Edin.ʳ in the autumn, to Look out for a Master in that Profession. In the mean time came a Letter from my Grand Father in Favour of his own Profession and that of my Father, written with so much Force and Energy, and stating so many Reasons for my Yielding to the wish of my Friends, and the Conveniency of a Family still consisting of 8 Children of whom I was the Eldest, That I Yielded to the Influence of Parental Wishes and Advice, which in Those Days, Sway'd the Minds of Young Men, much more than it Does now or has Done for many Years Past. I therefore Consented that my Name should this Year be Enroll'd in the List of Students of Divinity, tho' Regular Attendance was not enjoin'd.

[1739]

On the 13 of Jan.ʸ 1739, There was a total Eclipse of the Moon to view which M.ᶜLaurin Invited his senior scholars, of which I was one. About a Doz. of us Remain'd till near one a clock on the Sunday morning, when the Greatest Tempest arose that ever I Remember. Eight or Ten of us were so much alarm'd with the Fall of Bricks and Slates in the College Wynd, that we call'd a Council of War in a Stair Foot, and Got to the High Street safe, by walking in File Down the Cowgate and up Niddery's Wynd.

I pass'd most of the Summer of this Year in Dumfries Shire, where my Grand Father kept me pretty close to my Studies; Tho' I frequently walk'd in the afternoons to Dumfries, and brought him the Newspapers, from Provost Bell his Son-in-Law; who had by that time acquir'd the chief sway in the Burgh, Having Taken the Side of the Duke of Queensberry in opposition to Charles Erskine of Tinwald, at that time the Sollicitor. Geo. Bell was not a man of Ability, but he was successfull in Trade, was popular in his Manners, and having a Gentlemany Spirit was a Favourite with the Nobility and Gentry in the neighbourhood. He had a Constant Correspondence with the Duke of Q. and Retain'd his Friendship to his Death in 1757. What Bell wanted in Capacity or Judgment was fully Compensated by his Wife Marg.ᵗ Robison, the 2.ᵈ of my Mothers Sisters, and afterwards still more by my Sister Margaret, whom they Reard, as they had no Children, and when she grew up, added Beauty and Address, to a very uncommon Understanding. During the Period when I so much frequented Dumfries, There was a very agreable Society in that Town. They were not Numerous, But the few there was, were Better inform'd and more agreable in Society, than any to be met with in so Small a Town.

I Return'd home before Winter, but Did not attend the College tho' I was enroll'd a Student of Divinity. But my Father had promis'd to Ld Drumore the Judge and his Great Friend, that I should pass most of my Time with his Eldest Son Mr Hew Horn Dalrymple, who not liking to Live in Edin^r was to pass the Winter in the House of Walliford, which was adjacent to his Estate of Drummore where he had only a Farmhouse at that time with two Rooms on a Ground Floor, which would have ill agreed with Mr Horn's Health, which was Threatned with Consumptive Symptoms, of which Disease he Died five or six years afterwards, married but without Issue.

Mr Hew Horn Dalrymple had been Intended for the Church of England, and with that view had been Educated at Oxford, and was an accomplish'd Scholar. But his Elder Brother John having Died at Naples, he fell Heir to his Mother's Estate. He was five or six Years Older than I and Being Frank and Communicative, I Rec'd much Benefit from his Conversations which were Instructive, and his Manners which were Elegant. With this Gentleman I liv'd all Winter Returning generally to my Fathers House on Saturdays, when Ld Drummore Return'd from Edin^r and went Back again on Monday, when I Resum'd my Station. We past great part of the Day in Novr and Decr planting Trees Round the Inclosures at Drummore, which by their appearance at present, prove that they were not well chosen, for they are very Small of their Age. But they were too Old when they were Planted. After the Frost set in about Xtmass, we pass'd our Day very much in Following the Gray Hounds on Foot or on Horseback, and tho' our Evenings were Generally Solitary, between reading and Talking we never Tir'd. Mr Horn's Manners were as Gentle as his Mind was Enlightned. We had Little Intercourse with the Neighbours, except with my Fathers Family, Mr Cheap the Coll^{rs} where there were two Beautifull Girls, and with Mr Keith afterwards Ambassador, whose Wife's Sister was the Widow of Sir R^t Dalrymple, Ld Drummore's Brother.—They were twins, and so like Each, that even when I saw them first when they were at Least 30, it was hardly possible to Distinguish them. In their Youth, their Lovers, I have heard them say, always mistook them, when a sign or watchword had not been agreed on. Mr Keith was a very agreable Man, had much Knowledge of Modern History and Genealogy, and Being a pleasing Talker made an agreable Companion. Of him and his Intimate Friend Mr Hepburn of Keith it was said that the Witty Lady Dick (Ld Royston the Judge's Daughter) said[1] That Mr Keith told her nothing but what she knew before, tho' in a very agreable Manner—But that Hepburn never said any thing that was not new to her, thus Marking the Difference between Genius and Ability. Keith was a Minion of the Great Marischal Stair, and went abroad with him in 1743 when he Got the Command of the Army. But I observ'd that L⁴ Stairs Partiality to Keith made him no Great Favourite of the Dalrymples. Coll! Gardiner had been another Minion of L⁴ Stairs, but Being illiterate and considerd as a Fanatick, the Gentlemen I mention, had no Intimacy with him tho' they admitted that he was a very Honest and well-meaning Brave Man.

My Father had sometimes express'd a wish, that I should allow myself to be Recommended to Take Charge of a Pupil, as that was the most likely way to Obtain a Church in Scotland. But he Did not press me on this Subject, for as he had been four years in that Station himself, Tho' he was very Fortunate in his Pupils, he felt how Degrading it was. By that time I had been acquainted with a few Preceptors, had Observ'd how they were Treated, and contracted an abhorrence of the Employment. Insomuch that when I consented to follow out the clerical Profession, It was on Condition I should never be urg'd to Go into a Family as it was Call'd; and engag'd at the same time to make my expences as Moderate as Possible.*

[1740]

I pass'd the Summer of this Year as usual in the Neighbourhood of Dumfries, and kept up my connexion with the young people of that Town, as I had done formerly. I Return'd home in the autumn; and pass'd some part of the Winter 1740 in Edin! attending the Divinity Class, which had no attractions, as the Professor tho' said to be Learned was Dull and Tedious in his Lectures,[1] insomuch that at the End of seven Years, he had only Lectur'd half thro' Pictets Compound of Theology. I became acquainted however with several Students with whom I had not been Intimate, as I had pass'd the Greek Class, such as D⁻ Hew Blair, and the Bannatines and D⁻ Jardine, all my Seniors, and D⁻ John Blair, afterwards Prebendary of Westminster, and John Home and W™ Robertson. and Geo. Logan, and W™ Wilkie, &c. &c. There was one advantage attending the Lectures of a Dull Professor, viz. That he could form no School,

* This was the Winter of the Hard Frost which commenced in the End of Dec! 1739 and Lasted for 3 months. As there were no canals or Rivers of extent enough in this Part of the Country to encourage the fine exercise of Skating, we contented ourselves with the Winter Diversion of Curling[2] which is peculiar to Scotland, and became tolerable proficients in that manly exercise. It is the more Interesting That it is usual for the young Men of adjacent parishes to contend against each other, for a whole Winters Day, and at the End of it to Dine together with much Jollity.

and the Students were left entirely to themselves and naturally form'd Opinions more Liberal than those they Got from the Professor. This was the answer I gave to Pat. L.ᵈ Elibank one of the most Learned and Ingenious Noblemen of his time, when he ask'd me one Day many years afterwards, What could be [the] Reason that the young Clergymen of that Period, so far Surpass'd their Predecessors of his Early Days, in usefull Accomplishments and Liberality of Mind, viz. That the Professor of Theology was Dull and Dutch, and prolix. His L.ᵈship said he perfectly understood me, and that this entirely accounted for the Change.

[1741]

In Summer 1741 I Remain'd for most part at home, and it was about that time that my old Schoolmaster M.ʳ Hannan, having Died of a Fever, and M.ʳ John Halket having come in his place, I was Witness to a Scene that made a Strong Impression upon me. This M.ʳ Halket had been Tutor to L.ᵈ Lovats Eldest Son Simon, afterwards well known as Gen.ˡ Fraser. Halket had Remain'd for 2 Years with Lovat, and knew all his ways. But he had parted with him on his coming to Edin.ʳ for the Education of that Son, to whom he then gave a Tutor of a Superior Order, M.ʳ Hew Blair, afterwards the celebrated D.ʳ—But he still retain'd so much Regard for Halket, That he thought proper to fix his 2.ᵈ Son Alex.ʳ Fraser with him at the School of Prestonpans, Believing that he was a much properer Hand for Taming an untutor'd Savage, than the Mild and Elegant D.ʳ Blair.

It was in the Course of this Summer that Lovat brought his Son Alex.ʳ to be plac'd with Halket: from whom understanding That I was a Young Scholar Living in the Town who might be usefull to his Son, he order'd Halket to Invite me to Dine with him and his Company, at Lucky[1] Vints, a Celebrated Village Tavern in the West end of the Town. His Company consisted of L.ᵈ (M.ʳ Erskine of) Grange with three or four Gentlemen of the Name of Fraser, one of whom was his Man of Business, together with Halket, his Son Alex.ʳ and myself. The two old Gentlemen Disputed for some time which of them should say Grace; at Last Lovat yielded and Gave us two or 3 pious Sentences in French, which M.ʳ Erskine and I understood, and we only. As soon as we were Set Lovat ask'd me to send him a Whiting, from the Dish of Fish that was next me. As they were all Haddocks, I answer'd, That they were not Whitings, but according to the Proverb, He who got a Haddock for a Whiting was not ill off.[2] This saying takes its Rise from the Superiority of Haddocks to Whitings in the Firth of Forth. Upon this His Lordship Storm'd and Swore more than 50 Dragoons, He was sure they must be Whitings as he had bespoke them.

Halket Tip'd me the Wink, and I Retracted saying that I had but little Skill, and as his Lordship had bespoke them, I had certainly been mistaken. Upon this he Calm'd and I sent him one, which he was quite pleas'd with, Swearing again, That he never could Eat a Haddock all his Life. The Landlady told me afterwards that as he had been very Peremptory against Haddocks and She had no other, She had made her Cook carefully scrape out Sᵗ Peters mark on the Shoulders,[1] which she had often Done before with Success. We had a very good Plain Dinner, and as the Claret was excellent and Circulated Fast, the two old Gentlemen grew very Merry, and their Conversation became Youthfull and Gay. What I observ'd was That Grange without appearing to Flatter was very Observant of Lovat, and Did everything to please him. He had provided Geordy Sym, who was Lᵈ Drummore's Piper, to Entertain Lovat after Dinner: But tho' he was Reckon'd the Best Piper in the Country, Lovat Despis'd him and said He was only fit to play Reel's to Grange's Oister Women. He grew frisky at Last, however, and upon Kate Vint the Landladys Daughter coming into the Room, he insisted on her Staying to Dance with him. She was a Handsome Girl with Fine Black Eyes, and a Remarkable good Person. And tho' without the Advantages, of Dress or Manners, she by means of her Good Sense and a Bashfull Air, was very alluring. She was a Mistress of Lᵈ Drumore who liv'd in the Neighbourhood; and tho' her Mother would not part with her, as she Drew much company to the House, she was Said to be faithfull to him; except only in the Case of Capt. Merry, who Married her, and soon after went abroad with his Regᵗ—When he Died she Enjoyed the pension. She had two Sons by Drummore and one by Merry. One of the First was a pretty Lad and a Good Officer for he was a Master and Commander before he Died. Lovat was at this Time 75 Years and Grange not much Younger. Yet the wine and the Young Woman, Embolden'd them to Dance a Reel, Till Kate observing Lovats Legs as Thick as Posts she fell a Laughing and Run off. She mist her Second Course of Kisses as was then the Fashion of the Country, tho' she had endur'd the First. This was a Scene not easily Forgotten. Lovat was tall and stately, and might have been Handsome in his Youth, with a very Flat Nose. His Manner was not Disagreable, Tho' his Address consisted chiefly in Gross Flattery, and in the Due Application of money. He Did not make upon me the Impression of a Man of a Leading Mind; his Suppleness and Profligacy were apparent.

The Convivium was not over, tho' the evening approached. He Convey'd his Son to the House where his Son was to be Boarded, for Halket had not taken up House, and there while we Drank Tea, he won the Hearts of the Landlady, a Decent Widow of a Ship Master and her Niece, by Fair Speeches, Intermix'd with Kisses to the Niece, who was about 30, and such Advices as a Man in a State of Ebriety could give. The Coach was in Waiting. But Grange would not yet Part with him, and Insisted on his accepting of a Banquet from him at his House in Preston. Lovat was in a Yielding Humour, and it was agreed to. The Frasers who were on Horseback, were sent to Edin[r]. The Boy was left with his Dame, and Lovat and Grange and Halket and I went up to Preston, only a Quarter of a Mile Distant, and were Rec'd in Granges Library, a cube of 20 Feet in a Pavilion of the House which extended into a Small Wilderness of not more than Half an Acre, which was sacred to Grange's private Walks, and to which there was no Entry but through the Pavilion.* This Room had been well stor'd with Books from Top to Bottom, but by this time was much Thin'd, there Remaining only a large Collection of Books on Daemonologia, which was Granges Particular Study. In this Room, there was a fine Collation of Fruit and Biscuits, and a new Deluge of excellent Claret. A[t] Ten a clock the two old Gentlemen Mounted their Coach to Edin[r] and thus clos'd a very Memorable Day.

In the Following Winter viz. Nov[r] 1741 I attended the Divinity Hall at Edin[r] again for 3 or four Months, and Deliver'd a Discourse, De fide Salvifica, a very Improper Subject for so Young a Student, which attracted no attention from any one but the Professor, who was pleas'd with it as it Resembled his own Dutch Latin.

[1742]

The Summer 1742, I pass'd at home, making only a few Excursions into East-Lothian, where I had Sundry Companions. My Father ever attentive to what he thought was best for me, and Desirous to Ease himself as much as possible from the expence of my Education, availd himself of my Mothers being a Relation of the Hon[ble] Basil Hamilton's, for their Mothers were Cousins, applied to Duke Hamilton for one of the Bursaries Given by that Family by Dutchess Ann in the Former Century, to Students in Divinity, to pass two Winters in Glasgow College, and a third in some Forreign University. The Sallary for the 1st two year 100 Lib. Scots[1] ann[y] and for the 3[d] 400 Lib—which might have been competent, as far back as 1670, but was very far short of the most Moderate Expence, at which a Student could live in 1742—But I was pleasd with this plan as it

---

* This Wilderness was said to be his place of Retreat from his Lady when she was in her Fits of Termagancy, which were not unfrequent, and were said by his Minions to be Devoted to Meditation and Prayer. But as there was a Secret Door to the Fields, it was Reported That he had occasionally admitted fair Maidens to Solace him for his Sufferings from the Clamour of his Wife.

open'd a prospect of going abroad. The Presentation was obtain'd, and my Father and I set out on Horseback for Glasgow in the beginning of Nov.ʳ and arriv'd there next forenoon, having staid all night at Mr Dundas's at Castle Cary on the Old Roman Wall.¹ My Father Immediatly Repair'd to the College, to Consult with an old Friend of his, Mr Dick proffr of Nat. Philosophy, how he was to proceed with his Presentation. I was Surpris'd to see him Return soon after in a Great Flurry, Mr Dick having assur'd him that there was no vacant Bursary, nor would be till next Year. The next object was how to secure it, in which we were both much Interested, my Father to prevent my Deviating into some other Employment, and I for fear I should have been forc'd to become Tutor to some Young Gentleman, a Situation which as I then observ'd it, had become an Object of my Abhorrence. Several of my Companions had the same turn of Mind, for neither Robertson, nor I, Home nor Geo. Logan, were ever Tutors; we thought we had observ'd that all Tutors, had contracted a certain Obsequiousness or *Basesse*; which alarm'd us for ourselves. A little Experience corrected this Prejudice, For I knew many afterwards who had pass'd thro' that Station, and yet had retain'd a manly Independency both in Mind and Manners.

After a Hasty Dinner we Took to our Horses by 4 in the afternoon, and Riding all night by the nearest road which was as Bad as possible we arriv'd in Edinr by 8 in the Morning. My Father Drest himself and went Down to the Abbey,² where to his Great Joy he Found that Duke Hamilton was not set out for London, as he was affraid he might have been, and obtain'd a promise that the Presentation should be Renew'd next Year.

In compensation for this Dissappointment, I pass'd the greatest part of this Winter at my Grand Fathers at Tinwald, where I read for many hours of the Day; and generally took the weekly amusement of passing one Day and night at Dumfries where I met with agreable Society both Male and Female and Learn'd what was going on.³

[1743]

I Return'd to Edinr in March and attended the Divinity Hall for a few weeks. Living at Edinr continued still to be wonderfully Cheap as there were ordinaries for Young Gentlemen at 4ᵈ a piece, for a very Good Dinner of Broth and Beef, and a Roast and Potatoes every [Day], with Fish 3 or 4 times a week: and all the Small Beer you call'd for till the cloth was Remov'd. In the Summer* I past some time in E. Lothian, Frequently

---

* It was this Summer that my Father from Mr Keith afterwards ambassador Rec'd a Letter, Desiring I might be sent over to him Immediatly. He had been Sent for by

attending the Presbytery of Haddington, where by accident at that period There were not less than a Doz. Young Scholars, Preachers and Students in Divinity, who generally met there on the Presbytery Day. For two or 3 times we Dined with the Presbytery by Invitation, but finding that we were not very welcome Guests, and that whatever Number there was in company, they never allow'd them more than 2 Bottles of Small Lisbon Wine, we Bespoke a Dinner for ourselves in another Tavern; and when the Days were Short generally Staid all night. Very Early in the Afternoon Mr Stedman* a Minister of the Town, and one or two more of the Clergymen, us'd to Resort to our Company, and keep up an Enlightned and Joyfull Conversation† till Bedtime.‡ John Witherspoon was of this Party, he who was afterwards a Member of the American Congress, and Adam Dickson, who afterwards wrote so well on Husbandry. They were both Clergymens Sons, but of very Different Characters: The One Open and Frank and Generous, Pretending only to what he was, and supporting his title with Spirit, the Other Close and Suspicious, and Jealous, and always aspiring at a Superiority that he was not able to maintain. I us'd sometimes to go with him for a Day or two, to his Fathers House at Giffordhall, where we past the Day in Fishing, to be out of Reach of his Father who was very Sulky and Tyrannical, But who Being much Given to Gluttony, fell asleep Early and went always to Bed at 9, and being as Fat as a porpus, was not to be awak'd, So that we had 3 or 4 hours of Liberty every night to amuse ourselves, with the Daughters of the

Ld Stair, and went to Germany with him as his private Secretary. This was after the Battle of Dettingen. But I knew nothing of it for some years, otherwise I might probably have broke thro' my Fathers Plan. When Ld Stair Lost the Command of the army—Mr Keith Liv'd with him at London, and had a Guinea a Day confer'd on him till he was sent to Holland in 1746, or 47 as Resident. His Knowledge of Modern History and of all the Treaties &c. made him be valued.

* Mr Edward Stedman was 2^d Minister of Haddington and a Man of very Superior Understanding. He it was who first Directed Dr Robertson how to Obtain his Leading in the Church; and who was the Friend and Supporter of John Home, when he was in Danger of being Depos'd for Writing the Tragedy of Douglas. It was Stedman who with the Aid of Hugh Bannatyne, then Minister of Dirleton, and Robertson, Conducted the Affairs of the Presbytery of Haddington in Such a Manner, that they were never able to Reach John Home till it was Convenient for him to Resign his Charge.

† The chief Subjects were the Deistical Controversy and Moral Philosophy, as connected with Theology. Besides Stedman, Murray and Glen almost always attended us.

‡ By this time Even the 2^d Tavern in Haddington where the Presbytery Dined, having Quarrell'd with the first, had Knives and Forks for their Table. But Ten or 12 Years before that time, my Father us'd to Carry a Shagreen Case with a Knife and Fork and Spoon as they perhaps Do still on many parts in the Continent. When I attended in 1742, and 1743, they had still but one Glass on the Table which went Round with the Bottle.

Family, and their Cousins who Resorted to us from the Village when the Old Man was Gone to Rest. This John Lov'd of all things,* and this Sort of Company he enjoy'd in greater Perfection, when he Return'd my Visits, when we had still more Young Companions of the Fair Sex and no restraint from an austere Father. So that I always consider'd, the Austerity of Manners, and aversion to Social Joy which he Affected afterwards, as the Arts of Hypocrisy and Ambition. For he had a Strong and Enlighten'd Understanding far above Enthusiasm, and a Temper that Did not seem Liable to it.

In Nov.ʳ 1743 I went to Glasgow much more opportunely than I should have Done the preceding year, For the Old Professor of Divinity Mʳ Potter who had been a very short while there, Died in the week I went to College, and his Chair being in the Gift of the University, was immediatly Fill'd by Mʳ Wᵐ Leechman, a Neighbouring Clergyman, a Person thoroughly well Qualified for the Office, of which he Gave the Most Satisfactory Proofs, for a great many Years that he Continued Professor of Theology, which was till the Death of Principal Neil Campbell raisd him to the Head of the University. He was a Distinguish'd Preacher, and was follow'd when he was occasionally in Edin.ʳ—His appearance was that of an Ascetick reduc'd by Fasting and Prayer. But in aid of fine Composition, he Deliver'd his Sermons with such a Fervent Spirit, and in so persuasive a Manner as captivated every Audience. This was so much the case, that his Admirers regreted that he should be withdrawn from the Pulpit; For the Prof.ʳ of Theology has no charge in Glasgow, and preaches only occasionally. It was much for the Good of the Church however that he was rais'd to a Station of more Extensive Usefullness. For while his Interesting Manner Drew the Steady Attention of the Students, the Judicious Choice and Arrangement of his Matter Form'd the Most Instructive Set of Lectures in Theology, that had, it was Thought, ever Been Deliver'd in Scotland. It was no Doubt owing to him, and his Friend

* Thomas Hepburn a Distinguish'd Minister who Died Minister of Athelstaneford and was Born and Bred in the Neighbourhood, us'd to allege that a Dʳ Nisbet of Montrose, a Man of Some Learning and Ability which he us'd to Display with little Judgment in the Assembly, was Witherspoons Son, and that he was supported in this opinion by the Scandalous Chronicle of the Country. Their Features no Doubt had a Strong Resemblance but their Persons were unlike. Neither were their Tempers at all Similar. Any likeness there was between them in their Sentiments and Publick appearance might be accounted for by the Great Admiration the Junior must have had for the Senior, as he was bred up under his Eye, in the same parish in which he was much admir'd. Whether or not he was his Son, he follow'd his Example, for he became Discontented, and Migrated to America During the Rebellion, where he was Principal of [Carlisle] College for which he was well qualified in point of Learning: But no preferment nor Climate can Cure a Discont[ent]ed Mind, For he became Miserable because he could not Return.

and Colleague Mr Hutchison Proffr of Moral Philosophy, That a Better Taste and Greater Liberality of Sentiment, was Introduc'd among the Clergy in the Western Provinces of Scotland.

Able as this Gentleman was however, and highly unexceptionable, not only in Morals, but in Decorum of Behaviour, he was not allow'd to ascend his Chair without much Opposition, and even a Prosecution for Heresy. Invulnerable as he seem'd to be, the Keen and Prying Eye of Fanaticism, Discover'd a weak place, to which they Directed their attacks. There had been publish'd at Glasgow,* about that period a small pamphlet against the use of Prayer, which had circulated among the Inferior Ranks, and had made no small Impression, Being artfully compos'd. To counteract this Poison Leechman had compos'd and Publish'd his Sermon, on the Nature, Reasonableness and Advantages of Prayer, with an attempt to answer the Objections against it from Mat. 26. 41. In this Sermon, tho' admirably well Compos'd, in Defence of Prayer as a Duty of Natural Religion, the Author had forgot or omitted to State the Obligation on Christians to Pray in the Name of Christ. The Nature of his Subject Did not Lead him to state this part of a Christian's prayer, and perhaps he thought, That the Inserting any thing Relative to that point, might Disgust, or Lessen the Curiosity of those, for whose Conviction he had publish'd his Sermon. The Fanatical or Highflying Clergy in the Presbytery of Glasgow took advantage of this omission, and Instituted an Enquiry into the Heresy Contain'd in this Sermon, by Omission, which lasted with much Theological Acrimony on the Part of the Enquirers† till it was Finally Settled in Favour of the Proffr by the General Assembly 1744.‡

I attended Hutchesons Class this year with Great Satisfaction and Improvement. He was a Good Looking Man of an Engaging Countenance. He Deliver'd his Lectures without Notes walking Backwards and forwards in the Area of his Room—as his Elocution was Good and his Voice and Manner pleasing, he rais'd the attention of his Hearers at all times, and when the Subject Led him to Explain and Inforce the Moral Virtues and Duties, he Display'd a fervent and Persuasive Eloquence which was Irresistible. Besides the Lectures he Gave thro' the Week, he every Sunday at Six a clock, open'd his class Room to whoever chose to attend, when he Deliver'd a Set of Lectures on Grotius' De Veritate Religionis

---

* or in the neighbourhood of Dr Leechman's Church in the Country before he came to Glasgow.

† who were chiefly those who had Encourag'd Cambuslang Work[1] as it was Call'd two years before.

‡ Instead of Raising any anxiety among the Students in Theology, or Creating any Suspicion of Dr Leechman's Orthodoxy, This Fit of Zeal against him, tended much to Spread and Establish his Superior Character.

Christianæ, which tho' Learned and Ingenious were adapted to every Capacity. For on that evening he expected to be attended not only by Students but by many of the People of the City, and he was not Dissappointed. For this Free Lecture always drew Crowds of Attendants.

Besides Hutcheson and Leechman, There were at that period Several Eminent Professors in that University, Particularly Mr Robert Simpson the Great Mathematician, and Mr Alex^r Dunlop the Professor of Greek. The Last besides his Eminence as a Greek Scholar, was Distinguish'd by his Strong Good Sense and Capacity for Business, and Being a Man of a Leading Mind was suppos'd with the aid of Hutcheson to Direct and Manage all the affairs of the University; for it is a wealthy Corporation and has much Business, Besides the charge of Presiding over Literature and maintaining the Discipline of the College.

One Difference I remark'd between this university and that of Edin^r where I had been bred, which was that, altho' at that time, there appear'd to be a mark'd Superiority in the best Scholars and most Diligent Students of Edin^r, Yet in Glasgow Learning Seem'd to be an Object of more Importance, and the Habit of Application was much more general.— Besides the Instruction I Rec'd from Drs Hutchison and Leechman, I Deriv'd much pleasure, as well as Enlargement of Skill in the Greek Language, from Mr Dunlops Translations and Criticisms of the Great Tragick Writers in that Language. I likewise attended the Professor of Hebrew, a Mr Morthland, who was Master of his Business, having neglected that Branch at Edin^r the Professor Being then Superannuated.

In the 2^d week I was in Glasgow, I went to the Dancing Assembly with some of my New Acquaintance, and was there Introduc'd to a Married Lady, who claim'd Kindred with me, her Mothers Name being Carlyle of the Limekiln Family. She carried me home to sup with her that night, with a Brother of hers two Years younger than me, and some other young people. This was the Commencement of an Intimate Friendship, that lasted during the Whole of the Lady's Life, which was four or five and Twenty Years. She was Connected with all the Best Families in Glasgow, and the Country Round. Her Husband was a Good Sort of Man and very Opulent, and as they had no Children, he took pleasure in her exercising a Genteel Hospitality. By this Lady's Means I became acquainted, with all the Best Families in the Town; and by a Letter I had procur'd from my Friend James Edgar, afterwards a Commissioner of the Customs, I soon became well acquainted with all the Young Ladies who Liv'd in the College: He had studied Law the preceding Year at Glasgow, under Proff^r Hercules Lindsay, at that time of some Note. I ask'd him for a Letter of Introduction to some one of his Companions. He gave me one to Miss Mally Campbell, the Daughter of the Principal, and when I seem'd surpris'd at his choice, he added That I would find her not only more Beautifull than any Woman there, but more Sensible and Friendly, than all the Professors put together, and much more usefull to me. This I found to be Literally True.

The City of Glasgow at this time, tho' very Industrious and Wealthy and Commercial, was far Inferior to what it afterwards became both before and after the Failure of the Virginia Trade.[1] The Modes of Life too and Manners were Different from what they are at Present. Their Chief Branches were the Tobacco Trade with the American Colonies, and Sugar and Rum with the West India. There were not Manufactures Sufficient either there or at Paisley, to Supply an Outward Bound Cargo for Virginia. For this purpose they were oblig'd to have Recourse to Manchester. Manufactures were in their Infancy. About this time, the Incle[2] Manufactory was first begun by Ingram and Glasford, and was shewn to Strangers as a Great Curiosity. But the Merchants had Industry, and Stock and the Habits of Business; and were Ready to Sieze with Eagerness and prosecute with vigour, every new object in Commerce or Manufactures that promis'd Success. Few of them could be call'd Learned Merchants; Yet there was a weekly club, of which a Provost Cochran was the Founder, and a Leading Member, in which their Express Design was to Enquire into the Nature and principles of Trade in all its Branches, and to Communicate their Knowledge and Views on that Subject to each other. I was not acquainted with Provost Cochran at this time: But I observ'd that the members of this Society had the Highest Admiration of his Knowledge and Talents. I became well acquainted with him 20 Years afterwards, when Drs Smith and Wight were Members of the Club; and was made sensible that too much could not be said of his accurate and extensive Knowledge, of his agreable Manners, and Colloquial Eloquence. Dr Smith acknowleg'd his Obligations to this Gentleman's Information, when he was Collecting Materials for his Wealth of Nations: and the Junior Merchants who have flourish'd since his time and extended their Commerce far beyond what was then Dream't of, Confess with respectfull Remembrance, That it was Andrew Cochrane who first open'd and enlarg'd their Views.

It was not long before I was well Establish'd in close Intimacy with many of my Fellow Students, and soon felt the Superiority of an Education in the College of Edin^{r}, not in Point of Knowledge or acquirements in the Languages or Sciences, but in knowledge of the world and a Certain Manner and Address that can only be attain in the Capital. It must be confess'd that at this time they were far behind in Glasgow, not only in their Manner of Living, but in those Accomplishments and that Taste that belongs to people of Opulence, much more to persons of Education.

There were only a few Families of antient Citizens, who pretended to be Gentlemen—and a Few others who were Recent Settlers there who had obtain'd Wealth and Consideration in Trade. The Rest were Shopkeepers or Mechanics, or Successfull Pedlars, who occupied Large Ware-Rooms full of Manufactures of all Sorts, to Furnish a Cargo to Virginia. It was usual for the Sons of Merchants to attend the College, for one or two Years: and a few of them compleated their academical Education. In this respect the Females were still worse off, for at that period there was neither a Teacher of French nor of Musick in the Town. The Consequence of this was twofold. 1st the Young Ladies were entirely without accomplishments, and in general had nothing to Recommend them but Good Looks and Fine Cloathes, For their Manners were ungainly. 2dly The few who were Distinguish'd, Drew all the Young Men of Sense and Taste about them, for Being void of Frivolous Accomplishments, which in some respects make all Women Equal, they Trusted only to Superior Understanding and Wit, to Natural Elegance, and unaffected Manners.

There never was but one Concert During the two Winters I was at Glasgow, and that was Given by Walter Scott Esqr of Harden who was himself an Eminent performer on the Violin; and his Band of assistants Consisted, of two Dancing School Fidlers, and the Town Waits.

The Manner of Living too at this time was but Coarse and Vulgar. Very Few of the Wealthiest Gave Dinners, to any Body but English Riders, or their own Relations at Christmas Holidays. There were not half a Dozen Families in the Town who had Men Servants. Some of those were Intertain'd by the Professors who had Boarders. There were no Post-chaises in [those Days.] There were no Hackney Coaches in the Town, and only three or four Sedan chairs, for Carrying Midwives about in the Night, Old Ladies to Church, or to the Dancing assembly once a Fortnight.

The Principal Merchants fatigued with the Morning Business, Took an Early Dinner with their Families at Home, and then Resorted to the Coffee House or Tavern to Read the Newspapers, which they generally Did in Companies of 4 or 5 in Separate Rooms over a Bottle of Claret: or a Bowl of Punch. But they never staid Supper, but always went home by 9 a clock without Company or farther Amusement. At Last an Arch Fellow from Dublin a Mr Cockaine came to be Master of the Chief Coffee House, who Seduc'd them Gradually to Stay Supper, by placing a few nice cold things at first on the Table as Relishers to the Wine, till he Gradually Led them on to bespeak fine Hot Suppers, and to Remain till Midnight.

There was an Order of Women at that time in Glasgow, who Being either Young Widows not Wealthy, or Young Women unprovided for, were set up in Small Grocery Shops in various parts of the Town, who generally were protected and Countenanc'd by some Creditable Merchant. In their Back Shops much time and Money were Consum'd, for it being Customary then to Drink Drams,[1] and white Wine in the Forenoon, the Tipplers resorted much to those Shops where there were Back rooms—and the Patron with his Friends frequently pass'd the evening there also, as Taverns were not frequented by persons, who affected Characters of Strict Decency.

I was admitted a Member of two Clubs, one entirely Literary, which was held in the Porter's Lodge at the College; and where we Criticis'd Books, and wrote abridgements of them with Critical Essays: and to this Society we submitted, the Discourses which we were to Deliver in the Divinity Hall in our Turns when we were appointed by the professor. The other club met in Mrs Dugalds Tavern near the Cross weekly and admitted a Mixture of Young Gentlemen, who were not Intended for the Study of Theology.* These Societies contributed much to our Improvement, and as Moderation and Early Hours were Inviolable Rules of both Institutions, they Serv'd to open and enlarge our Minds.

* There met there John Bradefoot afterwards Minister of Dunsire, Jas Lesly of Kilmarnock, John Robertson of Dumblane, Jas Hamilton of Paisly and Rob. Lawson of London Wall.—There came also some young Merchants, such as Robin Bogle my relation, Jas and Geo. Anderson, Wm Sellers and Robin Craig—here we Drank a little Punch after our beef Steaks and pancakes, where the Expence never exceeded 1/6, seldom was more than one shilling. Our Conversation was almost entirely Literary, and we were of such Good Fame that some Ministers of the Neighbourhood when Occasionally in Glasgow frequented our Club—Hyndman had been twice Introduced by Members, and Being at that time Passing Trials as a Probationer before that Presbytery in which his Native Town of Greenock Lay, he had become well acquainted with Mr Robt Paton Minister of Renfrew, who tho' a Man well . . . and of Liberal Sentiments, was too much a Man of Worth and principle not to be offended with Licentious Manners in Students of Divinity. Hyndman by way of Gaining Favour with this man took occasion to Hint to him to advise his Nephew Robt Lawson not to frequent our Club, as we admitted of and encouraged Conversation not suitable to the profession we were to Follow. He mention'd two Instances, which Lawson said was one of them false, and the other Disguis'd by Exaggeration. Lawson who was a Lad of pure Morals told me this, and as the best antidote to this Injurious Impression which had been made chiefly against me, I beg'd him to Let his Uncle know, that I would accept of the Invitation he had Given thro' him to pass a night or two with him at Renfrew. We accordingly went next Sat. and met with a Gracious Reception: and staid all next Day and heard him preach, at which he was thought to excell, tho' he was almost the only person who Read in those Days, in which he truly excell'd, and Being a very Handsome Man, his Delivery much enhanced the value of his Composition. We heard him Read another night in his Study, with much Satisfaction, as he told us it was one of his best, and was a Good Model. To this we respectfully assented, and the Good Man was pleas'd. When we took Leave on Monday Morn. he politely requested another visit, and said to me with a Smile, he was now fortified against Tale Bearers.[2]

[1744]

Towards the end of the Session however I was Introduc'd to a Club, which gave me much more Satisfaction. I mean that of Mr Robert Simpson the Celebrated Proff^r of Mathematicks. Mr Robert Dick Proff^r of Natural Philosophy, an old Friend of my Fathers, one Evening after I Din'd with him, said he was going to Mr Roberts Club, and if I had a Mind he would take me there and Introduce me. I readily accepted the Honour. I had been Introduc'd to Mr Robert before in the College Court, for he was extremely Courteous, and shew'd Civility to every Student who fell in his Way, tho' I was not attending any of his classes.* He Rec'd me with Great Kindness, and I had the Good Fortune to please him so much, that he ask'd me to be a Member of his Friday's Club, which I readily agreed to. Mr Simpson tho' a Great Humourist, who had a very particular way of Living, was well Bred and Complaisant, was a comely Man of a Good Size and had a very prepossessing Countenance. He Liv'd entirely at the small Tavern opposite the College Gate, kept by a Mrs Millar. He breakfasted Dined and Sup'd there—and almost never accepted of any Invitations to Dinner: and paid no Visits but to Illustrious or Learned Strangers, who wish'd to see the University. On such Occasions he was always the Cicerone. He shew'd the Curiosities of the Colledge which consisted of a few Manuscripts, and a large Collection of Roman Antiquities from Severus's Wall, or Grahams Dyke in the Neighbourhood, with a Display of much Knowledge and Taste. He was particularly averse to the Company of Ladies, and except one Day in the Year, when he Drank Tea at Principal Campbells, and convers'd with Gaiety and Ease, with his Daughter Mally, who was always his 1st Toast, he was never in Company with them. It was said to have been otherwise with him in his Youth, and that he had been much attach'd to one Lady to whom he had made Proposals, but on her Refusing him he became Disgusted with the Sex. The Lady was Dead before I became acquainted with the Family. But the Husband I knew, and must confess that in her Choice the Lady had Preferr'd a Satyr to Hyperion.[1] Mr Simpson almost never Left the Bounds of the College, having a large Garden to Walk in, unless it was on Sat. when with two chosen Companions he always walk'd into the Country but no Farther than the Village of Anderston one mile off, where he had a Dinner bespoke, and where he always treated the Company, not only when he had no other but his two humble attendants, but when he casually added one or two more, which happend twice to myself. If any of the Club met him on Saturday night at his Hotel, he took it very Kind, for he was in Good Spirits, tho' fatigued with the Company of his Satellites,

* Having attended McLaurin in Edin^r for 3 Sessions.

and Reviv'd on the Sight of a fresh Companion or two for the Evening. He was of a Mild Temper and of an Engaging Demeanour, and was Master of all Knowledge, even of Theology, which he told us he had Learn'd by his Being one Year Amanuensis to his Uncle, the Professor of Divinity; which he Deliver'd in an Easy Colloquial Stile, with the Simplicity of a Child, and without the Least Symptom of Self-Sufficiency or Arrogance.

His club at that time Consisted chiefly of Hercules Lindsay Teacher of Law, who was Talkative and assuming, of James Moore, Proffessor of Greek on the Death of Mr Dunlop, a very Lively and Witty Man and a Famous Grecian, but a More Famous Punster, Mr Dick Professor of Nat. Phil. a very worthy Man, and of an agreable Temper, and Mr James Purdie the Rector of the Grammar School, who had not much to Recommend him, but his Being an adept in Grammar.* His most constant attendant however and Greatest Favourite was his own Scholar, Mr Mat. Stuart afterwards Proffr of Maths in the College of Edinr, much Celebrated for his Profound Knowledge in that Science. During the Course of Summer he was ordain'd Minister of Rosneath, but resided during the Winter in Glasgow College. He was of an amiable Disposition, and of a most Ingenuous Mind; and was highly Valued in the Society of Glasgow University. But when he was prefer'd to a chair in Edinr, Being of Diminutive Stature, and of an ordinary appearance, and having withall an Embarrass'd Elocution, he was not able to bring himself into Good Company, and Being Left out of the Society of those, who should have Seen thro' the Shell, and put a Due Value on the Kirnell, he fell into Company of an Inferior Sort, and adopted their Habits with too Great Facility.

With this Club, and an accidental Stranger at times, the Great Mr Robert Simpson Relax'd his Mind every evening, from the Severe Studies of the Day; For tho' there was properly but one Club night in the week, yet as he never Failed to be there, some one or two commonly attended him, or at least one of the two Minions he always commanded and whom he could Command at any time as he paid their Keeping.

The Fame of Mr Hucheson had fill'd the College with Students of Philosophy, and Leechman's high Character brought all the Students of Divinity from the Western Provinces, as Hucheson attracted the Irish. There were sundry young Gentlemen from Ireland with their Tutors, one of whom was Archd Mclaine, Pastor at the Hague, the Celebrated Trans-

---

* Having been ask'd to See a Famous Comet that appeard this Winter or the Following, thro' Professor Dicks Telescope, which was the best in the College at that time, when Mr Purdie Retir'd from Tak[ing] his view of it, he Turn'd to Mr Simson and said, Mr Robert, I believe it is Hic or Hæc Cometa a Comet. To settle the Gender of the Latin Name, was all he thought about this Great and Uncommon Phenomenon of Nature.

lator of Mosh[e]ims Ecclesiastical History.* With him I became better acquainted next Session, and I have often Regretted since, that it has never been my Lot to meet him, During the many times I have been for Months in London, as his enlightned Mind, engaging Manners, and animated Conversation, gave Reason to hope for excellent Fruit when he arriv'd at Maturity. There were of Young Men of Fashion attending the College, Walter Lord Blantyre, who Died young, Sir [Thomas] Kennedy and his Brother Davᵈ afterwards Lord Cassilis, Walter Scott of Harden, James Murray of Broughton &c. and Dunbar Hamilton, afterwards Earl of Selkirk. The Education of this Last Gentleman, had been Marr'd at an English Academy in Yorkshire. When his Father the Honᵇˡᵉ Basil H. Died, he came to Glasgow: But finding that he was so Illfounded in Latin as to be unfit to attend a Publick Class, he had resolution enough at the age of 15 to pass seven or 8 hours a Day, with Purdie the Gramarian, for the greater part of two Years, when having acquir'd Latin, he took James Moore the Greek Scholar for his Private Tutor, Fitted up Rooms for himself in the College, and Livd there with Moore in the most Retir'd Manner—visiting nobody but Miss M. Campbell, and Letting nobody in to him but Lᵈ Blantyre and myself, as I was his Distant Relation. In this Manner he liv'd for 10 Years, hardly Leaving the College for a few weeks in Summer, till he had acquir'd the Antient Tongues in Perfection, and was Master of Antient Philosophy. The Effect of which was, That with much Rectitude and Good Intention, and some Talents, he came into the World more fit to be a Professor than an Earl.

There was one advantage I Deriv'd from my Edinʳ Education which set me up a little in the Eyes of my Equals, tho' I soon Tir'd of the Employment. Proffʳ Leechman Devoted one Evening [a week] from 5 to 8 to Conversation with his Students, who assembled on Fridays about 6 or 7 together, and were first Rec'd in the Professors own Library. But Dʳ Leechman was not able to carry on Common Conversation; and when he spoke at all, it was a short Lecture. This was therefore a very Dull Meeting; and every Body Long'd to be Call'd in to Tea with Mʳˢ Leechman; whose Talent being Different from that of her Husband, she was able to Maintain a Continued Conversation, on Plays and Novels and Poetry and the Fashions. The Rest of the Lads Being for most part Raw and aukward, after trying it once in their Turns they became Silent, and the Dialogue Rested between the Lady and me. When she observ'd this, she Requested me to attend as her assistant every night. I Did so for a Little While, but it became too Intolerable not to be soon Given up by me.

What Dʳ Leechman wanted in the Talent for Conversation was Fully Compensated, by his Ability as a Professor. For in the Chair he shone with

* (Who had himself been bred at Glasgow College).

Great Lustre. It was owing to Hucheson and him, that a New School was form'd in the Western Provinces of Scotland, where the clergy till that Period were narrow and bigotted, and had never ventur'd to Range in their Minds, beyond the Bounds of Strict Orthodoxy. For tho' neither of these Professors taught any Heresy, yet they open'd and enlarg'd the Minds of the Students, which soon gave Them a Turn for Free Enquiry; the Result of which was Candour and Liberality of Sentiment. From Experience this Freedom of thought was not found so Dangerous as might at first be apprehended; For tho' the Daring Youth made excursions into the unbounded Regions of Metaphysical Perplexity, yet all the Judicious soon Return'd to the Lower Sphere of long Establish'd Truths, which they found not only more subservient to the Good Order of Society, but necessary to fix their own [Minds] in some Degree of Comfortable Stability.

Hucheson was a Great Admirer of Shaftsbury, and adopted much of his Writings into his Lectures; and to Recommend him more to his Students, was at great pains in Private to prove That the Noble Moralist was no Enemy to the Christian Religion; But that all appearances of that kind, which are very Numerous in his Works, flow'd only from an excess of Generous Indignation against the Fanaticks of Charles the 1st Reign. Leechman and he Both were suppos'd to Lean to Socinianism. Men of Sense however soon perceiv'd, That it was an arduous Task to Defend Christianity on that Ground, and were Glad to adopt more common and vulgar Principles, which were well Compacted together in an uniform System which it was not easy to Demolish.

Leechman's Manner of Teaching Theology was excellent and I found my Sphere of Knowledge in that Science, Greatly Enlarged, tho' I had attended the Professor at Edin.r pretty closely for two or three Years. But he Copied the Dutch Divines, and had he liv'd would have Taken 20 Years, to have Gone thro' the System, which Dr Leechman accomplish'd in two Years, Besides Giving us admirable Lectures, on the Gospels, on the proofs of Christianity, and the art of Composition. If there was any Defect, it was in the Small Number of Exercises prescrib'd to the Students, for one Discourse in a Session, was by no means sufficient to produce a Habit of Composition. Our Literary Clubs in some Degree supplied that Defect.*

---

* I had been call'd home to Prestonpans in Jan.y to see my Brother James, who was then Dying of a Consumption. He was in his 19t.h [Year] and Dyed in March. He had been Sent to London Several Years before to be bred to Business, but an accident threw him into bad Health and he had been at home for 2 Years, or more. He was not a lad of Parts, but Remarkably Handsome and agreable. I found him perfectly Reconcil'd to a premature Death.

I had left my original Companions at Edin.r, who had every Kind of Merit to Create Attachment, but I found a few in Glasgow University, who in some Degree supplied their places, who were worthy and able Young Men, and afterwards fill'd their Ranks in Society with Credit, tho' they had neither the Strength nor the Polish of the Blairs and Robertsons, and Fergusons and Homes. Near the end of the Session, I made an acquaintance with a Young Gentleman, which next Year grew into the strictest Friendship. This was W.m Sellar, then an apprentice in his 3.d or 4.th year with the Oswalds at that time the most Eminent Merchants in Glasgow. He was the Son of a W.S.1 in Edin.r, had been two or three Years at the College there, was Handsome and Wellbred and of very agreable Manners. Tho' not Learned he had a Philosophical and Observing Mind, and was Shrewd in Discerning Characters. This Young Man, my Junior by a Year or two, attach'd himself to me on our First Acquaintance, and I soon Repaid him with my Affection for I found that the Qualities of his Heart were not Inferior to those of his Understanding. He was daily Conversant with the Principal Merchants as I was with the Students and Members of the University; on whom our Observations were a Great Source of Instructive Entertainment. He had the Celebrated Jenny Fall, afterwards Lady Anstruther, a Coquette and a Beauty for Months together in the House with him, and as his person and Manners Drew the Mark'd Attention of the Ladies, he Deriv'd Considerable Emprovement from his Constant Intercourse with this Young Lady for she was Lively and Cliver no less than Beautifull. He had also the Benefit of M.r Richard Oswalds Conversation, a Man afterwards so much Celebrated as to be Employ'd by Government in Settling the Peace of Paris in 1783—This Gentleman was much Confin'd to the House with Sore Eyes, and yet was able to pass his time almost Entirely in Reading. And Becoming a very Learned and Intelligent Merchant, and Having acquird some Thousand Pounds, by his Being Prize Agent for his Cousins, whose Privateer had taken a Prize worth £15000, he a few years after this Period Establish'd himself at London, acquir'd a Great Fortune, which Having no Children of his own, he left to the Grandson of his Brother a Respectable Clergyman of the Church of Scotland; and thus founded that Family of Oswald who Continue to flourish in the Shire of Air.2

I liv'd this Winter in the same house with D.r Robert Hamilton Proff.r of Anatomy, an Ingenious and well bred Man, But with him I had little Intercourse, except at Breakfast now and then, for he always Dined abroad. He had a Younger Brother a Student of Divinity, afterwards his Fathers Successor at Bothwell, who was vain and shewy but who expos'd himself very much thro' a Desire of Distinction. He was a Relation of M.rs Leechmans, and it had been hinted to him, that the Proff.r expected a

Remarkable Discourse from him. He accordingly Deliver'd one which Gave Universal Satisfaction, and was much Extoll'd by the Professor. But very unfortunatly for Hamilton, half a Dozen of Students in Going down Streets, Resorted to a Booksellers Shop, where one of them taking a vol. from a Shelf, was struck on opening the Book to find the 1ˢᵗ Sermon from the Text he had just heard preach'd upon. He read on, and found it was verbatim from beginning to end, what he had heard in the Hall. He shew'd it to his Companions, who laugh'd heartily, and Spread the Story all over the Town before night. Not soon Enough to prevent the Vain-Glorious Orator, from Circulating two fine Copies of it, one among the Ladies in the College, and another in the Town. What aggravated the Folly and Imprudence of this Young Man, was, that he was by no means Difficient in parts, of which he gave us sundry Specimens. His Cousin and Namesake James Hamilton, afterwards Minister of Paisly, was much asham'd of him; and Being a much more Sterling Man, was able to keep down his Vanity ever after. He had submitted his Manuscript to the Club, and two or three Criticisms had been made on it, but he would alter nothing. After Dr Robert Hamiltons Death, which was premature, a Younger Brother succeeded him in the Anatomical Chair, who was very able—who Dying Young also, his Son was advanc'd, who was said to have surpass'd all his predecessors in ability. They were Descended of the Family of Hamiltons of Preston, a very antient Branch of Duke Hˢ Family.

Dr Johnstone who was said to be very Able, was at this time Professor of Medecine. But he was very old, and Died this Year, and was succeeded by Dr Wᵐ Cullen, who had been Settled at Hamilton: In those Days there were but few Students of Physick, in that University. Dr Cullen and his Successor Dr Black, with the Younger Hamiltons brought the School of Medecine more into Repute there.*

Tho' the Theological Lectures clos'd in the beginning of May, on

* In the Month of March or April this Year, having Gone Down with a Merchant to visit New Port Glasgow, as our Dinner was preparing at the Inn, we were alarm'd with the Howling and Weeping of half a Dozen of Women in the Kitchen; Which was so loud and lasting that I went to see what was the Matter; When after some time I Learn'd from the Calmest among them, That a Pedlar having Left a Copy of Peden's Prophecy's that Morning, which having read part of they found that he had predicted woes of every kind to the people of Scotland, and that in particular, that Clyde would be overflow'd with Blood in the Year 1744, which now being some months advanc'd they Believ'd that their Destruction was at hand. I was puzzled how to pacify them, but calling for the Book I found that the passage which had Terrified them, was contain in the 44ᵗʰ Paragraph of the Book, without any allusion whatever to the Year; and by this Means, I quieted their Lamentations. Had the Intended Expedition of Mareschal Saxe¹ been carri'd into execution in that year as was Intended their Fears might have been Realis'd.

account of some accidental circumstances, I Did not Get to my Fathers till the Middle of that Month. My Fathers Wish was that I should pass thro' my Trials to be admitted a Probationer[1] in Summer 1745, and Leave nothing undone but the finishing Forms, when I Return'd in 1746 from a forreign Protestant University, where I was bound to Go by the Terms of the Exhibition I held. I was to spend a part of this Summer 1744, in visiting the clergy of the Presbytery of Haddington, as the Forms requir'd that I should perform that Duty before I was admitted to Trials.

I made my Tour accordingly Early in Summer, and shall give a short Specimen of my Reception and the Characters I met with. I first past a Day at Aberlady, where Mr And. Dickson was then Minister, the Father of Adam Dickson, the Author of many excellent Works on Agriculture. Mr Dickson was a well bred Formal Old Man and was Reckon'd a Good Preacher tho' Lame Enough in the Article of Knowledge, or indeed of Discernment. Among the first Questions he put to me, was, Had I read the Famous Pamphlet, Christianity not founded on Argument. I answer'd that I had. He Replied that certainly That Elaborate Work, was the Ablest Defence of our Holy Religion, that had been publish'd in Our Times, and that the Author of it who was unknown to him Deserv'd the Highest praise.[2] I look'd surpris'd and was Going to make him an Answer, according to my Opinion, which was that it was the Shrewdest Attack that ever had been made on Christianity. But his Son observ'd me, and Broke in by saying That he had had some Disputes with his Father on the Subject, but had now Yielded and had come in to his Opinion. I only Subjoin'd That whoever saw it in that light, must subscribe to its Superiority. The Old Gentleman, was pleas'd, and went on Descanting on the Great Merit, of this New Proof of Reveald Religion, which was quite unanswerable. Having Settled that point, There was no Danger of my Differing from him in any other of his Notions.

Next Day I proceeded to Dirleton the Neighbouring Parish, where Mr James Glen was the Incumbent. This was a Man of Middle Age, Fat and unwieldy[3]. . . Good Natur'd and Open Hearted . . . very Social, tho' quick Temper'd and Jealous. He was a Great Master of the Deistical Controversy, had read all the Books, and never stop'd, for it was his first topick with me till he Compleatly Refuted Christianity not founded on Argument, which he said was truly very Insidious. There was not much time however this Day for Theology, as it happen'd to be his *Cherry Feast*, there being many Fine Trees of that Fruit in his Garden: When they were fully Ripe it was his Custom to Invite some of his Neighbours and their Families to pass the Day with him and his Daughters, and the only Son then at Home, Mr Alexr Glen who was a Student and two years

47

my Junior. We were a very large Company, among whom, were Congalton of that ilk, a very Singular Gentleman of very Good Parts, and extremely promising when he pass'd Advocate but who had become a Drunken Laird; tho' the Brilliancy of his Wit frequently broke thro' the Cloud. There were likewise 4 Miss Hepburns of Beanstone, who were Young and Handsome and Gay. The old people Dispers'd not long after Dinner, and went their Several Ways—Congalton and his Swaggering Blades went to the Village Changehouse, and Remaind there all night. There not being lodging in the House for us all, the young men Remaind as late as they could in the Parlour, and then had Mattresses brought in to sleep a while upon.

When I wish'd to Depart next Day, with the rest of the Company, the old man protested against that, for we had not yet sufficiently Settled the Deistical Controversy, and the Foundations of Moral Sentiment. I Consented, and as his Daughters had Detain'd two Miss Hepburns, I pass'd the Day very well, between Disputing with my Landlord, and walking about and Philandering with the Ladies. When I came to Leave him after Breakfast next Day, it was with the Greatest Difficulty he would part with me, and not till after he had taken my Sollemn promise to come soon back, as I was the only Friend he had left in the World. I at last escap'd after he had shed a Flood of Tears. I was uneasy and ask'd afterwards if he was not a very Solitary Man: No they said but that he was of a Jealous Temper, and thought he was hated, if he was not Resorted to more than it was possible.

The next Clergyman, Mr Geo. Murray of N. Berwick was in appearance quite the opposite of Mr Glen, for he was a Dry Wither'd Stick, and as Cold and Repulsive in his Manner, as the other was Kind and Inviting. But he was not the less to be depended on for that, for he was very Worthy and Sensible; Tho' at the Age of 50, as Torpid in mind as in body. His Wife however, of the Name of Reid the Former Ministers Daughter, by whose Interest he Got the Church, was as Swift to Speak as he was Slow. And as he never Interrupted her, She kept up the Conversation, such as it was without Ceasing, except that her Household Affairs took her sometimes out of the Room, when he began some Metaphysical Argument, But Drop'd it the moment she appear'd, for he said *Anny* Did not like Those Subjects. Worn out however with the Fatigues of the Cherry feast I Longd to be in Bed, and took the 1st opportunity of a Cessation in Anny's Clapper to request to be shewn to my Room—This was complied with about 11—But the worthy Man accompany'd me, and being at last Safe and at Liberty, we began a Conversation on Liberty and Necessity, and the Foundation of Morals, and the Deistical Controversy, that lasted till two in the Morning.

I Got away time enough next Day to reach Haddington before Dinner; Having past by Athelstaneford where the Minister Mr Robert Blair Author of The Grave, was said to be Dying Slowly; or at any Rate, was so Austere and void of Urbanity, as to make him quite Dissagreable to Young People. His Wife who was in every respect his Opposite, a Sister of Shirreff Law's, was Frank and Open and uncommonly Handsome. Yet even with her allurements, and his acknowledg'd ability, his House was unfrequented.

I pass'd on to Haddington and Dined with Mr Edward Stedman, a Man of first Rate Sense and Ability and the Leader of the Presbytery. We call'd on his Father in Law Mr Pat. Wilkie, who had as little Desire to examine Young Men, as he had Capacity to Judge of their profficiency. So that I had only to pay my Compliments, and pass an Hour or Two with Stedman, whom I knew well before and who with the Sombre Constrain'd Air of a Jesuit, or an Old Covenanter, had an Enlighten'd and Ardent Mind and Comprehended all things Human and Divine. From him I went Early in the Evening to Mr Barclay's at Moreham, a Good Sensible Man, But with not many Words or Topicks of Conversation, for he was a Great Mathematician. With the Help of his Wife and Daughter, we made a Shift however to Spend the Evening, and retir'd at an Early Hour.

I pass'd on next forenoon to Garvald, where Liv'd his Son in Law Mr Archd Blair, Brother of Mr Robert. He seem'd as Torpid as Geo. Murray, and not more Enlighten'd than Pat. Wilkie. He Conversd none; as we walk'd out before Dinner to see the Views which were not Remarkable, I thought I might try to *Examine him*, and put a Question to him as we Enterd the Church Yard, which he Answer'd when we Got to the Far End of the Glebe. His Wife however made it well up. This with other Instances Convinc'd me that it would have been better if the Wives had Preach'd and their Husbands Spun.

From hence I went to the next Manse which was Yester, where I had been very frequently before with John Witherspoon, afterwards the Celebrated Dr: The Father, who had very few Topicks to Examine on, as the Depth of his Reading was in the Sermons of the French Calvinist Ministers which he Preach'd Daily, was besides too Lazy to Engage in any thing so arduous as the Examination of a Student.—How to Eat and Drink and Sleep being his Sole Care: tho' he was not without parts, if the Soul had not been buried under a Mountain of Flesh.

The Next I went to was old Lundie of Saltoun, a Pious and Primitive Old Man, very Respectfull in his Manners and very Kind. He had been bred an old Scotch Episcopal, and was averse to the Confession of Faith. The Presbytery shew'd Lenity towards him so he Did not Sign it to his Dying Day, For which Reason he never would be a Member of Assembly.

The Last I went to on this Tour, was Mat. Simpson of Pencaitland, a Brother of Prof.ʳ Simpson who had been Suspended for Heresy, and an Uncle of the Celebrated Dʳ Robert Simpson of Glasgow. Their Father was Mʳ Pat. Simpson of Renfrew, who had been Tutor to some of the Family of Argyll—Mʳ Mat. was an old Man but very Different in his Manners from Mʳ Lundie, For he was Frank and Open and Familiar, as much as the other was Reserv'd and Dignified. He was an excellent Examinator for he answer'd all his own Questions, and Concluded all with a Receipt for making Sermons, which he said would serve as a General Rule, and answer well, be the Text what it would. This was to Begin first with an acc.ᵗ of the Fall of Man, and the Depravity of Human Nature, then, a Statement of the Means of our Recovery by the Grace of our Lᵈ Jesus Christ, and thirdly an application: consisting of Observations, or Uses or Reflections, or Practical Inferences, Tending to make us Good Men. For my Patient Hearing he made me a present of a Pen-case of his own Turning, and added If I would come and stay a week with him, he would Teach me to Turn, and Converse over the System[1] with me, for he saw I was tolerably well founded, as my Father was an able Calvinist. He said he would order his Son Patrick who was a more Powerfull Master of the Turning Loom than he was, to turn me a Nice Snuff Box or Egg Cup, which I pleas'd; But Pat was Lazy and Lik'd better to Go about with the Gun, from which he Did not restrain him, as he not only furnish'd his Sisters with Plenty of Partridges and Hares, but likewise Gratified the Lady Pencaitland with many. Thus ended my preparatory Trial by Visiting the Clergy: For with the two or three nearer home I was well acquainted.

Early in Nov.ʳ this Year 1744 I Return'd to Glasgow. As it was a hard frost, I chose to walk, and went the first Day, to my Friend Mʳ Hew Horns at Foxhall near Kirkliston. He had been Married for a Year or two to Miss Inglis a Daughter of Sir John Inglis, a handsome and agreable Woman. I perceiv'd that he was much chang'd and thought him in a very Dangerous Way. He was however very chearfull and pleasant, and sate up with me till eleven a clock. I Breakfasted with him next Morning, and then took my Leave with a forboding that I should see him no more. Which was verifi'd for he Gave Way, not many Months afterwards. In him I lost a most Valuable Friend. I walk'd to Whitburn at an Early Hour, But could venture no Farther, as there was no Tolerable Lodging House within my Reach. There was then not even a Cottage nearer than the Kirk of Shotts, and Whitburn itself was a Solitary House, in a Desolate Country.

Next Morning the Frost was Gone, and such a Deluge of Rain and Tempest of Wind, took possession of the atmosphere, as put an End to all

Travelling.—This was on Thursday Morning, and the wet thaw and bad weather Continuing, I was oblig'd to Remain there for Several Days, for there was in those Days, neither Coach nor Chaise on the Road, and not even a Saddle Horse to be had. At last on Sunday Morning Being the 4ᵗʰ Day, an open chaise Returning from Ediṇʳ to Glasgow took me in, and Convey'd me safe. I had pass'd my time more tolerably than I Expected, for tho' the Landlord was Ignorant and Stupid, his Wife was a Sensible Woman, and in her Youth had been Celebrated in a Song under the Name of the Bony Lass of Livingstone.[1] They had fine Children, but no Books but the Bible, and Sir Richᵈ Blackmore's Epick Poem of Prince Arthur which the Landlord brought in one Day, as the Name of a Song Book which he Said would Divert me, and so it Did, for I had not met with it before. The Walls and Windows, were all Scrawld with Poetry, and I amus'd myself not a little, in composing a Satyre on my Predecessors, which I also Enscrib'd on the Walls, to the Great Delight of my Landlady, who Shew'd it for many Years afterwards with vanity to her Travellers. When I came to pay my Reckoning to my astonishment, she only charg'd me three shillings and six pence for Lodging and Board for 4 Days—I had presented the little Girls with Ribbons I bought from a wandering Pedlar, who had taken Shelter from the Storm. But my whole Expence Maid-servant and all was only 5 sh.—Such was the Rate of Travelling in Those Days.

I had my Lodging this Session in a College Room which I had furnish'd for the Session at a Moderate Rent. I had never been without a Cough in the former Winter when I Lodg'd in a warm house in Kings Street, opposite to what was the Butchers Market in those Days. But such was the Difference between the air of the College, and the Lower Streets of Glasgow, that in my new apartment, tho' only Bare Walls, and 20 feet by 17, I never had a Cold or Cough all the Winter. John Donaldson a College Servant, lighted my Fire and made my Bed: and a Maid from the Land-lady who furnish'd the Room, came once a fortnight with Clean Linnen. There were two English Students of Theology, who liv'd on the Floor below and Nobody above me. I again attended the Lectures of Professors Leechman and Hutcheson, with much Satisfaction and Improvement.

Young Seller who I mentiond before became my most Intimate Friend. He came to me whenever he was at Leisure, and we pass'd our time very agreably together. He enlarg'd my Circle of Acquaintance, by Introducing me to the Ladies whom he Visited: and I introduc'd him to my two Intimates Miss Campbell, and Mrs D.[2] who he admitted were Superior to any of his Former Acquaintance. In an Excursion with him to Hamilton the Year before, he had made me acquainted with Dʳ Cullen, and now that he was come to Glasgow I Improv'd that acquaintance. I became Intimate with D^r McLain whom I mention'd before; and on his Suggestion, we proposd to act the Tragedy of Cato[1] to a Select Company in the College. Our Parts were allotted, and we Rehears'd it twice, tho' we never acted it before an Audience. McLean and I allotted the Parts: I was to be Cato, he was Marcus, our Friend Seller Juba, a Mr Lesly was to do Lucius, an English Student of the Name of Seddon was to be Syphax and Robin Bogle Sempronius—Miss Campbell was our Marcia, and Miss Wood Lucia. I have forgot our ... Portius. Tho' we never acted our play, we attain'd one of our chief purposes which was to become more Intimate with the Ladies. Ld Selkirk would not join us, tho' he took much pleasure in Instructing Miss Campbell.

In our Literary Club this Session we took to Reviewing of Books as a proper Exercise. Mr Thom, who was afterwards Minister of Govan, a Learn'd Man of a very particular tho' an Ingenious Turn of Mind, tho' much Senior to any of us was one of our Number, and had Great Sway among us. He had Quarrell'd with Hucheson, and having Heard me say that Huchesons Book on the Passions was not Intelligible, he assign'd [it] to me that I might understand it better. I accordingly Review'd it in a few pages, and took much Pains to unravel Certain Intricacies both of thought and expression that had Ran thro' it; This I Did with much Freedom, tho' not without Respect to the Author. This Essay pleas'd my Friends—and one of them, by Thom's Instigation Carried a Copy of it to Hucheson. He Glanc'd it over, and Return'd it saying that the young Gentleman might be in the Right, But that he had long ago made up his Mind on those Subjects, and could not now take the Trouble to Revise them.

Not long after this I had certain proof of the Gentleness and Candour of this Eminent Professor, For when I Deliver'd a Discourse in the Divinity Hall, it happen'd to please the Professor (Leechman) so much, That he Gave it very Liberal Praise both in Publick and Private; Insomuch that it was Borrow'd by one of his Minions, and handed about the College, with so much approbation that Mr Hucheson wishd to see it. When he read it, he return'd it with unqualified applause, tho' it containd some things, which a Jealous Mind might have Interpreted as an attack on his Favourite Doctrine of a Moral Sense. His Civility was now accompanied with some Degree of Confidence.

[1745]

I preservd my Intimacy with my Friends of last Winter, and added a few more Families to my Acquaintance which made the time pass very agreably. I had been introduc'd to Mr Purdie the Rector of the School, who having at N. Berwick Taught many of my Young Friends in the Lothians, and particularly the Whole Name of Dalrymple, he had half a Dozen or 8 Boarders, for whom his Daughters kept a very Good Table, Insomuch that I was often Invited to Dinner, and became Intimate in the Family. The Eldest Daughter who was a sensible prudent Woman, and M^{rs} of the House, Being about 40, sent for me one Sat. Morning in Haste and when I arriv'd, she Took me into a Room apart from her Sisters, who were Girls under 20; and there with many Tears inform'd me that Her Father having been much Intoxicated on the Friday or Sat. before, had never since been Sober—That he had not attended the School all the week, and that he now was firmly Determin'd to Resign his Office, as he was Sensible that he could not abstain from Dramdrinking. She added that he had not sav'd much money, having been held Down by some Idle and Wastefull Sons, and that they could ill afford to want the Emoluments of his Office. She concluded with telling me that she had previously Inform'd her Father that she was Going to Send for me and Impart his Secret to me for advice. To this he had not Objected: and when I was Carried to his Room he Rec'd me with Open Arms, told me his Dismal Case with Tears and Lamentations, and his firm Resolution to Resign, as he was Sensible he could not reform, and could no longer be of use. He concluded by asking for a Dram, which was the 2^d he had call'd for before 9 a clock. I Laugh'd and Rallied, and was Serious and Grave with him by Turns, and us'd every argument I could to Break him of his Habit—But to no purpose, for he answer'd all my arguments by the Impossibility of his ever Reforming, and consequently of ever appearing again in the world. He concluded with, Nelly give me a Dram, which she Durst not Refuse otherwise he would have Fir'd the House. To have time to Think and consult about him I went from him to the Breakfast Parlour. When I was leaving him he pray'd me to Return as soon as possible, as he could not Bear his own Thoughts alone.

When at Breakfast I thought of an expedient, that I imagin'd I could Depend upon for him, if it took Effect. I Communicated my plan to his Daughter, and she was pleas'd. When I went to him again, I told him that I was truly sorry I could not pass that Day with him, as I was oblig'd to go to Stirling by my Fathers orders upon Business, and that I had made Choice of that Day, as I could return without missing more than one Day of the College. I Added that I had never been there, but had not been able to find a Companion for which I was sorry. Nelly, said he with Great Quickness, Do you think I could sit on a Horse; If I could I would go with him and shew him the Way. I cajol'd him on this, and so Did his Daughter. And in short after an Early Dinner, while the Horses and a Servant were preparing, we set out for Stirling about one a clock, I having taken his word before his Daughter, That in all things he would comply with my will, otherwise I would certainly return.

I had much Difficulty to Get him to pass the little village publick Houses which were in our way without Calling for Drams. He made this attempt half a Doz. times in the first Stage—But I would not consent, and besides promis'd him he should have as much wine as he pleas'd. With much Difficulty I Got him to Kilsyth, where we stop'd to feed our Horses, and where we Drank a Bottle of Claret. In short I Got him to Stirling before it was quite Dark in the 2ᵈ week of April old Style.[1] He ate a Hearty Supper, and had another bottle of Claret, and confess'd he never slept sound but that night since he was taken ill. In short we Remain'd at Stirling all Sunday, attended Church, and had our Dinner and Claret, and our Walk on the Castle Hill in the Evening. I brought him to his own House on Monday by Five a clock; The Mans Habit was Broken, he was again of a Sound Mind, and he attended his School on Tuesday in perfect Health. As many of the Professors were Purdie's Friends, This successful act of Kindness to him Rais'd me in their Esteem, and atton'd for many Levities with which I had been Tax'd.

He liv'd many Years after this, but Did not Leave his Family Independent. One of his Daughters was Married Creditably in Edinᵣ—The Two Eldest came to Live there after his Death but were in Indigence. In the Year 1778, I happen'd to be for a few weeks at Buxton where I met with Sir Wᵐ Gordon K.B. who had been a Boarder at Purdie's, for two or three Years before 1745—and who was at Leyden with me in the End of that Year. Riding out with him one Day, he happen'd to ask me in what State Purdie's Family was Left. I told him what I knew, and added That they had a kind Remembrance of him, for that not many Months after he had Left them, I heard Nelly say with Tears in her Eyes, upon an Insult having been offer'd them by some of their Neighbours, That they Durst not have Done so if Willy Gordon had been in the House. He answer'd that the Father had very often lick'd him, but he had no Resentment as it was for his Advantage, and that the Daughters were Good Girls. He concluded by offering me a Sum of Money. I thought it better to accept of an Annual Pension of £10, which he Remitted to them by me for Several Years.

My Friendship with Mʳˢ D. and her Brother never Impair'd, tho' having a more Extended Acquaintance, than I had the preceding year, I was frequently engag'd when they wish'd to have me with them. They had made me acquainted with Mʳ Woods Family, where there were three or four very agreable Daughters, Besides the Governor of the Isle of Man, and Andrew the Clergyman, who Died Rector of Gateshead by Newcastle

in the Year 1772, by a Fever which he contracted by exerting himself
with the utmost Humanity to save his Parishioners on the Fatal Night
when the Bridge of Newcastle fell. There it was that I met with Coll! R!
Hepburn of Keith for the first time, since we had been at the same class
together in the Year 1736. We left Mr Woods Early in an Evening after
Drinking Tea, Returnd to Cockaines Tavern and Did not part till near 5
in the Morning. Most unfortunatly for me I had made an appointment
with Mr James Hog a Probationer and Tutor to the 4 Sons of Sir John
Douglas of Kilhead, to Ride Ten or 12 Miles with them on their Way to
Annandale, and I had hardly become Warm in Bed, when Rap, Rap he
came to my Door, and Insisted on my Getting up and fulfilling my Promise. Never in my Life had I such a Reluctance to fullfill any Promise, for
Hepburn had propos'd to make Rack-Punch[1] our Beverage after Supper,
which I had never Tasted before, and which had Given me the first
Headach I had almost ever Felt. There was no help for it—It was a Fine
Morning in the 2^d Week of May, we Breakfasted at Hamilton, and I Rode
6 Miles Farther with them, and Return'd. James Hogg was a man of a
Good Heart and uncommon Generosity. Sir John's affairs were compleatly Derang'd, and he could Raise no Money to carry on the Education
of his Boys. Hog had a little Patrimony of his own nearly £200 pounds.
Rather than his Pupils should suffer, two of whom were fit for College, he
came to Glasgow with all the Four and with a trusty old woman of a
Servant, he kept a small house for them in Kings Street, and Being an
excellent Œconomist Fed them well at the Least possible Expence. I frequently Din'd with him and them, and was astonish'd with his Good
Management. This he Continued all the next Year also, when Sir John
was sent to the Tower of London for Rebellious Practices. This Debt
together with arrears of Wages, was not paid till many Years afterwards
when Hog was Minister in Linlithgow, where he Died by a fall from his
Horse in Spring 177[8]. Had his Understanding been as strong as his
Heart was Generous, he would have been a first Rate Character.

In that week or that Immediatly Following, Will. Sellar and I, and
Robin Bogle of Shettelstoon, went on a Party with Ladies, two Miss
Woods, and Peggy Douglas of Mains, a Celebrated Wit and a Beauty
even then in the Wane. When we came to Hamilton she pray'd us to send
a Messenger a few Miles, to bring to us a Clergyman of a Neighbouring
Parish a Mr Tho? Cleland. He came to us when we were viewing the
Romantick Gardens of Barncluth which Ly between Hamilton and the
Dog-Kennell.[2] Thom Cleland was a Good Looking little Man, but his
Hair was becoming Gray, which no sooner Marg! Observ'd than she
Rallied him pretty Roughly (which was her Way) on his Being an old
Fusty Batchelor, and on his Encreasing Marks of Age, since she had seen

him not more than a Year before. After Bearing Patiently all the Efforts of her Wit—Marg! says he, you know that I am Master of the Parish Register, where your Age is Recorded, and that I know, when you must be with Justice Call'd an Old Maid in spite of your Favourite Airs. What Care I Thom, said she, for I have for some time Renounc'd your Worthless Sex, I have Sworn to be Dutchess of Douglas, or never mount a Marriage Bed. This Happen'd in May 1745; she made her purpose Good. When she made this Prediction she was about 30—It was fullfill'd a Few Years after.

I had an opportunity of Seeing the temper and spirit of the Clergy in the Neighbourhood of Glasgow, a 2⁴ time this Year by Means of a Trial of a Clergyman in the County of Air for Certain alleg'd Crimes, which came by appeal before the Synod of Glasgow. The person tried was a very Sensible Man of much Wit and Humour, who had made a But of a Neighbouring Clergym[a]n, who was weak and at the same time Good Natur'd, and had all the Qualities of a Butt. He was found out however to be a Man full of Deep Resentment, and so Malicious as to turn Frolick into Crime. After many very late Sederunts[1] of the Synod, and at last a Hearing of the General Assembly—The Affair was Dismiss'd, the Gentleman was settled in the Parish to which he was presented, and many Years afterwards Died Minister of Glasgow, where his Good Name had been so much traduc'd, much Regretted. A Caution to Young Men of Wit and Humour to Beware of Fools as much as Knaves.

I was Detain'd later at Glasgow, than I would have chosen that I might obtain my Credentials from the University as by the Tenor of the Act of Bursary, I was Oblig'd on this Third Year to repair to some foreign Protestant University. I had Taken my Degree of A. M. at Edin!, and had only to Get here my Certificate of attendance for two years, and my Latin Letter Recommending me to Foreign Academies. I must acknowledge, That I had profited much, by two years Study at Glasgow, in two Important Branches viz. Moral Philosophy, and Theology—along with which last, I Rec'd very excellent Instructions on Composition. For Leechman was not only fervent in Spirit when he Lectur'd, but ornamented all his Discourses with a Taste Deriv'd from his Knowledge of Belles Lettres.

In the Months of June and July 1745, I went through most of my Trials in the Presbytry of Haddington, as my Father was Resolv'd I should be ready to take out my Licence within a Month after my Return from abroad. In the Month of Aug! I went to Dumfrieshire to pass a few weeks there, and to take Leave of my Friends. About the End of that Month I Rec'd orders from my Father to Repair to Drumlanerick Castle to meet his Friend Dr John Sinclair M. D. who was to be some Days there on his way from Moffat to Dumfries: and after that to return home as soon as I could, as he Expected to be home, with my Mother from Lan[g]ton near

Dunse, where they were Drinking Goat Whey, about the 18th of next Month.

I accordingly Met Dr Sinclair at Dumlanerig, where I had been Frequently before, with my Friend James Ferguson of Craig-Darroch, who was then acting Commissioner for his Grace the Duke of Queensberry. He had been bred to the Law, but Relinquish['d] the Bar for this Employment, which seated him within a Few Miles of his own Estate which needed Improvement. His First Lady was a Sister of Sir Henry Nisbets, who Died Young. His 2^d was her Cousin a Daughter of the Honble Mr Baron Dalrymples. Dr Sinclair had been my Fathers Class Fellow, and had a great regard for him. He was an Elegant Scholar, and Remarkable for his perfect Knowledge of the Latin Tongue, which in those Days, was much Cultivated in Scotland. The Professors of Medecine then Taught in Latin, and Dr Sinclair was one of that First Set, who rais'd the Fame of the School of Medecine in Edin^r above that of any other in Europe. He and Dr John Clerk the Great Practising Physician had Found Moffat Waters agree with themselves, and frequented it Every Season in their Turns for a Month or Six Weeks, and by that Means Drew many of their Patients there, which made it be more frequented than it has been of late Years, when there is much better Accommodation.

I had promis'd Mr R. Bogle and his Sister to pass a Few Days with them at Moffat; on the Road to which I pass'd one Day with my Friend Wm Cunningham Minister of Durisdeer the Duke of Queensberrys Parish Church. He was Knowing and Accomplish'd, and pleasing and Elegant in his Manners, beyond most of the Scotch Clergymen of that Day. The Duchess of Q. (Lady K. Hyde) had Discover'd his Merit on her visits to Scotland and had him Constantly with her, so that he was Call'd the Duchesses Walking Staff. From his House I Cross'd to Moffat about 15 Miles off—But Did not Reach it that night on acc^t of a Thunder Storm, which had made the Waters Impassable. So that I was oblig'd to Lodge in what they call a Shealing,[1] where I was us'd with Great Hospitality and uncommon Politeness by a young Farmer and his Sister, who were then Residing there attending the milking of the Ewes, The Business of that Season in a Sheep Country.

When I got to Moffat, I found my Expecting Friends still there, tho' the News [had] arriv'd that the Chevalier Prince Charles had Landed in the North with a Small Train, had been Join'd by Many of the Clans, and might be expected to break Down into the Low Country, unless Sir John Cope who was then on his March North, should meet with them and Disperse them. I Remain'd only a few Days at Moffat, as the News became more Important and alarming Every Day, and Taking Leave of my Friends, I Got home to Prestonpans, in the Evening of the 12th of

Sepr My Father &c. were not returnd, but I was perfectly informd of the State of Publick Affairs, by many Persons in the Place, who told me, that Prince Charles had evaded Sir John Cope, who found himself oblig'd to March on to Inverness, not venturing to attack the Highlanders on the Hill of Corryarrock, and was then proceeding to Aberdeen where Transports were sent, to bring his Army by Sea to the Firth. I was also Inform'd that as the Highlanders were making Hasty Marches, The City of Edin.^r was putting itself in some State of Defence, so as to be able to Resist the Rebels in Case of an attack before Sir John Cope arriv'd.

On this News I repair'd to Edin.^r the next Day which was the 13th and meeting many of my Companions, found that they were Enlisting themselves in a Corps of 400 Volunteers which had been Embodied the Day before and were thought necessary for the Defence of the City. Mess.^s Wm Robertson, John Home, W^m McGhie, Hugh Bannatyne, Wm Cleghorn, Wm Wilkie, Geo. Logan and many others, had Enlis[te]d into the First or College Company as it was Call'd which was to be commanded by Provost Drummond, who was expected to Return that Day from London, where he had been for some time. On the 14th I Join'd that Company, and had arms put into my Hands; and attended a Drill Serjeant that afternoon and the next Day to Learn the Manual Exercise, which I had formerly been Taught by my Father, who had himself been a Volunteer in the End of Queen Ann's Reign, when there was an Alarm about the Pretender, But were oblig'd to hold their Meetings in Malt Barns in the Night and by Candlelight.

The City was in Great Ferment and Bustle at this time, for besides the Two parties of Whigs and Jacobites, of which a well inform'd Citizen told me, There were two Thirds of the Men in the City, of the First Description or Friends to Government, and of the 2.^d or Enemies to Government, two Thirds of the Ladies. Besides this Division, There was another between those who were keen for preparing with Zeal and activity to Defend the City, and those who were averse to that Measure, which was Provost Stuart and all his Friends. This appear'd so plainly from the Provost's Conduct and Manner at the time, That there was not a Whig in Town, who Did not suspect that he favour'd the Pretenders Cause;[1] and however Cautiously he acted in his Capacity of Chief Magistrate, there were not a few who suspected that his Backwardness and Coldness in the Measure of arming the People, was part of a plan to admitt the Pretender in to the City.

It was very true that a half armd Reg.^t of New Rais'd Men with 400 Volunteers of the City, and 200 from other places, might not be thought Sufficient for the Defence of the City, had it been Seriously besieg'd; Yet Considering that the Highlanders, were not more than 1800, and the half of them only arm'd; That they were averse to approach Walls, and affraid of Cannon; I am persuaded that had the Dragoons prov'd Firm, and resolute, instead of Running away to Dunbar to meet Sir John Cope,—It was more than two to one that the Rebels, had never approach'd the City, till they had Defeated Cope, which in that Case they would not probably have attempted. Farther I am of Opinion, That if that part of the Town Council who were Whigs, had found Good Ground to have [put] Stuart under arrest, that the City would have held out.

In this opinion of Stuart I was confirm'd when in London the Following Month of April. I happend to be in the British or Forrests Coffee House[1] I forget which, in the afternoon of the Day when the News of the Victory at Culloden arriv'd. I was Sitting at a Table with Dr Smollet and Bob Smith, The Duke of Roxburghs Smith, when John Stewart the Son of the Provost, who was then Confin'd in the Tower, after Turning Pale, and Murmuring many Curses, Left the Room in a Rage, and slap'd the Door behind him with much Violence. I said to my two Companions, That Lad Stewart is either a Madman or a Fool to Discover himself in this Manner when his Father is in the Tower on Suspicion. Smith who knew him best, acquiesc'd in my Opinion, and added that he had never seen him so much beside himself.

For a few Days past McLaurin the Proff^r had been Busy on the Walls on the Southside of the Town endeavouring to make them more Defensible, and had even Erected some small cannon near to Potterow Port[2] which I saw. I visited my old Master, when he was Busy, who seem'd to have no Doubt that he could make the Walls Defensible against a Sudden Attack, but complain'd of want of Service; and at the same time Encourag'd me and my Companions, to be Diligent in Learning the Use of Arms. We were Busy all Saturday when there arriv'd in Town Bruce of Kenneth with a Considerable Number of Volunteers, above 100, from his Country, and Sir Robert Dickson with 130 or 40 from Musselburgh and the Parish of Inveresk—This increas'd the Strength and added to the Courage of the Loyal Inhabitants.

On Sunday Morning the 15th however News had arriv'd in Town that the Rebel Army had been at Linlithgow the night before, and were on full March towards Edin^r—This alter'd the Face of Affairs, and made thinking people Fear that they might be in Possession of Edin^r before Cope arriv'd. The Volunteers Rendevous'd in the College Yard before 10 a clock to the Number of about 400—Capt Drummond appear'd at Ten, and walking up in Front of the Right of his Company where I stood with all my Companions of the Corps, he address'd us in a Speech of some Length, the purport of which was that it had been agreed by the General and the Officers of the Crown that the military Force should oppose the Rebels on their March to Edin.ʳ Consisting of the Town Guard, that Part of the New Regiment who had got arms, with the Volunteers from the Country— What he had to propose to us was, That we should Join this Force, and expose our Lives in Defence of the Capital of Scotland, and the Security of our Country's Laws and Liberties. He added That as there was a Majority for Leaving Some Men in Arms for the Defence of the City, That any persons chusing the one Service rather than the other, would bring no Imputation of Blame—But that he Hop'd his Company would Distinguish themselves by their Zeal and Spirit on this Occasion. This was answer'd by an Unanimous Shout of Applause.

We were March'd Immediatly up to the Land Mercat,¹ where we halted till the other Companies should Follow. They were late in making their appearances, and some of their officers coming up to us while in the Street, told us that most of the Privates were unwilling to March. During this Halt, Hamilton's Dragoons, who had been at Leith, march'd past our Corps on their Rout to Join Gardiners Reg.ᵗ who were at the Colt Bridge.² We cheer'd them in Passing with an Huzza—and the Spectators began to think at last, that some Serious Fighting was likely to Ensue, Tho' before this Moment, many of them had laugh'd at and Ridiculd the Volunteers. One Striking Example of this we had in our Company, for a Mʳ Hawthorn a Son of Baillie Hawthorne, who had laugh'd at his Companions among the Volunteers, Seeing us pass through the Luckenbooths³ in Good Order and with apparent military Ardour, Ran Immediatly upstairs to his Fathers House, and Fetching his Fowling piece and his Small Sword Join'd us before we left the Land Market.

While we Remain'd there which was Great part of an Hour, the Mob in the Street, and the Ladies in the Windows, treated us very variously, Many with Lamentation and even with Tears, and some with apparent Scorn and Derision. In one House on the South Side of the Street, there was a Row of Windows full of Ladies, who appear'd to Enjoy our March to Danger, with much Levity and Mirth—Some of our warm Volunteers Observ'd them, and threatned to fire in to the Windows if they were not Immediatly Let Down, which was Immediatly Complied with. In marching Down the Bow, a Narrow Winding Street the Scene was Different, for all the Spectators, were in Tears and uttering Loud Lamentations; Insomuch that, Mʳ Kinloch a Probationer, the Son of Mʳ Kinloch one of the high church Ministers who was in the 2.ᵈ Rank Just behind Hew Ballantine, said to him in a melancholy tone, Mʳ Hew, Mʳ Hew, Does not this Remind you of a Passage in Livy when the *Gens Fabii* March'd out of Rome to prevent the Gauls from Entering the City, and the Whole Matrons and Virgins of Rome were wringing their Hands and Loudly Lamenting the Certain Danger, to which that Generous Tribe was going

to be expos'd.[1] Hold your Tongue says Ballantine, otherwise I shall complain to the Officer, for you'll Discourage the Men. You must Recollect
the End of all M[r] Hew, *Omnes ad unum perieri*. This Occasion'd a Hearty
Laugh among those who heard it. Which being over, Ballantine Half
Whisper'd Kinloch, Robin, if you're affraid you had better steal off when
you can find an opportunity; I shall not tell that you are Gone till we are
too far off to Recover you.

We halted in the Grassmarket near the West Port, That the other
Bodies who were to Join us might come. On our March even our Company
had lost part of their Number, and none of the other Volunteers were
Come up. The Day being advanc'd to between 12 and one a clock, the
Brewers who liv'd in that End of the Street, brought out Bread and
Cheese, and Strong Ale and Brandy as a Refreshment for us, in the Belief
that we needed it, in Marching on Such an Interprise. While we Remain'd
in this Position my Younger Brother W[ll] then near 15, as promising a
Young Man as ever was Born, of a fine Genius, and an Excellent Scholar,
tho' he had been kept Back with very Bad Health, came up to me. He had
walk'd into Town that Morning, in his anxiety about me, and Learning
that I was with the Company on our March to Fight the Rebels, he had ran
Down with Great Anxiety from the House where I Lodg'd, to Learn how
things Realy Stood. He was Melancholy and much alarm'd. I withdrew
with him to the Head of a Neighbouring Close, and Endeavour'd to abate
his Fears, by assuring him, that our March was only a Feint, to keep back
the Highlanders, and that we should in a little While, be order'd back to
our Field for exercise in the College. His anxiety began to abate, when
thinking whatever should happen, It would be better for me to trust him
with a Portugal piece of 36 sh. and 3 Guineas that I had in my Pocket I
Deliver'd them over to him. On this he burst into Tears, and said that I
surely Did not think as I said, but Believ'd I was going out to Danger,
otherwise I would not so readily part with my Money. I comforted him the
Best Way I could, and Took back the greater part of the Money, assuring
him that I Did not believe yet that we would be Sent out or if we were I
thought that we should be in such force that the Rebels would not Face
us. The Young Man was Comforted, and I gave him a Rendezvous, for
7 at night.

While we were waiting for an additional Force, a Deputation of
the clergy, (the Forenoon Service being but ill attended on account of the
Ringing of the Fire Bell, which is the Great Alarm in Edin[r],) who were the
Two Wisharts and Wallace, and Glen and Logan &c.—came to us. D[r] W[m]
Wishart Principal of the College was their Prolocutor, and call'd upon us
in a most pathetick Speech to Desist from this Rash Interprise, which he
said was exposing the Flower of the Youth of Edin[r] and the Hope of the

Next Generation, to the Danger of being Cut off or made Prisoners, and Maltreated without any Just or Adequate Object—That our Number added so very little to the Force that was Intended against the Rebels, That withdrawing us, would make little Difference, while our Loss would be Irreparable and that at any rate a Body of Men in Arms, was necessary to keep the City Quiet During the absence of the Armed Forces and therefore [he] objected and besought the Volunteers and their Officers, to Give up all thoughts of Leaving the City Defenceless, to be a Prey to the Seditious. This Discourse, and others Similar to it, had an effect upon many of us, tho' Youthfull Ardour, made us Reluctant to abandon the prospect of shewing our Prowess. Two or three of the Warmest of our Youths Remonstrated against those unseasonable Speeches, and Seem'd Eager for the Fight. From that Moment, I saw the Impropriety of sending us out, But till the Order was Recall'd, it was our Duty to Remain in Readiness to Obey. We remain'd for near an hour Longer and were Join'd by another Body of Volunteers, and part of the New Regiment that was Raising. Not long after Came an Order for the Volunteers to March back to the College Yards, when Provost Drummond who had been absent return'd and put himself at our Head, and March'd us back. In the mean time the other Force that had been Collected with 90 Men of the Town Guard &c. &c. march'd out to the Coltbridge and Join'd the Dragoons, who were watching the Approach of the Enemy. Some of the Volunteers Imagin'd that this Manœevere about the Vol.ˢ was entirely of Drummonds, and that he had no Mind to Face the Rebels, tho' he had made a Parade of Courage and Zeal to make himself popular. But this was not the Man's Character. Want of Personal Courage was not his Defect. It was Civil Courage in which he Faild, for all his life he had a Great Deference to his Superiors. But I then thought, as I Do now, That his offer to Carry out the Vol.ˢ was owing to his Zeal and Prowess, for personally he was a Gallant Highlander, But on better Considering the Matter, after Hearing the Remonstrance of the Clergy, he Did not think That he could well be answerable for exposing so many Young Men of Condition to Certain Danger and uncertain Victory.

When we were Dismiss'd from the College Yards, we were order'd to Rendevous there again in the Evening, as Night Guards were to be posted Round the whole City. Twelve or 13 of the Most Intimate Friends, went to a late Dinner to a Mrs Turnbulls, then next House to the Tron-church. Many things were talk'd of with Great Freedom, for the Company were, Wᵐ Mᶜghie, Wᵐ Cleghorn, Wᵐ Robertson, John Home, Hugh Ballantine and I—The other Names I have forgot. Sundry proposals were made, one of which was that we should March off with our arms into England and Raise a Volunteering Spirit—Or at any Rate that we should Join Sir John

Cope's Army, and try to Get as many as possible to Follow us. As I had been Separated from my Companions for two Years, by my attendance at Glasgow, I had less Confidence to Speak my Mind, Especially as some of my warm associates, thought every body Cowardly, or a Secret Jacobite who did not agree with them. However perceiving that some of the Company Did not agree with the Chief Speakers, I ventur'd to State that before we Resolv'd to March off with our arms, we should take Care to have a Sufficient Number of Followers—For even if it were a Lawfull Act to March off with our arms without orders, we would appear Ridiculous and Contemptible, if there were no more of us than the present Company, and I Guess'd we could not Reckon on three or four more. This brought out McGhie and Hew Bannatine, who were consider'd as the Steadiest Men amongst us. This occasion'd a warm altercation for Cleghorn and Home in those Days were very Fiery. At Last however it was Settled, that we should try in the Course of next Day to find if we could prevail on any considerable number to Follow us; and if not That we should carry our arms to the Castle, that they might not fall into the Enemies Hands, and then make the best of our Way separately, to Sir John Cope's army and offer our Service.

When the Night Watch was Set, all the Company I have now mention'd were appointed to Guard the Trinity Hospital in Leith Wynd, which was one of the weakest parts of the City.[1] There 12 of us were plac'd under the Command of Lieut. Alexr Scott, a young Man of Spirit, a Merchant in the City, and not two or three Years Senior to the eldest of us. There we had nothing to do all night, but make Responses every half hour, as the *Alls Well*, came Round from the other Guards that were posted at certain Distances, so that a Stranger who was approaching the City, would have Thought it was Going to be Gallantly Defended. But we knew the Contrary, for Provost Stuart and all his Friends had been against making any preparation for Defence, and when they Yielded to the Zeal of their Opponents, they hung a Dead Weight upon every Measure. This we were all Sensible of at the time, and had no Doubt that they wish'd the City to fall into the Pretenders Hands, however Cautiously they might hide their Intentions.

At one a clock the Ld Provost and his Guard visited all the Posts and found us at Trinity Hospital very alert. When he was gone, Did you not see said John Home to me How pale the Traitor Lookd, when he found us so vigilant? No I Replied, I thought he look'd and Behav'd perfectly well: and it was the Light from the Lanthorn that made him appear Pale. When we were Reliev'd in the Morning, I went to my Lodging and tried to Get a Few Hours Sleep; But tho' [the] House was Down a Close, the Noise was so Great, and my Spirits so much agitated, that I Got no Sleep.

At Noon on the 16th when I went to the Streets I heard that Gen. Fowkes had arriv'd from London, Early and by Order of Gen! Guest [had] taken the Command of the 2ᵈ Regᵗ of Dragoons, who having Retir'd the night before from Corstorphine, where they left only a Guard, and had march'd with them to the Colt Bridge a mile nearer than Corstorphine and were Join'd by the same Body of Foot that had been with them on the 15th. The Rebels however were slowly approaching, and there was no News of Sir John Cope's arrival with the army from Aberdeen, and the General Opinion was that the Town would certainly be Given up. The Most Zealous Whigs, came now to think this necessary, as they plainly thought they Saw that Provost Stuart and his Friends, so far from Co-operating with their Zeal, Retarded every Measure.

But the fate of the City was Decided Early in the Afternoon, when the two Regts. of Dragoons, were seen about 4 a clock on their March from the Colt Bridge to Leith by the Long Dykes, as then Call'd, Now George Street in the New Town.[1] Then the Clamour arose that it would be Madness to think of Defending the Town as the Dragoons had fled. The Alarm Bell was Rung—a Meeting of Inhabitants with the Magistrates was Conveen'd first in the Goldsmiths Hall, and when the Crowd Increasd, in the New Church Aisle—The 4 Companies of Volunteers, Rendezvous'd in the Land Market[2]—and Growing Impatient sent two of their Lieutˢ to the Provost for orders, for the Capᵗˢ had been sent for to the Meeting. They soon Return'd without any orders, and said all was Clamour and Discordance. While they were absent two Volunteers in the Rear Rank just behind Quarrelld, when Debating whether or not the City should be Surrender'd, and were Going to Attack one another, one with his Musket and Bayount, and the other with his Small Sword, having flung Down his Musket—They were soon Separated without any Harm, and plac'd asunder from Each other. At this time a Man on Horseback whom nobody knew came up from the Bow, and Riding at a quick pace along the Line of Volunteers, Call'd out that the Highlanders were at hand, and that they were 16000 strong. This Fellow Did not stop to be examin'd, but made off at the Gallop. About this time a Letter had come Directed to the Provost Summoning the Town to Surrender, and alarming them with the Consequence in case any opposition was made.

The Provost made a Scrupulous Feint about reading the Letter, but this Point was soon carried and all Idea of Defence was abandon'd. Soon after Capᵗ Drummond Join'd us in the Lawnmarket, with another Capᵗ or two. He sent to Gen! Guest after Conversing a Little with the Lieutˢ to acquaint him that the Volˢ were coming to the Castle to Deliver their Arms. The Messenger soon Return'd, and we march'd up Glad to Deliver them lest they should have fallen into the Hands of the Enemy, which the Delay of Orders, seem'd to favour, Tho' not a little asham'd and afflicted at our Inglorious Campaign.

We endeavour'd to Engage as many as we could to meet us at Haddington and there Deliberate what was to be Done as we Conjectur'd that Sir John Cope would not Land nearer to the Town of Edin. than Dunbar, after it had surrender'd. Upon being ask'd by two of my Friends What I was to do, viz. Willm Robertson and Wm Cleghorn, I told them that I meant to Go that night to my Fathers at Prestonpans, where if they would Join me next Day, by that time Events might take place that would fix our Resolution. Our ardour for Arms and the Field was not abated.

As it was now the Dusk of the Evening, I went to a House near the Nether Bow Port, where I had appointed my Brother to meet me that we might walk home together, having foreseen the events that took Place, as the Rebels were so near the Town, I wish'd to take Road as soon as possible. But on attempting to Get out at the Gate, in the Inside of which Several Loaded Carts or Waggons were standing, I found the Gates Lock'd and the Keys Lodg'd with the Provost. The Carts were said to contain the Baggage of Sir John Cope's Army &c. and Each Party Interpreted the Shutting of the Gates according to their own Fancy. One Side thinking this was a Manœvre to Prevent their Reaching Sir John, and the other, to hinder them from falling into the Hands of the Enemy. Be that as it may, it was half past 8 a clock before the Gate was open'd, when as I heard, the Baggage was order'd back to the Castle—at a Later hour, they were Sent to Dunbar.

My Brother and I Set out immediatly, and after Passing thro' the Croud at the Head of the Cannongate, who were pressing both ways to Get out, and in, we went thro' the Abbey by St Ann's Yards, and the Duke's Walk, to Jocks Lodge,[1] meeting hardly a Mortal the whole way. When we came down near the Sands, I chose that way rather than the Road thro' the Whins, as there was no Moonlight, and the Whins were Dark and Solitary, and the Sands always Lightsome when the Sea is in Ebb, which was then the Case. We walk'd Slowly as I had been fatigu'd and my Brother not strong, and having met no Mortal, but one Man on Horseback as we Enter'd the Sands, Riding at a Brisk Trot, who haild us, we arriv'd at the west end of Prestonpans, having shun'd Muss^h by passing on the Northside without meeting or being overtaken by any Body. When we came to the Gate of Lucky Vents Court Yard,[2] a Tavern or Inn then much frequented, I was astonish'd to meet with the utmost alarm and confusion, the Officers of the Dragoons, calling for their Horses in the Greatest Hurry. On Stepping into the Court Lord Drumore the Judge saw me, whose House being near had come down to sup with the

Officers. He immediatly made up to me, and hastily Enquir'd whence I had come. From Edin.ʳ Direct. Had the Town Surrender'd. No! but it was expected to fall into the Hands of the Rebels, Early tomorrow. Were there any Highlanders on their March this Way. Not a Soul, I could answer for it, as I had left Edin.ʳ Past 8 a clock and had walk'd out Deliberately, and seen not a Creature but the Horseman in the Sands.

He turn'd to the Officers, and repeated my Intelligence, and asserted that it must be a false Alarm, as he could Depend on me. But this had no Effect, for they Believ'd the Highlanders were at hand. It was in vain to tell them, that they had neither Wings nor Horses, nor were Invisible. Away they went as fast as they could to their respective Corps, who on Marching from Leith, where they thought themselves not Safe, had Halted in an open Field above the west end of Prestonpans, between Prestongrange, and the Inclosures of Mr Nisbet, Lying west from the Village of Preston. On Enquiring what was become of Gardiner, Drumore told me that Being quite worn out on their arrival on that Ground, he had beg'd to Go to his own House within half a Mile, where he had been since 8 a clock and where he had Lock'd himself in, and could not be awak'd till four in the Morning, his usual Hour. I went thro' the Town to my Fathers—and before I Got there, I heard the Dragoons, Marching in Confusion, so Strong was their Panick, on the Road that Leads by the Back of the Gardens to Portseaton, Aberlady and N. Berwick all the way by the Shore. My Father and Mother were not yet come home.

Before Six on Tuesday Morning the 17th Mr James Hay, a Gentleman in the Town, who was afterwards a Lieut. in the Edin.ʳ Reg.ᵗ came to my bed side and eagerly Enquir'd what I thought was to be Done, as the Dragoons in Marching along in their Confusion had strew'd the Road Eastward with accoutrements of every Kind: Pistols, and Swords and Skull Caps[1] &c. I said that People should be Employ'd Immediatly to Gather them up and Send them after, which was Done, and amounted to what fill'd a Close Cart, and a Couple of Creels on Horseback.[2] By this time it was reported That the Transports with Cope were seen off Dunbar. But it was not this News, for it was not then come, That made the Dragoons scamper from their Ground on the Preceding Night. It was an unlucky Dragoon, who stepping a little aside for a Pease Sheaf for his Horse, for there were some on the Ground not led off, fell into a Coal Pit,[3] not fill'd up, when his Side Arms and Accounterments made such a Noise as alarm'd a Body of Men, who for two Days had been Compleatly Panick Struck.

About Midday I Grew anxious for the arrival of my Two Companions, Cleghorn and Robertson. I Therefore walk'd out on the Road to Edin.ʳ, when on Going as Far as where the Turnpike is now, below Drumore I met with Robertson on Horseback, who Told me that a little way behind him was Cleghorn, and a Cousin of his own a Mr Fraser of the Excise, who wish'd to accompany us to Sir John Cope's Camp. For it was now known that he was to Land that Day at Dunbar, and the City of Edin^r had been Surrender'd Early that Morning to the Highland Army.

We Waited till our Companions came up, and walk'd together to my Fathers House, where I had order'd some Dinner to be prepar'd for them by 2 a clock. They were Urgent to have it sooner, as they wish'd to begin our Journey towards Dunbar as long before Sunset as they could.

As we were finishing a small Bowl of Punch, that I had made for them after Dinner, James Hay, the Gentleman, I mention'd before, paid us a visit, and Immediatly after the ordinary Civilities, said Earnestly, That he had a small Favour to ask of us, which was, That we would be so Good as accept of a Small Collation, which his Sister and he had provided at their House (That of Charles Sherriff the Most Eminent Merch^t in the Place, who had Died not Long before, and left a Widow and 4 Daughters, with this Gentleman their Uncle to Manage their Affairs). We Declin'd accepting this Invitation for fear of Being too Late. He continu'd Strongly to Sollicite our Company, adding that he would Detain us a very Short While, as he had only 4 Bottles of Burgundy which if we Did not accept of, he would be oblig'd to Give to the Highlanders. The Name of Burgundy which some of us had never Tasted,[1] Dispos'd us to Listen to Terms, and we Immediatly adjourn'd to Mrs Shirreffs not an Hundred Yards Distant. We found very Good Apples and Pears and Bisket set out for us and after one Bottle of Claret to wash away the Taste of the Whiskey Punch, we fell to the Burgundy, which we thought Excellent, and in little more than an Hour, we were ready to take the Road, it being then not long after 5 a clock. Robertson mounted his Horse, and left us to Go Round by his House at Gladsmuir, to Get a little Money, as he had not wherewithall to Defray his Expenses, and mention'd an hour when he promis'd to meet us at Bangley Brae Foot, Maggie Johnstone's, a Publick House on the Road Leading to Dunbar, by Garlton Hills, a mile to the North of Haddington.*

When we came within Sight of the Door of this House, we Saw Robertson Dismounting from his Horse. We Got some Beer or Porter to Refresh after our walk, and having broken off in the Middle of a Keen Dispute between Cleghorn and a Recruiting Serjeant, whether the Musket and Bayonet, or Broad Sword and Target[2] were the best Weapons, we proceeded on our Journey, still a little Doubtfull if it was true That Sir John Cope had arriv'd. We proceeded Slowly, for it was Dark, till we came to Linton Bridge. Robertson with his usual prudence propos'd to stay all

---

* There were no Horses here for me, for tho' my Father kept two, he had them both at the Goat Whey Quarters.

night, it being ten a clock, and still Double beds for us all. Cleghorns Ardor and mine resisted this proposal, and Getting a Loan of Robertsons Horse, we proceeded on to the Camp at Dunbar, That we might be more Certain of Sir John's arrival. At Belton Inn within a mile of the camp, we were Certified of it, and might then have Turn'd in, but we obstinatly persisted in our plan, Fancying that we should find Friends among the officers, to Receive us into their Tents. When we arriv'd at the Camp we were not allow'd admittance, and the Officer on the Picket whom Cleghorn knew, assur'd us, that there was not an Inch of Room for us or our Horse Either in camp or at Dunbar, advis'd to Return. Being at last persuaded that Cope was Landed and that we had play'd the Fool, we first attempted Belton Inn, but it was chok'd full by that time, as we were convinc'd by 8 or ten Footmen Lounging in the Kitchens, on Tables and Chairs. We Tried the Inn at Linton with the same Success. At Last we were oblig'd to knock up the Minister, Mat. Reid, at two in the Morning; who taking us for Marauders from the Camp, kept us an hour at the Door. We were hardly well asleep, when about Six, Robertson came to Demand his Horse quite Stout and well refresh'd, as well as his Cousin Fraser, while we were Jaded and undone. Such is the Difference between Wisdom and Folly.

After Breakfasting however at the Inn, we set out again for Dunbar, in sanguine Hopes that we should soon return with the Army, and Give a Good Acc^t of Sir John Cope. In our way we visited the Camp, which lay a mile west from Dunbar. As soon as I arriv'd at the Town, I Enquir'd for Coll^l Gardiner, and went and visited him, at Mr Pyots the Minister of the Town, where he Lodg'd. He receiv'd me with Kindness, and Invited me to Dine with him at 2 a clock, and to come to him a little before the Hour. I went to him at half past one, and he took me to Walk in the Garden. He look'd Pale and Dejected which I attributed to his Bad Health and the Fatigue he had lately undergone. I began to ask him, if he was not now quite satisfy'd with the Junction of the Foot with the Dragoons and confident that they would Give a good account of the Rebels. He answer'd, Dejectedly, That he hop'd it might be so, But—and then made a long pause. I said that to be sure they had made a very Hasty Retreat: a Fowl Flight said he, Sandy, and they have not Recover'd from their Panick; and I'll tell you in Confidence that I have not above 10 Men in my Reg^t who I am Certain will Follow me, But we must Give them Battle Now, and Gods Will be Done! We were call'd to Dinner, where there was nobody, But the Family, and Cornet Kerr, a Kinsman of the Coll^l He assum'd an Air of Gayety at Dinner, and Enquiring of me the Adventures of the Night rallied me as a Raw Soldier in not taking up with the first Good Quarters I could get; and when the approaching Event was mention'd, Spake of Victory as a thing Certain, If God were on our Side. We Sate very short time after Dinner. The Coll! went to Look after his Reg! and prepare them for tomorrow's March, and I to look out for my Companions. On Finding them, it was agreed to Return back to Linton as between the Dragoons and the Concourse of Strangers there was not a bed to be had. We Return'd accordingly to Linton, and made Good our Quarters at the Ministers where we Remain'd till the army past in the Morning on their Route to Haddington. John Home had arriv'd at Dunbar on Wednesday and said he had Number'd the Highlanders, and thought they were about 1900—But that they were illarm'd, tho' that Defect was now Suppli'd at Edin!. There were many of the Volunteers all night at Linton, whom we saw in the Morning, and with whom we appointed to meet in the Inn at Haddington.

As the Army past about 11 or 12 a clock, we Join'd them and march'd along with them. They took the Hill Road by Charteris' Dykes, and when we were about Beanston I was accosted by Major Bowles, whom I knew, and who Desirous of some Conversation with me, made his Servant Dismount, and Give me his Horse, which I Gladly accepted of, Being a Good deal worn out with the Fatigue of the preceding Day. The Major was compleatly Ignorant of the State of the Country, and of the Character of the Highlanders. I found him perfectly Ignorant and Credulous, and in the power of every person with whom he Convers'd. I was not acquainted with the Discipline of Armies, but it appear'd to me, to be very Imprudent, to allow all the Common People to Converse with the Soldiers on their March as much as they Pleas'd; by which means their Panick was kept up, and perhaps their principles corrupted. Many People in East Lothian at that time were Jacobites—and they were most forward to mix with the Soldiers. The Commons in General as well as two thirds of the Gentry, at that period, had no aversion to the Family of Stuart, and could their Religion have been Secur'd, would have been very glad to see them on the Throne again.

Cope's Small Army Sate Down for the Afternoon and Night on an open Field on the west side of Haddington. We Volunteers, to the Number of 25, assembled at the Principal Inn—where also sundry officers of Dragoons, and those on the Staff, came for their Dinner. While our Dinner was preparing, an alarm was beat in the Camp, which occasion'd a Great hurry skurry in the Court Yard, with the Officers taking their Horses; which some of them Did with no small Reluctance, either thro' Love of their Dinner, or aversion to the Enemy. I saw Coll! Gardiner passing very slowly, and ran to him to ask What was the Matter. He said it could be nothing but a False Alarm and would soon be over. The Army however was Drawn out Immediatly and it was found to be a False Alarm. The

Honble Francis Charteris had been Married the Day before at Prestonhall, to Lady Fra[n]ces Gordon, the Dutchess of Gordon's Daughter; who was suppos'd to Favour the Pretender tho' she had a large Pension from Government. How that might be, nobody knew But it was alleg'd that the alarm Follow'd their Coach, as they Pass'd to their House at New Amis-field.

After Dinner Capt Drummond came to us at the Inn, to whom we unanimously Gave a Commission, to apply to the General for arms to us, and to appoint us a Station in the Line, as we had not only our Capt but one of our Lieut^s with us. Drummond Left us to make this Application, but was very long in Returning: and the answer he brought was not so agreable. It was That the General Did not think we could be so Serviceable by taking arms as we might be in Taking post Horses thro' the Night, and Reconnoitring the Roads Leading from the Enemy towards our army, and bringing an acct. of what movements there were. This was agreed to after some Hesitation—and 16 of us were Selected to Go out 2 and 2, one set at 8 in the Evening, and another at 12—Four of those were thought useless, as there were only three Roads, that could be reconnoitrd. I was of the 1st Set, being chosen by M^r W^m M^cghie as his companion, and we chose the Road by the Sea Coast, thro' Longniddery, Port Seaton and Prestonpans, as that with which I was best acquainted. We set out not long after 8 a clock and found every thing perfectly Quiet as we expected. At Prestonpans we Call'd at my Fathers and found that they had Return'd home on Wednesday, and having requested them to wait Supper till our Return, we Rode on to West Pans, in the County of Midlothian, near Muss^h, and still met with nothing on which to report; we return'd to Supper at my Fathers.—While we were there, an application was made to us by Baillie Hepburn, the Baron Baillie or Magistrate of the place, against a Young Gentleman, a Student of Medecine as he said, who had appear'd in arms in the Town, and pretended that he wish'd to be Conducted to Cope's Army. We went down from the Manse to a Publick House where this Gentleman was Confin'd. At the First Glance McGhie knew him to be a Student tho' not personally acquainted with him. He Got him Reliev'd Immediatly, and brought him up to Supper. McGhie took all the Pains he could to persuade this Gentleman whose Name was Myrie, to attach himself to the Vol^s and not to Join the Army. But he would not be persuaded; and actually Joind one of the Reg^ts on their March next Morning, and was sadly wounded at the Battle.*

---

* Francis Garden afterwards Ld Gardenstone, and Robert Cunningham afterwards the General in Ireland, follow'd D^r M^cghie and me, and were taken Prisoner and not very well us'd. They had gone as far as Crystalls Inn west of Muss^h and had Sate with a window open after Daylight, at a Regale of White Wine and Oysters, when they

When Mᶜghie and I Return'd to Haddington about one a clock, all the Beds were taken up, and we had to sleep in the Kitchen on Benches and Chairs. To our Regret we found that several Volˢ had Single Beds to themselves a part of which we might have occupied. Sir John Cope and his Army March'd in the Morning, I think not till 9 a clock, and to my great Surprise instead of Keeping the Post Road thro' Tranent Muir which was high ground and Commanded the Country South for Several Miles, as it Did that to the North for 2 or 3 Miles towards the Sea, they turn'd to the Right, by Elviston and the village of Trabroun, till they past Longniddery on the North, and Sᵗ Germains on the South, when on Entering the Defile made by the Inclosures there, they halted for near an Hour, and then March'd into the open Field, of 2 Miles in Length and 1½ Breadth extending from Seaton to Preston, and from Tranent Meadow to the Sea. I understood afterwards, that the Generals Intention was, (If he had any Will of his own) to Occupy the Field Lying between Walliford, Smeaton and Inveresk, where he would have had the River Esk Running thro Deep Banks in Front, and the Towns of Dalkeith and Mussᵇ at hand to supply him with provisions. In this Camp he could not have been Surpris'd, and in Marching to this Ground, the Road thro' Tranent was not more Distant by 100 Yards than that by Seaton. But they were too Late in Marching; for when they came to Sᵗ Germains their Scouts, who were chiefly Lords Home and Loudon brought them intelligence that the Rebel Army were on their March, on which after an Hours Halt, when by turning to the Left they might have Reach'd the high Ground at Tranent before the Rebels, they March'd on to that plain before Describ'd now call'd the Field of Battle. This Field was entirely clear of the Crops, the last Sheaves having been Carried in the Night before, and neither Cottage, Tree or Bush were in its Whole Extent, except one Solitary Thorn Bush, which Grew on the March between Seaton and Preston Fields, around and near to which Lay the Greatest Number of Slain, and which Remains there to this Day, tho' the Fields have been long Since Compleatly Inclos'd.

The Army march'd streight to the West End of this Field till they came near the Walls of the Inclosures of Preston, which reach'd from the Road Leading to the Village of Preston North of Tranent Meadow and Banktoun, down almost half way to Prestonpans, to which Town from this Inclosure there was no Interruption, and the whole projection of those Inclosures into the Plain to the East was not above 300 Yards. That part of it which belong'd to Preston Estate was Divided into 3 shots as it

---

were observ'd, by one of the Prince's Life Guards who was riding past not in uniform, but arm'd with Pistols—They took to their Horses, when he pretending to take them for Rebels they avow'd they were Kings Men, and were taken to the Camp at Duddingstone.

was call'd, or Rigg Lengths, the Undershot, the Middle and the Upper.[1] A cart road for carrying out Dung Divided the two First, which Lay Gently Sloping to the Sea, from where it was Separated by Garden Walls and a large Inclosure for a Rabbit Warren. The upper Shot was Divided from the Middle One by a foot path, and lay almost Level, sloping almost Imperceptibly to Tranent Meadow. This was properly the Field of Battle, which on acc! of the Slope was not seen fully from the Lower Fields or the Town. Near to those Walls on the East the Army form'd their First Line of Battle Fronting West. They were hardly Form'd, when the Rebel Army appeard on the high Ground at Birsley, South West of our Army about a Mile. On the sight of them our Army Shouted. They Drew nearer Tranent, and our Army shifted a little Eastward, to Front them. All this Took place by one a clock. Coll! Gardiner having Inform'd the General and his Staff that I was at Hand to execute any thing in my Power for the Good of the Service, There was sent to me a Message, to try if I could provide a proper Person, to venture up to the Highland Army to make his Observations, and particularly to Notice, if they had any cannon or if they were Breaking Ground any where. With some Difficulty I prevail'd with my Fathers Church Officer, a fine Stout Man, to make this Expedition which he Did Immediatly. A little farther on in the afternoon, the same Aid Du Camp (an uncle of Sir Ralph Abercrombies) came to request me to keep a Look out from the Top of the Steeple and Observe, if at any time, any Detachment from the Main Army was sent westwards. In the Mean time the Highlanders lay with their Right close to Tranent, and had Detach'd Some Company's Down to the Church Yard which was close by a Waggon Way, which Led Directly Down to our Army and Cross'd the Road Leading between Preston and Seaton, where Cope's 6 or 7 pieces of Canno[n] were plac'd, not above ⅓ of a Mile Distant from the Church. As the Highlanders appear'd, N. of the Church in the Church Yard, which was higher than the Waggon Way, the Cannon were Fir'd and Dislodg'd them from thence. Not long after this about 4 in the afternoon, The Rebels made a Movement to the West-ward to Birsley, where they had first appear'd, and our Army took their first position. Soon after this I observ'd from the Steeple, a large Detachment of Highlanders, about 3 or 400, Lodge themselves in what was Call'd the Thorny Loan, which Led from the W. End of Preston to the Village of Dauphiston,[2] to the S. West. I mounted my Horse, to make this known to the General and Met the Aid du Camp riding Briskly down the Field, and told him what I had seen. I immediatly Return'd to my Station in the Steeple. As Twilight approach'd I observ'd that Detachment withdrawn, and was Going up the Field to tell this when my Doughty arriv'd—who was going to tell me his Story, how numerous and Fierce the Highlanders were, how keen for the

John Home by W. Millar

David Hume by Allan Ramsay

Fight, and how they would make but a Breakfast of our Men. I made him go with me to the General to tell his own Story. In the Mean time I visited Coll. Gardiner, for a 3ᵈ time that Day on his Post, and found him Grave but Serene and Resign'd, and who Concluded by praying God to Bless me, and that he could not wish for a better night to ly on the Field, and then call'd for his Cloak, and other Conveniences for Lying down, as he said they would be awak'd Early enough in the Morning, as he thought by the Countenance of the Enemy. For they had now shifted their position to a Sloping Field E. from the Church, and were very near our Army, with little more than the Morass between. Coming down the Field I ask'd my Messenger, if they had not paid him for his Danger. Not a Farthing had they Given him, which Being of a piece with the Rest of the General's Conduct rais'd no Sanguine Hopes for tomorrow. I Gave the poor Fellow half a Crown which was half my Substance, having Deliver'd the Gold to my Father the night before.

When I Return'd to my Fathers House I found it Crowded with Strangers, some of them Volunteers, and Some Merse[1] Clergymen, particularly, Monteith and Laurie, and Pat. Simpson. They were very Noisy and Boastfull of their Atchievements, one of them having the Dragoons Broadsword, who had fallen into the Coalpit—and the other the Musket he had Taken from a Highland Soldier, between the Armies. Simpson who was Cousin to Adam Drummond of Meginch, Capᵗ and Paymaster in Lee's Regᵗ had Entrusted to him a pair of Saddlebags containing 400 Guineas, which Patrick not Imprudently Gave to my Father to keep all night for him, out of any Danger of Being Plunder'd. Perceiving that there would be no Room for me without Incommoding the Strangers, I stole away to a neighbouring Widow Gentlewomans, where I bespoke a Bed, and Return'd to Supper at my Fathers.—But no Sooner had I cut up the Cold Surloin which my Mother had provided, than I fell fast asleep, having been much worn out with all the fatigues of the Preceding Week. I retir'd Directly.

I Directed the Maid to awake me the Moment the Battle began, and Fell into a profound Sleep in an Inst.—I had no need to be awak'd, tho' the Maid was Punctual, for I heard the 1ˢᵗ Cannon that was fir'd, and started to my Cloaths, which as I neither Buckled nor Garter'd, were on in a moment, and Immediatly went to my Fathers not 100 Yards off— All the Strangers were Gone, and my Father had been up before Daylight and had Resorted to the Steeple. While I was conversing with my Mother, he Return'd to the House, and assur'd me of what I had Guess'd before, that we were Compleatly Defeated. I Ran into the Garden where there was a Mount in the S.E. Corner, from which one could see the Fields, almost to the Verge of that part where the Battle was Fought. Even at that time, which could hardly be more than Ten or 15 Minutes after Firing the First Cannon, The Whole Prospect was fill'd with Runaways, and Highlanders Pursueing them—Many had their Coats turned as prisoners, but were still trying to Reach the Town, in Hopes of Escaping. The Pursuing Highlanders, when they could not overtake, fir'd at them: and I saw two Fall in the Glebe. By and Bye a Highland Officer, whom I knew to be Lord Elcho pass'd with his Train, and had an air of Savage Ferocity, that Disgusted and alarm'd—He enquir'd fiercely of me, Where a publick House was to be found; I answer'd him very meekly, not Doubting but that If I had Displeas'd him with my Tone, his Reply would have been with a Pistol Bullet. The Crowd of Wounded and Dying now approachd with all their Followers, But their Groans and Agonies were nothing compar'd with the Howlings and Cries and Lamentations of the Women, which Suppress'd Manhood and Created Despondency. Not long after The Duke of Perth appear'd with his Train, who ask'd me in a very Different Tone, the Way to Collector Cheaps, to which House he had order'd our Wounded Officers, Knowing the Family were from Home. I answer'd the Questions of Victorious Clemency, with more assurance of personal Safety, than I had Done to unappeas'd Fury, and Directed him the Way to the House, which was hard bye that where I had Slept.*

* The Rebel Army had before Day March'd in 3 Divisions, one of which went streight Down the Waggon Way to attack our Cannon, the other two cross'd the Morass near Seaton House, one of which March'd North towards Portseaton, where the Field is Broadest, to attack our Rear, but overmarch'd themselves, and fell in with a Few Companies that were Guarding the Baggage in a small inclosure near Cockenzie, and took the whole. The Main Body march'd west thro' the Plain, and Just at the Break of Day attack'd our Army. After Firing once, they Run on with their Broadswords, and our People Fled. The Dragoons attempted to Charge under Coll! Whitney who was wounded, but wheel'd immediatly and rode off thro' the Defile between Preston and Banktoun to Dauphiston half a mile off. Coll! Gardiner with his Division attempted to Charge, but was only follow'd by 11 Men as he had foretold, Cornet Kerr being one. He Continued Fighting and had Rec'd several Wounds, and was at last brought down by a stroke of a Broad Sword over the Head. He was Carried to the Ministers House of Tranent, where liv'd till next Forenoon. His own House which was nearer was made an Hospital for the Highlanders—No person of our Army being Carried there, but the Master of Torphichen, who was so badly wounded, that he could be sent to no greater Distance. Some of the Dragoons fled as far as Edin!— and one stood all Day at the Castle Gate as Gen! Guest would not allow him to be taken in. A Considerable Body of Dragoons met at Dauphistone immediatly after the Rout, little more than half a Mile from the Field, where Cope Join'd them—and where it was said Lord Drummore offer'd to Conduct them back with assurance of Victory, when the Highlanders were busy with the Booty. But they could not be prevaild on, by his Eloquence, no more than by the Youthfull Ardour, of the Earls Home and Loudon. After a short Halt, they March'd over Falside Hill to Lauder. Sir Peter Halket a Cap! in Lee's Reg! acted a Distinguish'd part on this Occasion; for after the Rout he kept his Company together, and Getting behind a Ditch in Tranent

In the Mean time my Father became very uneasy Lest I should be ill-treated by the Rebels, as they would Discover that I had been a Vol. in Edin!—He therefore order'd the Horses to be Saddled, and telling me that the Sea was out, and that we could escape by the Shore without being Seen, we mounted taking a Short Leave of my Mother and the Young Ones, and took the way he had pointed out. We escap'd without Interruption, till we came to Portseton Harbour, a Mile off, where we were oblig'd to turn up on the Land, when my Father observing a Small Party of Highlanders, who were pursueing two or 3 Carts with Baggage, that were attempting to Escape, and coming up with the Foremost Driver who would not Stop when call'd to, they Shot him on the Spot. This Daunted my Father, who turn'd immediatly, and took the way we came. We were back again soon after when taking off my Boots, and putting on Shoes, I had the appearance of a person who had not been abroad. I then proposd to Go to Collector Cheaps House, where I understood there were 23 wounded officers, to offer my assistance to the Surgeons, Cunningham and Trotter, the 1st of whom I knew. They were Surgeons of the Dragoons and had Surrender'd that they might attend the Officers. When I went in, I told Cunningham (afterwards the Most Eminent Surgeon in Dublin) That I had come to offer them my Services, as tho' no Surgeon, I had better hands than a Common Servant. They were oblig'd to me, but the only Service I could do to them, was to try to find one of their Medecine Chests among the Baggage, as they could do nothing for want of Instruments. This I readily undertook provided they would furnish me with a Guard. This they hop'd they could Do, and knocking at the Door of an Inner Room, a Highland Officer appeard whom they Call'd Cap! Stewart. He was Good Looking, Grave and of Polish'd Manners. He answer'd that he would soon find a proper Conductor for me, and Dispatch'd a Servant with a Message. In the Mean time I observ'd a very Handsome young Officer Lying in an Easy Chair in a Faint, and seemingly Dying. They Led me to a Drawers Head,[1] where there lay a Piece of his Skull about 2 Fingers Breadth and an Inch and an Half Long. I Said, this Gentleman must Die. No said Cunningham, The Brain is not affected, nor any vital part. He has Youth and a fine Constitution on his Side, and could I but get my Instruments there would be no Fear of him. This Man was Cap! Blake. Cap! Stewarts Messenger arriv'd with a Fine Brisk little well Dress'd Highlander arm'd Cap a Pie with Pistols and Dirk and Broadsword. Cap! Stewart gave him his Orders, and we set off immediately.

Meadow, he kept Firing away on the Rebels, till they were Glad to Let him Surrender on Terms.

Never Did any Young Man more perfectly Display the Boastfull
Temper of a Raw Soldier new to conflict and victory than Did this High-
land Warrior. He said he had that Morning been Armour Bearer to the
Duke of Perth, whose Valour was as Conspicuous as his Clemency. That
now there was no Doubt of their Final Success, as the Almighty had
Bless'd them with this almost Bloodless Victory (on their part). That He
had made the Sun to Shine upon [them] uninterruptedly Since their
First Setting out, and That no Brawling Women had Curst, nor even a
Dog had Bark'd at them; That not a cloud had interpos'd between them
and the Blessings of Heaven! and that this Happy Morning—Here he was
Interrupted in his Harangue, by observing in the Street a Couple of
Grooms Leading 4 fine Black Horses. He Drew a Pistol from his Belt, and
Darted at the foremost in a Moment, Wha are you Sir, and whare are you
Going, and whom are you Seeking. It was answer'd with an uncover'd
Head and a Dastardly Tone, I am Sir John Cope's Coachman, and I am
seeking my Master. You'll not find him here Sir, But you and your man
and your Horses are my Prisoners. Go Directly to the Collectors House,
and put up your Horses in the Stable, and wait till I return from a piece of
Publick Service. Do this Directly as you Regard your Lives. They Instantly Obey'd. A few Paces farther on we met an Officer's Servant, with
Two Handsome Geldings and a large and full Clokebag. Similar Questions
and answers were made, and we found them all in the place to which they
were order'd, on our Return.

It was not long before we arrivd at Cockenzie; where, under the Pro-
tection of my Guard, I had an opportunity of seeing this victorious
Army. In General they were of Low Stature, and Dirty, and of a Con-
temptible Appearance. The Officers with whom I mix'd were Gentlemen
Like, and very Civil to me, as I was on an Errand of Humanity. I was
Conducted to Lochiel who was polish'd and Gentle, and who Order'd a
Soldier to make all the Enquiry he could about the Medecine Chests of the
Dragoons. After an Hours Search we Return'd without Finding any of
them. Nor were they ever afterwards Recover'd. This View I had of the
Rebel Army, Confirm'd me in the Prepossession, that nothing but the
weakest, and most unaccountable Bad Conduct, on our part, could have
possibly Given them the Victory. God Forbid that Brittain should ever
again be in Danger of Being over-run by such a Despicable Enemy. For at
Best the Highlanders were at that time but a Raw Militia, who were not
Cowards.

On our Return from Looking for the Medicine chests, we Saw walking
on the Sea-Shore at the E. End of Prestonpans all the Officers who were
Taken Prisoners to the N⁰—¹ Then saw I human Nature in its most Despicable abject form, for all most every aspect bore in it Shame, and

Dejection and Despair. They were Deeply Mortifyed with what had happen'd, and timidly anxious about the Future. For they were Doubtfull, Whether they were to be Treated as Prisoners of War, or as Rebels. I ventur'd to speak to one of them who was nearest me, a Major Severn, for Major Bowles, my acquaintance was much wounded, and at the Collectors. He answer'd some Question I put to him, with Civility, and I told him what Errand I had been on, and with what Humanity I had seen the wounded Officers Treated, and ventur'd to assert, that the Prisoners would be well us'd. The Confidence with which I spake, Seem'd to Raise his Spirits; which I compleated by Saying, That nothing could be expected but what had happened, when the Foot were so Shamefully Deserted by the Dragoons.

Before we Got back to the Collector's House, the wounded officers were all Dress'd, Capt Blake's Head was Trepan'd, and he was Laid in Bed, for they had Got Instruments from a Surgeon who Liv'd in the Town, of whom I had told Cunningham, and they were Order'd up to Bankton Coll! Gardiners House, where the Wounded Highlanders were, and the Honble Mr Sandilands. Two Capts of ours had been kill'd outright besides Gardiner viz. Capt Stewart of Physgill, whose Wife was my Relation, and who has a Monument for him Erected in the Ch. Yard of Prestonpans, by his Father in Law Pat. Heron of Heron Esqr The other was Capt Brymer of Edrom in the Merse.[1]

While we were Breakfasting at my Fathers Some Young Friends of mine Call'd, among whom was James Dunlop Junr of Garnkirk, my Particular Acquaintance at Glasgow. He and his Companions had Rode thro' the Field of Battle, and Being well acquainted with the Highland Chiefs assur'd us that there was no Danger as they were civil to every Body. My Father who was Impatient till he saw me Safe, Listen'd to this and Immediatly Order'd the Horses. We Rode thro' the Field of Battle where the Dead Bodies still lay between 11 and 12 a clock mostly Stript—There were about 200 we thought—There were only slight Guards, and a Few Straggling Boys. We rode along the Field to Seaton, and met with no Interruption till we came close to the Village, when 4 Highlanders Darted out of it, and Cried in a Wild Tone presenting their Pieces, Fourich, Fourich! i.e. Stop, Stop—By advice of our Glasgow Friends we stopt, and Gave them Shillings a piece, with which they were heartily Contented; we Parted with our Friends, and rode on, and Got to Mr Hamiltons Minister of Bolton, a solitary place, at a Distance from any high Road, by two a clock, and Remain'd there all Day. My Father having time to Recollect himself, fell into a new anxiety, for he then Call'd to Mind, that besides Sundry Watches and Purses, which he had taken to Keep, he also had Pat. Simson's 400 Guineas. After many proposals and projects, and among the Rest, my Earnest Desire to Return alone, it was at last agreed to write a Letter in Latin to John Ritchie the Schoolmaster, afterwards Minister of Abercorn, and Instruct him How to Go at night, and Secrete the Watches and purses if still there, and Bury the Saddle Bags in the Garden. Ritchie was also requested to come to us next Day.

My Father and Mr Hamilton Carried on the Work of that Day Sunday, with Zeal, and not only pray'd fervently for the King, But warn'd the People against Being Seduc'd by appearances that the Lord was with the Rebels and that their Cause would in the End be Prosperous. But no sooner had we Din'd than my Father Grew Impatient to see my Mother and the Children, Ritchie having Wrote by the Minister that all was Quiet. He wanted to Go alone, but that I could not allow. We set out in due time, and arriv'd before it was Dark, and Found the Family quite well, and my Mother in Good Spirits. She was Naturally Strong Minded, and void of Imaginary Fears; But she had Rec'd Comfort from the attention paid to her, For Capt Stewart, by the Duke of Perths Order as he Said, Gave one of his Ensigns a Mr Brydone a particular Charge of our Family, and Order'd him to Call upon her at Least twice a Day.

We soon began to think of my Fathers Charge of Watches and Money—and when it was Dark enough I went into the Garden to Look for the place where Ritchie had Buried the Saddle Bags—This was no Difficult Search, for he had wrote us, that they were below a Particular Pear Tree. To be sure he had Buried the Treasure, But he had left the Leather Belts by which they were fix'd, fully above Ground: So that had the Highlanders been of a Curious or Prouling Disposition, They must have Discoverd this Important Sum. Soon after this Ritchie arriv'd. He had set out for Bolton Early in the afternoon, but taking a Different Road, that was nearer for People on foot, he Did not Meet us; and had Return'd Immediatly. On Setting out, not 20 Yards from the Manse of Prestonpans, he was stopt by a single Highlander, who took from him all the Money he had, which was 6 shs But as he Spar'd his Watch he was Contented. Not long after came in my Mothers Guard Ensign Brydone, a well looking, sweet tempered young man, about 20 Years of Age. He was Capt. Stewarts Ensign—Finding all the Family assembled again, he resisted my Mothers Faint Invitation to Supper; she replied that as he was her Guard, she hop'd he would come as often as he could. He promis'd to Breakfast with us next Morning. He came at the hour appointed 9 a clock. My Mothers Custom was to Mask[1] the Tea before Morning Prayer, which she Did. And soon after my Father came into the Room, he call'd the Servants to Prayers. We Knelt Down, when Brydone turning awkwardly, his Broadsword, Sweep'd off the Table a china Plate with a Roll of Butter on it. Prayer being ended the Good Lady Did not forget her Plate,

But taking it up Whole, she said Smiling and with a Curtsey, Capt. Brydone this is a Good Omen, and I trust our Cause will be as Safe in the End from your Army, as my plate has been from the sweep of your Sword. The Young Man Bow'd, and sate down to Breakfast, and ate Heartily. But I afterwards thought, that the bad Success of his Sword, and my Mothers application, had made him thoughtfull, as Highlanders are very Superstitious. During the rest of the week while I remain'd at home finding him very Ignorant of History, and without Political Principles, unless it was a Blind attachment to the Chief, I thought I convinc'd him in the Many Walks I had with him that his Cause would in the End be unsuccessfull. I Learn'd afterwards, that tho' he March'd with them to England, he Retir'd before the Battle of Falkirk, and appeard no more. He was a Millar's son, near Drumond Castle.

On Tuesday and not sooner came many Young Surgeons from Edin.ʳ to Dress the Wounded Soldiers, most of whom Lay on Straw in the School Room. As almost all their Wounds were with the Broad Sword, they had Suffer'd little: The Surgeons Return'd to Edin.ʳ in the Evening and came back again for 3 Days—As one of these was Colin Simpson, a Brother of Patricks, the Clergyman at Fala, and apprentice to Adam Drummond their Uncle, we Trusted him and his Companions, with the 400 Guineas, which at Different times they Carried in their pockets, and Deliver'd it safe to Cap.ᵗ Adam Drummond of Megginsh, then a Prisoner in Queensberry House in the Cannongate.

I Remain'd at home all this week, about the End of which my Friend W.ᵐ Seller came from Edin.ʳ to see me, and press'd me much to come to Edin.ʳ to stay with him at his Fathers House. Having Several things to purchase to prepare for my Voyage to Holland, I went to Town on the following Monday, and Remain'd with him till Thursday. Besides his Father and Sisters, There Lodg'd in the House M.ʳ Smith, and there Came also to Supper every Night, his Son afterwards M.ʳ Seton of Touch having Married the Heiress of that Name. As Prince Charles had Issued a Proclamation, allowing all the Volunteers of Edin.ʳ 3 weeks During which they might pay their Court to him at the Abbey, and Receive a Free Pardon: I went twice Down to the Abbey Court with my Friend about 12 o clock to wait till the Prince should come out of the Palace, and Mount his Horse to Ride to the East Side of Arthur Seat to Visit his Army. I had the Good Fortune to see him both Days, one of which I was close by him, when he walk'd thro' the Guard to take his Horse. He was a Good Looking Man of about 5 Feet 10 Inches. His Hair was Dark Red and his Eyes Black; His Features were Regular, his Visage long, much Sunburnt and Freckled; and his Countenance Thoughtfull and Melancholy. He mounted his Horse, and Rode off thro' St. Ann's Yards and the Duke's Walk to his

Army. There was no Crowd after him, about 3 or 400 Each Day. By that time Curiosity had been Satisfy'd.

In the House where I Liv'd they were all Jacobites, and I heard much of their Conversation. When young Seller and I Retir'd from them at night, he agreed with me that they had less Ground for being so Sanguine and uppish than they Imagin'd. The Court at the Abbey was Dull and Sombre, the Prince was Melancholy. He Seem'd to have no Confidence in any Body, Not even in the Ladies who were much his Friends. Far Less had he the Spirit to Venture to the High Church of Edinr and take the Sacrament,[1] as his Great Uncle Charles 2d had done the Covenant, which would have Secur'd him the Low Country Commons, as he already had the Highlanders by attachment. He was thought to have Loiter'd too long at Edinr—and without Doubt, had he March'd Immediatly to Newcastle, he might have Distrest the City of London not a little. But besides that his Army wanted clothing and Necessaries, the Victory at Preston put an End to his Authority. He had not a Mind fit for Command at any time, far less to Rule the Highland Chiefs in Prosperity.

I Return'd to Prestonpans on Thursday, and as I was to set out for Newcastle on Monday to take Shipping for Holland, I sent to Capt Blake who was Recovering well, that if he had any Letters for Berwick I would take charge of them. He pray'd me to call on him Immediatly—He said he was quite well, and complain'd of nothing but the pain of a little Cut he had Got on one of his Fingers. He said he would trouble me with a Letter to a Friend at Berwick, and that it would be ready on Sat. at 4 a clock, when he beg'd I would call on him. I went at the Hour, and found him Dress'd and Looking Well, with a small Table and a Bottle and Glasses before him. What says I, Capt Blake are you allow'd to Drink Wine? Yes said he and as I expected you I postpon'd my Few Glasses, till I should Drink to your Good Journey. To be sure we Drank out the Bottle of Claret; and when I sent to Enquire after him on Sunday he said he had Slept better than ever. I never saw this Man more, but I heard he had sold out of the Army and was married. In Spring 1800, when the King was very ill and in Danger, I observ'd in the Papers that he had left a written Message mentioning the Wounds he had Rec'd at the Battle of Preston. On seeing this I wrote to him as the only Living Witness, who could attest the Truth of his Note Left at St James's. I had a Letter from him Dated the 1st of March that Year, wrote in High Spirits and Inviting me to Great George St Westminster, where he hop'd we would uncork a Bottle, with more pleasure than we had done in 1745, but to come soon for he was verging on 81.—He Died this Spring 1802.

On Monday Morn. the 9th of Oct Old Stile, my Father and I set out for Newcastle on Horseback, where we arriv'd on Wednesday to Dinner.

Having Secur'd my Passage on Board a Small Vessel Going to Rotterdam, that was to Sail whenever there was a Convoy, we Rode to Sunderland to visit some Emigrants, who we understood were there, and Found Old George Buchan, and his Brother in Law Mr Wm Grant, afterwards Ld Advocate, and Ld Prestongrange. We Din'd with them, and were told that Ld Drumore and many others of our Friends had taken up their Residence at Bishop Auckland, where they wish'd to have been, had there been Room. Next Day my Father and the Servant set out on their Journey home and I having been acquainted with some of the Common Council [of Newcastle] was invited to Dine with the Mayor at one of their Guild Dinners. A Mr Fenwick I think was Mayor that Year—I was Seated at the End of one of the Long Tables in the same Room, next Mr John Simson afterwards Alderman Simson, Sherriff of Newcastle for that Year. As I was fresh from Scotland, I had to answer all the Questions that were put to me, Concerning the affairs in Scotland; and I saw my Intelligence punctually Detailed in the Newcastle Journal Next Morning. Of that Company there was one Gentleman a Wine Mercht who was alive in the Year 1797 or 98, when Happening to Dine with the Mayor, the subject was talk'd of and he Recollected it perfectly.

At the Inn where I Slept I met with my Companion Bob Cunningham who had been a Volunteer in Edinr, and with Francis Garden was taken Prisoner by the Rebels as Narrated in Home's Hist.—[1] He and I sup'd together one of the Nights. He was Studying Law—But his Father Being an Officer and at that time Lieut. of Stirling Castle, he had a Military Turn, which was heightend by the Short Campaign he had made. He resented the Bad Usage his Fathers Nephew Murray of Broughton the Pretenders Secretary had Given him During the Day he was a Captive, and was Determin'd to become a Volunteer in some Regt till the Rebellion was suppress'd, but express'd a strong abhorrence at the Subordination in the Army and the Mortifications to which it expos'd a Man. I argued that he ought either to return Immediatly to his Studies, or Fix on the Army for his Profession, and Stated the Difference between Modern Armies, and those of Greece and Rome with which his Imagination was Fir'd, when a Man could be a Leading Citizen and a Great General at the same time. We Debated on this Point till two in the Morning, and tho' he Did not Confess he was Convinc'd, he went into the Army Immediatly, and Rose till he became General of Horse in Ireland. He was at the time I met him very Handsome, and had an Enlighten'd and ardent Mind. He went to Durham that Morning, and I never Saw him more.

On the Tuesday I was Summon'd to Go Down to Shields, as the Sloop had fallen Down[2] there, and was to sail immediatly with the London Convoy. I went down accordingly and had to Live for Six Days, with the

Rude and Ignorant Masters of Colliers. There was one Army Surgeon of the Name of Allan a Stirling Man, who had taken his Passage and had some Conversation—at last on Monday the 14th of Oc[t] I went on Board the Blagdon of Newcastle, Tim. Whinny Master, who Boasted that his Vessel had rode out the Great Storm of Jan[y] 29th 1739 at the Back of Inchkeith. She was Loaden with Kit's[1] of Butter and Glass Bottles—I was the only Passenger—There was besides the Master, a Mate and an Old Sailor and two Boys—as we Let the Great Ships Go out before us it was night almost before we Got over the Bar.

Next Day the Weather being calm and moderate we had an agreable Sail along the Coast of Yorkshire. In the Evening however the Gale rose, Seperated the Fleet of about 80 Sail, and Drove us off Shore. We pass'd a Dreary Night with Sickness and not without Fear: for the Idle Boys, had mislaid things and it was two hours before the Hatches could be clos'd. The Gale abated in the Morning, and about Midday, we made for the Coast again; But Did not come in with the Land till two a clock, when we Descried the Norfolk Coast, and saw Many Ships making for Yarmouth. About 10 at night we came up with them, and found them to be part of the fleet with which we had saild from Shields. Next Day, Friday the 18th we came into Yarmouth Roads, when the Master and I went a shore in the Boat. The Master was as much a Stranger there as I was, for tho' he had been often in the Roads, he never had Come on Shore. This Town is Handsome, and Lies in a Singular Situation. It stands on a Flat plain about a Q[r] of a Mile from the Sea. It is an oblong Square about a Mile in Length, and a 3[d] part as Broad. The Whole Length is Intersected by 3 Streets which are rather too Narrow; That next is well Built, and Lands on the Market place to the North, which is very Spacious and Remarkable well provided with every kind of vivre, ready for the Pot and the Spit. The Market Women are clean beyond Example, and the Butchers themselves, Dress'd with Great Neatness indeed—In short there was nothing to offend the Eye or any of the Senses in Yarmouth Market. Very Genteel Looking Women were providing for their Families. But the Key which is on the west side of the Town, and Lies parallel to the Beach is the most Remarkable thing about the Town, tho' there is a Fine Old Gothick Church in the Market place, with a very lofty Steeple, the Spire of which is crooked, and Likewise a fine Modern Chappel of Ease, in the Street Leading to it. The Key is a Mile Long, and is Form'd by a River, the Mouth of which above a Mile distant at the Village of Gorelston, forms the Harbour. The Largest Colliers can Deliver their Goods at the Key, and the street behind it has only one Row of the Handsomest Houses in the Town. As the Master and I knew nobody, we went into the House of a Robin Sad at the Sign of the 3 Kings, who standing at his own Door near the South End of the Key, had such an Inviting aspect and Manner, that I could not resist him. His House was perhaps not 2ᵈ Best, but it was cleanly and I staid 2 nights with him. He Entertain'd me much, for he had been several Years a Mate in the Mediteranean in his Youth, and was vain and Boastfull, and presumptuous, and Ignorant to my Great Delight.

In the Evening 2 Men had come in to the House, and had Drank a pot or two of Ale. He said they were Customhouse Officers, and was ill pleas'd as they Did not use to frequent his House. But they had come into the Common Room, on hearing of my Being in the House and tho' they Sate at a Distance from the Fireplace, where the Landlord and I were, they could hear our Conversation. Next Morning after 9 they came again, and with many Apologies addressing themselves to me said they had orders from the Commissioners to enquire my Name and Designation, as they understood I was Going beyond Sea to Holland. I had no Scruple in writing it down to them. They Return'd in half an Hour and told me that they were order'd to Carry me before the Lᵈ Mayor. I went accordingly down to Justice Hall, where I waited a little while in an antichamber, where I overheard my Landlord Sad under examination. He was very high and Resentfull in his Answers, and had a Tone of Contempt for [Men] who he said were unfit to Rule, as they Did not know the value of any Coins but those of England. He answer'd with a still more sawcy pride when they ask'd him what expence I made, and in the End told them exultingly, that I had order'd him to Buy the best Goose in the Market for tomorrow's Dinner. I was Call'd in and examin'd. The Mayor was an old Gray headed Man, of a mild address. He had been a Common Fisher, and had become very Rich, tho' he could not write, but sign'd his Name with a Stamp. After my examination, under which I had nothing to conceal, they told me as I was Going abroad, they were oblig'd to Tender me the Oaths[1] or Detain me. I objected to that as they had no Ground of Suspicion, and offer'd to shew them my Diploma as Master of Arts of the University of Edinʳ and a Latin Letter from the University of Glasgow to any Forreign University where I might happen to Go. They Declin'd looking at them, and Insisted on my Taking the Oaths: Which accordingly were administer'd, and I was Dismist. I Did not know that the Habeas Corpus was not then Suspended,[2] and that if they had Detain'd me, I could have Recover'd large expences from them. I amus'd myself in the Town till the Master Came on Shore when after Dinner we walk'd down to Garelstone, the Harbour at the Mouth of the River, where we heard of 3 vessels which were to Sail without Convoy on Monday with the Ebb-Tide.

I staid this Night with Landlord Sad, and Invited the Master to Dine with us next Day Being Sunday, when we were to have our Fine Goose Roasted. I went in the Morning to their Fine Chappel which was pannell'd with Mahogany, and saw a very populous Audience.—The Service and the Sermon were but So-So. Tim Whinny came in Good time, and we were on Board by 4 a clock, and fell down opposite the Harbour of Garelstone. As the 3 Colliers which were to venture over to Holland without Convoy, were bound for a Different Port from Helvoet which was our object, our Master spent all the Morning of Monday, making Enquiry for any ship that was Going where we were bound, and rangd the Coast Down as far as Lestoff[1] for this Purpose, but was Dissappointed. This made us so late of Sailing, That the 3 Ships which took thro' the Gat or opening between Sand Banks, were almost out of Sight before we ventur'd to Sail. Tim's Caution was increas'd by his having his whole property on Board, which he often Mention'd. At last after a Sollemn Council on the Quarter Deck, where I Gave my Voice Strongly for our Immediate Departure, we follow'd the Track of the 3 Ships, the last of which was still in Sight, and having a fine night with a Fair Breeze of Wind, we came within Sight of Land at 10 a clock. The Shore is so Flat, and the Country so Level, that one sees nothing on approaching it but tops of Steeples and Masts of Ships. Early in the afternoon I Got on Shore at Helvoet on the Island of Voorn, and put up at an English House, where one Fell was the Landlord; There I saw the First Specimen of Dutch Cleanliness, so little to be expected in a Small Seaport. As I wish'd to be as soon as I could at Rotterdam, I Quitted my Friend Tim Whinny to come up at his Leisure, and went on Board the Rotterdam Schout[2] at 9 in the Morning, and arriv'd there in a Few Hours. The Beauty of this Town and of the River Maas that flows by it and Forms its Harbour is well Known. The Sight of the Bombcase[3] and of the Canals that carry Shipping thro' the Whole Town Surpris'd and pleas'd me much. I had been Directed to put up at Cater's, an English House where I took up my Lodgings accordingly and adher'd to it in the two or three Trips, I made afterwards to this City, and found it an Exceeding Good House, where the expence was Moderate and every thing Good. In the Afternoon I enquir'd for Mr Robert Herries on whom I had my Credit, and found [his House] on the Scotch Dyke,[4] after passing in the Doit Boat,[5] over the Canal that Seperates it from the End of the Bombcase. From Mr Herries I met with a very Kind Reception. He was a Handsome Young Man of a Good Family in Annandale, who had not succeeded in Business at Dumfries, and had been sent over by my Uncle Provost Geo. Bell of that Town, as their Agent and Factor, as at that time they Dealt pretty Deep in the Tobacco Trade. He had immediatly assimilated to the Manners of the Dutch and was much Respected among them. He Liv'd in a very

Good House with a Mr Robertson and his Wife from Aberdeen, very Sensible Good Sort of people. They took very much to me, and Insisted on my Dining with them every Day. Next Door to them Liv'd a Mr Livingston from Aberdeen also, who was thought to be Rich. His Wife was the Daughter of Mr Kennedy one of the Ministers of the Scotch Church. She was a very Handsome and agreable Woman; and neither of the Ladies having Children, They had little care and Liv'd a very Sociable and pleasant Life; Especially my Landlady whose attractions consisted chiefly in Good Sense and Good Temper. Our Neighbour Being Young and Gay as well as Handsome, had not quite so much Liberty. Mr Herries advis'd me to Remain some Days, with them, Because Our King's Birthday having Happen'd lately, the British Students were to have a Grand Entertainment, it was better for me to escape the expence that might be Incurr'd by Going there too soon. Besides I had to Equip myself in cloaths and with a Sword, and other Necessaries, with which I could be better and cheaper Supplied at Rotterdam than at Leyden. I took their advice, and they were so obliging as to have New Company for me every Day; among whom were Mess^s Kennedy and Ainslie his Colleague. The First was popular, and Pompous, and Political, and an Irishman. The 2^d was a plain, Sensible Scotchman, less sought after but more respectable than his Colleague. During my Stay at Rotterdam, I was Informed of every thing, and saw every thing that was New or Curious.

Travelling in Holland by means of the Canals is Easy and Commodious, and tho' the Country is so flat, that one can See to no Distance, Yet the Banks of the Canals, especially as you approach the Cities, are so much adorn'd with pleasure Houses and Flower Gardens, as to furnish a constant Succession, not of the Grand and Sublime, or Magnificent Works of Nature, but of a profusion of the Rich and Gawdy Effects of Opulence without Taste. When I arriv'd at Leyden, which was in a Few Hours, I found my Lodgings Ready, having had a Correspondence from Rotterdam with Thos Dickson M.D. afterwards my Brother in Law. They were in the House of a Madam Vander Tasse, on the Long Bridge. There was in her House, Besides Dr Dickson, Dr John Gregory, Mr Nicholas Monckly, and a Mr Skirret, a Student of Law. Vandertasse's was an accustom'd Lodging House, her Father and Mother having carried on that Business, so that we liv'd very well there at a moderate Rate—That is 16 Stivers[1] for Dinner, 2 for Coffee, 6 for Supper and for Breakfast. She was a Lively little French Woman about 36, had been tolerably Well Looking, and was plump and in Good Condition. As she had only one Maid Servant, and five Gentlemen to Provide for, she Led an Active and Laborious Life; Insomuch that she had but little time for her Toilet, except in the article of the Coiff, which no French Woman omits. But on

Sundays when she had Leisure to Dress herself for the French Church, either in the Morning or Evening, Then, Who but Mademoiselle Vandertasse! She spoke English perfectly well, as the Guests of the House had been mostly British: But it had cost her Something to Learn the Language. As I had come Last, I had the worst Bedchamber. Besides Board, we paid pretty High for our Rooms, and Dearest of all for Fewel, which was chiefly Peat. We had very Good Small Claret, at a Shilling a Bottle; Giving her the Benefit of our Exemption from Town Duty, for Sixty Stoups of Wine, for every Student.[1] Our House was in high Repute for the best Coffee so that our Friends were pleas'd when they were Invited to partake with us in that Delicious Beverage. We had no Company to Dinner, but in the Evenings about a Dozen of us met at one anothers Rooms in Turn 3 Times a Week and Drank Coffee and Smoak'd tobacco, and Chatted about politicks, and Drank Claret, and supped on Bukkam (Dutch Red Herrings)[2] and Eggs and Sallad, and never Sate later than 12 a clock. At Mr Gowans the Clergyman, never later than 10, unless when we Deceiv'd him, by making such a Noise, when the Hour was Ringing as prevented his Hearing it.

Tho' I had not been acquainted with John Gregory formerly, which was owing to my two Winter's Residence at Glasgow when he was in Edin^r, Yet as he knew most of my Friends there, we soon became Intimate together and Generally pass'd two Hours every forenoon in Walking. His Friend Monckly, Being very Fat and a Bad Walker could not follow us. There were at this time about 22 British Students at Leyden, of whom Besides the 5 at our House already nam'd were, the Honble Charles Townshend, afterwards, a Distinguish'd Statesman, and Husband to Lady Dalkeith the Mother of the Duke of Buccleuch, Mr James Johnstone Junr of Westerhall, Dr Anthony Askew, John Campbell Junr of Stonefield, his Tutor Mr Morton, afterwards a Professor at St Andrews, John Wilkes, his Companion Mr Bland and their Tutor Mr Lyson, Mr Freeman from Jamaica, Mr Doddeswell Brother of Mr Dodeswell afterwards Chancellor of the Exchequer, Mr Wetherall from the West Indies, Dr Charles Congalton to this Day a Physician in Edin^r, an Irish Gentleman Keeffe, I think in his House, Willy Gordon, afterwards K.B. with 4 or 5 more whose Names I have forgot, and who Did not associate with my Friends.

On the First Sunday Evening I was in Leyden I walk'd round the Cingle, a fine Walk on the outside of the Rhine, which formd the Wet-Ditch of the Town, with John Gregory, who Introduc'd me to the British Students as we met them, not without Giving me a Short Character of them, which I found in general a very Just Outline. When we came to John Wilkes, whose Ugly Countenance in Early Youth was very Striking,

I ask'd Earnestly who he was; his Answer was that he was the Son of a London Distiller or Brewer, who wanted to be a Fine Gentleman and Man of Taste, which he could never be, for God and Nature had been against him. I came to know Wilkes very well afterwards, and found him to be a Sprightly Entertaining Fellow, too much so for his Years, as he was but 18—For even then he shew'd Something of Daring Profligacy for which he was afterwards Notorious. Tho' he was fond of Learning, and passionatly Desirous of being thought Something Extraordinary, he was unlucky in having an old Ignorant Pedant of a Dissenting Parson for his Tutor. This Man a Mr Leeson, or Lyson, had been singled out by the Father as the Best Tutor in the World for his most promising Son, Because at the Age of 3 score, after studying Controversy for more than 30 Years, he told his Congregation that he was going to Leave them, and would tell them the Reason next Sunday: When Being fully Conven'd, he told them that with much anxiety and care he had Examin'd the Arian Controversy, and was now Convinc'd that the Creed he had read to them as his Creed was False, and that he had now adopted that of the Arians, and was to bid them farewell. The People were shock'd with this Creed, and not so sorry as they would otherwise have been to part with him, for he was a good natur'd well meaning Man. His Chief Object seem'd to be to make Wilkes an Arian also, and Teas'd him so much about it, that he was Oblig'd to Declare, that he Did Not Believe the Bible at all, which produc'd a Quarrel between them—and Wilkes for Refuge went Frequently to Utrecht, where he met with Immateriallity Baxter, as he was Call'd, who then attended Lord Blantyre and Mr Hay of Drummellier, as he had formerly done John Lord Gray. This Gentleman was more to Wilkes's Taste than his own Tutor for tho he was a profound Philosopher and a hard Student, he was at the same time a Man of the World, and of such pleasing Conversation as attracted the Young. Baxter was so much pleas'd with Wilkes, that he Dedicated one of his Pieces to him. He Died in 1750—Which fact Leads me to Correct an Error, in the Acc^t of Baxter's Life in which he is much Prais'd for his Keeping well with Wilkes, tho' he had given so much umbrage to the Scotch. But this is a Gross Mistake, For the People of that Nation, were always Wilkes's Favourites, till 1763, thirteen Years after Baxter's Death, when Wilkes became a violent Party Writer, and wish'd to Raise his Fame and Fortune on the Ruin of Lord Bute.

Wilkes was very fond of Shining in Conversation very prematurely, for at that time he had but little Knowledge, except what he Deriv'd from Baxter, in his frequent visits to Utrecht. In the Art of Shining however, he was much outdone by Charles Townshend, who was not above a Year older, and had still less Furniture in his Head. But then his person and

manners were more engaging; he had more Wit and Humour, and a Turn
for Mimickry, and above all, had the Talent of Translating other Mens
Thoughts, which they had produc'd in the Simple Style of Conversation,
into the most charming Language, which not only took the Ear, but
elevated the thoughts. No person I ever knew, nearly Equald Charles T.
in this Talent but Dʳ Robertson, who tho' he had a very great fund of
Knowledge and Thought of his own, was yet so passionately fond of
Shining, that he Siez'd what was Nearest at Hand, the Conversation of
his Friends of that Morn. or the Day before, and Embellish'd it with such
Rich Language, that they hardly knew it again themselves. Insomuch
That he was the greatest Plagiary in Conversation, that ever I knew. 'Tis
to this probably that his Biographer alludes, his *Strong Itch* for Shining,*
when he Confesses that he lik'd his Conversation best, when he had not an
audience.¹ Gregory's Chum Dʳ Monckly, had this Talent too, and exercis'd it so as to bring on him the Highest Ridicule. He was in reallity, an
Ignorant vain Blockhead, who had the most passionate Desire of Shining,
which Gregory was Entirely above. His usual Method was to Get Gregory
into his Room either before or after Breakfast, when he Settled with him
what were to be the Leading Topicks of the Day, especially at our Coffee,
or our Club Suppers, For I soon Broke him of his attempt to Shine at
Dinner. Having thus Settled everything with Gregory and heard his
Opinion, he Let him go a Walking with me, and Jotted Down the Topicks
and Arguments he had heard. The very prospect of the Glory he was to
Earn in the Evening, made him Contented and Happy all Day. Gregory
kept his Secret, as I Did, who was Generally Let in to it in our Walk, and
pray'd not to contradict the Fat Man—Which I seldom Did when he was
not too provoking. Unfortunaty one Night Gregory took it in his Head
to Contradict him, when he was Harranguing very pompously, on Tragedy or Comedy or some Subject of Criticism. The Poor Man Look'd as
if he had been Shot—and after Recovering himself, said with a Ghastly
Smile, Surely this was not always your Opinion. Gregory persisted, and
after saying That Criticism was a Subject, on which he Thought it Lawfull to change, he entirely Refuted the poor undone Dʳ. Not another word
Did he utter the Whole Evening. He had his Coffee in his Room next

---

* Being on one occasion Invited to Dine with Pat. Robertson his Brother, I miss'd
my Friend whom I had met there on all former Occasions. I have not Invited him
today says Peter, for I have a very Good Company, and he'll let no body speak but
himself. I saw him once overpowered. He was staying with me for a Week, and I
carried him to Dine with our Parish Club, who were fully assembled to see and hear
Dʳ Robertson. But Dʳ Finlay of Drummore took it in his head to come that Day,
where he had not been for a Year before, who Took the Lead, Being then Rich and
Selfsufficient, tho' a Great Babbler, and Entirely Dissappointed the Company—and
Gave us all the Headach—

Medallion of Adam Smith by James Tassie

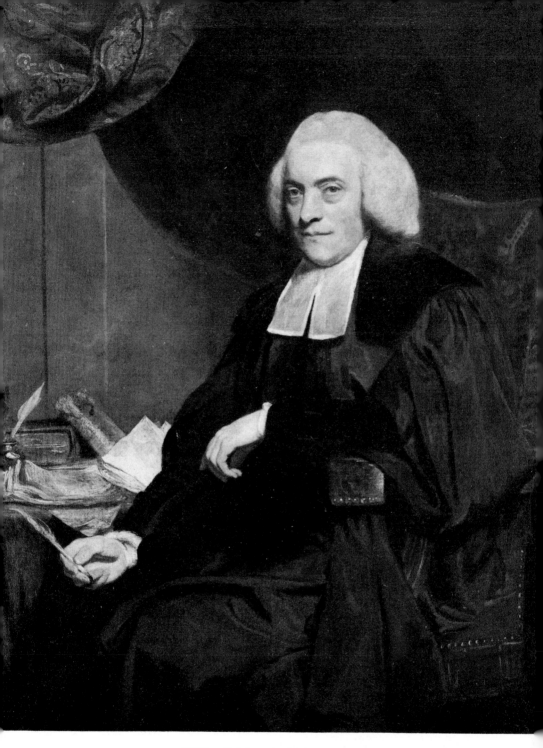

William Robertson by Sir Joshua Reynolds

Morning, and sent for Gregory before he Left the Parlour. I waited for an Hour, when at last he Join'd me, and told me that he had been Rated at no allowance by the Fat Man—and when he Defended himself by Saying that he had gone far beyond the Bounds prescrib'd, The Poor Soul fell into Tears, and Said He was undone, as he had Lost the only friend he had in the world. It cost Gregory some time to comfort him, and to exhort him—By exacting from him some Deference to himself at our Future Parties, (for the Blockhead till then had never so much as said, What is your opinion on this Subject Dr G.). A New Settlement was made between them, and we went on very well. For when some of the Rest were Debating Bona Fide, with the absurd animal, I who was in the Secret gave him Line and Encouragement, till he had Got far beyond his Depth, while Gregory was Sitting Silent in a Corner, and never Interpos'd, till he was in Danger of Being Drown'd in the Mud. This may seem a Cruel Amusement—But I forgave Gregory for there was no Living with Monckly without it.

We pass'd our time in General very agreably, and very profitably too, for ten or 12 of us held Meetings at our Lodgings, thrice a Week in the Evenings, when the Conversations of Young Men of Good Knowledge, intended for Different professions, could not Fail to be Instructive. Much more so than the Lectures, which except two, that of Civil Law, and that of Chemistry, were very Dull. I ask'd Gregory why he Did not attend the Lectures, which he answer'd by asking in his turn why I Did not attend the Divinity Professors (for there were no less than four of them). Having heard all they could say in a much better form, at home, we went but rarely and for Form's Sake only to Hear the Dutchmen.

At this time we were in great anxiety about the Rebellion, and were frequently 3 or 4 Weeks without getting a Packet from England. Insomuch that Gregory and I agreed to make a trip to Rotterdam, to Learn if they had heard any thing by Fishing Boats. We went one Day and return'd the Next without Learning anything. We Din'd with my agreable Friends on the Scotch Dyke, Harris and Robertson. In Returning in the Shuyt, I said to Gregory that we would be laugh'd at for having gone so Far, and brought back no News: But if he would Support me I would Frame a Gazette. He promis'd, and I immediatly wrote a Few Paragraphs which I said I had Copied from Allan the Bankers private Letter he had Got by a Fishing Boat. This was to Impose on Dr Askew for Allan was his Banker. I took Care also, to Make Admiral Townshend Take 2 Ships of the Line at Newfoundland, for he was Charles Townshends Uncle, and so on with the Rest of our Friends. On our arrival They all assembled at our Lodging and our News pass'd Current for all that Day. At night we Disclosd our Fabrication, Being able to hold out no Longer.

On another occasion I went Down with Dr Askew, who as a Learned Man of 28, had come over to Leyden to Collate Manuscripts of Æschylus for a new edition. His Father had Given him £10,000 in the Stocks, So that he was a Man of Importance. When Gregory and I were alarm'd at the expensive Suppers some of our Friends gave from the Tavern, we went to Askew whose turn was next, and easily persuaded him, to Limit his Supper to Eggs and Buccam and Sallad, which he accordingly Gave us next night, which with Tobacco of 40 Stivers a Lib. and very Good Claret pleas'd us all. After this no more Fine Suppers were presented. And Gowans the old Minister of the Scottish Church, ventur'd to be of our Number and was very pleasant. Askews Errand at this time, was to cheat his Banker Allan, as he said he would draw on him for an £100— which he Did not want, because Exchange was at that time against Holland. In vain Did I try to persuade him, that the Banker would take care, not to Lose by him. But he persisted, Such Being the Skill in Business of this Eminent Grecian. He had some Drollery, but neither much Sense nor usefull Learning. He was much alarm'd when the Highlanders got as far as Derby, and believ'd that London would be taken and the Bank Ruin'd. I endeavour'd in vain to Raise his Spirits. At last I told him, that personally I Did not much Care, for I had nothing to Lose—and would not return to Brittain under a Bad Government. You are the very Man I want says he, for I have 4 or 500 £. worth of Books, and some Name as a Greek Scholar: We'll begin Bookselling and you shall be my Partner and Auctioneer. This was soon Settled and as soon forgot, when the Rebels March'd back from Derby.

I went twice to the Hague, which was then a very Delightfull place. Here I met with my Kinsman Willy Jardine, now Sir W^m who was a Cornet in the Prince of Orange's Horse Guards, and then a very Handsome Genteel Fellow, for as Odd as he has turn'd out since. Tho' I had no Introduction to any Body there, and no Acquaintance but the two Students who accompanied me the first time, I thought it a Delightfull place. A Ball that was Given about this time by the Imperial Ambassador, on the Empress's Birth Day, was Fatal to one of our Students, a very Genteel Agreable Rake as ever I saw from the W. Indies. At a preceding Dancing Ass[embly] he had been taken out by a princess of Waldeck, and had acquitted himself so well, that she procur'd him an Invitation to the Birthday Ball, and engag'd him to Dance with her.—He had Run himself out a good Deal before, and a Fine Suit of White and Silver—which Cost £60—compleated his Disstress, and he was oblig'd to Retire without shewing it to us more than once. There was another West Indian there, a Mr Freeman, a Man of Fortune, Sedate and Sensible. He was very Handsome and well made. Having been 3 Years in Leyden, he was the best Scater there. There was an E. India Cap[t] Resident in that City, whom the Dutch set up as a Rival to Freeman; and they Frequently appear'd on the Rhine together. The Dutchman was Tall and Jolly, but very Active with all. All the Ladies however Gave the Palm to Freeman, who was so Handsome, and having a Figure much like Garrick, all his Motions were perfectly Genteel. This Gentleman after we left Leyden, Made the Tour of Italy, Sicily and Greece, with Willy Gordon and Dod-deswell—The former of whom told me long afterwards, That he had Died soon after he Return'd to Jamaica, which was Gordon's own Native Country, Tho' his Parents were Scot[c]h, and Cousins of Gordon of Hawhead, in Aberdeenshire. He was too Young and too Dissipated to attend our Evening Meetings. Neither Did Charles Congalton, who was one of the best young men I have ever Known. His pretence was that he could not Leave his Irish Chum of the Name of Keeffe, but the Truth was, that having been bred a Jacobite, and having many Friends and Rela-tions in the Rebellion, he Did not like to keep company with those who were Warm Friends of Government. Dickson and he were my Compan-ions on a Tour to Amsterdam where we staid only three Days, and were much pleas'd with the Magnificence and Wealth and Trade of that City. Dickson was a very Honest Fellow, but rather Dull and a hard Student. As I commonly Sate up an Hour after the Rest had Gone to their Rooms, chatting or reading French with Madamoiselle, and as Dickson's apart-ment was next the Parlour, he Complain'd much of the Noise we made Laughing and Talking because it Disturb'd him, who was a Midnight Student. He [Broke in] once upon us with Impertinent Curiosity, But I Drove him to his Bed, and by Sitting up an hour Longer that night, and making more noise than usual, we Reduc'd him to patience and close Quarters ever after, and we made Less Noise. I mention'd some where That Mademoiselle had paid for her English, which was true, for she had an affair with a Scotch Gentleman ten or 12 Years before and had follow'd him to Leith on pretence of a promise, of which however she made nothing but a piece of Money.

At Christmas time three or four of us past 3 Days at Rotterdam where my Friends were very Agreable to my Companions. Young Kennedy whom we had known at Amsterdam, was visiting his Father at this time, as well as Young Anslie, the other Ministers Son, which Emprov'd our Parties. M[rs] Kennedy the Mother was ill of a Consumption, and British Physicians Being in Great Credit There, Monckly who was call'd D[r] tho' he had not taken his Degree, Being always more forward than any Body in Shewing himself off, was pitch'd upon by M[r] Kennedy to visit his Wife. Gregory who was realy a Physician, and had acquir'd both Know-ledge and Skill, by having been an Apprentice in his Brothers Shop at

Aberdeen, and visited the Patients with him, was kept in the Back Ground. But he was anxiously consulted by Monckly twice a Day, and taught his Lesson, which he Repeated very exactly, for I heard him two or three times being a Familiar in the House, while the Good D.ʳ was unconscious that I knew of his Secret Oracle. For all this, Monckly was only Ridiculous on account of his Childish Vanity and his Love of Shewing himself off. He was in reality a very Good Natur'd and obliging Man of much Benevolence, as well as Courtesy. He practis'd afterwards in London with Credit, For they Cur'd him of his affectation at Batsons.¹ He Died not many years after.*

[1746]

Gregory tho' a far abler Man and not less a Man of Learning for his Age, than of Taste, in the Most Important Qualities was not Superior to Monckly. When he was afterwards tried by the ardent Spirits of Edin.ʳ and the Prying Eyes of Rivalship, he Did not escape without the Imputation of Being Cold, and Selfish, and Cunning with all. His pretensions to be more Religious than others of his Profession, and his constant Eulogiums on the Female Sex, as at least Equal if not Superior to the Male, were suppos'd to be Lures of Reputation, or professional arts to Get into Business. When those Objections were made to him at Edin.ʳ I was able to take off the Edge from them, by assuring them that his Notions and Modes of Talking were not newly adopted for a Purpose, For that when at Leyden at the age of 21 or 22, he was equally Incessant and Warm on those Topicks, Tho' he had not a female to Flatter, nor ever went to Church, but when I Drag'd him to please old Gowans. Having Found Aberdeen too Narrow a Circle for him, and having tried London for a twelvemonth without Success, for Being ungainly in his Person and Manner, and no lucky accident having befallen him, he could not make his way suddenly in a Situation, where External Graces and address, Go much farther, than Professional Learning or Professional Skill. D.ʳ Gregory however was not without address. For he was much a Master of Conversation on all Subjects, and without Gross Flattery, obtain'd even more than a favourable Hearing to himself: For never Contradicting you at first but rather assenting, and yielding as it were to your Knowledge

---

* At this time 5 or 6 of us made an agreable Journey on Skates to see the Painted Glass in the church at Tergou. It was Distant 12 Miles. We left Rotterdam at 10 a clock, saw the church and Din'd, and Return'd to Rotterdam between five and six in the evening—It was Moonlight and a Gentle Breeze in our Back, so that we Return'd in an Hour and a Quarter.

and Taste, he very often brought you Round to think as he Did, and to Consider him as a Superior Man. When he Settled in Edin? The Poker Club[1] was Highly Fashionable, of which he was very anxious to be a Member. As one of his Most Intimate Friends I made Interest for him, and he was Elected. But strange to tell, he never attended but twice, for what Reason was left to Conjecture.* In all my Dealings with him, for he was my Family Physician, I found him Friendly and affectionate and generous.

An unlucky accident happen'd about the End of Jan? which Disturb'd the Harmony of our Society, and Introduc'd uneasiness and Suspicion among us. At an evening Meeting where I happen'd not to be, Charles Townshend who had a Great Deal of Wit, which he was fond to shew even sometimes at the expence of his Friends, Tho' in reality one of the best Natur'd of Men, took it in his Head to make a But of James Johnstone afterwards Sir James of Westerhall. Not Contented with the Smartness of his Raillery, Lest it should be Obscure, he frequently accompanied it with that Motion of the Tongue in the Cheek which explains and aggravates everything. He Continued During the Evening to Make Game of James; who slow of apprehension, and unsuspicious, had taken all in Good part. Some one of the Company however, who had felt Charles's Smartness, which he Did not chuse to Resent, had Gone in the Morning to Johnstone, and open'd his Eyes on Townshend's Behaviour over Night. Johnstone tho' not apt to take offence was prompt enough in his Resentment when Taken, and Immediatly Resolv'd, to put Charles's Courage to the Test. I was sent for next forenoon by 12 a clock to Charles's Lodging, who Look'd pale and undone, more than I had ever Seen him. He was Liable at that time to Convulsion Fits, which seldom Fail'd to attack him after a late Supper. I ask'd him what was the Matter with him; he answer'd that he had been Late up and had been ill. He next ask'd me, If I had ever observ'd him use James Johnstone with ill natur'd Raillery or Sarcasm in Company or Ridicule him behind his back. I answer'd him that I had never perceiv'd any thing between them, but that Playsome Kind of Raillery so frequent among Good Friends and Companions, and that when Johnstone was absent, I had never heard him Ridicule him but for Triffles, in spite of which I conceiv'd that he had a Respect for him. Upon this he shew'd me a letter from Johnstone, Taxing him for having often Treated him with Contempt in Company, and particularly for his Behaviour the Night before, which having been made to advert to by a friend, who was sharper Sighted than him, and which had brought sundry

* Professor Ferguson told me not long ago, that he was present the 2ᵈ time Dʳ Gregory attended the Poker, when Enlarging on his Favourite Topick, the Superiority of the Female Sex, he was so laughd at and run down That he Never Return'd.

things to his Recollection, which tho' he Did not mind at the time, were fully explain'd by his Behaviour to him the Night before. The Letter Concluded with a challenge. And what answer are you to make to this said I; Not Fight to be Sure said he, for I have no Quarrel with Johnstone, who is the best Natur'd Man in the World. If you can make it up, and keep it secret it may Do; otherwise you'll be Disshonour'd by the transaction: I added, find out the Malicious Scoundrel if you can, who has acted like a vile Informer, and take Vengeance of him. He seem'd quite Irresolute and I left him with this Advice, either to make it up, or put it over as soon as possible. He made it up to be sure, but it was in a manner that Hurt him, for Johnstone and he went Round all the Lodgings in Leyden, and Enquir'd of every Body if any of them had ever heard or seen him Ridicule Johnstone. Every Body said no, to this, and he and Johnstone became the Greatest Friends. But it Did him more harm than it would, or ought to have Done at his Raw Age, If he had not afterwards betray'd want of firmness of Character. This was a Pity, for he had unbounded Capacity and Application, and was good temper'd and affectionate.

This accident in some measure Broke the Bond of our Society, But it was of little Importance to us who meant to Leave Leyden very Soon. Gregory and I had agreed to Go to London together, and when Monckly heard of this Resolution he Determin'd to Accompany us. His Monitor had advis'd him to take his Degree in Leyden, But the Honest Man Did not chuse to stand the Examination, and he knew that by paying a little more he could get his Diploma Sent after him. Dickson Remain'd to take his Degree, as he regarded the additional Guineas, much more than he fear'd the Examination. Gregory with a Degree of Malice Due the Fat Man for his Vanity and Presumption, press'd him very much to abide the Trial, and Blazon'd to him the Inglorious Retreat he was about to make. But it would not Do, as Gregory knew perfectly before Hand. About the End of Feb.ʸ or beginning of March, we Set out on our Return to Brittain; when passing two Days very agreably with our Friends at Roterdam, we fell down to Helvoet, and took our passage on Board the Packet which was to Sail for Harwich next Morning. On the Journey and Voyage Monckly assum'd his proper Station which was that of Treasurer and Director—and to say the truth he Did it well, for except in one Instance he manag'd our Affairs with a Decent Oeconomy, no less than with the Generosity that became his assum'd office. The exception to this was his allowing himself to be Impos'd on by the Landlord of the Inn at Helvoet, in Laying in seastores for our Voyage, for he said he had known Packets on the Sea for a Week by Calms &c. The Director Elect therefore Laid in a cold ham and a Couple of Fowls with a Surloin of Beef, 9 Bottles of Wine

and 3 of Brandy, None of all which we were able to Taste except a little of
the Brandy to settle our Stomachs.

We Sail'd from Helvoet at 8 in the Morning, and having a fine Brisk
Gale quite Fair, we arriv'd on the Coast of England by 8 in the Evening:
Tho' having Made the Land too far to the Northward, it was near 12
before we Got down to Harwich. We had beds in the Cabbin, and were all
so heartily Sea Sick, that we were hardly able to lift up our Heads the
Whole Day. We had one Cabbin Passenger who was afterwards much
Celebrated. When we were on the Quarterdeck in the Morning, we
observ'd 3 Forreigners of Different Ages, who had under their care a
Young Person of about 16 very Handsome indeed whom we took for a
Hanoverian Baron Coming to Brittain to pay his Court at S!̠ James's.
The Gale Freshen'd so soon, that we had not an opportunity of Conversing with those Forreigners, when we were oblig'd to Take to our Beds in
the Cabbin. The Young Person was the only one of the Strangers, who
had a Birth there, because as we suppos'd it occasion'd an additional
Freight. My Bed was Directly opposite to that of the Stranger. But we
were so Sick that there was no Conversation among us, till the Young
Forreigner became very frightend in Spite of the Sickness, and call'd out
to me in French, if we were not in Danger—Her voice betraid her Sex at
once no less than her Fears; I consold her as well as I could, and soon
brought her above the Fear of Danger. This Beautifull Person was
Violletti the Dancer, who was engagd to the Opera in the Hay-Market—
This we were made certain of by the Man who Call'd himself her Father,
waiting on us next Day at Harwich, Requesting our Countenance to his
Daughter, on her First appearance and on her Benefit. I accordingly was
at the Opera the first Night she appear'd where she was the First Dancer,
and Maintaind her Ground till Garrick Married her. I never saw her
afterwards till the Year 1758, when I was frequently at her House in
London, and pass'd one Compleat Day at their House at Hampton, with
John Home and D.r Robertson, L.d Chancellor Loughborough and his
Brother and two of the Adams's, Robert and James—as it was so long
since I had met with her, I took no Notice and she Did not seem to Know
me.

We had so much trouble about our Baggage, that we Did not Get from
Harwich till one aclock, and I was oblig'd to Leave Leeson's Picture,
which I had undertaken to Carry to London for John Wilkes. We pass'd
the Night at Colchester, where the Forreigners were likely to be Roughly
Treated, as the Servants at the Inn took offence at the Young Woman in
Mens Cloaths, as one Room was only bespoke for all the Four. We inter-
fer'd however, when Monckly's Authority Back'd by us, prevented their
Being Insulted. They Travell'd in a Seperate Coach from us, but we made

the Young Lady Dine with us Next Day, which secur'd her Good Treatment. We were so late in Getting to London that we Remain'd all Night together in an Inn in Friday S⸞ and when we Seperated Next Day, with a Promise of Seeing one another often, Yet so Great is the City of London, and so Busy is every Body Kept there, That Intimate as we had been, it was 3 weeks or a Month before we met again. We had not yet found out the British Coffee House, where so many of our Countrymen assemble Daily.[1]

I Got a Coach and went Directly to New Bond Street to my Cousin Cap⸞ Lyon's, who had been Married for a few Years to Lady Catharine Bridges, a Daughter of the Marquiss of Carnarvon, and Grandchild of the Duke of Chandos—Lyon's Mother was an acquaintance of the Marchioness, the young Lady's Mother of the Dysart Family, who had Fallen in Love with Lyon, who was one of the Handsomest Men in London, But he escap'd by Marrying the Daughter, who tho' not Handsome was Young and Alluring, and had a Prospect of a Great Fortune, as she had only one Sister who was Deform'd. Here I Renew'd my Acquaintance with my Aunt Lyon, who was still a Fine Woman—Her Elder Sister M⸞ˢ Paterson, the Widow of a Cap⸞ Paterson of the Bannockburn Family, a very plain looking sensible woman, kept House with her, while the Son and his Family Liv'd in the Next House which belong'd to M⸞ˢ Lyon. Lady Catharine by this time had two Girls, 3 and 4 years of age, as Beautiful Children as ever were Seen. They had bespoke for me a Small Lodging in little Madocks S⸞ within Sight of the Back of their House. Lyon was a cheerfull fine fellow as ever was Born, who had just return'd with his Troop of the Horse Guards from Flanders, where he and they had been for two Compaigns under the Duke of Cumberland. With them and their Friends I past part of my time. But having found some of my Old Friends lounging about the British and Forrests Coffee Houses, in Cockspur Street Charing Cross, viz. John Blair afterwards a Prebendary of Westminster, Robert Smith, afterwards Distinguish'd by the appellation of the Duke of Roxburgh's Smith, who introduc'd me to D⸞ʳ Smollet with whom he was Intimate, and Charles Congalton arriving in a Few Weeks from Leyden, who was a Stranger as well as myself in London, I was at no loss how to pass my Time agreably, when Lyon and his Family were engag'd in their own Circle.

By him however I was Introduc'd to some Families of Condition and was Carried to Court of an Evening for Geo. 2ᵈ at that time had evening Drawing Rooms, where His Majesty and Princess Emilia, who had been a Lovely Woman, play'd at Cards, and the Courtiers Saunter'd for an Hour or two. This was a very Insipid Amusement. I went with Lyon also and his Lady to a Ridotta at the Hay Market,[2] a Ball where there were not fewer than 1500 people; and which R! Keith the ambassador told me in the Entry, was a strong proof of the Greatness and Opulence of London, for he had stood in the Entry he said, and seen all the Ladies come in, and was certain that not one half of them were of the Court End of the Town, for he knew every one of them. Lady Catherine Lyon whom I Squir'd that night and with whom I Danc'd Introduc'd me to many of her Acquaintance, and among the Rest to Lady Dalkeith and her Sisters, the Daughters of John Duke of Argyle, who she said were her cousins. What is worth observing, the Countess was then with Child of Henry Duke of Buccleugh who was Born on the 14ᵗʰ of Sept! thereafter, who was my much Respected Patron and highly Honour'd Friend.

Cap! Lyon Introduc'd me to his Friends and the Officers of the Horse Guards with whom I liv'd a Good Deal. The Troop he belongd to which I think was Lᵈ Tyrawley's was one of the two who had been abroad in Flanders, between whom and those at home, there was a Strong Emulation, who should Entertain most expensively, when on Guard. Their parties were Generally in the Evening, when they had as expensive Suppers as could be Got from a Tavern; amongst other Things, Champagne and Ice Creams, both of which were new to me and the last then rare in London. I had many very agreable Parties with those Officers, who were all Men of the World, and some of them of Erudition, and Understanding. One I must particularly Mention, was Cap! Elliot, afterwards Lord Heathfield, the Celebrated Defender of Gibraltar. A Parcel of us happen'd to meet in the Park in a fine evening in April, who on asking each other how they were engag'd, Seven or Eight of us agreed, to Sup at the Cardigan, at Charing Cross, among whom Elliot was one. Lyon and I undertook to Go Directly to the House and Bespeak a Room, and were soon after Join'd by our Company, and two or three more of their Friends whom they had met in their Walk. We pass'd the Evening very pleasantly, and when the Bill was Call'd for, a Mʳ Phillips who was in the Chair, and who by the Death of a Relation that Morning had Succeeded to an Estate of £1000 a year wish'd to pay the whole Reckoning as he said it was a triffle, which was Resisted—He then said he would play Odds or Evens with all the Company in their Turns, whether he or they should pay— This was agreed to: and he contriv'd to Lose to Every Body, except Cap! Elliot, who said he never play'd for his Reckoning. I observ'd on this afterwards to Lyon that this appear'd Particular, and that Elliot tho' by his Conversation a very Sensible Man, yet Did not Yield to the Humour of the Company, which was to Gratify Phillips. He answer'd me, That tho' Cap! Elliot was some what Singular and Austere in his Manners, yet he was a very worthy and able Officer, for whom he had Great Esteem. This Trait of Singularity, Occur'd to me, when he became so

Distinguish'd an Officer, whom I should rather have Noted as Sour and Intractable.

John Blair had past his trials as a Preacher in Scotland, but having a few hundred pounds of Patrimony, chose to pay a visit to London, where he Loiter'd till he spent it all. After some time he thought of compleating and Publishing his Chronological Tables, the plan of which had been Given him by Dᵣ Hugh Blair, the Celebrated Preacher. He became acquainted with the Bishop of Lincoln, with whom he was soon a Favourite; and having been ordain'd by him, was presented to the Living of Burton Cogles in his Diocese. He was afterwards Teacher of Math. to the Duke of York, the Kings Brother, and was by his Interest prefer'd to be a Prebendary of Westminster. He was a Lively agreable Fellow, and one of the most Friendly Men in the World. Smith had been abroad with the young Laird of McLeod of that period, and was call'd home with his Pupil, when the Rebellion began. He had been ill-rewarded and was on his shifts at that time in London. He was a Man of superior understanding and of a most Gentlemany address. With Smollet he was very Intimate. We Four with one or two more frequently resorted to a Small Tavern in the Corner of Cockspur Sᵗ at the Golden Ball, where we had a frugal Supper, and a little punch as the finances of None of the Company were in very Good Order. But we had rich enough Conversation on Literary Subjects, which was enliven'd by Smollets agreable Stories, which he told with peculiar Grace.

Soon after our acquaintance Smollet shew'd me his Tragedy of James the 1ˢᵗ of Scotland, which he never could bring on the Stage, for which the Managers could not be blam'd. But it sour'd him against them, and he appeald to the Publick by Printing it—But the Publick seem'd to take part with the Managers.

I was in the Coffee House with Smollet when the News of the Battle of Culloden arriv'd, and when London all over was in a perfect uproar of Joy—It was then that Jack Stuart the son of the Provost behaved in the Manner I before mention'd (page 59). About 9 a clock I wish'd to Go home to Lyon's in N. Bond Sᵗ as I had promis'd to Sup with him that night, it being the anniversary of his Marriage Night, or the Birthday of one of his children. I ask'd Smollet if he was ready to Go, as he liv'd at Mayfair—He said he was, and would conduct me. The Mob were so Riotous, and the Squibs so Numerous and Incessant, that we were Glad to Go into a Narrow Entry to put our Wigs in our Pockets, and to take our Swords from our Belts and walk with them in our Hands, as every Body then wore Swords—and after Cautioning me against Speaking a Word, Lest the Mob should Discover my Country and become Insolent—For John Bull says he is as Haughty and Valiant tonight, as a few Months ago he was abject and cowardly, on the Black Wednesday when the Highlanders were at Derby. After we Got to the Head of the Haymarket, thro' Incessant Fire, The Dr Led me by narrow Lanes where we met Nobody but a few Boys at a Pitifull Bone Fire, who very civilly ask'd us for 6^d which I Gave them. I saw not Smollet again for some time after, when he Shew'd Smith and me the Manuscript of his Tears of Scotland, which was publishd not long after, and had such a Run of Approbation.[1] Smollet tho' a Tory was not a Jacobite, but he had the Feelings of a Scotch Gentleman, on the Reported Cruelties that were said to be exercis'd after the Battle of Culloden.

My Cousin Lyon was an Englishman Born, tho' of Scottish Parents, and an officer in the Guards and Perfectly Loyal—and yet even he Did not seem to Rejoice so Cordially at the Victory as I expected. What's the matter says I, has your Strathmore Blood Got up that you are not pleas'd with the Quelling of the Rebellion? God knows says he, I heartily Rejoice that it is Quell'd, But I'm sorry that it has been accomplish'd by the Duke of C[umberland] for if he was before the most Insolent of all Commanders, what will he be now? I afterwards found that this Sentiment, prevail'd more than I had Imagin'd: (and yet tho' no General he had certainly more Parts and Talents, than any of his Family).

I was witness to a Scene in the British Coffee House which was afterwards explain'd to me. Capt David Cheap who was on Ansons Voyage,[2] and had been wreck'd on the Coast of Chili, and was Detain'd there for some time by the Spaniards, had arriv'd in London and frequented this Coffeehouse. Being a Man of Sense and Knowledge, he was employ'd by Ld Anson to look out for a Proper Person to write his voyage, the Chaplain whose Journal furnish'd the Chief Materials being unequal to the work. Capt Cheap had a predilection for his Countrymen, and having heard of Guthrie, the Writer of the Westminster Journal &c., he had come down to the Coffee House that evening to Enquire about him, and if he was pleasd with what he heard, would have been Introduc'd. Not long after Cheap had Sate Down, and call'd for Coffee, Guthrie arriv'd Dress'd in Lac'd Clothes, and talking Loud to every Body, and soon fell a wrangling with a Gentleman about Tragedy and Comedy and the unities &c. and Laid Down the Laws of the Drama in a peremptory manner, supporting his argument with Cursing and Swearing. I saw Cheap was astonish'd, when Rising and Going to the Bar he asked who this was, and finding it was Guthrie whom he had come down to Enquire about, he paid his Coffee and slunk off in Silence. I knew him well afterwards, and having one Day ask'd him if he remember'd the Incident, he told me that it was true, that he came there with the Design of talking with Guthrie, on the Subject of the Voyage, but was so much disgusted with his vapouring[1] Manner, that he thought no more of him.

As I have Mention'd Cap! Cheap whom I met in Scotland 2 Year after this, when he came to visit his Relations: I met him often at his Half Brother's Geo. Cheap Collector of the Customs at Prestonpans, and in Summer at Goat Whey Quarters,[2] where I liv'd with him for 3 Weeks; and became very confidential with him. He had a Sound and Sagacious Understanding and an Intrepid Mind, and had Great Injustice Done to him, in Biron's acc! of that [voyage] which Major Hamilton, who was one of the Unfortunate People in the Wager,[3] told me was in many things False or exagerated. One Instance I remember, which is this, That Cheap was so selfish that he had Conceald 4 Libs. of Seal in the Lining of his Coat to abstract from the Company for his own Use. He no Doubt had the piece of Seal, and Cap! Hamilton saw him Secrete it. But when they had Got Clear of a Cazique,[4] who plunder'd them of all he could, the Cap! Producing his Seal, said to his Companions, That Devil wanted to Reduce me to his own Terms by Famine, but I outplotted him, for with this Piece of Seal we could have held out 24 hours Longer. Another Trait of his Character Cap! Hamilton told me which was, That when they arriv'd in Chili to the N? of Eleven who had adher'd to Cheap, and were truly, for Hunger and Nakedness, worse than the Lowest Beggars; and were Delighted with the arrival of a Spanish officer from the Governor, who presented Cheap with a Petition, which he said he behov'd to Sign, otherwise they could not be taken under the Protection of the Spanish Governor—Cheap having Glanc'd this Paper with his Eye, and throwing it Indignantly on the Ground, said sternly to the Officer, That he would not sign such a paper, For the Officers of the King of England could Die of Hunger, but they Disdain'd to Beg. Hamilton and Biron and all the People fell into Despair, for they believ'd that the Cap! was Gone Mad, and that they were all undone. But it had a quite Contrary Effect, for the Officer now treated him with unbounded Respect, and Going hastily to the Governour, Return'd Immediatly with a Blank Sheet of Paper, and Desir'd Cap! Cheap to Dictate, or Write his Request in his own Way. Hamilton added that Biron and he Being then very Young, about 16 or 17, they frequently thought they were Ruin'd by the Captains Behaviour which was often Mysterious and always Arrogant and High; But that yet in the Sequel, they found that he had always acted under the Guidance of a Sagacious Foresight. This was marking him as a character Truly fit for Command. Which was the Conclusion I Drew from my Intercourse with him in Scotland.*

* On my Enquiring at Hamilton what had made Biron so severe he said he believ'd it was that the Cap! one Day, had call'd him Puppy when he was Petulant

As I had seen the Chevalier, Prince Charles frequently in Scotland, I was appeal'd to, if a Print that was selling in all the Shops was not like him. My answer was, that it had not the Least Resemblance. Having been taken one night however to a meeting of the Royal Society by Microscope Baker, There was Introduc'd a Hanoverian Baron, whose likeness was so strong to the Print which passd for the Young Pretender, that I had no Doubt, that he Being a Stranger, the Printsellers, had Got him Scetch'd out, that they might make something of it before his Vera Effigies could be had. Experiments in Electricity were then but New in England, and I saw them well exhibited at Mr Bakers, whose wife by the by, was a Daughter of the Celebrated Daniel Defoe.

I Din'd frequently with a club of Officers mostly Scotch, at a Coffee house in Church Court in the Strand, where Charles Congalton Lodg'd, and who Introduc'd me to the club, many of whom were old acquaintance, such as Capt Henry Fletcher, Boyd Porterfield and sundry more who had been Spar'd the Fatal Battle of Fontenoy. We had an excellent Dinner at 10^d, I thought as Good as those in Holland at a Guilder. The Company however were so much pleas'd, that they voluntarily rais'd it to 18^d pence, and they were right for as they Generally went to the play at 6 a clock, the advance of the Ordinary left them at Liberty, to forsake the Bottle Early.

The Theatres were not very attractive this Season, as Garrick was Gone over to Dublin. There still remain however what was enough for a Stranger, Mrs Pritchard and Mrs Clive, and M^clin who were all excellent in their way.[1] But I had seen Hughes and Mrs Hamilton in Edin^r, and whether or not it might be owing to the Force of First Impressions, I then thought, that they were not surpass'd by those I saw in London.*

At that particular time, Strangers were excluded from the House of Commons, and I had not then a strong Curiosity for that kind of entertainment. I saw all the Sights as usual for Strangers in London, and having procur'd a Small Pamphlet which Describ'd the Publick Buildings

---

and Feeling himself in the Wrong, he Endeavour'd to make up with Biron by Greater Civility, which the other Rejecting, Cheap kept him at a Greater Distance. He entirely clear'd Cheap from any Blame for shooting Cozens, into which he was Led by unavoidable circumstances, and which compleatly reestablish'd his Authority.

* Of the Literary People I met with at this time in London I must not forget Thomson the Poet and Dr Armstrong. Dickson had come to London from Leyden with his Degree of M.D. and had been Introduc'd to Armstrong who was his Countryman. A Party was form'd at the Ducie Tavern at Temple Bar, when the Company was Armstrong and Dickson and And. Millar, with Murdoch his Friend—Thompson came at last, and Dissappointed me both by his Appearance and Conversation. Armstrong bore him Down, having Got into his Sarcastical Vein, by the Wine he had Drank before Thomson Join'd us.

with taste and Discernment, I visited them with that in my hand. On Sundays I went with Lyon and his Family to S! George Church in Hanover Square. Sometimes I went to S! James' Church to Hear D[r] Secker who was then Rector of that Parish, and a Fine Preacher.

I was twice at the Opera, which seem'd so very far from Real Life and so unnatural, that I was pleas'd with Nothing, but the Dancing, which was exquisite, especially that of Violetti.

[Vau]xhall furnish'd Early in May a fine entertainment. But I was now urg'd by my Father to Return Home and accordingly Charles Congalton and I Left London about the middle of May on Horseback, and Having Windsor and Oxford to See, we took the West Road, and were Delighted with the Beauty of the Country. At Windsor which charm'd us we met with some old Acquaintance, D[r] Francis Home and D[r] Adam Austin, who were then Surgeons of Dragoons, and who when afterwards settled in Edin[r] as Physicians became Eminent in their Line. At Oxford we knew nobody but D[r] John Smith, M.D. who was a Glasgow exhibitioner, and then taught Mathematicks with Success in Oxford. He was a Good kind of Man, and became an Eminent Practitioner. He went about with us, and shew'd us all the Colleges, with which we were really astonish'd. We took the road by Warwick, and were much [pleas'd] with that Town and L[d] Brooks Castle. When we came to Litchfield we met as we expected with John Dickson of Kilbucho M.P. who accomp[ani]'d us during the Rest of the Jorney till we arriv'd in Scotland. As Three make a better Travelling Party than 2, our Society was Emprov'd by this Junction. For tho' Kilbucho was a Singular Man, he knew the Country which he had often Travell'd; and his absurdities which were Innocent, amus'd us. As well as he knew the Country however, when we came to the River Esk and to the usual place of Passing it, for there was then no Bridge, opposite Gratney Green, altho' he had insisted on our Dissmissing the Guide we had brought from some Distance to Shew us the Road, yet nothing could persuade him (not even his Servant) to Venture in to that Ford, which he profess'd he knew so well. The Tide was not up, but the River was a little Swoln. Congalton and I became impatient of his Obstinate Cowardice, and thinking we Observ'd the Footstep of a Horse on the opposite Side,* we Ventur'd in together and Got Safe thro', while the Gallant Knight of the Shire for the County of Peebles, with his Squire, Stood on the Bank till he Saw us safe through. This Disgusted us not a little—But as I was to part with him at Gratney, and Go round by Annan and Dumfries to visit my Friends, I had only half an Hour more of his Company, which I pass'd in Deriding his Cowardice. Congalton

* What we thought a Horsefootstep turn'd out a piece of Sea Ware which the Tide had left.

anxious to Get soon to Edin.^r accompanied him by the Moffat Road. But strange to tell of a Scotch Laird, when they came to the Crook inn, within a Few Miles of Kilbucho, which lies about half a mile off the Road as it approaches Broughton, he wishd Congalton a Good Evening, without having the Hospitality to ask him to Lodge a Night with him, or even to Breakfast as he past next Morning. I was happy to find afterwards that all the Tweedale Lairds were not like this Savage.

I pass'd only two Days at Dumfries, and Tinwald, at which last place, my Old Grandfather, who was then 72, was Rejoic'd to see me and not a little proud to find that his arguments had prevaild, and had Sufficient Force, to prevent my Deviating into any other Profession than the Clerical. When I Returnd to my Fathers House I found all the Family in Good Health, except my Brother William, who was then in his 16th Year, and had all the Appearance of Going into a Decline. My Favourite Sister Catherine had fallen a Prey to the Same Disease in Feb^{ry}—I had Describ'd to Gregory when at Leyden the State of her Health, and the Qualities of Mind and Temper that had attach'd me to her So Strongly. He said that I would never see her again, For those exquisite Qualities were Generally attach'd to such a Frail Texture of Body, as promis'd but Short Duration. William was as remarkable in one Sex as she was in the other, an Excellent Capacity for Languages and Science, a Kind and Generous Temper, a Magnanimous Soul, and that Superior Leading Mind, that made him always be lookt up to by his Companions, with a Beautifull Countenance, and a Seemingly Well-form'd Body, [which however] were not proof against the Slow but Certain Progress of that Insidious Disease. He Liv'd to Novr 1747, and then to my infinite Regret, Gave way to Fate.

I had only one Sermon to Deliver before the Presbytery of Haddington to become a Preacher, which was over in June. My First Appearances were attended to with much expectation; and I had the Satisfaction to find that the First Sermon I ever preach'd, but on Trials, which was on a Fast Day before the Sacrament at Tranent, had met with universal approbation. The Genteel People of Prestonpans parish were all there; and one Young Lady to whom I had been Long attach'd, not having been able to Conceal her Admiration of my Oratory, I Inwardly Applauded my own Resolution, of adhering to the Promise I had made my Family to persevere in the Clerical Profession.

I Revisited Dumfries and Tinwald again, to Preach two Sundays for my Grandfather who Gave me his Warmest Approbation. One Mr Wm Stewart an old Clergyman, who heard me on a Weekday at Dumfries Gave me more Self-Confidence, for he was a Good Judge without Partiality. I Return'd home, and continued Composing a Sermon now and then which I first preach'd for my Father and then in the Neighbourhood.

Our Society was still pretty Good, for tho' Hew Horn was no more and Mr Keith had left us, and Cheap's Eldest Son Alex^r had been kill'd at the Battle of Fontenoy, Mr Wm Grant then Ld Advocate had bought Preston-grange, and Resided much there. Ld Drumore too was still in the Parish and with both of them I was in Good Habits. Hew Bannatine had been ordain'd Minister of Ormiston, who was a first rate Man, for sound understanding and Classical Learning, Robertson was at Gladsmuir, and in Jany 1747, John Home was Settled at Athelstaneford:[1] So that I had Neighbours and Companions of the first Rank in point of Mind and Erudition.

In Harvest of this Year I was presented by John Hay Esqr of Spot to the Church of Cockburnspath. As my Father and Grandfather were always against resisting Providence, I was Oblig'd to Accept of it. It was an obscure Distant Place, without Amenity, Comfort or Society, where If I had been Settled, I would have more probably fallen into Idleness and Dissipation, than a Course of Study.[2] For preferment is so Difficult to be Obtain'd in our Church, and so triffling when you have obtain'd it, that it requires Great Energy of Mind, Not to fall asleep when you are Fix'd in a Country charge.

[1747]

From this I was Relievd by Great good Luck. There was a Mr Andrew Gray, afterwards Minister of Abernethy, who was a very Great Friend of my Fathers. He had been preaching one Sunday in the Beginning of 1747 for Fred. Carmichael Minister of Inveresk, and staid with him all night. From him he had drawn the Secret, that President Forbes, who liv'd in his Parish, had Secur'd for him a Church that was recently vacant in Edin^r. Gray who was very friendly and Ardent, and knew my Fathers connexions, Urg'd him without Loss of time, to apply for Inveresk. By this time I had preach'd thrice at Cockburnspath, and was very accept-able to the People. My Father was unwilling to take any Step about a church, that would not even be vacant for a Year to come. But Gray was very urgent, and back'd all his other Arguments with my Father with the Idea, that his not Doing his utmost, would be peevishly rejecting the Gift of Providence when within his Reach. My Father at last Mounted his Horse, for that he would have done, had the Distance been but $\frac{1}{4}$ of a Mile only, and away he went and found Ld Drumore on the point of Going to Edin^r for the Week. My Father open'd his Budget—which he receivd Most Cordially, and told him there was Great probability of Success, for that he was well enough to write both to the Duke of Buccleuch the Patron and to the Duke of Q.ʸ his Brother in Law—Besides that provost Bell of Dumfries had every thing to say with the Duke of Q. In a few Posts, there were Favourable Answers from Both the Duke's, and a Promise of Inveresk.*

In the preceding Winter I had preach'd 3 times at Cockburnspath, and was so acceptable to the People, that I should have an unanimous Call, which was on the point of being Moderated, when the Promise of Inveresk was obtain'd. My Father wish'd me to Let my Settlement Go on, But I Resisted that as I thought it was Tampering with People, to enter into so close a Relation with them, that was so soon to be Dissolv'd. The Puzzle was how to Get off from the Presbytery of Dunbar, who were Desirous of having me among them. But I soon solv'd the Difficulty, by Saying to Lᵈ Drumore and my Father, That nothing could be so Easy, for as I had accepted of the Presentation by a Letter of acceptance, I had nothing to Do but to withdraw that acceptance. This I accordingly Did in Janʸ or Febʸ 1747—at this period it was that John Home was Settled in Athelstaneford, which he Obtaind by the Interest of Alexʳ Home Esqʳ of Eccles, afterwards Sollʳ Genⁱ, with Sir Francis Kinloch, who was his Uncle. He was still alive as well as his Lady, but his Son David who was the Year before Married to Harriet Cockburn, the Sister of Sir Alexʳ, were living in the House of Gilmerton, which as it had been always Hospitable, was render'd more agreable by the Young People, For the Husband was Shrewd and Sensible, and his Wife Beautifull, Lively and Agreable, and was aspiring at some knowledge and Taste in Belles Lettres. This House for that reason, became a Great Resort of John Home and his Friends of the Clergy.

This Summer 1747 past as usual in visiting Dumfries-shire where I had many Friends and Relations; where in addition to the Rest I became well [acquainted] with Mʳ Wᵐ Cunningham, at that time Minister of Durrisdeer and one of the Most Accomplish'd and Agreable of our Order. When the Dutchess of Queensbery was at Drumlanerick,¹ where she was at least for one summer after he was Minister, she soon Discover'd his Superior

* Lᵈ Drumore was a true Friend of my Father and had in Summer 1746 Recommended me to Lᵈ Stair for one of his Churches that was about to be Vacant, by the Translation of the Minister, and I preach'd a Day at Kirkliston before his Lady with that view. But the Translation Did not take place at that time; Mʳ John Hay of Spot the Son of Lᵈ Alexʳ Hay presented me to Cockburnspath and on that I would have been Settled; But the Crown soon after I Gave it up, commenc'd a Prosecution against Mʳ Hay, and were found to have the Right.

Mʳ John Hay of Spot was a very Good Man, tho' not of Remarkable Talents. He Died unmarried and the Estate went to his Brother William.—My Father had been their Tutor in the years 1714 and 15, and they Retaind the Greatest regard for him.

Merit, and made him her Daily Companion, insomuch that the Servants and Country people, Call'd him her Grace's Walking Staff. My Cousin Wᵐ Wight afterwards Proffʳ at Glasgow, was a Great Favourite of this Gentleman, and us'd to live much with him in Summer, During the vacation of the College of Edinʳ, and was very much Improv'd by his Instructive Conversation.

My Sister Margᵗ who had been brought up by her aunt Bell who had no children, was now past 15 and already Disclos'd all that Beauty of Person, Sweetness of Temper and Disposition, and that Superiority of Talents, which made her afterwards be so much admir'd and Gave her a Sway in the politicks of the Town which was Surprising in so Young a Female. Her Uncle Geo. Bell was the Political Leader, who was Govern'd by his Wife, who was sway'd by her Niece and Frank Paton Surveyor of the Customs, who was a very able Man, and who with my Sister, were the Secret Springs of all the Provosts Conduct. Dʳ Thoˢ Dickson who was his Nephew, by his Sollicitation, after trying London for [9] Years, was pre-vaild on by his Uncle Provost Bell to come down to Dumfries [in] 1755 to try his Fortune as a Practitioner of Physick, but Dʳ Eben. Gilchrist was too well Establish'd, and the Field too Narrow, for him to do any thing; so at the End of a Year he Returnd to London again where he Did better. During that Year however, he Did what was not very agreable to me, he Gain'd my Sisters affection, and a promise of Marriage, tho' in point of Mind, there was a very Great Inequality. But he had been the only young Man in the Town, whose Conversation was enlighten'd enough for her Superior Understanding; and she had been pester'd by the Courtship of Several Vulgar and Illiterate Blockheads, to be clear of whom she engag'd herself, Tho' that could not be fulfil'd for four years or more, when their uncle the Provost was Dead, and Dickson in better Circumstances.

In the end of this Year my Brother Wᵐ Died at the Age of 17, who in spite of his long Bad Health, was likely to have acquird as much Learning and Science, as with his Good Sense would have made him a Distinguish'd Member of Society. He was much regretted by all his Companions, who Lov'd him to excess. His own chief regret was that he was not to Live to see me Minister of Inveresk, the Prospect of which Settlement as so near my Father had Given him much Satisfaction.*

* I had for 3 weeks this Summer been at the Goat Whey with Mʳ Cheap's Family at a place call'd Ducheray at the Head of the Forth, where I met Capᵗ David Cheap above mentioned. There was also the Magnet which Drew me after her with unseen tho' Irresistable Power; the Star that sway'd and Guided all my actions. And there I hop'd that by acquiring the Esteem of the uncle, I had the better chance of obtaining my Object. In the first I Succeeded, but in the Last I finally Faild, tho' I Did not Desist from the pursuit for Several Years after.

When Mr Fred. Carmichael was Translated to Edin^r and the time Drew near when I was to be presented to Inveresk, There arose much murmuring in the Parish against me as too Young, and too full of Levity and too much addicted to the Company of my Superiors to be fit for so Important a Charge; together with many Doubts about my Having the Grace of God, (an Occult Quality, which the People cannot Define, But surely is in full opposition to the Defects they saw in me).[1] A Part of my Early History, was on this Occasion, of more Effect than can be conceiv'd. There was one Ann Hall a Sempstress who had liv'd close by the Manse of Prestonpans, when I was a Boy. She was by this time Married at Dalkeith, and a Seceder of the Strictest Sect,[2] and a Great Leader among her Own People. As many People from Inveresk Parish frequented her Shop at Dalkeith on Market Days, the Conversation Naturally fell on the Subject of who was to be their Minister.—By this time I had been presented, But they said it would be up hill work, for an opposition was Rising against so Young a Man, to whom they had many Faults, and that they expected to be able to prevent the Settlement. Your Opposition, will be altogether in vain says Mrs Ann, For I know that it is fore-ordain'd that he shall be your Minister. He foretold it himself when he was but Six Years of Age, and you know that *out of the Mouths of Babes and Sucklings &c.*[3] The Case was that soon after I had read the Bible to the old wives in the Churchyard, as I mention'd (pp. 4–5), I was Diverting my self on Mrs Ann's Stairhead[4] as was often the case; she came to her Door, and Stroaking my Head and Caressing me, she call'd me a fine Boy, and hop'd to Live to see me my Fathers Successor. No, No, says I (I suppose alarmd at the thoughts of my Father Dying so soon), I'll never be Minister of that Church, But yonders my Church, pointing to the Steeple of Inveresk, which was Distinctly seen from the Stairhead. She held up her Hands with Wonder, and Stor'd it up in her Heart. And telling this Simple Story 20 times every Market Day to Musselburgh People for several Months, it made such an Impression, That the Opposition Died away. The Reign of Enthusiasm[5] was so Recent, that such accidents still made an Impression on the Populace.

[1748]

After all the Forms were Gone Through, and about a Year had Elaps'd after the Translation of Mr Frederick Carmichael to Edin^r I was ordaind Minister of Inveresk on the 2^d of Augt O.S. 1748, by Mr Robt Paton Minister of Laswade, as Honest and Gentlemany a Person, as any of his cloth, with the almost universal Good Will of the Parish. The only person of Consideration who was not present at the Ordination was Sir James Dalrymple of Newhailles, who had taken umbrage at his being Refus'd the Presentation, when he had applied for it to Gersham Carmichael the Brother of Frederick. He and his Family however attended the Church on the 1st Sunday after the Ordination, when he came Round and Welcom'd me to the Parish, and Invited me to Dine with him next Day; which I Did and continued ever after in perfect Friendship with him till his Death in 1751.

Sir James Dalrymple was the Son of Sir David, who had been Kings Advocate from 1709, to 1720, and was the Youngest, and as was said the Ablest of all the Sons of the First Lord Stair. He had loaded himself with Debt in the South Sea,[1] but his Son Sir James was Auditor of the Exchequer, which enabled him to keep up the Rank of his Family. He was Hospitable and Gentlemany and very Charitable, but Died in 1751. He Died of a Lingering Disorder, an anasarga,[2] and wish'd me to be often with him when he was ill, and tho' he never wish'd me to pray with him, when we were left alone, always Gave the Conversation a Serious Turn and talk'd like a Man who knew he was Dying. His Lady, Lady Christian Hamilton a Sister of the Celebrated Ld Binning, who Died before him, had warnd me against Speaking to him about Death, for Jamy she said was Timid; so I allowd him always to Lead the Conversation. One Day we were talking of the Deistical Controversy and of the Progress of Deism, when he told me that he knew Collins, the author of one of the Shrewdest Books against Reveal'd Religion. He said he was one of the Best Men he ever had known, and Practis'd every Christian Virtue without Believing in the Gospels, and added, that tho' he had swum ashore on a plank, for he was sure he must be in Heaven, yet it was not for other People to throw themselves into the Sea at a venture. This prov'd him to be a sincere tho' Liberal Minded Christian. I was sorry for his Death, for he was respected in the Parish and had treated me with much Kindness.

There was a Mr James Graham, advocate, Living here at this time, a Man of Distinguish'd Parts and Great Business. He was raisd to the Bench in 1749, and Died in 1751—He had one Daughter, Mrs Baron Mure. He was an Open Friendly Man, and Gave me every Sort of countenance both as his Minister and Friend, and was a Man of Publick Spirit. He was Liable in a very Great Degree to a Nervous Disorder which opprest him with Low Spirits. He knew when he was Going to fall ill, and as it sometimes confin'd him for 3 Months, he Sent Back his Fees to the Agents, who all of them waited till he recover'd, and applied to him again. He was Dugalstone's Brother, and a very powerful Barister.

Lord Elchies a Senior Judge Liv'd at Carberry in the Parish—and was in all respects a most regular and exemplary Parishioner. His Lady was Dead, who was a Sister of Sir Robert Dicksons; and his Family Consisted of three Sons and three or four Daughters unmarried; for some of the Elder Daughters were married. He came every Sunday with all his Family to Church and Remaind to the afternoon Service. As he liv'd in the House of Carberry, he had the Isle in the Church which belong'd to that Estate, where there was a very Good Room where he Retir'd to a Cold Colation, and took Sir R! Dickson and me always with him, when I Did not preach in the afternoon. He was an Eminent Judge, and had Great Knowledge of the Law. But tho' he was held to be a Severe Character I found him a most agreable Good-temper'd Man in Society. He attended as an Elder at the time the Sac[rament] of the Lords Supper was administred, and follow'd one Practice in which he was Singular—It is the Custom for Elders to Serve Tables in Sets, and by Turns that all may Serve, and None be fatigued. When it was his turn to Retire to his Seat, he Enter'd it as it was close by the Communion Table, but never sat Down till the Elements were Remov'd, which could not be Less than an Hour and an Half. I mention'd this Singularity to him one day wishing to have it explain'd, when he said, that he thought it Irreverent for any one who minister'd at the Table to Sit Down, while the Sacred Symbols were present. He remov'd to the House of Inch nearer Edin!, when an owner came to live at Carberry in the year 1752 and Died of a Fever in 1754, Being one of 9 Judges who Died in the Course of 2 Years or a little more. His Eldest Son was Mr Baron Grant, His 2^d Robert Cap! of a Fifty Gun Ship Died Young—Andrew the 3^d Surviv'd his Brothers and Died as the Baron did in Granada.

Sir Robert Dickson of Carberry Bar! was Great Grandson of Dr David Dickson a Celebrated Proff! of Divinity in Edin! who was one of the Committee who attended the Scotch Army in England in Char! the 1^s^ts time, and Got his Share of the Sum that was paid for Delivering the King to the English Army. His having acquird an Estate in those Days Does not imply that he had acquird much Money, for Land was very cheap in those Days. There was annex'd to the Estate the Lordship of Inveresk, now in the Duke of Buccleuch, with the Patronage of the Parish.

This Sir Robert being a weak vain Man had Got thro' his whole Fortune. [The Estate] was Sold, and he now liv'd in a House in Inveresk opposite to Mr Colts call'd Rosebank, Built near 100 Years before by Sir Tho! Young Knight. (John Home's Mother told me she had liv'd a Summer in that house about 1707, or 8.) Sir R! Dicksons Lady was a Daughter of Douglas of Dornoch, a worthy and Patient Woman, who thought it her Duty not only to Bear, but Palliate the Weaknesses and Faults of her Husband. They had one Son Robert who was in the same

Classes at the College with me, and was very promising. He went Young to the E. Indies to try to Mend their Broken Fortunes, and Died in a few Years. There were three or four Daughters. Sir Robert had obtain'd an office in the Customs or Excise of about £180, on which by the Good Management of his Wife and Daughters he in those Days Liv'd very Decently; and was Respected by the Common People, as he had been once at the Head of the Parish. He Lov'd twopenny[1] and Low company; which contributed to his popularity, together with his being Mild and Silent even in his Cups.

Colin Campbell Esq.ʳ who had been Collector at Prestonpans and was promoted to the Board of Customs in 1738, Liv'd now at Pinkie House, and had several Sons and Daughters, my Early Companions. There liv'd at that time in the Corner of Pinky House by himself Arch.ᵈ Robertson Commonly Call'd the Gospel, Uncle to the Celebrated Dʳ Robertson: a very Singular Character who made Great part of our Amusement at Pinky House as he came thro' a passage from his own apartment, every night to Supper, and Din'd there likewise as often as he pleas'd, for which he paid them a Cart of Coals in the Week, as he took Charge of Pinky Coal, which his Brother in Law Wᵐ Adam architect and he had a Lease of. He was a Rigid Presbyterian and a severe old Batchelor, whose Humours Diverted us much. He was at first very fond of me, because he said I had Common Sense, but he Doubted[2] I had but little of the Grace of God in me —and when Dʳ Geo. Kay one of his Great Friends pos'd him on that notion, he could not explain what he meant, But answer'd that I was too Good Company, to have any Deep Tincture of Religion. Kay then ask'd if he thought he had any Grace, as he had seen him much amus'd and pleas'd when he sang, which was more than I could Do. He Replied that his Singing tho' so excellent, Did not much raise him in his Opinion.

There was likewise Living at Inveresk at this time John Murray Esq.ʳ Clerk of Session, of the Ochtertyre Family, who having been a Rake and Spendthrift, had married Lucky Thom a Celebrated Tavern keeper to clear £4000 of Debt that he had Contracted to her. She was Dead, but there was a fine Girl of a Daughter, who kept house for her Father. There was very Good Company, especially of the Jacobite Family, came about the House where I was very often.

There was likewise Mʳ Oliver Colt who resided in the Family House in Inveresk, who in two or 3 years, afterwards, by the Death of an Uncle and Brother had Come to a large Fortune. He was Descended of those Clergymen of the Parish, the first of whom was ordain in 1609, whose Father I have heard was a professor at St Andrews.

Oliver was a Man of Mean Appearance and Habits, and had pass'd

much of his time with the Magistrates and Burghers of Muss[h], and having
Humour, was a Great Master of their Vulgar Wit. When he grew Rich, he
was Deserted by his Old Friends, and had not Manners to Draw better
Company about him. Insomuch that Having been confin'd for a Good
While to his House by illness, tho' not keeping his Room, when an Old
Lady a M[rs] Carse went in to ask for him, he complaind bitterly that it was
the 43[d] Day that he had been confin'd and no Neighbour had ever come
near him. He married afterwards a Lady of Quality and had Enough of
Company. His Son Robert who Died in 1798, was one of the best and
worthiest Men that ever the Parish Bred in my Time, and I was much
afflicted with his Early Death.

The Magistrates and Town Council, were at this time less respectable
than they had been, for the Whigs in 1745, had turn'd out the Jacobites
who were more Gentleman like than their Successors, and were overlook'd by Government as Muss[h] was only a Burgh of Regality,[1] Depend-
ant on the Duke of Buccleuch. The New Magistrates, were of very Low
Manners and Habits—But Good Whigs and Presbyterians. All of the
Burghers except two of the Old Magistrates Smart and Vernon, still
preserv'd the old Custom at their Family Feasts, of making the Company
pay for their Drink. There were few or no Shops in the Town and but one
in each of the Streets of Muss[h] and Fisherow, where even a Lib. of Sugar
could be Bought, and that always 1[d] per Lib. Dearer than at Edin[r] so that
they had very little Sale at a time when a woman would have Run to
Edin[r] with her Basket, and brought ½ C. weight for a Groat, which Did
not rise to above 6[d] till after the Year 1760.

There were no Lodging Houses at this time in the Town; and as it was a
Dragoons Q[rs] where Generally two Troops Lay, the Officers were oblig'd
to accept of their Billets in Burghers Houses. The only Lodging I remem-
ber was in a Bye S[t] between Muss[h] and Newbigging, where the Late Gen[l]
Geo. Ward and his Chum Lodg'd for a Year, and where a Corporal and his
Wife would not think themselves well accomodated Now.*

I have not yet Mention'd the two most able Inhabitants here at this
time, who were Alex[r] Wood, Surgeon, and Commissioner Cardonnell.
Sandy Wood was very Young, not above 21 or 22, But there being an
opening here, by means of the Illness of the Senior Practitioner, Wood
was Invited out, by a few of the Principal People, and Got Immediatly
into Some Business. His Father an Opulent Farmer in the Neighbourhood of Edin[r] had bound him an Apprentice to his Brother a Surgeon
well Employ'd by people of Inferior Rank, and Surgeon to the Poorhouse,

* As in those Days the Dragoons Generally Staid two Years in Scotland and Did
not always change Quarters at the end of a Year, I became Intimate with Ward then
a Lieut., a Sensible Man and a Good Scholar, and pleasant Company tho' he Stutter'd.

then recently Erected. Sandy Wood was a Handsome Stout Fellow, with fine Black Eyes and altogether of an agreable and Engaging Appearance. He was perfectly Illiterate in every thing that Did not belong to his own Profession; In which even he was by no means a Great Student.

Some Scrapes he Got into with Women Drove him from this place in two or three Years for his Good. One Gentlewoman he Got with child and Did not Marry. When he had Got over this Difficulty another fell with Child to him, whom he Married. She Died of her Child, and Sanders was soon after Call'd to a Birth[1] in Edin.r on the Death of his Uncle.

Sanders Supplied his Want of Learning, with Good Sense, and a Mind as Decisive as his Eye was Quick. He knew the Symptoms of Diseases with a Glance; and having no Superfluous Talk about Politicks or News, for Books very few of the Profession knew any thing about, he wasted no time in Idle Talk like many of his Brethren, but pass'd on thr[o'] Steep and Narrow Lanes and upright Stairs of Six or Seven Stories High, by which means he Got soon into Good Business. And at Last his Hands being as Good as his Eyes, on the Death of Geo. Lauder, he became the Greatest and most Successfull Operator for the Stone, and all other Difficult Cases. His Manners were careless and unpolish'd, and his Roughness often offended—But it was soon Discover'd that in spite of his usual Demeanor, he was remarkably tender-hearted, and never Slighted any Case where there was the Least Danger. I found him always a very honest friendly and Kind Physician. He is Doing Business yet in his 74th Year, and tho' his Faculties are Impaird and his Operations long over, he Gives Satisfaction to his Patients. He has always been convivial, Belongs to many Clubs and Sings a Good Song.

The other person was Mansfelt Cardonnell Esq.r Commissioner of the Customs. His Father Adam De Cardonnell[2] (for they were French Protestants by Descent) had been Secretary to the Duke of Schomberg who was kill'd at the Battle of the Boyne at the age of 80. He had been affronted the Day before by King W.m not having Entrusted him as usual with his Plan of the Battle, as Adam Cardonnell told his Sons. Another Brother James was Secretary to the Duke of Marlborough, and had made a Large Fortune. His Daughter and Heiress, was Lady Talbot (Family now L.d Dinevor). My Friends Mother was a Natural Daughter of the Duke of Monmouth, and as he was by some other Line related to Waller the Poet, he us'd to Boast of his being Descended from the Usurper as well as the Royal Line.[3] He was not a Man of much Depth or Genius; But he had a Right Sound Understanding and was a Man of Great Honour and Integrity and the most agreable Companion that ever was. He excell'd in Story telling like his Great Grand Father Charles the 2.d—But he Seldom or ever repeated them and indeed had such a Collection, as serv'd to

Season every Conversation. He was very Fond of my Companions, particularly of John Home, who was very often with me. On a very limited Income he liv'd very Hospitably; he had many children but only one Son and a Daughter Remain'd. The Son is now Adam De Cardonnell Lawson of Chirton, close by Shields, a fine Estate that was left him, by a M⁣r Hilton Lawson a Cousin of his Mothers whose Name was Hilton of the Hilton Castle Family near Sunderland.

There was another Gentleman, who I must mention who then Liv'd at Loretto,[1] a M⁣r Hew Forbes a Principal Clerk of Session. He was a Nephew of the Celebrated President Duncan Forbes, and had at the Request of his uncle purchas'd Loretto from John Steel, a minion of the Presidents, who had been a Singer in the concert, but had lost his voice and was patroniz'd by his Lordship and had for some years kept a Celebrated Tavern in that House. Hew Forbes was the 2⁣d of three Brothers whom I have Seen together, and to my Taste had more Wit and was more agreable than either of them. Arthur the Eldest, Laird of Pittencrieff and a Coll⁣l [in] the Dutch [Service] was a Man of Infinite Humour, which Consisted much in his Instantaneous and Lively Invention of Fictions and Tales, to Illustrate or Ridicule the Conversation that was Going on. And as his Tales were Inoffensive tho' totally void of truth, they afforded Great Amusement to Every Company. The Third Brother John, was the General who Retriev'd our affairs in N. America after Braddocks Defeat. He was an accomplish['d] agreable Man. But there appear'd to me to be more Effort and less Naiveté in his Conversation, than in that of Hew, whose Humour was Genuine and Natural.

With so many resident Families of Distinction, my Situation was Envied as superior to most Clergymen, for Good Company and agreable Society. And so it was at that period, preferable to what it has often been since, when the Number of Genteel Families were Doubled, or Tripled as they have long been. But tho' I liv'd very well with the upper Families, and could occasionally Consort with the Burghers, some of whom tho' unpolishd were sensible people, yet my Chief Society was with John Home, and Robertson and Bannatine, and Geo. Logan, who were Clergymen about my own age and very accomplish'd.

In the Month of Oc⁣r this Year I had a very agreable Jaunt to Dumfriesshire, to attend the Marriage of my Cousin Jean Wight, with John Hamilton the Minister of Bolton. She was very Handsome, Sprightly and agreable, about 20. He tho' a Sensible Knowing Man was . . . [*MS illegible*]. John Home was his best Man, I was the Lady's attendant of the same occupation, according to the Fashion of the times. We set out together on horseback, but so Contriv'd it, that we had very little of the Bridegroom; For Being in a Greater haste to get to his Journey's End than we were, he was always at the Baiting place an hour before us, where after our Meal, we linger'd as long after he had Departed.

Our Grand Father Robison wish'd to Sollemnize this first Marriage of any of his Grandchildren at his own House at Tinwald; which tho' an ordinary manse had 30 People to Sleep in it for two or three nights. John Home and I had been one Day in Dumfries with the Bridegroom, where we met with Geo. Bannatyne, our Friend Hews Brother at that time Minister of Craigie. As he was an old Schoolfellow of Hamilton's we Easily induc'd him to ask him to the Marriage; and George having a Great Deal of Falstaffian Humour, help'd much to Enliven the Company. Home and he and I with Willy Wight, the Bride's Brother then a fine Lad of 18, had to Ride 4 miles into Dumfries to our Lodgings at Provost Bell's another Uncle of mine, after Supper; Where Bannatyne's vein of Humour kept us in perpetual Laughter.*

John Home too was an admirable Companion, and most acceptable to all Strangers, who were not offended with the Levities of a Young Clergyman, for he was very Handsome and had a fine person, about 5 F. 10½ Inches, and an agreable catching address. He had not much Wit and still less Humour, but he had so much Sprightlyness and Vivacity, and such an expression of Benevolence in his Manner, and such an unceasing Flattery of those he lik'd (and he never kept company with any Body else), the kind Commendations of a Lover, not the adulation of a Sycophant, That he was truly Irresistable, and his Entry to a Company was Rec'd, like letting in the Sun into a Dark Room.

After passing 8 Days at Dumfries with such a variety of amusement as would fill half a Vol. of a Novel we return'd with our Young Couple home to E. Lothian, and pass'd two or three Days with them at their Residence.

There was an assistant Preacher here when I was ordain'd whose

---

* I shall take this Opportunity of Correcting a Mistake into which the English Authors [fall], in which they are Supported by many of the Scotch Writers, particularly by those of the Mirror,¹ which is that the People of Scotland have no Humour. That this is a Gross Mistake, could be prov'd by Innumerable Songs, and Ballads, and Stories, that are prevalent in the South of Scotland, and by every Person old enough to Remember the times when the Scottish Dialect was spoken in purity in the Low Country; and who have been at all conversant with the Common People. Since we began to affect Speaking a Forreign Language, which the English Dialect is to us, Humour it must be Confest is less apparent in Conversation.

The Ground of this pretension in the English to the Monopoly of Humour, is their Confounding two Characters together, that are quite Different, the Humourist and the Man of Humour. The Humourist prevails more [in] England than in any Country, because Liberty has long been universal there, and Wealth very General, which I hold to be the Father and Mother of the Humourist. This mistake has been confirmd by the Abject Humour of the Scotch, who till of late Years, allow'd John Bull out of Flattery, to profess Every Quality to which he pretended.

Name was Geo. Anderson the Son of a Clergyman in Fife, and by his Mother, Grandson of a Proff.r Campbell of Edin.r who made [a] Figure in the Divinity Chair, towards the End of the 17th Century. His Aunt was the Mother of Dr John Gregory of Edin.r—But he had not partaken of the Smallest Spark of Genius from Either of the Families. He was Good Natur'd and Laborious in the Parish however, and likely to fall into the Snare of such kind of People, by partaking of their Morning Hospitality, viz. a Dram, very usual in those Days. He was Reckon'd an excellent Preacher by the Common People, because he got a Sermon faithfully by Heart (his Fathers I suppose) and Deliver'd it with a Loudness and Impetuosity, surpassing any Schoolboy, without making a Halt or Stop, from beginning to End. This Galloping Sort of Preaching pleas'd the Lairds as well as the People, for Sir David Kinloch was much taken with him, and he would have been popular in all respects had not his Conversation and Conduct betray'd his Folly. With a very Small Income, he ventur'd a handsome Sempstress Peggy Derquier, the Daughter of a Swiss Ensign who had Got into the British Army. They had children and a very Slender Subsistence, not above [£] 40 per annum; so that I was oblig'd to look about for some better birth for them. At Last in 1757, a place Cast up in S. Carolina, to which he and his Family were with Difficulty Sent out, as a Sum of Money had to be Borrow'd to fit out him and his Wife and 2 Children for the voyage. I was one of his Securities for the Money, and Lost nothing but the Interest of £50 for two Years. His Wife was Mettlesome, and paid up the Money the Year after he Died; which was not above 2 years, for poor George being a Guzzling Fellow could not remain long enough from Charlestown near which his Meetinghouse was, till he Recover'd his Strength after a Severe Fever: the Rum punch Got the better of him and he Relaps'd and Died. His Widow, being still Handsome and Broody, Married well next time, and Got her Children well provided for.

In a Ludicrous Poem which John Home wrote on the March of his Volunteers to the Battle of Falkirk, he gives Anderson his Character under the Nickname of Lungs, For the Wags call'd him Carlyle's Lungs, on account of his Loud Preaching, of which I remember one Line, 'And if you Did not Beat him Lungs was pleas'd'. Like other Gluttons Lungs was a Coward, the first Man at Leith after the Battle, for he was a Vol. in the Company of which Home was Lieut: and shew'd his activity chiefly in providing the Company with Victuals and Drink, in Begging of which he had no Shame.

In winter 1748, I Remain'd much at home in my own Parish, performing my Duties, and becoming acquainted with my Flock. The Cheaps took a House in Edin.r this Winter to Entertain Capt. Cheap, who being a

Man past 50, and a Good Deal worn out, his very Sensible Niece Thought he would never Marry, and therefore brought her Young Female Companions about to amuse him. Among the rest she had much with her the Widow Brown, Amy Clerk that was, whose Husband Major Brown [was killed at the Battle of Falkirk]. She was a handsome Lively Coquette as ever was, Being of a Gay temper and a slight understanding. My sagacious Friend had taken her Measures ill indeed, for as she Told me afterwards, she never Dream't, that her Grave Respectable Uncle would be Catch'd with a Woman of Mrs Brown's Description. But he was so Captivated at the very first Glance, That he very soon propos'd Marriage; and having executed his Design and taken the House of Preston for next Summer, They came and liv'd there for Several Months, where I saw them frequently, and was ask'd to Marry a Niece of hers with a Gentleman at Dunbar, which I accordingly Did. They went to Bath and London, where his Niece Join'd them in Winter 1749.

[1749]

It was in the General Assembly of this Year that some Zealous West Country Clergyman form'd the Plan of applying to Parliament for a General Augmentation of Stipends by Raising the Minimum from 800 Merks to 10 Chalders of Grain or its Value in Money.[1] The Clergy having Shewn Great Loyalty and Zeal During the Rebellion of 1745, which was acknowledg'd by Government, They presum'd that they would obtain Favour on this Occasion. But they had not Consulted the Landed Interest nor even Taken the Leaders among the Whigs along with them, which was the cause of their miscarriage. The Committee appointed by this Assembly to prepare the form of their application brought it in to next Assembly, and by a very Great Majority agreed to send Commissioners to London the Session thereafter to prosecute their Claim; which when it faild rais'd some ill Humour, for they had been very Sanguine. Dr Pat. Cuming who was then the Leader of the Moderate Party, Lent his whole aid to this Scheme, and was one of the Commissioners.—This Gave him still a greater lead among the Clergy. The same thing Happen'd to Ld Drumore the Judge who espous'd their Cause Warmly. On the other hand Principal Wishart and his Brother George Followed Dundas of Arniston, the 1st President of that name, and Lost their Popularity. Of the two B^rs W^m and Geo. Wishart, Sons of Principal Wishart, Willm the Eldest, and Principal of the University of Edin^r, was the most Learned and Ingenious; but he had been for 17 Years a Dissenting Minister, in London, and Return'd with Dissenting Principles. He had said some things rashly, while the Augmentation Scheme was Going on, which Betray'd Contempt of the Clergy; and as he was Rich, and had the expectation of still more, Being the Heir of his two Uncles, Admiral and Gen! Wisharts of Queen Ann's Reign, his Sayings Gave still Greater Offence. George the Younger B.ʳ was Milder and more Temperate, and was a more Acceptable Preacher than his Brother, tho' Inferior to him in Genius. But his Understanding was Sound, and his Benevolence unbounded, so that he had many Friends. When his B.ʳ who Misled him about Ecclesiastical Affairs Died in 1754, he Came back to the Moderate Party, and was much respected among us.

About this Period it was that John Home and I Being left alone with D.ʳ Pat. Cuming after Synod Supper, he prest us to Stay with him a little longer; and During an hour or two's Conversation, Being Desirous to please us, who he thought might be of some Consequence in Church Courts, he threw out all his Lures to Gain us to be his Implicite Followers. But he faild in his purpose, having Gone too far in his animosity to Geo. Wishart, for we Gave up the Principal, That we said to each other when we parted, that we would Support him when he acted Right, but would never be Intimate with him as a Friend.

It was the Custom at this Time, for the Patron's of Parishes, when they had Litigations about Settlements which sometimes lasted for years, To open Publick Houses to Entertain the Members of Assembly, which was a very Gross and Offensive Abuse. The Duke of Douglas had a case of this kind, which lasted for 3 assemblies; on which Occasion it was that his Commissioner White of Stockbridge open'd a Daily Table for a Score of People which vied with the L.ᵈ Commissioner's for Dinners, and Surpass'd it far in Wine.* After the Case was finish'd, Stockbriggs kept up his table while he liv'd for the Honour of the Family, where I have often Din'd after his Grace's Suit was at an end. There was another of the same kind, that lasted Longer, the Case of S.ᵗ Ninians, of which Sir Hew Paterson was Patron.[1]

John Home, and Robertson, and Logan and I enter'd into a Resolution to Dine with None of them, while their Suits were In Dependance. This Resolution we kept Inviolably when we were Members, and we were follow'd by many of our Friends. D.ʳ Pat. Cuming Did not like this Resolution of ours as it shew'd us to be a little untractable. But it added to our Importance and after that No Man, Not even L.ᵈ Drumore, to whom I was so much oblig'd, and who was a keen Party man, ever Sollicited my Vote in any Judicial Case.†

* White who was a Low Man, was Delighted with the respect which the Dinners procur'd him.

† The Lord President Dundas, who led the opposition to the Scheme of Augment-

In Winter 1749 it was that John Home went to London with his Tragedy of Agis, to try to bring it on the Stage, in which he fail'd;[1] which was the Cause of his turning his Thoughts on the Tragedy of Douglas, after his Return. He had a Recommendation to M[r] Littleton, afterwards L[d] Littleton, whom he could not so much as prevail with to Read his Tragedy. And his Brother afterwards a Bishop, would not look at it, as he said he had turn'd his Thoughts to Natural History. Home was enrag'd but not Discourag'd—I had given him a letter to Smollet,[2] with whom he Contracted a Sincere Friendship, and he Consol'd himself for the Neglect he met with by the warm Approbation of the D[r] and of John Blair, and his Friend Barrow an English Physician, who had escap'd with him from the Castle of Down:[3] and who made him acquainted with Collins the Poet, with whom he Grew very Intimate[4]—He extended not his acquaintance much farther at this Time, except to a Governor Melville a Native of Dunbar of whom he was Fond; and pass'd a Good Deal of time with Cap[t] Cheap's Family which was then in London. I had Several Letters from him at that time which Display'd the Character he always Maintain'd, which was a thorough Contempt of his non-approvers, and a Blind Admiration of those who approv'd of his Works and Gave him a Good Reception: Whom he attach'd still more to him by the most Caressing Manners, and the Sincere and Fervent Flattery of a Lover. In all the Periods of his Long Life, his Opinions of Men and Things, were only Prejudices.

[1750]

It was in the Year 1750 I think, that he gave his Manse (for he boarded himself in a House in the Village) to M[r] Hepburn of Keith and his Family, a Gentleman of Pristine Faith, and Romantick Valour, who had been in both the Rebellions in 1715 and 45; and had there been a 3[d] as was projected at this time, would have Join'd it also. Add to this that M[r] Hepburn was an accomplish'd Gentleman, and of a Simple and Winning Elocution, who said nothing in Vain. His Wife and his Daughters by a former Lady, Resembled him, in his Simplicity of Mind, But propagated his Doctrines with more Openess and Ardour, and an Higher Admiration of Implicite

---

ation, was accounted the First Lawyer this Country ever had bred, was a Man of a high and ardent Mind, a most persuasive Speaker, and to me who met him but seldom in Private, one of the Ablest Men I had ever seen. He Declin'd soon after this, and was for two or three years laid aside from Business before his Death.

The Earl of Marchmont appear'd in this Assembly, who had been very Ignorantly Extoll'd by Pope, whose Hemisticks stamp'd Characters in those Days.[5]

Loyalty, and Romantick Heroism. It was the Seductive Conversation of this Family, that Gradually Soften'd and Cool'd M[r] Home's aversion to the Pretender and to Jacobites, for he had been a very Warm Whig in the time of the Rebellion, and prepar'd him for the Life he afterwards Led.*

It was from his having Heard M[rs] Janet Denoon, M[r] Hepburn's Sister in Law, Sing the Old Ballad of Gil Morrice,[1] that he first took the Idea of his Tragedy of Douglas, which 5 Years afterwards, he carried to London, for he was but an Idle Composer, to offer it to the Stage, but with the Same Bad Success as Formerly.[2] The Length of time he took however tended to bring it to perfection. For want of Success, added to his Natural Openess, made him communicate his Compositions to his Friends, whereof there were some of the Soundest Judgment, and of the Most Exquisite Taste. Of the first Sort were D[rs] Blair and Robertson and M[r] Hew Bannatine, and of the 2[d] Pat. Lord Elibank, the Hepburn Family and some Young Ladies with whom he and I had become Intimate, viz. Miss Hepburn of Monkrigg L[d] Milton's Niece; Miss Eliza Fletcher, afterwards M[rs] Wedderburn, his Youngest Daughter; and Miss Campbell of Carrick, at that time their Great Friend. As Home himself wrote a Hand that was hardly Legible, and at that time could ill afford to hyre an ammanuensis, I Copied Douglas several times over for him, which by means of the Corrections of all the Friends I have mention'd, and the Fine and Decisive Criticisms of the Late Sir Gilbert Elliot, had attain'd to the perfection with which it was acted. For at this time Home was tractable, and listen'd to our Remarks.

It was at this Period that Geo. Logan, the Son of a Minister in Edin[r] of note, was presented to the Church of Ormiston, vacant by the Translation of M[r] Hew Bannatine to Dirleton. Logan was a Man of parts and Genius, and of a particular Turn to Mathematical, and Metaphysical Studies. But he was of an Indolent and Dilatory Disposition. When he past Trials

---

* M[r] Home in his History of the Rebellion has prais'd this Gentleman for an Act of Gallant Behaviour, in becoming Gentleman Usher to Prince Charles, by ushering him in to the Abbey with his Sword Drawn.[3] This has been on false Information, for his Son Coll. Riccard Hepburn, Denied to me the Possibility of it, his Father being a Person of Invincible Modesty, and void of all Ostentation. The Coll[l] added That it was his Fathers Fortune to be prais'd for Qualities he had not possess'd—For Learning for Instance, of which he had no Great Tincture but in Mathematicks, while his Prime Quality was omitted, which was the most Equal and Placid Temper with which ever Mortal was Endow'd. For in his whole Life, he was never once out of temper nor Did ever a muscle of his Face alter on any Occurrence. One Instance of a Serving Boy's having raisd much Disturbance one Day in the Kitchen or Hall: His Father rose to see what was the matter, when he found the Boy had wantonly run a Spit thro' the Dog who Lay Sprawling—He said not a Word, but took the Boy by the Shoulder, Led him out of the House Door, and lock'd it after him, and Return'd in Silence to play out his Game of Chess with his Daughter.

before the Presbytery of Dalkeith, he met with unexpected Opposition. When he came to the Last of his Discourses, which was the Popular Sermon,[1] from Heb. 2. 10 was appointed to him. He came home with me, and enquiring if my Popular Sermon when I was Licens'd by the Presbytery of Haddington was not on the Same Text, which was the Case, he prest me to Lend it to him, as it would save him much trouble; to which I with Reluctance consented. He Copied it almost verbatim, and Deliver'd it at our Next Meeting. Being averse to Logan, many of them thought there was Heresy in it, and insisted on an Enquiry, and that a Copy should be Deposited with the Clerk. This enquiry went on for several Meetings, till at last Logan being Impatient, as he had a Young Lady engag'd to Marry him, he took the first Opportunity of appealing to the Synod. After Several Consultations with our Ablest Divines, which were Doctors Wishart and Wallace, with Proff.r Goldie, and Mess.s Dalgliesh of Linlithgow, Nassmith of Dalmeny, and Stedman of Haddington, it was agreed that Logan's Sermon was perfectly Orthodox, and that the Presbytery in their Zeal had run into Heretical Opinions, in so much that those Friends were clear in their Judgement, that the Pannel should be assoilzi'd,[2] and the Presbytery taken to Task. But the Motive I have already Mentiond, induc'd young Logan to be Desirous of making Matters up without Irritating the Presbytery, and therefore it was agreed that he should make a slight apology to the Presbytery and that they should be ordain'd to proceed in the Settlement. Yet in spite of this Sacrifice to Peace the Zealots of the Presbytery still endeavour'd to Delay the Settlement, by Embarrassing him on what is Call'd the Extempore Tryals; But as he was an able and a Learned young Man, he baffled them all in an examination of three hours, 4 or 5 times Longer than usual, when he answer'd all their Questions and Refuted all their Cavils in such a Masterly Manner, as turn'd the Chase in the opinion of Bystanders, and made the Presbytery appear to be Heretical instead of the Person accus'd.

Among the accusers of Logan the most violent were, Plenderleath of Dalkeith, Primrose at Crichton, Smith at Cranston, Watson at Newbottle, and Walker at Temple. The first had been a Minion of D.r Geo. Wisharts, and set out as one of the most Moral Preachers, at the very Top of the Moderate Interest, and Giving offence by his Quotations from Shaftsbury. But Being very weak both in Body and Mind, he thought to compensate for his Dissability, by affecting a Change of Sentiment, and coming over to the popular side, both in his Sermons, and his votes in the Courts. He was truly but a poor Soul, and might have been pardon'd but for his Hypocrisy. Primrose was a Shallow Pedant, who was puff'd up by the Flattery of his Brethren, to think himself an Eminent Scholar because he was pretty well acquainted with the System,[3] and a person of a high

Independant Mind because he was Rich, and could speak Impertinently to his Heritors, and build a Manse of an uncommon Size, and pay for the overplus. He had a fluent Elocution, in the Dialect of Murrayshire, Embellish'd with English of his own Invention. But with all this he had no Common Sense. Smith was a sly Northern, seemingly very temperate, but a Great Counsellor of his Neighbour and Countryman Primrose. Watson was a Dark Inquisitor of some Parts. Walker was a Party Enthusiast, with nothing but Heat without Light. John Bonar at Cockpen, tho' of the High Party, was a man of Sense and an excellent Preacher. He was temperat in his Opposition. Robin Paton tho' Gentlemany was feeble in Church Courts. His Father was just Dead. So that I had no Zealous Supporter but Rab Simson and David Gilchrist at Newton. On those Inferior Characters I need not Dwell.

Logan was assoil[z]ied, and Settled at Ormiston, and Married: Not 3 years after which he Died, of a high Brain Fever. John Home and I felt our Loss. A strong proof of our Opinion of his Ability, was that a very short time before his Death, we had prevaild with him, to make David Hume's Philosophical Works his Particular Study, and to Refute the Dangerous Parts of them. A Task for which we thought him fully Equal. This was 16 or 18 Years before Beattie Thought of it. Dr Wight and I saw [Beattie] frequently at Aberdeen in 1765, or 66, when he open'd his Design to us, from which we Endeavour'd to Dissuade him, Having then a Settled Opinion That such Metaphysical Essays and Treatises, as they were Seldom Read, Certainly never Understood, but by the Few whose Minds were nearly on a Level with the Author, had best be left without the Celebrity of an Answer.

It was on occasion of this Trial of Logan, that we first took umbrage at Robert Dundas Junr of Arniston, then Sollicitor General, who could Easily have Drawn off the Presbytery of Dalkeith from their Illiberal pursuit, and was applied to for that purpose by some Friends, who were Refus'd. His Father the President was by that time Laid aside.

[1751]

It was in the Year 1751, or 52, I think, that a few of us of the Moderate party, were for two or three Days united in a Case that came before the Synod of Lothian in May with Dr Alex^r Webster, the Leader of the High Flying Party.[1] Webster with a few more of his Brethren, whereof Drs Jardine and Wallace were two, had objected to Mr John Johnstone a new Chaplain of the Castle's being admitted to a Seat in the Presbytery of Edin^r. They were Defeated in the Presbytery by a Great Majority, on which they appeal'd to the Synod, when a few of us taking part with the Minority, had an opportunity of seeing Webster very closely.

Our Conclusions on this Acquaintance were, (and we never alter'd them) That tho' he was a Cliver Fellow, an excellent and Ready Speaker, Fertile in Expedients and prompt in Execution, Yet he had by no Means a Leading or Decisive Mind, and Consequently was unfit to be the Head of a Party.—He had no Scruples for with a little temporary Feeling, he seem'd to be entirely without Principle. There was at this Time a Mr John Hepburn, Minister in the Old Grayfriars, who tho' he never appear'd to Take any Share in Ecclesiastical Affairs but by his vote, was in Secret, Webster's Counsellor and Director: So that while he liv'd, he Did well as the Ostensible Head of his Party.* But when he Died, not long after, [Webster] fell into the Hands of Dr Jardine who Manag'd him with Great Dexterity. For he allow'd him to adhere to his Party, but Restrain'd him from Going too Far. As Jardine was Son in Law to Provost Drummond with whom Webster wish'd to be well, Jardine who had much Sagacity, with Great Versatility of Genius, and a Talent for the Management of Men, had not such a Difficult Task as one would have Imagin'd. Webster had publish'd a Satyrical Sermon against Sir Robt Walpole, for which he had been Taken to Task in the Genl Assembly, by the Earl of Isla, by this time Duke of Argyle, and of Great Political Power in Scotland. Webster in Case of accidents wish'd to have a Friendly Mediator between him and the Duke. This is the true Key to all his Political Dissingenuity.

Webster had justly obtain'd much respect among the Clergy, and all Ranks indeed, for having Establish'd the Widows fund, For tho' Dr Wallace who was an Able Mathematician had made the Calculations, Webster had the Merit of carrying the Scheme into Execution. Having Married a Lady of Fashion, who had a Fortune of £4000, (an Estate in those Days) he kept better Company than most of the Clergy. His appearance of Great Strictness in Religion, to which he was bred under his Father who was a very popular Minister of the Tolbooth Church, not acting in Restraint of his Convivial Humour, he was held to be excellent Company even by those of Dissolute Manners. While being a 5 Bottle Man, he could Lay them all under the Table. This had [brought] on him the Nickname of Dr Bonum Magnum in the Time of Faction; But never being indecently the worse of Liquor, and a Love of Claret to any Degree not being Reckon'd in those Days a Sin in Scotland, all his excesses were pardon'd.[1]

When it was Discover'd that Jardine Led him, his Party became Jealous; and it was no wonder, for he us'd to undermine them by his

* Mr Hepburn was Grandfather of the Present Earl of Hyndford, and the Son of a Celebrated Mountaineer[2] in Galloway, the Rev. Mr John Hepburn in Q. Ann's time.

Speeches, and vote with them to Save Appearances. But the truly upright and Honble Men among them, such as Drs Erskine and Hunter &c., could not think of Parting with his Abilities, which both in the Pulpit and the Assembly Gave some Lustre to their Party. He could pass at once from the most unbounded Jollity to the most fervent Devotion; Yet I believe that his Hypocrisy was no more than Habit Grounded merely on Temper, and that his aptness to pray, was as Easy and Natural to him, as to Drink a Convivial Glass. His familiar Saying however, that it was his Lot to Drink with Gentlemen and to Vote with Fools, made too full a Discovery of the Laxity of his Mind. Indeed he liv'd too Long to preserve any Respect: For in his Latter Years his Sole Object seem'd to be where to find Means of Inebriety; which he at last too often Effected, for his Constitution having lost its vigour, he was sent home almost every evening, like other Drunkards who could not boast of Strength. Besides the £4000, he Got with his Lady, he spent £6000 more which was left him by Miss Hunter one of his Pious Disciples, which Legacy Did not raise his Character. In aid of his Fortune, when it was nearly Drain'd, he was appointed Collector of the Widows Fund, when a Mr Stewart Died who was the First, and likewise Obtain'd one of the Deaneries from the Crown. When the New Town of Edin^r came to be plan'd out,[1] he was Employ'd by the Magistrates, which Gratified his two Strongest Desires, his Love of Business and of Conviviality, in both of which he excell'd. The Business was all Done in the Tavern, where there was a Daily Dinner, which Cost the Town in the Course of the Year £500, the whole of an additional Revenue which had been Discover'd a little while before by Buchan, the Towns Chamberlain. He had done many Private and Publick Injuries to me, in Spite of the Support I and my Friends had Given him in his Cause before the Synod in May 1752,* for which I Did not spare him, when I had an

---

* As John Home and I had made Speeches in his Support at the Synod, he thought he could do no less than Invite us to Dinner on the Day after. We went accordingly, and was well enough Receiv'd by him, while his Lady treated us not only with Neglect, but even with Rudeness, while she Carress'd with the utmost Kindness Adams of Falkirk, the very person, who by Dissobeying the Assembly, and Escaping unhurt in 1751, Drew the Thunder of the Church on Gillespie the Following Year.

Another Instance of Webster[s] Hostility to me happen'd some time afterwards. His Colleague Mr Wm Gusthart, who was a very old Man and Liv'd for many Summers in my Parish, and at last the whole Year Round, Engag'd me to Preach for him in the Tolbooth Church one Sunday afternoon. I was averse to this Service, as I knew I would not be acceptable in that Congregation. But being urg'd by the old Man and his Family I agreed, and went to Town and preached to a very thin Audience. I was afterwards certainly inform'd that Webster had sent round many of his Principal Families, warning them that I was to do Duty for his Colleague, and Hoping that they would not Give Countenance to a Person who had attended the Theatre. This I think was in 1759, two years after I had foil'd the high Party in the General Assembly. This

Opportunity, by treating him with that rough raillery, which the Fashion of the times authoris'd, which he bore with Inimitable Patience. And when I rose into some Consideration he rather Courted than Shun'd my Company, with the perfect knowledge of what I thought of him. There was a few of us, who besides the Levity of Youth and the Natural Freedom of our Manners, had an express Design to throw Contempt on that vile Species of Hypocrisy, which magnified an Indecorum into a Crime, and Gave an Air of false Sanctimony and Jesuitism to the Greatest part of the Clergy, and was thereby pernicious to Rational Religion. In this plan we Succeeded: For in the Midst of our Freedom, having preserv'd respect, and attain'd a Leading in the Church, we freed the Clergy from many unreasonable and Hypocritical restraints.

I have Dwelt Longer on Dr Webster than on any other person, because such Characters are extremely pernicious, as they hold up an example to unprincipled Youth, how far they may play fast and Loose with profess'd principles, without being entirely undone; and how far they may proceed in Dissipation of Manners without entirely forfeiting the Publick Good Opinion. But Let the Young Clergy Observe, that very few Indeed, are Capable of Exhibiting for their Protection such usefull Talents or of Displaying such agreable Manners, as Dr Webster Did in Compensation for his Faults.*

It was in this Year 1751 that the Foundation was laid for the Restoration of the Discipline of the Church the next Year, in which Dr Robertson and John Home and I had such an active Hand. Mr Adams at Falkirk had Dissobey'd a Sentence of the Genl Assembly appointing the Presbytery

---

I consider'd as Most Malicious, and with this I frequently Tax'd him in very plain Terms indeed.

* In 1751 the Schoolmaster of Muss^h Died, a Mr Munro, who had only 7 Scholars and one Boarder, he and his Wife had become so unpopular. As the Magistrates of Musselburgh came in place of the Heritors as Patrons of the School, by a Transaction with them about the Mortcloths,[1] the Emoluments of which the Heritors Gave up, on the Towns agreing to pay the Sallary, I took the Opportunity this Gave me as Joint Patron to persuade them, as their School had fallen so Low, to fill it up by a comparative Trial[2] [before] a committee of Presbytery with Sir David Dalrymple and Dr Blair, as assessors, when a Mr Jeffrey from the Merse shew'd so much Superiority, that he was unanimously Elected. He soon rais'd the School to some Eminence, and Got about 25 or 30 Boarders the 2^d Year. When he Died 8 or ten years afterwards, his Daughters by my advice took up the 1st Female Boarding School that ever was there —which has been kept up with Success ever since. And such has been the Encouragement, that two others have been well Supported. On Jeffery's Death, John Murray succeeded him who Did also well. When he Grew old I got him to resign on a Pension, and had John Taylor to Succeed him who has Surpast them all, having Got as Far as 70 Boarders; his Wife being the best Qualified of any person I ever knew in her Station.

of Linlithgow to Settle Mr Watson, Minister of the Parish of Torphichen, to which he had been presented, and for which after Trial he was found fully Qualified. Mr Adams had been appointed Nominatim by the Act of Assembly to preside at this Ordination. This was the 2^d Year this Presbytery had Dissobey'd because there was an Opposition in the Parish. This had happen'd before, and the plea of Conscience had always brought off the Dissobedient. The Assembly had fallen upon a wretched expedient to Settle Presentees who were in this State. They appointed a Committee of their Number, who had no Scruple to Obey the Sentence of the Supreme Court, to Go to the Parish on a Certain Day and Ordain the Presentee. This had been done in Several Instances, with the very worst effect; For the Presbyteries having preserv'd their own Popularity by their Resistance they had no Interest in Reconciling the Minds of the People to their New Pastor; and accordingly for most part Cherish'd their Prejudices, and Left the unfortunate Young Man to fight his way without help in the Best Manner he could. This was a Great abuse and was likely to Destroy the Subordination of Church Courts, which of old had been the Great boast of our Presbyterian Form of Government, and had been very Compleat and perfect in early times. The Departure from that Strictness of Discipline, and the adoption of expedients in Judicial Cases, was of very Recent Growth, and was chiefly owing to the Struggle against Patronages, after their Restoration in the 10th of Q. Ann.[1] So that the Assembly had only to recur to her first Principles and Practice to Restore her Lost Authority. So far was it from being true that Dr Robertson was the Inventor of this System as was afterwards believ'd, and as the strain of Dugald Stuarts Life of Robertson has a tendency to Support.

The Rise of the Attempt to Revive the Antient Discipline in this Assembly was as Follows. Some Friends and Companions, having been well inform'd, That a Great Majority of the Genl Assembly 1751 were certainly to Let Mr Adams of Falkirk, the Dissobedient Brother, Escape with a very Slight Censure, a Select Company of 15, were Calld together in a Tavern, a night or two before the Case was to be Debated in the Assembly, to Consult what was to be Done. There met accordingly at a Tavern, The Right Honble The Lord Provost Drummond, The Honble Wm Master of Ross, Mr Gilbert Elliot Junior of Minto, Mr Andrew Pringle Advocate, Mr Jardine, Mr Blair, Mr Robertson, with John Home, Adam Dickson of Dunse, Geo. Logan of Ormiston, Alex^r Carlyle of Inveresk, and as many more as made 15, Two of whom viz. Logan and Carlyle were not members of Assembly. The Business was talk'd over and having the Advice of those two able Lawyers Mess^s Elliot and Pringle, we were confirm'd in our Opinion that it was necessary to use every Means in our Power, to Restore the authority of the church, otherwise her Government would be Degraded, and every thing Depending on her authority would fall into confusion. And tho' Success was not expected at this Assembly, as we knew that the Judges and many other respectable Elders beside the opposite Party of the Clergy, were resolv'd to Let Mr Adams and the Disobedient Presbytery of Linlithgow escape with a very slight Censure, (an admonition only) Yet we Believ'd that by keeping the object in view, Good Sense would prevail at last and Order be restor'd. We Did not propose Deposition, but Suspension for Six Months, which we thought was meeting the Opposite Party half way. John Home agreed to make the Motion and Robertson to Second him. Neither of them had ever spoken in the Assembly till then, and it was till that period unusual for Young Men to begin a Debate. They pluck'd up Spirits however, and perform'd their Promise, and were very ably Supported by Mess^s Pringle and Elliot, and one or two more of those who had Engag'd with them. When they came to Vote however, 2 of the 18 lost heart, and could not vote in opposition to all the Great Men of the Assembly. Those two were Mess^s John Jardine and Hew Blair, who soon repented of their Cowardice, and Join'd Heartily in the Dissent from a Sentence of the Commission, in March 1752, which brought on the Deposition of Gilespie, and re-establish'd the Authority of the Church. Adam Dickson of Dunse, who had been ill Treated by John Home's Friends in that Presbytery, when he was Presented to That Parish, was the first who voted on our Side. Home made a Spirited Oration, tho' not a Business Speech, which Talent he never attain'd: Robertson follow'd him, and not only Gain'd the attention of the Assembly, but Drew the Praise of the best Judges, particularly of the Ld President Dundas, who I overheard say That Robertson was an admirable Speaker and would soon become a Leader in the Church Courts.

Altho' the associated Members lost the Question by a very Great Majority, yet the Speeches made on that Occasion, had thoroughly Convinc'd many of the Senior Members, who tho' they persisted in their Purpose of Screening Adams, yet Laid to heart what they heard, and were prepar'd to follow a very Different Course with the Next Offender. Adams's own Speech, and those of his Apologists, had unequal Effect, with those on the other Side, in bringing about this Revolution in the Minds of Sensible Men. For the Plea of Conscience, was their only Ground, which the more it was urg'd, appear'd the more absurd, when applied to the Conduct of Subordinate Judicatories, in an Establish'd Church.

This Occasional Union of some of the young clergymen, with the Young Lawyers and other Elders of Rank, had another happy effect, for it made them well acquainted with Each other. Besides Casual Meetings they had two nights set apart During every Ass^y when Mess^s Ross, Elliot and Pringle, with additional Young Elders as they came up, Sup'd together and Confer'd about the Business with their Friends of the Assembly 1752, and whoever they thought were Fit associates. Thus was anticipated what took place on a Larger Scale a few Years afterwards, by the Institution of the Select Society. Till this Period the Clergy of Scotland, from the Revolution Downwards, had in Gen! been little Thought of, and Seldom admitted into Liberal Society. One Cause of which was, That in those Days a Clergyman was thought Prophane who affected the Manners of Gentlemen or was much Seen in their Company. The Sudden Call for young Men to fill up vacancies at the Revolution, oblig'd the Church to take their Intrants from the Lower Ranks, who had but a Mean Education.*

As it was about this Period that the Gen! Assembly became a Theatre for Young Lawyers to Display their Eloquence and Exercise their Talents, I shall mention the Impression which some of them made on me in my Early Days. The Lord President Arniston, the Father of a 2ᵈ President of the same name Robert Dundas, and of Lᵈ Viscount Melville by Different Wives, had been Kings Advocate in the Year 1720, which he had lost in 1725 by his opposition to Sir Rᵗ Walpole and Lord Isla, was one of the ablest Lawyers this Country ever produc'd, and a Man of a high Independant Spirit. His appearance was against him, for he was ill looking, with a large Nose and small Ferret Eyes, Round Shoulders, a Harsh Croaking Voice, and altogether unprepossessing; yet by the time he had utter'd three Sentences, he Rais'd attention, and went on with a torrent of Good Sense and Clear Reasoning, that made one totally forget the First Impression. At this Assembly he did not speak, and soon after fell into a Debility of Mind and Body, which Continu'd to 1753, when he Died.† Hew Dalrymple, Lᵈ Drumore, who was much Inferior to him in Talents, was a very popular Speaker, tho' neither an Orator nor an Acute

---

* It must be observ'd too that when Presbytery was re-establish'd in Scotland at the Revolution after the Reign of Episcopacy for 29 Years more than two 3ᵈˢ of the People of the Country, and most part of the Gentry were Episcopals. The Restoration of Presbytery by King William being chiefly owing to the Duke of Argyle, Marchmont, Stair, and other Leading Nobles who had suffer'd under Charles and James, and who had promoted the Revolution with all their Interest and Power.

† I never happen'd to be in Company with this Lᵈ President but once, which was at a Meeting of Presbytery for Dividing the Church of Newbottle. The Presbytery and the Heritors who attended, were quite puzzled how to proceed in the Business—and Arniston who was an Heritor was late in Coming. But he had no sooner appear'd, than he undid all that we had been trying to do, and putting the Meeting on a right Plan, Extricated and Settled the Business in a short time. To the Superiority of his Mind, he added experience in that Sort of Business. There was a Dinner provided for us in the Marquiss's House, where Sandy MᶜMillan W.S. presided in the absence of the Marquiss, when I was quite Delighted with the Presidents Brilliant Parts and fine Convivial

Reasoner. He was the Lay Leader of the Moderate Party; and Arniston was Inclin'd to favour the other Side, tho' he could not follow them, in their Settled opposition, to the Law of Patronage. Drumore Devoted himself During the Assembly to the Company of the Clergy, and had always two or 3 Elders who Follow'd him to the Tavern, such as Sir James Colquhoun, Colin Campbell Com.ᵣ of Customs &c.* I heard Lord Isla once Speak in the assembly, which was to Correct the Petulance of Alex.ᵣ Webster, which he did with Dignity and Force, but was in the Wrong to Committ himself with a Light Horseman, who had nothing to Lose. I heard L.ᵈ Marchmont Likewise speak on the Motion for an augmentation, which he Did with much Elegance, and a Flowing Elocution, but entirely without Sense or Propriety; Insomuch that he by his speech forfeited the Good Opinion of the Clergy, who had been preposess'd in his Favour, by Pope's Panegyrical Line.† M.ᵣ Gilbert Elliot shew'd himself in the Assembly's Equal to the Station to which he afterwards attain'd as a Statesman, when Sir Gilbert, by his Superior Manner of Speaking. But Andrew Pringle Sollicitor Gen.ˡ and afterwards Lord Aylmer, excell'd all the Laymen of that Period, for Genuine Argument and Eloquence; and when on the Bench, he Deliver'd his Opinion, with more Dignity, Clearness and Precision, than any Judge I ever heard either in Scotland or England. It was a Great Loss to this Country, that he Did not Live to fill the Presidents Chair, and Indeed had not Health to Go thro' the Labour of it, otherwise it was believ'd that he would have Set an Example of Elegance and Dignity in our Law proceedings, that could not Easily have been Forgotten.

In those Respects the Bench has been very unlucky, For however Great Lawyers, or Impartial Judges the Succeeding Presidents may have been in the Qualities I have Mention'd they have all been inferior even to the First President Arniston, who could not be call'd an Elegant Speaker, with all his other Great Qualities. In those Days there were very

---

Spirit. I was Earnestly Invited to Go to him at Arniston, where I should probably have been very often, had not this Happen'd a very short While, not above a Month or so, before he fell into Debility of Mind, and was Shut up.

* Drumore's Speaking was not Distinguish'd for any thing but Ease and Popularity, and he was so Deservedly a Favourite with the Clergy, that taking up the Common Sense of the Business, or Judging from what he heard in Conversation the Day before, when Dining with the Clergy of his own Side, he usually made a Speech in every Cause, which Generally seem'd to Sway the Ass.ˡʸ tho' there was not much arg.ᵗ—He us'd to Nod to Arniston with an Air of triumph (for they were Relations and very Good Friends) as much as to Say, "Take you that Robin".

† 'Polwarth is a slave'.[1] Pope according to his Manner intended this as a Panegyrick on his Patriotism and Independence—But this was the Voice of Party. For Marchmont in Reality was as much a Slave of the Court as any Man of his time.

Few Good Speakers among the clergy, as no young man almost ever ventur'd to Speak, but when at the Bar, till after 1752. The Custom Invariably was for the Moderator to Call for the Opinions of two or three of the old men, at the Green table, who were nearest him, and after them one or two of the Judges, or the Kings Advocate and Sollicitor, who were Generally all of a Side, and were very seldom oppos'd or answer'd but by James Lindsay, and one or two of his Followers. With respect to Lindsay, I have to add that he was a Fine Brisk Gentlemanlike Man who had a Good Manner of Speaking, But being very unlearn'd, could only pursue a single Track. He set out on the Popular Side, in Opposition to Patronage, But many of his Private Friends being on the other Side, and Church Preferment Running Chiefly in that Direction, he came for two or three years over to them: But on Drysdale's Getting the Deanery During the Marquiss of Rockingham's Administration, he took Pet and Return'd to his old Party. The Ground of his Patriotism was thus unveild, and he was no longer of any Consequence, tho' he Thought he could sway the Burgh of Lochmabin, where he was Minister at that time. He was a very Pleasant Companion; But Jealous and Difficult, and too Severe a Rallier.

The Clergyman of this Period who far Outshone the Rest in Eloquence was Principal Tullidelph of St Andrews. He had fallen into Bad Health or Low Spirits before my time, and seldom appeard in the Assembly. But when he did he far excell'd every other Speaker. I am not certain if even Ld Chatham in his Glory had more Dignity of Manner, or More Command of his Audience, than he had. I'm certain he had not so much Argument, nor such a Convincing Force of Reasoning. Tullidelph was Tall and Thin like Pitt, with a Manly and Interesting Aspect; and Rising slowly and Beginning in a very Low Tone, he soon Swell'd into an Irresistable Torrent of Eloquence, and in my Opinion was the Most Powerfull Speaker ever I heard. And yet this Great Man was overcome and Humbled by the Buffoonery of a Man much his Inferior in Everything but Learning. This was John Chalmers Minister of Ely. Tullidelph soon Gaind the Leading of his University and of the Presby. of St Andrews, and Likewise of the Synod of Fife. But Being of a Haughty and Overbearing Disposition, (Like Chatham) he soon Disgusted his Colleagues both in the University and Presby: of which the Younger Brethren made a Cabal against him, in which Chalmers was the Principal Agent. Tho' he was far behind the Principal in Eloquence, he was Superior to him in some things Especially in antient Learning—But his Chief Mode of Attack was by a species of Buffoonery, which totally unhing'd the Principal, who was very Proud and Indignant of Opposition. Chalmers watch'd his Arguments, and by turning them all into Ridicule, and shewing that they prov'd the very reverse of what he Intended, he put Tullidelph in such a Rage as Totally

Disabled him—and made him in a short time absent himself both from Presbytery and Synod. He at last became Hypychondriack, Sate up all night writing a Dull Commentary on the Gospels, and Lay in Bed all Day.

After this Period however when the Young Clergy Distinguishd themselves, and particularly after the Assembly 1753 when Alexr Webster being Moderator He on the very first Question Drop'd the old Mode of Calling upon the Senior Members, The Young Clergy began to feel their own Importance in Debate, and have ever since Continued to Distinguish themselves, and have Swayd the Decision of the Assembly. So that the supreme Ecclesiastical Court has long been a School of Eloquence for the Clergy as well as a Theatre for the Lawyers to Display their Talents.

It was in the Assembly 1752 That the Authority of the Church was Restor'd by the Deposition of Gillespie. Robertson and John Home having been Dissenters with some others from a Sentence of the Commission in March that Year, in the affair of the Settlement of Inverkeithing, Similar to that of Torphichen in 1751, had enter'd a Complaint against the Commission which gave them an Opportunity of appearing and pleading at the Bar of the Assembly, which they Did with Spirit and Eloquence. The Minds of the Leaders of the Assembly having been now totally chang'd, a vigorous measure was adopted by a Great Majority— The Presby. of Dumfermline were brought before the Assembly and peremtorily ordered to admit the Candidate 3 Days after, and report to the Assembly on the Following Friday. They Dissobey'd and Mr Gillespie was Depos'd. I was for the first time a Member, and my Friend and Copresbyter Geo. Logan. It was thought proper that on the 1st Days Debate, the Speaking should be left to the Senior Clergy and the Lay Members. But when at a General Meeting of the Party after Gilespie was Deposd, it was mov'd that it would be proper to propose next Day that the Assembly should proceed to Depose one or two more of the offending Brethren, Mr Alexr Gordon of Kintore, and Geo. Logan and I were pointed out as proper persons to make and second the Motion. I accordingly began, and was seconded by Gordon, in very vigorous Speeches, which Occasion'd a Great Alarm on t'other Side, as if we were Determind to Get Rid of the Whole *Presby*. But this was only *in Terrorem*, for by Concert one of our Senior Brethren with much Commendation of the two Young Men, Calmly propos'd that the Assembly for this time should rest contented with what they had Done, and wait the Effects of the Example that had been Set. After some Debate this was Carri'd. Logan not having Done his part—I ask'd him why he had been Silent. He answer'd that Gordon and I had spoken in such a Superior Manner, that he thought he would appear Inferior, and had not the Courage to Rise. As it was the 1st time I had ever open'd my mouth in the Assembly for I was not a member till that year,

I was encourag'd to Go on by that Reply from my Friend. At the same time I must observe, that many a time, as in this Case, the Better Man is Dazzld and Silenc'd perhaps for Life, by the more forward Temper and Brilliant appearances of his Companions. My admiration of Robertson and Home with whom I was Daily versant at that time, and who communicated their Writings to me, made me Imagine that I was Incapable of writing any thing but Sermons; Insomuch that till the year 1757, I wrote nothing else but some Juvenile Poems.[1] Dr Pat Cuming was at this time at the Head of the Moderate Interest, and had his temper been Equal to his Talents might have kept it Long, for he had both Learning and Sagacity, and very agreable Conversation, with a Constitution able to bear the Conviviality of the times.

[1753]

It was this Year that the 1st Reg^t of Dragoons lay at Musselburgh, with some of the Officers of which I was very Intimate, particularly with Charles Lyon the Surgeon, who was a very sensible, handsome and agreable young Man. He afterwards became an officer, and Rose to the Rank of a Lieut. General. He was at York when Capt Burton and Wind fought a Duel in which the 1st was Run thro' the Lungs and Recover'd. Lyon wrote to me twice a week, as I had a Great Regard for Burton, and had foretold the Duel. He was afterwards well known by the Name of Genl Phillipson. The Celebrated Major Johnstone so much admir'd for his Beauty, and for his Many Duels, was of this Reg^t and one of the best Naturd Men in the Intercourse of Friends, that ever I met with. George the 2^d had put a cross to his Name, on his Behaving very Insolently at one of the Theatres to a Country Gentleman, and afterwards Wounding him in a Duel. In George the 3^{ds} time John Home got the Slur taken off, and he was promoted. He was of the Family of Hilton, which is Descended from that of Westerhall, and Hew Bannatyne had been his Travelling Tutor abroad.

The Parish of Inveresk this Year 1753 Lost a very respectable Member. For the Estate of Carbery being sold to a Mr Fullerton who Came to Live at it, Lord Elchies left the place and went to Inch, where he Died soon after. His place was in some Respects fill'd by his Son Mr John Grant, afterwards Baron Grant, coming to Live at Castle Steads; with whom and his Lady Ld Milton's Eldest Daughter I fell into Habits of Great Intimacy. He was a Worthy Good Man, of Considerable Parts, but of a Weak and Whimsical Mind. He was at this time Chief Commissioner for the Duke of Buccleuch; and much Emprov'd the Family Gallery in the Church, where he attended Regularly.[1] I was frequently ask'd to Dine [at Carbery] while she staid there, and by that means became well acquainted with the Fletchers, whom I had not visited before—For their House was not in my Parish, and I was not forward in pushing myself into acquaintance elsewhere, without some proper Introduction. From this period I became Intimate with that Family, of which Lord Milton himself, and his Youngest Daughter Betty, afterwards Mrs Wedderburn of Gosford, were my much Valued Friends.

For two Summers about this time I went for some Weeks to Dunse Well, which was in high vogue at this Period, when I was often at Polwarth Manse, the Dwelling of M^r and Mrs Home, the last of whom was Aunt to Mary Roddam, the young Lady whom I afterwards Married, and who had liv'd there since the Death of Father and Mother in the Years 1744 and 1745—John Home past half his time in this House, Mr Wm Home a Brother of the Laird of Bassindean being his Cousin, and Mrs Home (Mary Rodham) a Superior Woman.

By frequenting this House, where John Home Resided half his time, I was Introduc'd to the Earl of Marchmont whose Seat was hard by. His 2^d Lady who was Young and Handsome, but a Simple and Quiet Woman[2] —and 3 Daughters he had by his Former Lady, were all under Due Subjection, for his Lordship kept a High Command at home. The Daughters were all Cliver, particularly Lady Marg^t, and stood less in awe than the Countess, who had it not been for her only Child Ld Polwarth, then an Infant, would have Led but an Uncomfortable Life. The Family of Marchmont, which rose to the Peerage at the Revolution, and to the ascendant in the County, thro' the Weakness and Jacobitism of the More Antient Earls of Home from whom they were Descended, to preserve their Superiority Paid Great Court to the County, and particularly to the Clergy, because they were the only Staunch Friends to Government. Marchmont was lively and Eloquent in Conversation, with a Tincture of Classical Learning and some Knowledge of the Constitution, especially of the Forms of the House of Peers; But his Wit appeared to me to be Petulant, and his Understanding Shallow. His Twin Brother Hume Campbell, then Lord Register[3] for Scotland and one of the most Eloquent Lawyers in the House of Commons, seemed to me to be a Man of Sounder Judgment than his Brother. His want of Manhood however had been Disclos'd, by his Receiving an Insult from Wm Pitt the Father, which he had probably been tempted to Inflict on his having Heard what had happen'd to him in Edin^r in his youthfull Days.

In one of the Summers in which I was in that part of the Country, the Ld Register Gave a Ball and Supper in the Townhall of Greenlaw, which I mention, because I had there an opportunity of Conversing, with Lady

Murray, and her Friend Lady Harvey, who was understood to be one of the Most Accomplish'd and Witty Ladies in England. There were in this Neighbourhood several very agreable Clergymen. Chatto was very acute and Sensible, Redpath Judicious and Learned—Dickson an able Ecclesiastick, and a Master in Agriculture.

In one of those Years it was, when Dunse Well was most frequented, that the Marchmont Family for several weeks attended, and came to Dunse, and Breakfasted at a Small Tavern by the Bowling Green—we generally Sate Down 24, or 25 to Breakfast in a very Small Room—Marchmont and his Brother behav'd with Great Courtesy, Seldom Sitting Down, but aiding the Servants. Francis Garden was there, and Increas'd the Mirth of the Company. Most of the Company Remain'd all the Forenoon at the Bowling Green, where we had very Agreable Parties.

In one of these Years it was that Smollet visited Scotland for the 1st time, after having left Glasgow immediatly after his Education was finish'd, and his engaging as a Surgeon's Mate on Board a Man of War, which Gave him an Opportunity of Witnessing the Siege of Carthagena, which he has so minutely Describ'd in his Roderick Random.[1] He came out to Musselburgh, and pass'd a Day and a Night with me, and went to Church and heard me preach. I Introduc'd him to Cardonnell the Commissioner, with whom he sup'd and [they] were much pleas'd with Each other. Smollet has Revers'd this, in his H. Clinker[2] where he makes the Commissioner his Old Acquaintance.*

Smollet was a Man of very agreable Conversation, and of much Genuine Humour, and tho' not a profound Scholar, Possess'd a Philosophical Mind, and was capable of making the Soundest Observations on Human Life, and of Discerning the Excellence, or Seeing the Ridicule of Every Character he met with. Fielding only excell'd him in Giving a Dramatick Story to his Novels, but in my Opinion was Inferior to him in the true Comick Vein. He was one of the many very pleasant men with whom it was my Good Fortune to be Intimatly Acquainted. Mr Cardonnell whom I have mention'd was another who excell'd like Smollet in a Great Variety of pleasant Stories.† David H[u]me and Dr John Jardine,

---

* He went west to Glasgow and that neighbourhood to visit his friends and Returned again to Edinr in Oct. when I had frequent meetings with him—One in particular in a Tavern where there supped with him Comr Cardonell Mr Hepburn of Keith John Home and one or two more. It was upon this occasion that Keith was so much pleased with Cardonell that he said if he went into rebellion again it should be for the Grandson of the Duke of Monmouth. Cardonell and I went with Smollet to Sir David Kinlochs and passed a day there after which John Home and Logan and I conducted him to Dunbar and staid all night.[3]

† Sir Hew Dalrymple of N. Berwick had as much Conversation and wit as any Man of his time having been long a M.P.

were likewise both Admirable, and had the Peculiar Talent of Rallying their Companions on their Good Qualities. Dr Wm Wight and Thos Hepburn were also Remarkable, the one for Brilliancy, Vivacity and Smartness, the other for [the] Shrewdness of [his] Remark, and irresistable Repartees.

The Right Honble Charles Townshend and Pat. Ld Elibank, were likewise admirable, for tho' the first was inferior in Knowledge to the Second, yet he had such flowing Eloquence, so fine a Voice and such Richness of Expression, Joind to Brilliant Wit, and a True Vein of Mimick[r]y, as Made him Shine in every Company. Elibank was more Enlighten'd and more profound, and had a Mind that Embrac'd the Greatest Variety of Topicks, and produc'd the most Original Remarks. He was rather an Humourist than a Man of Humour. But that Bias of his temper, Led him to Defend Paradoxes and uncommon Opinions, with a Copiousness and Ingenuity that was Surprising. He had been a Lieut. Coll! in the Army and was at the Siege of Carthagena, of which he left an Elegant and Xenophon-like acct.[1] (which I'm affraid is Lost). He was a Jacobite, and a Member of the Famous Cocoa Tree Club,[2] and Resign'd his Commission on some Disgust. Soon after the Rebellion 1745 he took up his Residence in Scotland; and his Seat being between Dr Robertson[s] Church and John Home's he became Intimately Acquainted with them, who Cur'd him of his Contempt for the Presbyterian Clergy, made him change or [Mellow] Down many of his Original Opinions and prepar'd him for Becoming a most agreable Member of the Literary Society of Edinr, among whom he liv'd during the Remainder of his Life admiring and admir'd. We used to say of Elibank, that were we to plead for our Lives, he was the Man with whom we would wish to Converse for at least one Whole Day before we Made our Defence.

Dr McCormick who Died Principal of St Andrews, was rather a Merry Andrew, than a Wit—But he left as many Good Sayings behind him, which are Remember'd, as any Man of his time. Andrew Gray, Minister of Abernethey, was a Man of Wit and Humour, which had the Greater Effect, that his person was Diminutive, and his Voice of the Smallest Treble.

Lindsay was a Hussar in Raillery who had no mercy, and whose Object was to Display himself and humble the Man he play'd on. Monteith was more than his Match, for he Lay by, took his opportunity of Giving him such Southboards[3] as Silenc'd him, for the Whole Evening. Happily for Conversation, this Horseplay Raillery, has been left off for more than 30 Years, among the Clergy and other Literati. Drumore of the Class of Lawyers, who Got the Epithet of Monk from Quin at Bath on account of his pleasing Countenance, and Bland Manner, was a first Rate at the Science of Defence in Raillery; he was too Goodnatur'd to attack. He had the Knack not only of pleasing fools with themselves, but of making them tolerable to the Company. There were two Men however, whose Coming into a Convivial Company pleas'd more than anybody I ever knew; the one was D[r] Geo. Kay a Minister of Edin[r] who to a Charming Vivacity when he was in Good Spirits, added the Talent of Ballad Singing, better than any Body ever I knew. The other was John Home who with little Wit and no Humour, by a Sprightly Expression of Benevolence to his Friends, Diffus'd a Joy at his Entry, which was like Opening a Window in a Dark Room to Let in the Sun.

I should not Omitt Lord Cullen here, tho' he was much my Junior, who in his Youth possess'd the Talent of Mimickry beyond all Mankind[1]— For his was not meerly an Exact Imitation of Voice and Manner of Speaking, but a perfect Exhibition of every Mans Manner of thinking, on ever[y] Subject. I shall mention two or three Instances, Lest his wonderfull powers should fall into Oblivion.

When the Hon[ble] James Stuart Wortley liv'd with D[r] Robertson, the D[r] had sometimes, tho' rarely to Remonstrate and admonish the Young Gentleman on some parts of his Conduct. He came into his Room between ten and Eleven in the Morning, when M[r] Stuart was still in bed, with the windows shut, and the Curtains Drawn close, when he took the opportunity in his Mild and Rational Manner (for he could not chide) to Give him a Lecture on the Manner of Life he was Leading. When he was Done, This is rather too much my D[r] Doctor said James, for you told me all this not above an Hour ago. The case was that Cullen had been beforehand with the D[r] and Siezing the Opportunity, Read his Friend such a Lecture, as he thought the D[r] might probably Do that Morning. It was so very like in Thought and in Words, that Stuart took it, for a second visitation from the D[r].

I was witness to another exhibition similar to this. It was one Day in the Gen[l] Assembly 1765 when there happen'd to be a Student of Physick who was siez'd with a Convulsion-fit, which occasion'd much commotion in the House and Drew a Score of other English Students around him. When the Assembly adjournd about a Doz. of us went to Dine in the Poker Club Room at Nicholson's,[2] when D[r] Robertson came and told us that he must Dine with the Commissioner, but would Join us soon. Immediatly after we Din'd, somebody wish'd to hear from Cullen what Robertson would say about the Incident that had taken place—which he Did Immediatly Lest the Principal should come in. He had hardly Finish'd, when he arriv'd. After the Company had Drank his Health Jardine said Slyly, Principal, was it not a strange Accident that Happen'd today in the Assembly? Robertson[s] Answer was exactly in the Strain and almost in the very Words of Cullen—This rais'd a very Loud Laugh in the Company—When the D^r more Ruffled than I ever almost saw him, said with a severe look to Cullen, I perceive somebody has been ploughing with my Heifer before I came in.

On another occasion he was ask'd to exhibit, when he answer'd, that his subjects were so much hackney'd that he could not Go over them with Spirit, but if any of them would mention a New Subject, he would try to please them. One of the Company mention'd the Wild Beast in the Gevaudon,[1] when after Laying his Head on the Table not for more than two or three Minutes, he lifted himself up and said Now I have it, and Immediatly Gave us the Thoughts of the Judges Affleck, Kaims, and Mon[bo]ddo, and Dr Robertson, with a characteristical exactness of Sentiment, as well as Words and Tone and Manner, as astonish'd the Company. This happen'd at Dr Blairs who then Liv'd in James's Square.

This was a very pleasing but a Dangerous Talent for it Led to Dissipation. When he had left off his usual Mode of Exhibition when call'd upon, yet he could not restrain himself from Displaying in his Common Conversation, in which he Intermingled Specimens of his superlative art, as the characters came in his way, which to me was much [more] agreable, than the Profess'd Exhibition. As he was more knowing and accomplish'd than almost any Judge in his time, had all other Qualities been of a Piece, his Company would very long have been Courted. In giving some account of those very Pleasant Characters, which it was my Good Fortune to Know, I have anticipated Several Years, For, Mr Robert Cullen for Instance, Did not begin to be known till after 1760—But I shall now Return to my Narrative.

It was in the General Assembly 1753, as I have before Mention'd, that Dr Webster being Moderator, he put an End to the Antient Mode of Calling up Principals and Professors, and Judges &c. to Give their Opinions, on Cases which came before the Assembly, by Declaring that he would call upon no Person, but would expect that every Member, should freely Deliver his Opinion when he had any to offer. This brought on the Junior Members, and much Animated and Improv'd the Debates. The Old Gentlemen at first were Sulky and held their Tongues. But in two or three Days they found them again, Lest they should lose their ascendant.* At this Assembly it was that an attempt was made, to have Gillespie the Depos'd Minister Restor'd. But as he had not taken the Proper Steps to Conciliate the Church, but on the Contrary had Continued to preach and had set up a Separate Congregation, the Application

---

* I never afterwards saw the practice revived of calling upon Members to speak, except once or twice when Principal Tullidelph attended, whom every body wished to hear, but who would not rise without having that piece of respect paid to him.

by his Friends was refus'd by a Great Majority, and was never Repeated.

Baron Grant having bought Castlesteads, and come to Live in the Parish, I was much with him and his Lady, which Led me to be frequently at Bru[n]stane also, the Seat of Ld Milton,[1] the nephew of the Famous Patriot And. Fletcher of Saltoun, and the Successor to his Estate. He had been Ld Justice Clerk and Political Manager of this Country under Lord Isla and now that his L.^dship had been Duke of Argyle, since 1744, [when] his Brother John Died, their Influence was Compleatly Establish'd. The Duke had Early made Choice of Fletcher for his Coadjutor, and had prov'd his Sagacity, by making so Good a Choice; For Ld Milton was a Man of Great Ability in Business, a Man of Good Sense and of excellent Talents for Managing Men. For tho' his Conversation was on a Limited Scale, because his Knowledge was very much so, Yet being possess'd of Indefeasable Power at that time in Scotland and keeping an excellent Table, his Defects were Overlook'd and he was held to be as agreable as he was able. His Talents had been illustrated by the Incapacity of the Tweedale Ministers who were in Power During the Rebellion, and who had been oblig'd to Resort to Milton for Intelligence and Advice. When the Rebellion was suppress'd, and the Duke of Argyle brought again into Power, he and Fletcher very wisely gaind the Hearts of the Jacobites, which were still very numerous, by adopting the Most Lenient Measures, and taking the Distress'd Families under their Protection, while the Squadrone[2] Party Continued as Violent against them as ever. This made them almost universally Successfull in the Parliamentary Election, which follow'd the Rebellion, and Establish'd their Power till the Death of the Duke which happen'd in 1761.

His [Ld Miltons] youngest Daughter, afterwards Mrs Wedderburn, was one of the first Females in point of Understanding as well as Heart, that ever fell in my way to be Intimately acquainted with. As there was much Weakness and Intrigue in the Mother and some other Branches of the Family, she had a Difficult part to act. But she perform'd it with much address, For while she preserv'd her Fathers Predilection and Confidence, she Remain'd well with the Rest of the Family. The Eldest Brother Andrew liv'd for most part with the Duke of Argyle at London as his Private Secretary; and was M.P. for E. Lothian; and tho' not a Man who produc'd himself in Publick Life, was sufficiently knowing and accomplish'd, to be a very amiable member of Society. After the Death of the Duke of Argyle in 1761, and of his Father in 1767, he Liv'd for Most Part at his Seat at Saltoun in E. Lothian. He was succeeded as M.P. for that County by Sir Geo. Suttie, who had been a Lieut. Coll.^l in the Army, and who with many others left the service in Disgust with the Duke of Cumberland, who tho' he had been always Beat in Flanders, had Dissoblig'd

Sundry Officers of Good Promise. This Sir George however was much overrated—He was held to be a great officer, because he had a way of thinking of his own, and had Learn'd from his Kinsman, Mareshall Stair, to Draw the Plan of a Campaign. He was held to be a Great Patriot because he wore a Course Coat and unpowder'd Hair, while he was Looking for a Post with the utmost anxiety. He was Reckon'd a Man of Much Sense, because he said so himself, and had such an Embarrass'd Stuttering Elocution that one was not sure but it was true. He was understood to be a Great Improver of Land, because he was always Talking of Farming and had Invented a Cheap Method of Fencing his Fields, by combining a Low Stone Wall and a Hedge together, which on Experiment Did not answer. For all those Qualities, he Got Credit for some time. But nobody ever mention'd the Real strength of his Character, which was that of an uncommonly Kind and Indulgent Brother, to a Large Family of Brothers and Sisters, whom he allowd During his absence in a five years war to Dilapidate his Estate, and Leave him less than half his Income. Lord Stair had been Catch'd with the Boldness of his cousin in attempting to make a plan of a Campaign, which had Given the Young Man a false measure of his own Ability.

It was in the Year 1753 that we had Lost two of the most Considerable Parishioners, Sir James Dalrymple of Newhailles, and James Graham, Lord Easdale as I formerly Mention'd.

At this Time David H[u]me was Living in Edinʳ and composing his History of Great Brittain.* He was a Man of Great Knowledge and of a Social and Benevolent Temper, and truly the Best Natur'd Man in the World. He was Branded with the Title of Atheist, on account of the many attacks on Reveald Religion, that is to be found in his Philosophical Works, and in many Places of his History. The Last of which are still

---

* David Hume During all his Life had wrote the most pleasing and agreable Letters to his Friends. I have preserv'd two of those, but I lately saw two of more Early Date in the Hands of Mʳ Sandiland Dysart Esqʳ W.S. to his Mother who was a friend of Davids and a very accomplish'd Woman. One of them Dated in 1751 on occasion of his Brother Hume of Ninewells Marriage, and the other in 1754 with a Present of the 1ˢᵗ Vol. of his History.[1] Both of which are written in a vein of Pleasantry and playfullness, which nothing can exceed; and which makes me think that a Collection of his Letters would be a valuable present to the World, and present throughout a very pleasing Picture of his Mind.

I have heard him say, That Baron Montesquieu[2] had said to him, when he ask'd him if he Did not think, that in France there would soon be a Revolution Favourable to Liberty, he answer'd No, for their Noblesse had all become Poltroons.

He said that the Club in Paris (Baron . . . . .) to which he belong'd were of Opinion that Christianity would be abolishd in Europe by the End of the 18ᵗʰ Century, and that they Laugh'd at Andʸ Stuart for making a Battle in Favour of a Future State, and Call'd him L'ame Immortelle.

more objectionable than the First, which a friendly Critick might Call only Sceptical. Apropos of this, when Mr Robt Adam the celebrated architect [and his Brother] Liv'd in Ed^r with their Mother, an aunt of Dr Robertson, and a very respectable woman, she said to her Son, I shall be glad to see any of your Companions to Dinner, But I hope you will never bring the Atheist here to Disturb my Peace. But Robert soon fell on a Method to reconcile her to him, for he introduc'd [him] under another Name, or Conceal'd it carefully from her. When the Com[pany] parted she said to her Son, I must confess that you bring very agreable Companions about you, But the Large Jolly Man who sate next me is the most agreable of them all. This was the very Atheist (said he) Mother that you was so much affraid of. Well says she, you may bring him here as much as you please, for he's the most agreable Facetious Man I ever met with. This was truly the case with him, for tho' he had much Learning and a Fine Taste, and was professedly a Sceptick, tho' by no means an Atheist, he had the Greatest Simplicity of Mind and Manners with the utmost Facility and Benevolence of Temper of any Man I ever knew. His Conversation was truly Irresistable, For while it was enlighten'd it was naive almost to puerility.* At this period when he first Liv'd in Edin^r and was

---

* I was one of those who never believ'd that Dav^d H. Sceptical Principles had laid fast hold on his Mind; But thought that his Books proceeded Rather from affectation of Superiority, and Pride of Understanding and love of Vain Glory. I was confirm'd in this opinion after his Death, by what the Honble Pat. Boyle one of his most Intimate Friends told me many years ago at my House in Muss^h when he us'd to come and Dine the 1st Sunday of every Genl Assembly after his Brother Ld Glasgow ceas'd to be Ld High Com^r—When we were Talking of David Mrs C. ask'd Mr B. If he thought he was as Great an Unbeliever, as the World took him to be. He answer'd that the World Judg'd from his Books, as they had a Right to do; But he thought otherwise who had known him all his Life, and mention'd the Following Incident. When Dav^d and he were both in London at the Period when Davids Mother Died, Mr Boyle hearing of it, soon after went into his apartment, for they Lodg'd in the Same House, when he found him in the Deepest Affliction and in a Flood of Tears. After the usual Topicks of Condolance, Mr Boyle said to him, My Friend you owe this Uncommon Grief to your having thrown off the Principles of Religion, for if you had not, you would have been consol'd by the Firm Belief That the Good Lady who was not only the best of Mothers, but the most Pious of Christians, was now Compleatly Happy in the Realms of the Just. To which David Replied, Though I Threw out my Speculations to Entertain and Employ the Learned and Metaphysical World, yet in other things, I Do not think so Differently from the rest of Mankind as you may Imagine. To this my Wife was a Witness—and this Conversation took place, on the year after David Died, when Dr Hill who was to preach, had Gone to a Room to Look over his Notes.

David, who Delighted in what the French Call Plaisanterie, with the aid of Miss Nancy Ord one of the Chief Baron's Daughters, contriv'd and executed one that Gave him very Great Delight. As the New Town was making its progress westward, he built a House in the S. West Corner of St Andrews Square. The Street Leading South to Princes S^t had not yet Got its name affix'd tho' the Magistrates intended . . . But they

writing his History of England, his circumstances were narrow, and he accepted the office of Librarian to the Faculty of Advocates, worth £40—p^r ann. But it was not for the Sallary, that he accepted this Employment; but that he might have Easy access to the Books in that Celebrated Library, for to my Certain Knowledge he gave every farthing of it to Family's in Distress. Of a piece with this temper was his Curiosity and Credulity, which were without Bounds. A Specimen of which shall be afterwards Given, when I come down to Militia and the Poker.[1] His Oeconymy was strict, as he lov'd independency, and yet he was able at that time to Give Suppers to his Friends in his small lodging in the Cannongate. He took much to the Company of the younger Clergy, not from a wish to bring them over to his Opinions, for he never attempted to overturn any Mans principles, but they best understood his Notions, and

---

Got a Workman Early one Morning, to Paint on the Cornerstone of Davids House, St Davids Street. Where it Remains to this Day.

He was at first quite Delighted with Ossians Poems and gloried in them. But on Going to London, he went over to the other side, and loudly affirm'd them to be Inventions of Macpherson.[2] I happen'd to say one Day when he was Declaiming against M^{c}pherson, That I had met with nobody of his opinion but Wm Caddell of Cockenzie and President Dundas—which he took ill, and was some time of forgetting. This is one Instance, of what Smellie says of him, that tho' of the best temper in the World yet he could be touch'd with Opposition or Rudeness. This was the only time I had ever Observ'd Davids Temper change. I can call to mind an Instance or two of his Good natur'd Pleasantry. Being at Gilmerton where David H[u]me was on a Visit, Sir D. Kinloch made him Go to Athelstaneford Church, where I preach'd for John Home. When we met before Dinner, What Did you mean, says he to me, by treating John's Congregation today with one of Cicero's Academicks? I Did not think that such Heathen Morality would have pass'd in E. Lothian. On Monday—when we were assembling to Breakfast, David Retir'd to the end of the Dining Room; when Sir Dav^d Enter'd, What are you Doing there Davy, come to your Breakfast. Take away the Enemy first, says David. The Bar^t Thinking it was the Warm Fire, that kept Davy in the Lower End of the Room, Rang the Bell for a Servant to Carry some of it off. It was not the Fire that Scard Dav^d but a Large Bible that was left on a Stand at the Upper End of the Room, a Chapter of which had been read at the Family Prayers the Night Before. That Good Custom not being then out of use, when Clergymen were in the House. Add to this John Home saying to him at the Poker Club when every Body wonder'd what could make a Clerk of Sir Wm Forbess's run away with £900; I know that very well says John Home to David, For when he was Taken, There was found in his Pocket, your Philosophical Works, and Boston's Fourfold State of Man.

Dav^d H[u]me like Smith had no Decernment at all of characters. The only two Clergymen whose Interest he Espous'd, and for one of whom he provided, were the two Silliest Fellows in the Church. With every Opportunity, he was ridiculously shy of asking Favours, on account of preserving his Independence, which always appear'd to me to be a very foolish Kind of Pride. His Friend John Home, with not more benevolence, but with no scruples from a wish of Independence for which he was not born, avail'd himself of his Influence, and provided for Hundreds, and yet he never ask'd any thing for himself.

could furnish him with Literary Conversation. Robertson, and John Home and Bannatyne and I liv'd all in the Country, and came only periodically to the Town; Blair and Jardine both liv'd in it—and Supper being the only Fashionable meal at that time, we Din'd where we best could, and by Cadies[1] assembled our Friends to meet us in a Tavern by nine aclock—and a Fine time it was when we could Collect David H[u]me and Adam Smith, and Adam Ferguson, and L.d Elibank and D.r Blair and Jardine on an Hours warning. I Remember one Night, That Dav. Hume who having din'd abroad came Rather late to us, and Directly pull'd a large Key from his Pocket which he Laid on the Table—This he said was Given him by his maid Peggy, (much more Like a Man than a Woman) That she might not sit up for him, for she said, When the Honest Fellows came in from the Country, he never Return'd home till after one aclock. This Intimacy of the Young Clergy with David Hume Enrag'd the Zealots on the Opposite Side, who little knew how Impossible it was for him, had he been willing, to Shake their Principles.

As M.r Hume's Circumstances Improv'd, he Enlarg'd his Mode of Living and instead of the Roosted Hen, and Minc'd Collops, and a Bottle of Punch, he Gave both Elegant Dinners and Suppers, and the Best Claret. And which was best of all, he furnish'd the Entertainment, with the most Instructive and pleasing Conversation, for he assembled whomsoever were most knowing and agreable, among either the Laity or Clergy. This he always Did, but still more unsparingly, when he became what he Call'd Rich. For Innocent Mirth and Agreable Raillery, I never knew his Match—Jardine who sometimes bore Hard upon him, for he had much Drollery and Wit tho' but little Learning, never could overturn his Temper. L.d Elibank Resembled David in his Talent for Collecting agreable Companies together, and had a House in Town for Several Winters, Chiefly for that Purpose.

Adam Smith, tho' perhaps only 2.d to David in Learning and Ingenuity, was far Inferior to him in Conversation Talents. In that of Publick Speaking they were Equal—David never tried it, and I never heard Adam but once, which was at the 1.st Meeting of the Select Society[2] when he open'd up the Design of the Meeting—His Voice was harsh and Enunciation Thick, approaching to Stammering. His Conversation was not Colloquial, but Like Lecturing, in which I have been Told he was not Deficient, especially when he Grew Warm. He was the most absent man in Company that I ever saw, Moving his Lips and Talking to himself, and Smiling, in the midst of large Company's. If you awak'd him from his Reverie, and made him attend to the Subject of Conversation, he Immediatly began a Harangue and never stop'd till he told you all he knew about it, with the utmost Philosophical Ingenuity. He knew nothing of

Characters, and yet was ready to Draw them on the Slightest Invitation—But when you check'd him or Doubted, he retracted with the utmost Ease, and Contradicted all he had been saying. His Journey abroad with the Duke of Buccleuch Cur'd him in Part of those Foibles. But still he appear'd very unfit for the Intercourse of the World as a Travelling Tutor. But the Duke was a Character both in Point of Heart and Understanding to surmount all Disadvantages.[1] He could Learn nothing ill from [this] Philosopher of the utmost Probity and Benevolence. If he [Smith] had been more a man of Address and of the World, he might Perhaps have Given a Ply to the Duke's Fine Mind, which was much better when Left to its own Energy. Ch. Townshend had chosen Smith not for his Fitness for the Purpose, but for his own Glory in having Sent an Eminent Scottish Philosopher to Travel with the Duke.* Tho' Smith had some little Jealousy in his Temper, he had the most unbounded Benevolence. His Smile of Approbation was truly Captivating. His affectionate Temper was prov'd by his Dutiful Attendance on his Mother. —One Instance I Remember which mark'd his Character. John Home and he travelling Down from London together in 64 or 65[2] met Dav.ᵈ Hume Going to Bath for the Recovery of his Health. He anxiously wish'd them both to Return with him. John agreed, But Smith excus'd himself on account of the State of his Mothers Health whom he needs must See. Smith's Fine Writing is chiefly Display'd in his Book on Moral Sentiment, which is the pleasantest and most Eloquent Book on the Subject. His Wealth of Nations, from which he was Judg'd to be an Inventive Genius of the First Order, is Tedious and Full of Repetition. His separate Essays in the 2.ᵈ Vol. have the Air of being Occational Pamphlets, without much force or Determination. On Political Subjects his opinions were not very Sound.

D.ʳ Adam Ferguson was a very Different kind of Man. He was the Son of a Highland Clergyman who was much respected, and had Good Connections. He had the Pride and High Spirit of his Countrymen. He was

---

* Smith had from the Duke a Bond for a Life Annuity of £300—Till an office of Equal Value was Obtain'd for him in Brittain. When the Duke Got him appointed a Commissioner of the Customs in Scotland, he went out to Dalkeith with the Bond in his Pocket, and offering it to the Duke told him that he Thought himself Bound in Honour to Surrender the Bond, as his Grace had now Got him a Place of £500—The Duke answer'd that M.ʳ Smith seem'd more Carefull of his Honour than of his, which he found wounded by the Proposal. Thus Acted that Good Duke who being entirely void of Vanity Did not value himself on Splendid Generosities. He had Acted in much the Same Manner to D.ʳ Hallam who had been his Tutor at Eton. For when M.ʳ Townshend propos'd Giving Hallam an annuity of £100 when the Duke was taken from him, No, says he, it is my Desire that Hallam may have as much as Smith, it being a Great Mortification to him, That he is not to Travel with me.

142

bred at St. Andrews University and had Gone Early into the World, for Being a Favourite of a Dutchess Dowager of Athole, and bred to the Church, She had him appointed Chaplain to the 42^{d} Reg^{t} then Commanded by Ld John Murray her Son, when he was not more than 22—The Dutchess had Impos'd a very Difficult task upon him, which was to be a kind of Tutor or Guardian to Ld John, That is to say to Gain his Confidence, and keep him in Peace with his officers, which it was Difficult to do. This however he actually accomplish'd, by adding all the Decorum belonging to the Clerical Character, to the Manners of a Gentleman: The Effect of which was, that [he was] highly respected by all the Officers, and ador'd by his countrymen the Common Soldiers. He remain'd Chaplain to this Reg^{t} and went about with them till 1755, when they went to America, on which occasion he resign'd, as it did not suit his views to attend them there. He was a Year or two with them in Ireland—and likewise attended them on the expedition to Bretany under Genl Sinclair,[1] where his Friends Dav^{d} H[u]me and Coll^{l} Edminstone also were. This turn'd his Mind to the Study of War, which appears in his Roman History, where many of the Battles are better Describ'd than by any Historian but Polybius, who was an Eye Witness to so many. He had the Manners of a Man of the World, and the Demeanor of a High-bred Gentleman, Insomuch that his Company was much Sought after—For tho' he Convers'd with Ease, it was with a Dignified Reserve. If he had any Fault in Conversation, it was of a piece with what I have said of his temper, for the Elevation of his Mind, prompted him to such sudden transitions, and Dark Allusions, That it was not always easy to follow him tho' he was a very Good Speaker. He had another Talent unknown to any but his Intimates, which was a Boundless Vein of Humour, which he Induldg'd when there were none others present, and which flow'd from his Pen in every familiar Letter he wrote. He had the Faults however that belong'd to that Character, for he was apt to be Jealous of his Rivals, and Indignant against assum'd Superiority. His wife us'd to say, that it was very fortunate that I was so much in Edin^{r}, as I was a Great Peacemaker among them. She Did not perceive that her own Husband was the Most Difficult of them all. But as they were all Honourable Men, in the highest Degree, John Home and I together kept them in very Good Terms. I mean by them Smith and Ferguson and David Hume; For Robertson was very Goodnatur'd, and soon Disarm'd the Failing of Ferguson of whom he was affraid.* With respect to Taste we held David H[u]me and Ad.

* David H[u]me said Ferguson had more Genius than any of them, as he had made himself so much Master of a Difficult Science, viz. Natural Philosophy, which he had never Studied but when at College, in 3 Months so as to be able to Teach it.

The time came when Those who were overaw'd by Ferguson Repaid him for his

Smith Inferior to the Rest, for they were both prejudic'd in Favour of the French Tragedies, and Did not sufficiently appreciate Shakspear and Milton. Their Taste was a Rational Act, rather than the Instantaneous Effort of fine Feeling.

With Respect to Robertson and Blair[1] their Lives and Characters have been so fully expos'd to Publick View by Professor Dugald Stuart in a Long Life of Robertson, where tho' the Picture is rather in Disjointed Members, yet there is hardly any thing omitted, that tends to make a Judicious Reader Master of the Character. D[r] Blair's Character is more obvious in a Short, but very Elegant and true Acc[t] of him Drawn by D[r] Finlayson. John Hill is writing a more Diffuse Acc[t] of the Latter, which may not be so like.[2] To the Character of Robertson, I have only to add here, That tho' he was truly a very Great Master of Conversation, and in General perfectly agreable, Yet he appear'd Sometimes so very fond of Talking, even when Shewing off was out of the Question, and so much addicted to the Translation of other Peoples Thoughts, that he sometimes appear'd tedious to his Best Friends. He was very much a Master of Conversation, and very Desirous to Lead it, and to make Dissertations and Raise Theories that Sometimes provok'd the Laugh against him.*

Haughtiness—For when his Roman History was publish'd at a period when he had lost his Health, and had not been able to Correct it Diligently, by a certain propensity they had unknown to themselves acquir'd to Disparage every thing that Came from Ferguson, they Did his Book more hurt, than they could have Done by Open Criticism. It was provoking to hear those who were so ready to give Loud Praises to very Shallow and Imperfect English Productions, to Curry Favour, as we suppos'd with the Booksellers and Authors concern'd, Taking every Opportunity, to undermine the Reputation of Fergusons Book. It was not a Roman History, said they, (which it Did not say it was): His Delineation of the Constitution of the Republick is well s[k]etchd but for the Rest, It is any thing but History, and then it is so Incorrect that it is a perfect shame. All his other Books met with the same Treatment. While at the same time, there were a few of us, who could not refrain from saying that Fergusons was the best History of Rome; That what he had omitted was Fabulous or Insignificant, and what he had wrote more profound in Research into Characters, and Gave a more Just Delineation of them, than any Book now extant. The same thing we said of his Book on Moral Philosophy, which we held to be the Book that Did the Most Honour of any to the Scotch Philosophers, Because it Gave the most perfect Picture of Moral Virtues, with all their Irresistable Attractions. His Book on Civil Society ought only to be Consider'd as a College Exercise, and yet there is in it a Turn of Thought, and a Species of Eloquence, peculiar to Ferguson. Smith had been weak enough to accuse him of Having Borrowd some of his Inventions without owning them. This Ferguson Denied, but own'd he Deriv'd many Notions from a French author and that Smith had been there before him. Dav[d] H[u]me Did not Live to see Fergusons History, otherwise his Candid Praise would have prevented all the Subtle Remarks of the Jealous or Resentfull.

* One Instance of this was, when he had Gone a Jaunt into England, with some of Henry Dundas Lord Melville's Famil[y], [Dundas] and M[r] Baron Cockburn and Robert

He was the best temper'd Man in the World, and the young Gentlemen who had Liv'd for years in his House Declar'd they never saw him once Ruffled. His Table which had always been Hospitable even when his Income was Small, became full and Elegant, when his situation was Improv'd. As he Lov'd a Long Repast as he Call'd it, he was as Ready to Give it at Home, as to Receive it Abroad. The Softness of his Temper, and his Habits at the Head of a Party, Led him to Seem to promise what he was not able to Perform, which Weakness rais'd up to him some very Inveterate Enemies; while at the same time his true Friends saw that those Weaknesses, were rather amiable than Provoking. He was not so much belov'd by Women as by Men, which he laughingly us'd to say, was owing to their Rivalship as Talkers, but was much more owing to his having been very little in Company with Ladies in his Youth. He was Early Married, tho' his Wife (a very Good one) was not his First Choice, as Stewart in his Life would make us Believe. Tho' not very complaisant to Women, he was not Beyond their Regimen, any more than Dr George Wishart, for Instances of both their Frailties on that Side could be Quoted.*

Sinclair were on Horseback, and seeing a Gallows on a Neighbouring Hillock, they rode Round to have a Nearer View of the Felon on the Gallows. When they met in the Inn, Robertson Immediatly began a Dissertation on the Character of Nations, and how much the English like the Romans, were harden'd by their Cruel Diversions of Cockfighting, Bullbeating, Bruising; For had they not observ'd 3 Englishmen on Horseback Do, what no Scotchman &c. Here Dundas had Compassion, and said, What, Did you not know Principal that it was Cockburn and Sinclair and me? This put an End to Theories &c. for that Day.

* 'Tis as well to mention them here. In the Year 78, when Drs Robertson and Drysdale had with much pains prepar'd an Assembly, to Elect young Mr Robertson into the Procurator's Chair, and to Get Dr Drysdale Chosen Principal Clerk to the Assembly, as Colleague and Successor to Dr George Wishart, It was necessary that Dr Wishart should Resign in order to his being Re-Elected with Drysdale. But this, when first appli'd to, he Positively refus'd to Do, Because he had Given his Word to Dr Dick That he would Give him a years warning before he Resign'd. In spite of this Declaration a Siege of Amazons was laid to the Honest Man. After Several Hearings, in which Female Eloquence was Display'd in all its Forms, and after many Days, he Yielded as he Said himself, to the Earnest and Violent Sollicitations of Dr Drysdale's Family. He never after had any Intercourse with that Family, nor Saw them more. Mr James Lindsay, Told me this anecdote.

Dr Robertson's weakness was as Follows. He had engag'd Heartily with me when in 1788 I Stood Candidate for the Clerkship, Dr Drysdale having Shewn evident Marks of Decline. In the Year 1787, I had a long Evening's Walk with the Procurator, when after Mentioning every Candidate for that office we could think of, the Procurator at last said that no body had such a good chance of [it as] myself. After a long Discussion I yielded; and we in Due [Form] Communicated this Resolution to his Father who Consented with all his Heart, and gave us much advice and some aid. When the Vacancy happen'd in 1789, Robert Adam assisted his Brother in Law with all his

Robertson's Conversation was not always so Prudent as his Conduct; one Instance of which, his always asserting that any Minister of State who Did not take Care of himself, when he had an opportunity, was no very Wise Man; This Maxim shock'd most Young People, who Thought the Doctors Standard of Publick Virtue was not very high. This Manner of Talking, likewise Seconded a Notion that prevail'd, that he was a very Selfish Man. With all these Defects, his Domestick Society was pleasing Beyond Measure; For his Wife tho' not a Woman of Parts, was well suited to him, who was more fitted to Lead than to be Led, and his Sons and Daughters Led so happy a Life, That his Guests, which we were often for a week together, met with nothing but welcome and peace and joy. This Intercourse was not much Diminish'd by his having not put any Confidence in me, when he left the Business of the Church, farther than Saying that he Intended to do it. Tho' he knew that I was much resorted to for advice when he retir'd, he never talk'd to me on the Subject, at which I was somewhat Indignant. His Deviations in Politicks, Lessen'd the Freedom of our Conversation, tho' we still continued in Good Habits. But ever after he left the Leading in Church affairs, he appear'd to me to have Lost his spirits, and still more, when the Magistrates Resorted to Dr Blair instead of him, for advice about their choice of Professors and Ministers. I had Discover'd his having Sacrific'd me to Mrs Drysdale in 1789; But was long acquainted with his Weaknesses, and Forgave him— Nor Did I ever up[b]raid him with it but in General Terms, Such as that I had Lost the Clerkship by the Keeness of my Oponents and the Coldness of my Friends. I had such a Conscious Superiority over him in that affair, That I [did] not Chuse to put an old Friend to the Trial of Making his Fault Greater by a Lame Excuse.

Dr Blair was a Different Kind of Man from Robertson, and his Character is very justly Delineated by Dr Finlayson, so far as he goes. Robertson was Most Sagacious, Blair was Most Naive. Neither of them could be said to have either Wit or Humour; of the latter Robertson had a Small Tincture, Blair had hardly a Relish for it. Robertson had a Bold and Ambitious Mind, and a strong Desire to make himself Considerable. Blair was Timid and Unambitious, and withheld himself from Publick Business of every kind, and seem'd to have no Wish but to be admir'd as a Preacher, chiefly by the Ladies. His Conversation was so Infantine,

---

Interest which was Considerable. In the mean time the same Influence was us'd with Dr Robertson as had been with Dr Wishart, in a still more Formidable Shape, for Mrs Drysdale was his Cousin German, and Threaten'd with the Eternal Hate of all the Family. He also Yielded—and Robt Adam when seriously [urged] with a View to Drop his Canvas, if Robertson advise to: No, Robertson bade, Go on, as he thought he had the Best Chance. R. Adam told this to Proff^r Ferguson when he Sollicited his Vote.

That many People thought it impossible at first Sight, That he could be a Man of Sense or Genius. He was as Eager about a New Paper to his Wife's Drawing Room, or his own New Wig, as about a New Tragedy or a New Epic Poem. Not Long before his Death I call'd on him, when I found him restless and Fidgetty—Whats the Matter with you today, says I, my Good Friend, are you well? O! yes, says he, but I must Dress my self, For the Dutchess of Leinster has order'd her Grand Daughters, not to Leave Scotland without seeing me.—Go and Dress yourself D.ʳ and I shall read this Novel, for I am Resolv'd to see the Dutchess of Leinster's Grand Daughters for I knew their Father and Grand Father. This being Settled, the young Ladies with their Governess arriv'd at one, and Turn'd out poor little Girls of 12 and 13, who could hardly be suppos'd to carry a well turn'd Compliment, which the D.ʳ Gave them in Charge to their Grand Mother.*

Robertson had so Great a Desire to Shine himself that I hardly ever saw him Patiently Bear any Body Else's shewing off but D.ʳ Johnson and Garrick. Blair on the Contrary, tho' capable of the most profound Conversation, when Circumstances Led to it, had not the least Desire to Shine; But was Delighted Beyond Measure, to shew other People in their best Guise to his Friends. Did not I shew you the Lyon well today, us'd he to say after the exhibition of a Remarkable Stranger. For a vain Man, he was the Least Envious I ever knew. He had truly a Pure Mind, in [which] there was not the least Malignity: For tho' he was of a Quick and Lively Temper and apt to be Warm and Impatient about triffles, his Wife who was a Superior Woman, only laugh'd, and his Friends Join'd her. Tho' Robertson was never Ruffled he had more Animosity in his Nature than Blair. They were both Reckon'd Selfish by those who Envied their Prosperity; but on very Unequal Grounds, for tho' Blair

---

* Blair had lain under obligation to L.ᵈ Leven's Family for his first Church, which he Left within the Year. But tho' that connexion was so soon Disolv'd, and tho' Blair took a Side in Church Politicks wholly opposite to L.ᵈ Leven's, the D.ʳ always behav'd to the Family with Great Respect, and kept up a visiting Correspondence with them all his Life. Not so Robertson with the Arniston Family, who had Got him the Church of Gladsmuir. The First President [Dundas] soon after fail'd and Died; Not however till he had mark'd his appro[ba]tion of Robertson in Assembly 1751—His Successor's manner had not been pleasing to him, so that he was alienated till Harry grew up.[1] But him he Deserted also on the Change in 1782, Being Dazzl'd with the Prospect of his Sons having Charge of Ecclesiastical Affairs as his Cousin John Adam was to have of Political, During Rockingham's New Ministry.—This threw a cloud on Robertson which was never Dispel'd.—Blair had for a year been Tutor to Simon Fraser, Lord Lovats Eldest Son, whose Steady Friendship he preserv'd to the Last, tho' the General was not Remarkable for that Amiable Weakness. Witness the Saying of a Common Soldier whom he had often promis'd to make a Serjeant, but never perform'd: O! Simon, Simon, said he, As long as you Continue to Live, Lord Lovat is not Dead!

talk'd selfishly enough sometimes, yet he never faild in Generous Actions. In one Respect they were quite alike. Having been bred at a time, when the Common People thought to play with Cards or Dice was a Sin, and every body thought it an Indecorum in Clergymen, they could neither of them play at Golf or Bowls, and far less at Cards or Backgammon, and on that account were very unhappy, when from home, in Friends Houses in the Country in rainy weather.* As I had set the first example of Playing at Cards at home with unlock'd Doors, and so Reliev'd the Clergy from Ridicule on that Side, They both Learn'd to play at Whist after they were 60; Robertson Did very well, Blair never shone. He had his Country Quarters for two Summers in my Parish, where he and his Wife were quite Happy—We were much together. Mrs C. who had wit and humour in a high Degree, and an acuteness and extent of Mind that made her fit to Converse with Philosophers, and indeed a Great Favourite with them all, Gaind much upon Blair, and as Mrs B. alledg'd could make him believe whatever she pleas'd. They took Delight in raising the Wonder of the sage Dr—Who told you that story my Dear Dr—No, says he, Don't you Doubt it for it was Mrs C. who told me. On my Laughing—and So, So, said he, I must hereafter make allowance for her Imagination.

Five or Six Days before he Died, finding him well and in Good Spirits, I said to him, since you Don't chuse to Dine abroad in this season (Decr) you may at least Let a Friend or two Dine with you. Well, well, come you and Dine with me tomorow—Looking Earnestly at Miss Hunter his Niece. I am engag'd tomorow, But I can Return at 4 today. He Lookt more Earnestly at his Niece. What's to hinder him, said She? Meaning to answer his Look, which said Have you any Dinner today,

* Robertson's translations and Paraphrases on other People's thoughts, were so Beautifull and so harmless, that I never saw any Body Lay claim to their own. But it was not so when he forgot himself so far, as to think he had been present where he had not been, and Done what he had not the least hand in: one very singular Instance of which I Remember. Hugh Bannatyne, and some Clergymen of Haddington Presbytery, came to Town in great haste on their Being Threatened with having their Goods Distraind for Payment of the Window Tax.[1] One of them Call'd on me as he Past, But as I was abroad, He Left a Note, or told Mrs C, to come to them Directly. I Rode Instantly to Town and Met them—and it was agreed on to Send immediatly to the Sollicitor James Montgomery—A Cady[2] was Dispers'd[3] but he could not be Found, till I at last heard his Voice, as I past the Door of a Neighbouring Room. He came to us on being Sent to. He Immediately Granted the Alarm'd Brethren a Sist.[4] Not a week after 3 or 4 of the same Clergymen Dining at the Drs House where I was, the Business was talk'd of, when he Said, Was not I very fortunate in Ferretting out the Sollr at Walkers,[5] when no Cadie could find him? No, No, Says I, Principal, (we had sent to the Dr but he could not come), It was I who had that Good Luck, and you were not so much as at the Meeting. Well well, replied he, I have heard so much about it, that I thought I had been there.

Betty? I Retᵈ accordingly at 4, and never past 4 hours more agreably with him, nor had more enlighten'd Conversation. Nay more, 3 Days before his Death, he sent to John Home a Part of his History with 2 or 3 pages of Criticism, on that Part of it that Relates to Provost Drummond in which he and I thought John egregiously Wrong.

It was long before Blairs Circumstances were Full, yet he liv'd handsomly, and had Literary Strangers at his House as well as Many Friends. A Task Impos'd on both Robertson and Blair was Reading Manuscript prepar'd for the Press, of which Blair had the Greatest Share of the Poetry, and Robertson of the other Things—and were Both Kind encouragers of young Men of Merit.[1]

In John Home's younger Days he had a Good Share of Wit, with much Sprightliness and Vivacity, (Insomuch that his Entrance into any Company, was like Letting in the Sun into a Dull Room) So that he Infus'd Joy, and a Social Exertion[2] wherever he Came. His address was Cordial and Benevolent; which Inspir'd his Companions with Similar Sentiments. Superior Knowledge and Learning except in the Department of Poetry, he had not, but such was the Charm of his fine Spirits in those Days, That when he left the Room, prematurely, which was but seldom the Case, the Company Grew Dull again, and Soon Dissolv'd. As John all his Life had a Thorough Contempt for such as Neglected or Disapprov'd of his Poetry he treated all who approv'd of his Works with a Partiality, which more than approach'd to Flattery. The effect of this Temper was, that all his Opinions of men and things, were Prejudices, which tho' it Did not Disqualify him for writing admirable Poetry, Yet made him unfit for writing Historys or other Prose Works. He was in no Respect a Man of Business, tho' he now and then spoke with some Energy and Success in the Genˡ Assembly—But he had no turn for Debate, which made me Glad, when he was Dissappointed in his Wish of Obtaining a Seat in the House of Commons, which was owing to the Good Sense of Sir Gilbert Elliot, and Sir Wᵐ Pulteney.

This has been a long Digression from my Narration, but having Noted down one Character, I thought it best to Go on with a few more Least I should forget some particulars, which then occurr'd to me.

[1754]*

In the year 1754 I Remember nothing Remarkable in the Genˡ Assembly. But this was the year in which the Select Society[3] was Estab-

* It was in the Year 1754, that my Cousin Capᵗ Lyon Died at London of a High Fever. His Wife Lady Catherine Bridges had conducted herself so very loosely and ill,

lish'd, which Improv'd and Gave a Name to the Literati of this Country th[e]n beginning to Distinguish themselves. I gave an acc^t of this Institution, and a List of the Members to Dugald Stuart, which he Inserted in his Life of Robertson. But that List Did not contain the whole of the Members; some had Died before the List was printed, and some were admitted after it was. Of the First were Lord Dalmeny the Elder Brother of the Present Ld Roseberry, who was a Man of Letters, and an amateur, and tho' he Did not speak himself, Generally Carried home 6 or 8 of those who Did to sup with him. There was also a Peter Duff a Writer to the Signet, who was a shrewd sensible Fellow, and pretending to be unlearnd, Surpris'd us with his Observations in Strong Buchan.[1] The Duke Hamilton of that Period, a Man of Taste and Letters could he have kept himself Sober, was also a Member and spoke there one Night.* The Earl of Hopetoun was Commissioner of the General Assembly. The Earl of Dumfries had wish'd for it—But some of the Ministers Discover'd that it would be proper to Dissappoint him, by a little Intrigue, Contriv'd to Get the King to Nominate Hopetoun, who accepted it for one Year, and Entertain'd his Company in a sumptuous Manner. At his Table I saw the Dutchess of Hamilton (Mary Gunning) without Doubt the Most Beautiful Woman of her time.

In the End of Summer, Lady Dalkeith the Duke of Buccleuch's Mother who had been a Widow since the Year 1750, came to Dalkeith, and brought with her the Honble Mr Stuart M^{c}kenzie and his Lady, the Countesses Sister, and Remain'd there for two Months. They had publick Days twice in the Week and I frequently Dined there. The Countess was well bred and agreable, and acting Plays being the Rage at the time among People of Quality, She Propos'd to act a Tragedy at Dalkeith House viz. The Fair Penitent,[2] in which Her Ladyship and M^r M^{c}kenzie

---

That it was suspected that she wish'd for his Death. But it was a Brain Fever of which he Died, and as his Wife had sent for Dr Monro, the Physician employ'd about the Insane, his Mother in the Rage of her Grief allegd'd that his Wife had Occasion'd his Death. Her two Children Died not long after. Lady [Catherine] Confirm'd all her Mother in Law's Suspicions by marrying a Mr Stanhope, one of her Many Lovers. By this time a large Fortune had fallen to her. She was truly a worthless woman, to my Knowledge. Lyon and his Children were buried in the Duke of Chando's Vault at Cannons, by his Grace's Order.

* Ld Dalmeny Died in 1755. Mr Robert Alexander Wine Merchant, a very Worthy Man, but a Bad Speaker, Entertain'd us also with Warm Suppers and excellent Claret, as a Recompense for the Patient Hearing of his Ineffectual Attempts, when I often Thought he would have Beat out his Brains on account of their Constipation.

The Conversation at those Convivial Meetings, frequently Improv'd the Members more by free Conversation, than the Speeches in the Society. It was those Meetings in particular, That Rub'd off all Corners as we call it, by Collison, and made the Literati of Edin^r Less Captious and Pedantick than they were Elsewhere.

were to have Principal Parts. Mr John Grant advocate, then Chief Manager of the D. of Buccleuchs Estate, and Living at Castlesteads, was to play the Part of the Father, and it was Requested of me to assist him in preparing his Part. I found him a Stiff Bad Reader, of Affected English, which we call Napping,[1] and Tolerably Obstinate. But Luckily for Both Master and Scholar, the Humour was soon chang'd, by Somebody's Representing to her Ladyship, That her Acting Plays would Give offence. Mr Mckenzie was very agreable, his Vanity having Carried it so Far above his Family Pride, as to make him wish to please his Inferiors. I was Simple enough then to think that my Conversation, and Manners had not been Dissagreable to him, so that when I was at London 4 years after, I attempted to avail myself of his acquaintance. But it would not Do, for I was chil'd to Death on my First Approach. So that all my Intimacy vanish'd in a few Jokes, which sometimes he Condescended to make when he met me in the Streets, and which I Rec'd with the Coldness They were Entitled to.

By this time John Home had almost Finish'd his Tragedy of Douglas, for on one of the Days that I was at Dalkeith House, I met Sir Gilbert Elliot, who on my Telling him that I had 3 acts of it written in my Hand, Came round with me to my House in Musselburgh, where I read them to him, to his Great Delight. This was in July or August 1754. I Do not Rem[em]ber whether or not he saw the two last acts at this time. I should think not: for I Remember, that I wrote 3 acts of it a Good Many Months afterwards to be sent up Suddenly to Sir Gilbert, while a Writers Clerk wrote out Fair the other two acts.

In Febry of this Year Home and I made Great Losses, by the Death of Friends. Geo. Logan, Minister of Ormiston, was seiz'd with a Brain Fever, of which he Died in a Few Days. I was sent for by his Wife, and Remain'd by his Bedside, from 5 in the afternoon, till one in the Morning, when he expir'd. He Rav'd the whole time, except During the Few Minutes in which I pray'd with him. I am not sure that he knew, for he soon relaps'd into his Ravings again, and never Ceas'd till the Great Silencer Came. I have Given the Character of his Mind before.[2] The Grief of his Wife, who never Could be Comforted, tho' she liv'd to an advanc'd age, was a Proof of his Kind and Affectionate Temper. They had no Children.

After my Friends Death I had Return'd home on Sunday Morning to Do Duty in Inveresk Church, and in the Evening about 6 John Home, to whom I had sent an express, arriv'd from Polwarth. On Hearing the Bad News he had almost Fainted, and threw himself on the Bed, and sob'd and weep'd, and after a while, I rais'd him by asking If he could think of no Misfortune Greater than the Death of Logan? He started up and

Cried, is my Brother David Gone? I had Rec'd an Express from his Brother George in Leith that afternoon, to tell me of their Brother David's Death on the Voyage. He was John's only Uterine Brother alive, had been at home the Autumn before, and was truly a fine Spirited promising Young Man. He had Gone out that fall 1ˢᵗ Mate of an Indiaman. After another short Paroxysm of Grief, for his stock was almost Spent before, he Rose and took his Supper; and insisting on my making a Good Bowl of Punch, we talk'd over the Perfections of the Deceased, went to Bed and Slept Sound. In the Morning he was taken up with the Suit of Mourning he was Going to Order, and for which he went to Edinᵣ on Purpose. I mention those Circumstances, to shew that there are very Superior Minds on which the Loss of Friends makes very little Impression. He was not Likely to feel more on any Future Occasion than on this: For as People Grow Older, not only Experience Hardens them to Such Events, but Growing Daily more Selfish, They feel less for other People.

[1755]

In the Month of Febᵧ 1755 John Home's Tragedy of Douglas, was completely well prepar'd for the Stage, and had Receiv'd all the Corrections and Improvements, that it needed, by many excellent Criticks who were Mʳ Homes Friends whom I have Mention'd before, and with whom he Daily Liv'd. He accordingly set out for London, and were I to Relate all the Circumstances Serious and Ludicrous which attended the Outset of this Journey, I am persuaded they would not be exceeded by any Novellist who ever has wrote, since the Days of the Inimitable *Don Quixote*. Six or Seven Merse¹ Ministers, the half of whom had Slept at the Manse of Polwarth, bad as it was, the Night before, set out for Wooller Haugh Head² on a Snowy Morning in Febʳʸ. Before we had Gone far we Discover'd that our Bard had no Mode of Carrying his Pretious Treasure, which we thought enough of, But hardly foresaw, That it was to be Pronounc'd a Perfect Tragedy by the Best Judges. For when David Hume Gave it that Praise, he Spoke only the Sentiment of the Whole Republick of Belles Lettres. The Tragedy in one Pocket of his Great Coat, and his Clean Shirt and night Cap in the other, tho' they Ballancd each other, was Thought an unsafe Mode of Conveyance; and our Friend [who] like most of his Brother Poets was unapt to forsee Difficulties and Provide against them, had neglected to Buy a pair of Leather Bags as he past thro' Haddington. We bethought that possibly James Landreth Minister of Simprin, and Clerk of the Synod, would be provided with such a Conveniency for the Carriage of his Synod Minutes, and having no Wife, no Atra Cura,[1] to Resist our Request, we unanimously turnd aside half a mile to Call at James; and concealing our Intention at first we easily persuaded the Honest Man to Join us in this Convoy to his friend Mr Home—and then Observing the Danger the Manuscript might Run in a Great Coat Pocket in a Journey of 400 Miles, we enquir'd if he could Lend Mr Home his Valise only as Far as Wooler, where he would purchase a new pair for himself. This he very cheerfully Granted. But while his Poney was preparing, he had another Trial to Go through; for Cupples, who never had any Money, Tho' he was a Batchelor too, and had twice the Stipend of Landreth, took the latter into another Room, where the Conference Lasted longer than we wishd for; so that we had to Bawl out for them to Come away. We afterwards understood, that Cupples having only 4 Sh. was pressing Landreth to Lend him half a Guinea, That he might be able to Defray the expence of the Journy. Honest James, knew that John Home, If he Did not Return his own Valise which was very Improbable, would provide him in a Better pair, had Frankly Agreed to the 1st Request, But as he knew Cupples never paid anything, he was very Reluctant to part with his half Guinea. However having at last Agreed, [we] at last set out and I think Gallant Troops, but so and so accoutred, to make an Inroad on the English Border. By Good Luck the River Tweed was not come Down,[2] and we Cross'd it safely at the Ford near Norham Castle, and as the Day Mended we Got to Wooller Haughhead by 4 aclock, where we Got but a So and So Dinner, for it was but a miserable House in those Days. But a Happier or more Jocose and merry Company could hardly be assembled.

John Home and I who slept in one Room, or perhaps in one Bed as was usual in those Days, were Disturb'd by a Noise in the Night, which Being in the Next Room, where Laurie and Monteith [were], we found they had Quarrell'd and fought and the former [had] Push'd the Latter out of Bed; after having Acted as Mediators in this Quarell we had Sound Sleep till Morning. Having Breakfasted as well as the House could afford, Cupples and I who had agreed to Go two Days Journy farther with Mr Home, Set off Southwards with him, and the Rest Return'd by the way they had come to Berwickshire again.

Mr Home had by that time Got a very Fine Galloway from his Friend Robert Adam, when he was Setting out for Italy. John had Call'd this Horse Piercy, who tho' only 14½ Hands high, was one of the Best Trotters ever was seen, and having a Good Deal of Blood in him, when he was well us'd, was Indefatigable. He Carried our Bard for many Years, with much Classical Fame, and Rose in Reputation with his

Master. But at last made an Inglorious End.* I had a fine Galloway too, tho' not more than 13 and ½ hands, which tho' much slower than Percy, Easily went at the Rate of 50 Miles a Day on the Turnpike Road, without being at all Tir'd.

Cupples and I attended Home as far as Ferry hill, about 6 Miles, where after Remaining all night with him, we Parted next Morning, he for London and we on our Return home. Poor Home had no better success on this occasion than before, with still Greater Mortification, for Garrick after Reading the Play Return'd it with an Opinion, that it was totally unfit for the Stage. On this occasion Home wrote a Pathetic Copy of Verses, address'd to Shakespear's Image in Westminster Abbey.

Cupples and I had a Diverting Journey back, for as his Money had Fail'd, and I had not an overflow, we were oblig'd, to feed our Horses in Newcastle without Dining, and to make the best of our Way to Morpeth, where we got an excellent Hot Supper. Next Day Staying too long in Alnwick to visit the Castle, we Lost our Way in the Night, and were in some Hazard; and it was past 12 before we Reach'd Berwick; but in those Days nothing came wrong to us. Youth and Good Spirits, made us Convert all Maladventures into Fun. The Virgins Inn, as it was Call'd, being at that time the best and on the S. Side of the Bridge, made us forget all our Dissasters.

On this Year it was in the time of the Sitting of the Gen! Assembly that L.ᵈ Drumore Died at the Age of 63—He had Gone the Western Circuit, and by Drying up an Issue in his Leg, Being a Corpulent Man who needed such a Drain, he Contracted a Gangrene, of which he Died in a few Weeks very much Regreted. More indeed than any Man I ever knew, his having Got a Legacy from   the Year before, and built

---

* Piercy's End. Robert Adam on his Setting out for London to Go to Italy, and some of his Brothers, with John, and Commissioner Cardonnell, had Din'd with me one day. Cardonnell, while their Horses were Getting Ready, insisted on our Going to his Garden to Drink a Couple of Bottles of some French White Wine, which he said was as Good as Champaigne. We went with him, but when we Sate down in his arbor we miss'd Bob Adam. We soon finish[d] our Wine which [we] Drank out of Rumers,¹ and Return'd to the Manse, where we found Robert Galloping round the Green on Piercy like a Madman, which he Repeated after Seeing us for at Least 10 Times. Home stopt him and had some talk with him. So the Brothers at last went off quietly for Edin.ʳ while Home remain'd to stay all night, or Go home. He told me what had put Robert into such Trim. He had been making Love to my Maid Jenny, who was a Handsome Lass, and had even Gone the Length of offering to Carry [her] to London, and Pension her there—all his offers were Rejected which had put him in a Flurry. This happen'd in Summer 1754—Many a time Piercy Carried John to London, and once in six Days. He sent him at Last to Sir Dav.ᵈ Kinloch, that he might end his Days in peace and ease in one of the Parks of Gilmerton. Sir David tir'd of him in a Few Weeks, and sold him to an Egg Carrier, for 20 sh.

himself a Comfortable House on his Small Estate, where he only had a Cottage Before, and where he had Slept only two or three Nights before his illness, was a circumstance that made his Family and Friends feel it the More. He had been married to an advocate's Daughter of Aberdeenshire of the Name of Horn, by whom a Good Estate came into his Family. By her he had 5 Sons, and three Daughters. Three of the Sons in Succession, Inherited the Name and Estate of Horn. After Ld Drummore became a Widower, he attach'd himself to a Mistress; which to do so openly as he Did, was at that time Reckon'd a Great Indecorum at least, in one of his Age, and Reverend Office. This was all that could be laid to his charge, which how[eve]r Did not Abate the Universal Concern of the City and Country when he was Dying. His Cousin Ld Cathcart was Commissioner that Year for the 1st time. His Eldest Son at his Death was Lieut. Gen! Horn Dalrymple, his 2d David D. some time afterwards Lord Westhall, his youngest Campbell, who was Distinguish'd afterwards in the West Indies, and was a Lieut. Coll! and Governour of Guadaloupe.*

[1756]

In the Year 1756 Hostilities were begun between the French and British after they had Given us much provocation in America. Braddock an officer of the Guards, very Brave, tho' unfit for the Business on which he was sent, having been Defeated and Slain at fort Dequesne (a misfortune afterwards repaird by Gen! John Forbes) Reprisals were Made by the Capture of French Ships without a Declaration of War. The French Laid Siege to Minorca, and Admiral Byng was sent with a Fleet of 13 Ships of the Line to Throw in Succours and Raise the Siege. The expectation of the Country was Rais'd very high on this Occasion, and yet was Dissappointed.

Concerning this I Remember a very Singular Anecdote. During the Sitting of the Gen! Assembly that year, by Desire of James Lindsay, a Company of 7 or 8 all clergymen Sup'd at a Punch-house in the Bow¹ kept by an old Servant of his, who had also been with Geo. Wishart. In that time of Sanguine Hopes of a Compleat Victory, and the Total Defeat of the French Fleet, all the company exprest their full belief that the next Post would bring us Great News, except John Home alone who

---

* At my Fathers Desire who was Minister of the Parish where Drumore resided I wrote a character of him which he Deliver'd from his Pulpit, the Sunday after his Funeral. This was Printed in Scots Mag. for June 1755, and was commended by the Publisher and well Recd by the Publick.—This was the first time I had seen my prose in Print, and it gave some Confidence in my own Talent.

persisted in Saying, That there would be no Battle at all, or at the best If there was a Battle, it would be a Drawn One. John's Obstinacy provok'd the Company, insomuch, that James Landreth, the Person who had Lent him the Valise the Year before, offer'd to Lay an half Crown Bowl of Punch, That the 1ˢᵗ Mail from the Mediterranean would bring us the News of a Compleat Victory. John took this Bett; and when he and I were walking to our Lodging together, I ask'd what in the World had made [him] so Positive. He answer'd that Byng was a Man, who would Shun Fighting if it were Possible: and that his Ground of Knowledge was from Admiral Smith, who a few Years Back had Commanded at Leith, who Lodg'd with his Friend Mʳ Walter Scot, [and] who when he was Confin'd with the Gout, us'd to have him to come and chat with him, or play at Cards when he was able: and That talking of the characters of Different Admirals, he had Told him That Byng tho' a much admir'd Commander and Manœverrer of a Fleet, would Shun Fighting whenever he could. The Gazette soon clear'd up to us the Truth of this assertion, tho' the First Accounts made it be Believ'd that the French were Defeated. A Full Confirmation of this Anecdote, I heard two Years afterwards, when Returning from London in May 1758, with John Home, Wᵐ Robertson, and James Adam. . . .[1]

It was During this Assembly, That the Carriers Inn in the Lower part of the West-Bow, Got into some Credit and was Call'd the Diversorium. Thoˢ Nicholson was the Man's Name, and his Wife's Nelly Douglas. They had been Servants of Lᵈ Elliocks, and had taken up this Small Inn, in which there was three Rooms, and a stable below for 6 or 8 Horses. Thoˢ was a Confus'd Rattling Coarse Fellow. Nelly was a Comely Woman, a Person of Good Sense and very Worthy. Some of our Companions frequented the House, and Home and I suspected that it was the Handsome Landlady, who had attracted their Notices. But it was not so. Nelly was an Honest Woman, But she had prompted her Husband to Lend them two o[r] 3 Guineas on Occasions, and Did not Suddenly Demand Repayment. Home and I follow'd Logan and James Craig, and William Cullen, and were pleas'd with the House. He and I happening to Dine with Dʳ Robertson, at his Uncle's who Liv'd in Pinkie House, a week before the Genˡ Assʸ of that year, some one of us propos'd, to order Thoˢ Nicholson, to lay in 12 Doz. of the same Claret, then 18/- pr Dozen, from Mʳ Scott winemercᵗ, at Leith, for in his House we propos'd to make our Assembly Parties. For being out of the way, we propos'd to have Snug Parties of our own Friends. This was accordingly executed. But we could not be conceald. As it happens in such Cases, the out of the way place, and mean House, as the attempt to be Private, made it be the more frequented. And no wonder, when the Company Consisted of

Robertson and Home and Ferguson and Jardine and Wilkie with the addition of Dav.ᵈ H[u]me, and L.ᵈ Elibank and the Master of Ross and Sir Gilbert Elliot.

Home and I were witness to a comical Circumstance at [t]his Assembly. There was a M.ʳ Pat. Grant Minister of   who had been Presented to Nigg in Ross shire;[1] and was to have been settled peacably there, but for a Report That he had Preach'd when Drunk in one of the churches of Edin.ʳ and had behav'd in such a manner as to Give Great Offence. This was Enquir'd into by the Presbytery of Edin.ʳ by Desire of the Presbytery of [?Tain], when it was Provd that M.ʳ Grant had Dind with the Presbytery of Edin.ʳ on the Day he had Given Offence, That he had left the Presbytery very soon after Dinner, and was not in the Least Intoxicated. This seem'd to Clear him; but he had Gone to the Grass Market to purchase a Horse before his Sermon; and there it was believ'd he had Got More Drink. Be that as it may, when a Company of between 40 and 50 were Consulting in a Tavern, How he should be assoilzied,[2] and while Pat. Cuming was haranguing warmly in his Favour, There stood a Conveniency behind a Skreen, which nobody in the Room could see but John and me, who had come in Late, when Grant who had been Moving about, talking to Different People in Whispers, Retir'd to it, not to use it as we Suppos'd he would, but as a Bason into which he Copiously Disgorg'd the Contents of his Stomach. Home and I Did not Disclose what we had Seen; and it was agreed to acquit him.

In Oc.ʳ 1756[3] John Home had been taken by L.ᵈ Milton's Family to Inveraray, to be Introduc'd to the Duke, who was much taken with his Liveliness, and Gentlemanlike Manners. The Duke's Good Opinion made Milton adhere more firmly to him, and assist in bringing on his Play in the End of that Season.

It was in the end of this Year 1756 that Douglas was first acted at Edin.ʳ. M.ʳ Home had been unsuccessful in London the year before, but he had been introduc'd to the Duke of Argyle, and was well with Sir Gilbert Elliot, M.ʳ Oswald of Dunnikier, and had the Favour and Friendship of Lord Milton here and all his Family; and it was at Last agreed among them That since Garrick could not yet be . . . with to Get Douglas acted, that it should be brought on here, for if it succeeded on the Edin.ʳ Theatre, Then Garrick could Resist no Longer.

There Happen'd to be a pretty Good Set of Players here, for Digges whose Relations had Got him Debar'd[4] from the London Theatres had come Down here, and perform'd Many Principal Parts with Success. He was a very Handsome Young Man at that time, with a Genteel Address. He had Drunk Tea at Mally Campbell[s] in Glasgow College when he was an Ensign in the Year 1745—I was there, and thought him very agreable.

He was however a Great Proffligate and Spendthrift, and [Poltroon] I'm affraid into the Bargain. He had been on the Stage for some time, having been Oblig'd to Leave the Army. Mrs Ward Turn'd out an exceeding Good Lady Randolph. Love perform'd Glenalvon well, Mr Haymen the Old Shepherd, and Digges himself Young Douglas. I attended two Rehearsals with our Author and Ld Elibank, and Dr Ferguson and David Hume, and was truly astonish'd at the Readiness with which Mrs Ward conceiv'd the Lady's Character, and how happily she Deliver'd it.* The Play had unbounded Success for a Great Many Nights in Edin^r and was attended by all the Literati, and most of the Judges, who except one or two had not been in use to attend the Theatre. The Town in Genl was in an uproar of Exultation, That a Scotchman had written a Tragedy of the First Rate, and that its Merit was first Submitted to their Judgment.[1] There were a few Opposers however among those who pretended to Taste and Literature, who Endeavour'd to Cry Down the Performance in Libellous Pamphlets and Ballads, (for they Durst not attempt to oppose it in the Theatre itself), and were openly Countenanc'd by Robert Dundas of Arniston, at that time Ld Advocate, and all his Minions or Expectants. The High Flying Set,[2] were unanimous against it, as they thought it a Sin for a Clergyman to write any Play, Let it be ever so Moral in its Tendency. Several Ballads and Pamphlets were publish'd on our side in answer to the Scurrili[ti]es against us, one of which was written by Adam Ferguson, and another by myself. Ferguson was Mild and Temperate, and besides other arguments Supported the Lawfullness and Use of Dramatick Writers, from the example of Scripture, which he Exhibited in the Story of Joseph and his Brethren, as having truly the Effect of a Dramatick Composition. This was much read among the Grave and Soberminded, and Converted Some, and Confirm'd Many in their Belief of the Usefullness of the Stage. Mine was of such a Different Nature, That many people read it at First as Intended to Ridicule the Performance, and bring it into Contempt. For it was Entitled, An Argument to Prove, that the Tragedy of Douglas, Ought to be Publickly Burnt by the Hands of the Hangman. The Zeal and Violence of the Presbytery of Edin^r, who had made Enactments, and Declarations to be read in the Pulpit provok'd me to Write this Pamphlet, which in the Ironical Manner of Swift, Contain'd a Severe Satire on all our Opponents. This was so well Conceal'd however, That the Pamphlet being publish'd

---

* To be near Digges Lodgings in the Canongate, where the first Rehearsals were Perform'd, the Gentlemen mention'd with two or 3 more Din'd together at a Tavern in the Abbey two or 3 Times, where Pork Griskins[3] Being a Favourite Dish, This was Call'd the Griskin Club, and excited much Curiosity, as every thing Did in which Certain People were Concern'd.

when I was at Dumfries about the End of January visiting Provost Bell who was on his Deathbed, some Copies arriv'd there by the Carrier, which being open'd and Read by my Sister and Aunt when I was abroad, they conceiv'd it to be Serious, and that the Tragedy would be quite Undone, till Mr Stewart the Controller of the Customs, who was a Man of Sense and Reading, came in, who soon undecievd them, and convincd them that Douglas was Triumphant. This Pamphlet had a Great Effect, by Elating our Friends, and perhaps more in exasperating our Enemies. Which was by no Means Soften'd by Ld Elibank and David Hume &c. Running about and Crying it up as the first performance the World had seen for half a Century.[1]

What I really Valued myself most upon how[eve]r was half a sheet which I pen'd very suddenly. Diggs rode out one forenoon to me Saying, That he had come by Mr Home's Desire to Inform me, that all the Town had seen the Play, and that it could run no Longer, unless some Contrivance was fallen upon to make the Lower Orders of Tradesmen and apprentices come to the Playhouse. After Hearing several ways of raising the Curiosity of the Lower Orders, I Desir'd him to take a walk for half an Hour, and Look at the View from Inveresk Church Yard, which he Did; and in the mean time, I Drew up what I Entitled, A full and True History of the Bloody Tragedy of Douglas, as it is now to be seen acting at the Theatre in the Cannongate. This was cried about the Streets Next Day, and fill'd the House for 2 nights more.

I had attended the Playhouse not on the 1st or 2^d but on the 3^d night of the Performance, being well aware that all the Fanaticks, and some other Enemies, would be on the Watch, and make all the Advantage they possibly could against me. But 6 or 7 Friends of the Authors, Clergymen from the Merse, having attended, who Reproachd me for my Cowardice, and above all the Author himself, and some Female Friends of his, having Heated me by their upbraidings, I went on the 3^d night, and having taken Charge of the Ladies, I drew on myself all the Clamour of Tongues, and Violence of Prosecution which I afterwards underwent. Every thing relating to this is pretty Correctly Narated in the Scotch Mag^e for the Year 1757. I believe I have already mention'd that Dr Pat. Cuming having become Jealous of Wm Robertson and John Home and myself on acct. of our Intimacy with Ld Milton, and Observing his Active Zeal about the Tragedy of Douglas, took into his Head that he could blow us up, and Destroy our Popularity, and Consequently Disgust Ld Milton with us. Very Warmly with all the Friends he could Get to follow him, particularly Hyndman his second, [he] Join'd with Webster and his Party, in Doing every thing they could to Depretiate the Tragedy of Douglas, and Disgrace all its Partisans. With this View besides the Act of the Presbytery of Edinʳ which was Read in all the Churches, and that of the Presby. of Glasgow who follow'd them, [they] had Decoy'd Mʳ Thoˢ Whyte Minister of Liberton, who had attended the Play, Honest but a Quiet Man, to Submit to a Six Weeks Suspension for his having attended the Tragedy of Douglas, which he had Confest he had done.[1] This they Contriv'd as an Example for prosecuting me, and at least of getting a Similar Sentence pronounc'd against me by the Presbytery of Dalkeith. On Returning from Dumfries in the 2ᵈ Week of Febʸ [1757] I was surpris'd to find not only the amazing Hue and Cry that had been Rais'd against Douglas but all the Train that had been laid against me, and a summons to attend the Presbytery to answer for my Conduct on the 1ˢᵗ Day of March.

[1757]

On Deliberating about this Affair with all the Knowledge I had of the Laws of the Church, and the Confidence I had in the Good Will of my Parish, I took a firm Resolution not to Submit to what I saw the Presbytery Intended, but to Stand my Ground, on a firm Opinion that my Offence was not a foundation for a Libel,[2] but if any thing at all a mere Impropriety, or Offence against Decorum, which ought to be Done at Privy Censures, by an admonition. This Ground I took and never Departed from it. But I at the same time resolv'd to mount my Horse, and visit every Member of Presbutery, especially my opponents, and by a free Confession, Endeavour to bring them over to my opinion. They Receiv'd me Differently, Some with a Contemptible Dissimulation, and others with a Provoking Reserve and Haughtiness. I saw that they had the Majority of the Presbytery on their Side, and that the Cabal was Firm, and that no Submission on my Part, would Turn them aside from their Purpose. This Confirm'd my Resolution not to Yield, but to Run every Risk, Rather than Furnish an Example of tame Submission not merely to a Fanatical but an Illegal Exertion of Power, which would have stampd Disgrace on the Church of Scotland, kept the younger Clergy for half a Century Longer in the trammels of Bigotry or Hypocrisy, and Debar'd every Generous Spirit from entering into Orders. The Sequel of the Story is pretty fully and correctly Stated in the Scots Mag. for 1757. To which I shall only add a few Particulars which were less known.

Joseph MᶜCormick at this Time Tutor to Young Mʳ Hepburn of Clarkington, and afterwards Principal of Sᵗ Andrews United Colleges, had enter'd on trials before the Presbytery of Dalkeith, and had two or three times attended the Tragedy of Douglas. This he told them himself, which threw them into a Dilemma, out of which they Did not know how to escape. To take no Notice of his having attended the Theatre, while they were prosecuting me, was a very Glaring Inconsistency. On the other hand, to send him out as a Probationer, with the Slur of an Ecclesiastical Censure on his Char was Injustice to the Young Man, and might Disoblige his Friends. So Reason'd the Jesuits of Dalkeith Presbytery. McCormick himself, shew'd them the way out of this Snare, into which their Zeal and Hypocrisy had Led them, after allowing them to flounce about in it for a Qr of an Hour (as he told me afterwards with Infinite Humour), for he then Represented, That his Pupil and He, having some time before Gone into their Lodgings in Edinr for the Remainder of the Season, he would be much oblig'd to the Presbytery of Dalkeith, if they would Transfer him to the Presbytery of Edinr to take the Remainder of his Trials. With this proposal, they very cheerfully clos'd, whilst McCormick Inwardly Laugh'd, (for he was a Laughing Philosopher) at their Proffligate Hypocrisy.*

* It is proper to Mention here that During the Course of this trial I Receiv'd Several Anonymous Letters, from a Person Deservedly high in Reputation in the Church, for Learning and Ability, and Liberality of Sentiment, the late Dr Robert Wallace, which Supported me in my Resolution, and Gave me the Soundest Advice with respect to the management of my Cause. I had Rec'd two of those Letters, before I knew from whence they came, when on Shewing them to my Father he knew the Hand, as the Dr and he had been at College together. This Circumstance prevented my Father from wavering to which he was Liable, and even Strengthen'd my own Mind.

It is Necessary likewise to advert here to the Conduct of Robert Dundas of Arniston, at that time Kings Advocate, as it accounts for that animosity, which arose against him among my Friends of the Moderate Party, and the Success of Certain Satirical Ballads and Pamphlets, which were publish'd some Years after. This was his Decided Opposition to the Tragedy of Douglas: which was perfectly known from his own Manner of Talking, Tho' more Cautious than that of his Minions, who Opend loud against Home and his Tragedy, and likewise from this Circumstance that Thos Turnbull his Minister, who took my Side in the Presbytery, Being influenc'd by his Brother in Law Dr Wallace, Fell ever after out of Favour at Arniston. And what was worse, Dr Wallace, who was of Ld Advocate's Political Party, Incur'd his Displeasure so much, that During the Remainder of his own Life, Geo. Wallace Advocate, who was under the Protection of the Family of Arniston, was totally Neglected. This piece of Injustice was not repaird till after his Death, when his Son Robert, of the most amiable and Liberal Mind, Gave him a Judges Place in the Commissariot of Edinr. It was farther prov'd by the unsuccessfull application of my Friend Mr Baron Grant, who was his Intimate Friend and Companion, to allay the Heat of the Presbytery of Dalkeith, and Induce them to withdraw their Prosecution, which a Nod from him would have Done.

This Conduct of Dundas, might in Part be Imputed to his want of Taste and Discernment in what Related to Belles Lettres, and to a certain Insolence of Temper which could endure no one that Did not bend to him, or to his Jealousy of Sir G. Elliot

Cuming and Webster and Hyndman, and a Fiery Man at Leith whose Name I forget, were the Committee who Drew up the Libel. Webster who had no Bowels, and who could Do Mischief with the Joy of an Ape, Suggested all the Circumstances of Aggravation, and was Quite Delighted when he Got his Colleagues of the Committee to Insert such Circumstances as my Eating and Drinking with Sarah Ward, and Taking my place in the Playhouse, by Turning Some Gentlemen out of their Seats and Committing a Riot, &c.

At a very full Meeting of my Friends in Boyds large Room in the Cannongate the Night before the Synod Met, I propos'd Dr Dick who had Recently been admitted a Minister in Edin^r for the Moderators Chair. I had prepar'd my Friends before hand for this proposal; and was Induc'd to Do it for Several Reasons. One was to exclude Robertson, whose Speaking would be of more Consequence if not in the Chair. Another was to shew my Friend Dick to the Rest, and to make them Confidential with him, and to fix so able an assistant in our Party. He was accordingly Elected without opposition, and perform'd his Duty with the utmost Spirit and Manhood. For besides preserving Gen! Good Order, he with uncommon Decision, and Readiness, Severely Rebuk'd Hyndman, when he was very offensive. The Lachité[1] of Hyndman's Mind, which was well known to Dick and me, made him Submit to this Rebuke from the Chair, Tho' in Reallity he was not out of Order. What a Pity it was that Robertson afterwards Lost this Man, in the Manner I shall afterwards Mention.

It was Remark'd that there were only 3 of Majority in the Synod for the Sentence which my friends had Devi[s]ed, assisted by the very Good Sense of Prof^r Robert Hamilton, and his Intricate and Embarrass'd Expression, which Conceald while it Palliated, and that two of those three, were John Home the author, and my Father.—But neither of their votes could have been rejected, and the Moderators Casting Vote would have been with us.

My Speech in my own Defence in the Synod which I Drew up rather in the form of a Remonstrance than an Argument, Leaving that for Robertson and my other Friends, made a very Good Impression on the Audience. John Dalrymple Junr of Cranstoun, was my advocate at the Bar and did Justice to the Cause he had voluntarily Undertaken, which while it serv'd me Effectually, Gave him the first opportunity he had of

---

and Andrew Pringle who were our Zealous Friends, or his Hatred to Ld Milton who so warmly patroniz'd John Home. 'Twas amusing to Observe During the Course of the Summer, when Wilkies Epigoniad appear'd, how Loud the Retainers of the House of Arniston were in its Praise, Saying they knew how to Distinguish between Good and Bad Poetry, and now they had Got something to Commend.

Displaying his Talents before a popular assembly. Robertsons was a Speech of Great Address, and had a Good Effect. But none was better than that of And.ᵂ Pringle Esq.ʳ The Sollicitor, who I think was the most Eloquent of all the Scottish Bar in my time. The Presbytery Thought fit to appeal. When it came to the Assembly, the Sentence of the Synod was ably Defended; and as a Proof that the Heat and Animosity Rais'd against the Tragedy of Douglas and its Supporters were artificial and Local, the Sentence of the Synod was affirmd by 117 to 39.—When it was over Primrose, one of my Warmest Opposers, turn'd to me, and Shaking Hands, I wish you Joy Said he of this sentence in your Favour, and if you hereafter chuse to Go to every Play that is acted, I shall take no Notice. Next Day on a proposal which was Seconded by Geo. Dempster my firm Friend, the Assembly Pass'd an Act Declaratory* Forbidding the Clergy to Countenance the Theatre. But Primrose was in the Right, For Manners are Stronger than Laws—and this Act which was made on Recent Provocation, was the only Act of the Church of Scotland against the Theatre, so was it totally Neglected. Altho' the Clergy in Edin.ʳ and its Neighbourhood had abstain'd from the Theatre, because it Gave Offence, yet the more Remote Clergymen when Occasionally in Town, had almost universally attended the Playhouse. And now that the Subject had been Sollemnly Discuss'd, and all men were convinc'd, that the violent proceedings they had witness'd were the Effects of Bigotry, or Jealousy, mixd with Party Spirit and Cabal, The More Distant Clergy Return'd to their usual amusement in the Theatre, when Occasionally in Town. It is Remarkable that in the year 1784, when the Great Actress M.ʳˢ Siddons 1.ˢᵗ appear'd in Edin.ʳ During the Sitting of the Gen.ˡ Assembly, That Court was Oblig'd to fix all its Important Business for the Alternate Days, when she Did not Act, as all the Younger Members Clergy as well as Layity took their Stations in the Theatre on Those Days by 3 in the afternoon. Doctors Robertson and Blair, tho' they Both visited this Great Actress in Private, often Regretted to me, that they had not siez'd the Opportunity which was Given them by her Superior Talents and unexceptionable Character, of Going Openly to the Theatre, which would have put an End to all future Animadversions on the Subject. This Conduct of theirs was keeping the Reserve of their own Imaginary Importance to the Last, and their Regreting it was very Just, for by that time they Got no Credit for their abstinence; and the Struggle between the Liberal, and Restraind and affected Manners of the Clergy, had been long at an End, by my having

* There is a Great Difference between such an Act, and a Law of the Church, for the Latter cannot pass till having been sent to all the presbyteries, it has been approv'd of by a Majority.

firmly Stood my Ground, and been so well Supported by so Great a Majority in the Church.*

One event was Curious in the Sequel. Mr John Home, who was the author of the Tragedy, and of all the Mischief Consequent upon it, while his Presbytery of Haddington had been from time to time Obstructed in their Designs, by the Good Management of Stedman, and Robertson, and Bannatyne, were now preparing in Earnest to Carry on a Prosecution against him, on the 7th of June that year, he Gave in to them a Demission of his Office, and he withdrew from the Church, without the least animadversion on his Conduct.† Which threw Compleat Ridicule on the Opposite Party, and made the Flame which had been rais'd against me appear Hypocritical and Odious to the Last Degree.

One of the chief Actors in this Farce, Suffer'd most for the Duplicity of his Conduct,‡ For he who was at the Head of the Moderate Party, through Jealousy or Bad Temper, Having with some of his Friends Headed the Party against the Tragedy of Douglas, His Followers in the Highlands and Remoter Parts, of the Moderate Party, were so much offended with his Hypocritical Conduct as they Call'd it, that they left him ever after, and Join'd with those whom he had taken so much pains to Disgrace, Whilst he and the other Old Leaders themselves United with their former Opponents. With respect to Webster, best known at that time by the Designation of Dr Bonum Magnum, his Proteus-like Character Seldom Lost by any Transaction, and in this Case, he was only Acting his Natural Part which was that of running Down all

---

* Of the Many Exertions I and my Friends have made for the Credit and Interest of the Clergy of the Church of Scotland, There was none more Meritorious or of Better Effects than this. The Laws of the Church were sufficiently Strict, to prevent Persons of Conduct realy Criminal from Entering into it: And it was of Great Importance to Discriminate the artificial virtues and vices, form'd by Ignorance and Superstition, from Those that are Real, Lest the Continuance of such a Bar should have Given Check to the Rising Liberality of the young Scholars, and prevented those of Better Birth, or more Ingen[i]ous Minds, from Entering into the Profession.

† Mr Home after the Great Success of his Tragedy of Douglas at Edin^r went to London Early in 1757, and had his Tragedy Acted in Covent Garden, for Garrick tho' now his Friend, could not possibly Let it be perform'd in his Theatre, after having pro[no]unc'd it unfit for the Stage, where it had Great Success. This Tragedy still Maintains its Ground, has been more frequently acted, and is more popular than any Tragedy in the English Language—[1]

‡ [Cuming.] Mr Alex^r Wedderburn, afterwards Ld Chancellor and Earl of Roslyn, Not having come Down time enough to Speak or Vote in the Cause, (by Design or not is more than I know) But appearing on the Day after took an opportunity to Give Peter Cuming a Very Compleat Dressing. Peter was Chaplain to Ld Grange for some years, before he was Settled at Kirknewton, and after my Father at Lochmabin—from whence he was brought to Edin^r.

Indecencies in Clergymen but those of the Table, and Doing Mischief like a Monkey for its own Satisfaction.

After John Home Resignd his Charge, he and Adam Ferguson Retir'd to a Lodging at Braid for 3 months to Study, where they were very Busy. During that time Mrs Kinloch of Gilmerton was Brought to Bed of her 8 Child, and Died immediatly after. This was a very Great Loss to her Family of 5 Sons, and 3 Daughters;* as her Being withdrawn from the Care of their Education, accounts Better for the Misconduct and Misery of four of her Sons, than the Gen! Belief of the Country That the House of Gilmerton could Never Thrive, after the Injustice Done to their Eldest Son, by Sir Francis and his [Wife] and their Son David, who was Involv'd in their Guilt, and was Made an Heir to the Estate Instead of his Brother. These Superstitious Notions however illfounded may sometimes, perhaps check the Doing of atrocious Deeds. But what shall we say when Sir Francis who succeeded his Father Sir Dav^d who Liv'd to 84, surviv'd him only a few Days, Tho' he was the most able, the most Ingenious, the most worthy and virtuous Young Man of the whole Country to which he belong'd, and Died by Fratricide,[1] a Crime rare every where, and almost unknown in this Country.

Home being very Busy with some of his Dramatick Works and not having Leisure to attend Sir Dav^d in his Affliction which was sincere, applied to me to make an excursion with him into the N. of England for a week or two, to amuse him. I consented, and when I went to Gilmerton by Concert, I found that the Bar! had Conjoin'd two other Gentlemen to the Party—my Friend Mr Baron Grant, and Mr Montgomery afterwards Chief Baron and Sir James, who was my Friend ever after. Those two Gentlemen were on Horseback, and Sir Dav^d and I in his Post-Chaise, a vehicle which had but Recently been brought into Scotland, as our Turnpike Roads, were but in their Infancy. We went no Farther than Sir John Halls at Dunglas the first Day; and as we pretended to be Enquiring into the State of Husbandry, we made very short Journeys, turning aside to See any thing Curious in the Mode of Improvement of Land that fell in our way, sometimes staying all night in Inns, and sometimes in Gentlemens Houses as they fell in our way: For Sir Dav^d was well known to many of the Northumbrians, for his Hospitality and Skill in Cattle. We went no farther than Newcastle, and its environs, and Return'd after a Fortnight's very agreable amusement. On this Expedition I made some very agreable Acquaintance, of which I afterwards availd myself: Ralph Carr an eminent Merchant still alive in Aug! 1804, and his Brother in Law Mr Withington, Stil'd the Honest Attorney

* No Greater Misfortune can befal any Family, when Children are in their Infancy, than the Loss of a Mother of Good Sense, and Dignity of Manners.

of the North, and his Son John, an accomplish'd Young Man who Died a few years ago and was the Representative of the antient Family of that Name.*

It was in the end of this Year that I was Introduc'd to Arch^d Duke of Argyle who usually past some Days at Brunstane Lord Milton's Seat, within two Miles of me, as he went to Inveraray and Returnd. It was on his way back to London that I was sent for one Sunday Morning, to come to Brunstane that day to Dine with the Duke. That I could not Do as I had to Do Duty at my own church in the afternoon, and Dinner in those Days was at two aclock. I went up in the Evening, when the Duke was taking his nap as usual in an elbow chair, with a Black Silk Cap over his Eyes. There was no Company but Lord and Lady Milton, Mr Fletcher and the young Ladies, with Wm Alstone, who was a Confidential and Political Secretary of Miltons.

After a Little I observ'd the Duke Lift up his Cap, and seeing a Stranger in the Room, he pull'd his Cap over his Eyes again, and Beckkon'd Miss Fletcher to him, who told him who I was. In a Little While he Got up, and advancing to me and taking me by the hand, said he was Glad to see me But that between Sleeping and Waking he had taken me for his Cousin the Earl of Home, who I still think you Resemble, but that could not be, for I know that he is at Gibraltar. When we Return'd to our Seats, Mally Fletcher, whisperd me that *my Bread was Baken*, for that Lord Home was one of his Greatest Favourites. This I laugh'd at, for the Old Gentleman had said that as an Apology, for his having Done what he might think not quite polite in calling Mally Fletcher to him, and not taking any Notice of me for a Minute or two afterwards. The Good Opinion of that Family was enough to Secure me a favourable Reception at first, and I knew he would not like me worse for having Stood a Battle with and Beat the H. Flyers of our Church whom he abhor'd. For he was not so accessible by Peter Cuming as Lord Milton was: whom he had tried to persuade, That his having Joind the Other Party, was out of tenderness to me, for it was the Intention of the High Flyers to Depose me, if he had not Moderated their Counsels. But I had a Friend behind the Curtain in his Daughter Miss Betty, whom he usd to take out in the Coach with him alone, to Settle his Mind, when he was in any Doubt or Perplexity, for like all other Ministers he was surrounded with Intrigue and Deceit. Ferguson was besides now come into Favour with him, for his Dignified and Sententious Manner of Talking,

---

* Some time this Summer after a Convivial Meeting Dr Wight and I were left alone for an hour or two with Alex^r Wedderburn, who open'd himself to us, as much as he was capable of Doing to any body, and the Impression he left corresponded with the Cha^r he had among his Intimates.[1]

had pleas'd him no Less than John Home's pleasantry, and unveild Flattery. Milton had a Mind sufficiently acute to Comprehend Ferguson's profound Speculations, Tho' his own Forte Did not ly in any kind of Philosophy, but the Knowledge of Men and the Management of them, while Ferguson was his admiring Scholar in Those Articles. He had been much Teaz'd about the Tragedy of Douglas, for Cuming had still access to him at Certain Hours, by the Political Backdoor from Gray's Close, and had alarm'd him much; Especially Immediatly after the Publication of my Pamphlet, *An Argument* &c., which had Irritated the Wild Brethren so much, said Peter, That he could not answer for what mischief might follow. When he had been by such means [kept in] a very Fretfull Humour, he came up into the Drawing Room, where Dav^d Hume was, with John and Ferguson and myself, on Davids saying something with his usual Good Humour to smooth his wrinkly Brow, Milton Turn'd to him with Great Asperity and said That he had better hold his Peace on the Subject for it was owing to him and keeping Company with him that such a clamour was rais'd. David made no Reply, but soon after took his Hat and Cane, and Left the Room, never more to Enter the House again. Which he never did, tho much pains was [taken] afterwards, for Milton soon repented. And David would have Return'd, But Betty Fletcher Oppos'd it, rather foregoing his Company at their House, than Suffer him to Degrade himself. Such was the Generous Spirit of that young Lady. Had it not been for Ferguson and her, John Home and I would have been expel'd also.

[1758]

Early in the Year 1758 my Favourite in the House of Brunstane chang'd her Name for on the 6th of February She was Married to Capt John Wedderburn of Gossford, much to the Satisfaction of Ld Milton and all her Friends, as he was a Man of superior character, had then a Good Fortune, and the Prospect of a Better, which was fulfill'd not long afterwards, when he Succeeded to the Title and Estate of Pitferran by the Name of Sir John Halket. As I was frequently at Brunstane about this time, I became the Confident of Both the Parties: and the Bride was Desirous to have me to Tie the Nuptial Knot. [But] this faild thro' Ld Miltons Love of Order, which made him employ the Parish Minister Bennet of Duddingston. This she wrote me with much Regret on the Morning of her Marriage, But added as on that Day, she would become Mistress of a House of her own, she Insisted that I should meet her there, and Receive her when she Enter'd the House of Gosford.[1]

About the end of Feby or the beginning of March this year, I went to London with my Eldest Sister Margaret, to Get her Married with Dr Thos Dickson M.D.—(This Match I would have Oppos'd because there was a Great Inequality of Mind and Manners between the Parties. But having talk'd to my Sister with serious anxiety, I found she was unalterably Engag'd, and then Did my best to Reconcile her Father and Mother and her Aunt Mrs Bell to the Marriage, who were all of them averse to it.) My Sister was truly a very Superior Woman, as I have formerly Mention'd, and having been frequently Sought in Marriage, and particularly by two Wealthy Men of Narrow Education and Vulgar Manners, and having Rec'd something like persecution from her Uncle and Aunt for having Refus'd them, she took the Resolution of Engaging herself with Dr Dickson, That she might be no more Solicited on that Hand.[1]

My Sister came to my Fathers in the beginning of Feb^ry and I made Ready to Go with her to London at the time appointed.—We set out about the End of Feb^ry and it is to be noted that we could get no Four Wheel'd Chaise till we Come to Durham, Those Conveyances being then only in their Infancy, the 2 Wheel'd Close Chaise, which had been us'd for some time, and was Call'd an Italian Chaise, having been found very Inconvenient. Turnpike Roads were only in their commencement in the North. Dr Dickson with a Friend met us at Stilton. We arriv'd safe at my Aunt Lyon's in New Bond Street, She Being then alive as well as her Sister Mrs Paterson. To the proper Celebration of our Marriage there were 3 things wanting: a Licence, a Parson, and a Best-Maid. For the Last, The Honble Miss Nelly Murray, Ld Elibanks Sister afterwards Lady Stuart, and still alive in Sepr 1804, offer'd her services, which Did us Honour, and pleas'd my two Aunts very much especially Mrs Lyon, whose Head was constantly Swimming with Vanity, which even her uncommon Misfortunes after having fulfill'd the utmost Wish of Ambition had not Cur'd. A License was easily bought at Drs Commons, and Dr John Blair, afterwards a Prebend of Westminster, my particular Friend, was easily prevaild with to Secure the Use of a Church and Perform the Ceremony.

This Business being put Successfully over in a few Days, and having Seen My Sister and her Husband into Lodging in the City, till their House was Ready, I took up my abode at my Aunts and Occasionally at John Home's Lodging in S. Audly Street, which he had taken to be near Ld Bute who had become his Great Friend and Patron, Having Introduc'd him to the Prince of Wales, who had Settled on him a Pension of £100 per Annum.

Dr Robertson having Come to London at this time to offer his History

Hugh Blair by Sir Henry Raeburn

Archibald, third Duke of Argyll by Allan Ramsay

of Scotland to Sale, where he had never been before, we went to *See the Lions* together, and had for most part the same acquaintance. Dr Wm Pitcairn a very Respectable Physician in the City, and a Great Friend of Dr Dicksons, was a Cousin of Dr Robertsons whose Mother was a Pitcairn. We became very Intimate with him. Drs Armstrong and Orme were also of their Society. Pitcairn was a very Handsome Man a little Turn'd of 50, of a very Gentlemanlike Address. When he Settled first in London he was Patronis'd by an Alderman Behn, who Being a Jacobite, and not Doubting that Pitcairn was of the Same Side as he had Travel'd with Duke Hamilton, he set him up as a Candidate for Bartholomew's Hospital. During the Canvas, the Alderman came to the D^r and ask'd him with Impatient Heat, if it was true that he was the Son of a Presbyterian Minister in Scotland, which Pitcairn not being able to Deny, the other Conjur'd him, to Conceal that Circumstance like Murder, otherwise it would Infallibly Blow them up. He was Elected Physician to that Hospital, and soon Rose in to Great Business in the City.

Dr Pitcairn was a Batchelor and liv'd Handsomly, But chiefly Entertaind young Scotch Physicians who had no Establishment. Of Those Drs Armstrong and Dickson were much with him. As our Connexions Drew Robertson and me frequently to the City, before my Sisters House was Ready, by Earnest Invitation we both took up our Lodging at his House. We never Saw our Landlord in the Morning, for he went to the Hospital before 8 a clock: But his Housekeeper had orders to ask us at Breakfast, If we intended to Dine there, and to tell us whom her Master expected. The D^r always Return'd from his round of visits before Three, which was his Hour of Dinner, and quite Happy if he found us there. Exactly at 5 his Chariot came to the Door to Carry him out on his afternoon visits. We sate as long as we lik'd at Table and Drunk excellent Claret. He Return'd soon after 8 a clock. If he found his Company still together, which was sometimes the case, he was highly pleas'd. He immediatly enter'd into our Humour, ate a Bit of Cold Meat, and Drank a little Wine, and went to bed before ten a clock. This was a very uncommon Strain of Hospitality, which I am Glad to Record, on Repeated Tryals, Never was exhausted. He liv'd on in the same Manner till 1782, when he was past 80, and when I was in London for the last time. He was then perfectly Entire and made his Morning tour on Foot. I Din'd once with him at that Period in his own House with a large Company of Ladies and Gentlemen, and at Dr Arnt. Hamilton's his Cousin of St Martin's church, on both of which Occasions he was Remarkably Gay. He Surviv'd for a Year or two Longer. Dr David Pitcairn the Son of his Brother the Major, who was killd early in the American Rebellion, was Heir, both of his Fortune and Professional Merit.

With Robertson and Home in London I pass'd the time very agreably. For tho' Home was now entirely at the Command of Ld Bute, whose Nod made him Break every Engagement, for it was not Given above an Hour or two before Dinner, Yet as he was sometimes at Liberty, when the Noble Lord was to Dine Abroad, Like a Horse Loosen'd from his Stake he was more Sportfull than usual. We had Sir Dav.^d Kinloch likewise who had come to Consult Physicians, and Dr Charles Congalton who was his attendant. With them we met often at the British.¹ Charles was my old Companion and a more Naive and Ingen[u]ous Soul never was Born. I said to him one day, Charly, How Do [you] like the English, Now that you have Seen them twice for two or three months. I cannot answer your Question replied he, for I am not acquainted with any of them. What, not acquainted, said I? Yes says he, I have seen half a Dozen of them Calling on Sir David, but I never Enter into Conversation with the John Bulls, for to tell you the truth, I Don't yet well understand what they say.

I shall here Mention one anecdote, which struck me as a proof of wonderfull Carelessness of Physicians. Supping one night with Duncan Forbes, with Sir David, Lord Elliock and sundry Physicians, while four of us were playing at whist, Ld Elliock took up a Book, and after Reading a while, Call'd out, Sir David here is your Case and a perfect Cure for it, that I find in this Book. He then read an account of the Great Effect of the Waters of Barege in the South of France for such Complaints as the Baronet Labour'd under. Have you heard of this before, Sir David? No, never, answerd he. Is it new to the Faculty, said he to Armstrong who was sitting near him. No, Reply'd the Crusty Doctor, but we never thought of Prescribing it, as we knew That he was such a Coward that he would rather be Damn'd by a Fistula, than Cross the Channell in a Packet Boat, especially in time of a French War. Sir David, Having his Pride irritated by this attack, Did Go to Barege, and Compleated a Cure which had been made by Dr Ward.

The 1st Wm Pitt had at this time Risen to the Zenith of his Glory, when Robertson and I after frequent attemp[t]s to hear him Speak, when there was nothing passing in the House that Call'd him, we at last heard a Debate on the Habeas Corpus Act, which Pitt had new model'd in order to Throw a Slur on Lord Mansfield, who had taken some Liberties it was alledg'd with that Law which made him unpopular. We accordingly took our places in the Gallery, and for the 1st 3 Hours were much Dispos'd to Sleep, by the Dull Tedious Speeches of 2 or 3 Lawyers till at Last the Attorney Gen! afterwards Lord Camden rose and Spoke with Clearness, Argument and Eloquence. He was answer'd ably by Mr York Soll.^r Gen!. Dr Hay the Kings Adv. in Doctors Commons spake next with a Clea[r]ness, a Force and Brevity, which pleas'd us much. At Length Mr Pitt rose, and with that commanding Eloquence in which he excell'd he Spake for half an hour with an overpowering Force of persuasion, more than the clear Conviction of Argument. He was Oppos'd by Several Speakers to none of whom he vouchsafd to make an answer, But to James Oswald of Dunnikier, who was a very able man, tho' not an Eloquent Speaker. With all our Admiration of Pitts Eloquence which was surely of the highest Order Robertson and I felt the same S[en]timent which was a Desire to Resist a Tyrant, who like a Domineering Schoolemaster kept his Boys in Order by raising their Fears without wasting Argument upon them. This Haughty Manner, is Necessary perhaps in every Leader of the House of Commons; . . . Civil and Condescending, he soon loses his authority and is trampled upon. Is this common to all pol[itical] assemblies? or is it only a part of the character of the English, in all ordinary political affairs, till they are heated by faction or alarm'd by Danger, to Yield to the Statesman who is most assuming?

Sir Gilbert Elliot of Minto was at this time One of the Lords of the admiralty, and we were frequently with him. He was a very accomplish'd and sensible man, and John Home had not found him a Cold Friend as he was supos'd to be, for by his means chiefly he had been put under the Protection of Ld But[e], a Favour which John Did not coldly return; for on the accession of the prince of Wales, Home who was then in full confidence with his Lordship Recommended the Bar^t most effectually to him, a clear proof of which I saw on a Letter from Ld Bute to Home.

Dr John Blair who on account of a Certain Petulant and Wrangling Humour was Dislik'd by many People, particularly by Smollet, in spite of Bob Smiths Intimacy with both, had been put about the Duke of York as his Math. Teacher and was afterwards his Secretary, had been also Recommended to that Situation by Sir G. Elliot thro' Home, and was not ungratefull. Blair was a Good Natur'd pleasant Fellow, and very agreable to every Body who could Bear his Flippancy of Speech. He was indeed one of the Most Friendly Men in the World, as he Shewd in Many Instances, from purchasing a pair of Shoes or Stockings, for any of his Old Companions, or pro[v]iding them a Settlement for Life. He Got to be a Prebendary in Westminster by the Interest of the Duke of York and had his Royal Highness Liv'd, would have been promoted to the Bench of Bishops. He was Senior to J. Home and me, but we were well acquainted at College. He had been bred to Our Church of which he was only a Probationer. He went only to see London, but prolongd his visit till he had spent his Patrimony of £300, and then was put on his Shifts.

But by his Talents and Alacrity Got the Length he Did. He Died of the Influenza in 1782.

John Douglas who has for some time been Bishop of Salisbury and who is one of the most able and Learned Men on that Bench, Had at this time but small preferment. He had been Tutor to Lord Pulteney, and was at this time secretary to Ld Bath and Liv'd with him, by which means he had acquir'd a very exact knowledge of the Court, as well as of Both Houses of Parliament, and all their Connexions. I became acquainted with him at this time, and preserv'd my Conexion with him which I valued much by Sundry Meetings, and frequent Correspondence. He is still Living tho' Two Years older than me, and much weaken'd by the Gout. His Sister Mrs Anderson, who at this time kept the British Coffee House, was like her Brother, a person of Superior Character.

Robertson had never seen Smollet, and was very Desirous of his Acquaintance. By this time the D^r had retir'd to Chelsea, and came Seldom to Town. Home and I however found that he came once a Week to Forrests Coffee House,[1] and sometimes Din'd there; so we manag'd an Appointment with him, on his Day when he agreed to Dine with us. He was now become a Great Man, and Being much of a Humourist was not to be put out of his way. Home and Robertson and Smith and I met him there, when he had Several of his Minions about him, to whom he prescrib'd tasks of Translation, Compilation or Abridgment, which after he had seen, he Recommended to the Booksellers. We Din'd together and Smollet was very Brilliant. Having to stay all night that we might spend the evening together, he only beg'd Leave to withdraw for an Hour that he might Give audience to his Mirmydons; we Insisted that if his Business [would admit] it should be in the Room where we sate. The Doctor agreed and the Authors were introduc'd to the N? of five I think, most of whom were soon Dismiss'd. He kept two however to Supper, whispering to us that he Believ'd They would amuse us, which They according[ly] Did, for they were Curious Characters.

We past a very pleasant and Joyfull Evening. When we Broke up Robertson exprest Great Surprize at the polish'd and agreable Manners and the Great Urbanity of his Conversation. He had Imagin'd that a Mans Manner must bear a Likeness to his Books; and as Smollet had Describ'd so well the Characters of Ruffians and Proffligates, that he must of Coarse Resemble them. This was not the first Instance we had of the Rawness in Respect of the World, that still Blunted our Sagacious Friends Observations.

As Ferguson had one Day in the week when he could be in Town we establish'd a club at a Coffee House in Saville Row or Sackvill Street, where we could meet him at Dinner, which we Did every Wednesday at 3 aclock. There were J. Home and Robertson and Wedderburn and Jack Dalrymple and Bob Adams, Ferguson and myself. Wedderburn brought with him an attorney of the Name of Dagg, a little odd looking Silent Fellow to be sure, whom none of us had ever seen before, and about whom Wedderburn had not Condescended to explain himself. Somebody was appointed to talk to him, and to express the uneasiness of the Club at his bringing an utter Stranger among them. His answer was that Dagg was a very important Friend of his, who was extremely Desirous to meet that Company, and that he would answer for his Silence and Discretion. He added that he pray'd the club to admit him, for he Learn'd more from him of the Forms of English Law, in his Walk from and Return to the Temple, than he could do by a Weeks Reading. This excuse was admitted, tho' some of us thought it a Lame One, and Smeld of an assum'd Superiority that we Did not admit of. As Ferguson Rode back to Harrow, we always parted between 5 and 6 a clock, and it will hardly be now believ'd that our Reckoning never exceeded 5/- apiece. We had a very Good Dinner, and plenty of Punch &c. tho no Claret for that Sum.

Having met we Generally went that night to Drury Lane Theatre, Garrick Being in Town now, who had been absent when I was formerly in London. I had frequent opportunities of Being in Company with [th]is Celebrated Actor, of whom Mr Home was now in Full possession, Tho' he had rejected his Tragedy of Douglas [as] totally unfit for the Stage. I am affraid it was not his own more mature Judgment that brought him Round, but his Idolatry to the Rising Sun, For he had Observ'd what a Hold Home had Got of Lord Bute, and by his Means of the Prince of Wales. As Garricks Vanity and Interestedness had made him Digest the Mortification, of Seeing Douglas already become the most Popular play on the Stage, so John Homes Facility, and the Hopes of Getting him to play in his Future Tragedies, made him forgive Garricks former want of Taste and Judgment, and they were now become the Greatest Friends in the World. If anything had been wanting to Compleat Garricks Conquest of Home, it was making Choice of him, as his 2d in a Quarrel he had with Calcraft (for John was very Heroick) which never came to a Duel, as well as Several other Quarrels of the same Kind, and with the same issue, in which John was chosen Second.

Garrick tho' not of an understanding of the First, nor of the highest Cultivated Mind, had Great Vivacity and Quickness and was very Entertaining Company. Tho' Vanity was his Prominent Feature, and a Troublesome and Watchfull Jealousy the Constant Visible Guard of his Reputation to a Ridiculous Degree; Yet his Desire to Oblige, his Want of Arrogance, and the Delicacy of his Mimickry, made him very agreable. He had no affected Reserve, but on the least Hint would Start up at any time, and Give the Company one of his best Speeches. As Garrick had been in Dublin when I was in London in 1746, I assiduously attended him at this time, and Saw him in all his Principal parts both in Tragedy and Commedy. He us'd to say himself that he was more at home in Comedy than in Tragedy, and I was of his Opinion. I thought I could conceive something more Perfect in Tragedy, But in Comedy he compleatly filld up my Ideas of Perfection. There may be a Deception in this for every well Educated person, has form'd to himself some Idea of the characters both in antient and modern Tragedy, and if the Actor falls short of that, he is thought to be Deficient in Judgment. Whereas Comedy Being an Imitation of Living Manners as they Rise[1] in Succession among Inferior Orders of Men, The Spectator can have formd no Rule or Standard of Judgment previous to the Representation, But must accept of the Picture the Actor Gives him, and must approve of it, if it is Lively tho' it should not be true.

Garrick was so friendly to John Home, that he Gave a Dinner to his Friends and Companions, at his House at Hampton, which he Did but Selldom. He had told us to bring Golph Clubs and Balls, that we might play at that Game on Molesly Hurst. We accordingly Set out in Good time, 6 of us in a Landaw; and as we past thro' Kensington the Coldstream Reg.t were changing Guard, and Seeing our Clubs Gave us 3 cheers in Honour of a Diversion peculiar to Scotland.[2] So much Does the Remembrance of ones Native Country Dilate the Heart, when one has been sometime absent. The same Sentiment, made us open our purses and Give our Countrymen wherewithal to Drink the Land of Cakes.[3] Garrick met us by the way, so Impatient he seem'd to be for his Company. There were John Home, and Robertson, and Wedderburn, and Robert and James Adam, and Dav.d Wedderburn &c.*

Immediatly after we arriv'd we cross'd the River to the Golphing Ground which was very Good. None of the Company could play but J. Home and myself and Parson Black from Aberdeen, who Being chaplain to a Reg.t During some of the Duke of Cumberlands Campaigns, had been pointed out to his Royal Highness as a proper person to Teach him the Game of Chess. The Duke was such an apt Scholar that he never lost a Game after the First Day; and he Recompens'd him for Having Beat him so Cruelly by procuring for him the Living of Hampton, which is a Good One. We Return'd and Din'd sumptuously, and M.rs Garrick

* Coll.! Dav.d Wedderburn, who was kill'd when Commander of the army in Bombay in [1773], was held by his Companions to be in evry respect as cliver and able a Man as his Elder Brother the Chancellor, with a much more Gay, Popular and Social Temper.

the only Lady, now Grown Fat, tho' still very Lively, Being a Woman of uncommon Good Sense, and now Mistress of English, was in all respects most agreable Company. She Did not Seem at all to Recognise me, which was no wonder, at the End of 12 years, Having Thrown away my Bag-Wig and Sword and appearing in my own Grisly Hairs, and in Parsons clothes. Nor was I Likely to Remind her of her former state.[1]

Garrick had built an Handsome Temple with a Statue of Shakespear in it, in his Lower Garden on the Banks of the Thames, which [was] Separated from the upper one by a High Road, under which there was an arch-way which united the two Gardens. Garrick in Compliment to Home, Had order'd the wine to be Carried to this Temple, where we were to Drink it under the Shade of the Copy of that Statue, to which Home had addrest his Pathetick Verses, on the Rejection of his Play. The Poet and the Actor were Equally Gay and wellpleased with Each Other on this Occasion, with much respect on the one hand, and a Total Oblivion of animosity on the other. For Vanity is a Passion that is Easy to be Intreated, and unites freely with all the Best affections. Having Observ'd a Green Mount in the Garden opposite the Arch-Way, I said to our Landlord, that while the Servants were preparing the Collation in the Temple I would Surprise him with a Stroke at the Golph, as I should Drive a Ball thro' his Archway into the Thames, once in three Strokes. I had measurd the Distance with my Eye in walking about the Garden, and accordingly at the 2ᵈ Stroke made the Ball alight in the Mouth of the Gateway, and Roll Down the Green Slope into the River. This was so Dextrous that he was quite Surpris'd, and beg'd the Club of me, by which Such a Feat had been performd. We past a very agreable afternoon, and it is hard to Say, which were Happier, The Landlord and Landlady, or the Guests.

There was a Club in London where Robertson and I never faild to attend as we were adopted Members while [we] Staid in [Town]. It was held once a week in the British Coffee House, at 8 in the evening. The Members were Scotch Physicians from the City and Court End of the Town. Of the first set were Pitcairn, Armstrong, Orme, Dickson; of the 2ᵈ were [William] Hunter, Clephan, Mʳ Graham of Pall-Mall &c.—all of them very agreable Men. Clephan especially, was one of the most Sensible, Learned and Judicious Men I ever knew, an admirable classical Scholar and a Fine Historian. He often Led the Conversation, but it was with an Air of Modesty and Deference to the Company which added to the Weight of all he Said. Hunter was Gay and Lively to the Last Degree, and often Came into us at 9 aclock, Fatigued and Jaded. He had had no Dinner, but Sup'd on a Couple of Eggs, and Drank his Glass of Claret, for tho' we were a Punch Club, we allowd him a Bottle of what he lik'd best. He repaid us with the Brilliancy of his Conversation. His Toast was, may no English Nobleman Venture out of the World without a Scottish Physician as I am sure there are none who Venture in. He was a Famous Lecturer in Anatomy. Robertson and I exprest a wish to be admitted one Day. He appointed us a Day, and Gave us one of the Most Elegant, Clear, and Brilliant Lectures on the Eye, that any of us had ever heard. One Instance I must Set Down of the Fallacy of Medical Prediction. It was this. Dr Hunter by his Attendance on Lady Ester Pitt, had frequent Opportunities of Seeing the Great Orator when he was ill of the Gout, and thought so ill of his Constitution, that he Said more than once to us, with Deep Regret, That he did not think the Great Man's Life worth two Years Purchase. And yet Mr Pitt Liv'd for 20 Years, for he Did not Give way to Fate till 1778.

As soon as my Sister Got into her House in a Court in Aldermanbury, Dr Dickson and She Gave a Dinner to my Friends, with two or 3 of his. There were Doctors Pitcairn, Armstrong, Smollet, and Orme, together with Dr Robertson and John Blair, Home and myself. We past an exceedingly pleasant Day, altho' Smollet had Given Armstrong a Staggering Blow at the Beginning of Dinner, by asking him some Questions about his Nose which was still patch'd on account of his having Run it thro' the Side Glass of his Chariot when Somebody come up to Speak to him. Armstrong was naturally Glumphy, and this I was affraid would have Silenc'd him all Day. But he knew that Smollet Lov'd and Respected him, and soon Recover'd his Good Humour and became Brilliant. Had not Smollet Call'd him Familiarly John, soon after his Joke on his Nose, he might have been Silenc'd for the Day. My Sister, who had one Lady with her, one of Pitcairns nieces I believe, was happy and agreable, and highly pleasing to her Guests, who Confess'd they had Seldom Seen such a Superior Woman.

There was a Friend of Dickson's, a Mr Jackson a Dumfries Man, and an Irish Factor[1] as they are Call'd, who was a Great Humourist, who tho' he had no Carriage, kept 6 Hunting Horses. This Man offer'd to mount us on his Horses and Go with us to Windsor. After a Breakfast Dinner at his Partners   we Set out on the 16th Day of April, the warmest that had been that Season. As the Great Road was very Dissagreable, Jackson who knew the environs of London better than Most People as he belong'd to a Hunt, took us thro' Green Lanes as soon as he Could and Giving us a little Wine and Water when he pleas'd, which was he Said whenever he came to Good Port, he Landed us at Staines Bridge in a very Good Inn across the Bridge. His Servant who rode an unruly Horse, had been thrown from him half an Hour before we Reachd Stains. He was very much Hurt about the Head, and with Difficulty we brought him along at a slow pace. When we arriv'd Jackson Sent immediatly for the Nearest Surgeon, who was a Mr Green—This Man examin'd the Ser^t and found he was not Dangerously Hurt, and Jackson invited [him] to Stay Supper, which he Did, and turn'd out a very Sensible Conversable Man. He Spoke English so well that [we] could not have Detected him to be a Scotch Man, far Less an Aberdeens Man which he was. But he had Gone very Young into the Navy as Surgeons Mate, and had entirely lost his Mothers Tongue. Almost the only Instance I ever knew of any one from that Shire. There was a Poor Scotch Presbyterian who had a very Small Living. Jackson had a small present of 2 Guineas to Give him, for the Humourist was not ungenerous. He sent for him in the Morning and promisd him a Sermon in his Meeting House for it was Sunday, and kept him [to] breakfast. I had been prepar'd to Do this Duty, For Jackson and I slept in the same Room, and he had Requested it as a Favour, as he Said the Meeting and the Audience were very poor Indeed. I was Drest and went down to Breakfast and Introduc'd to Mr Colstream. Soon afterwards came Robertson undrest and with his night cap on, and Being introduc'd to Coldstream, took no farther notice of him (not his usual Manner) and Breakfasted in Silence. When the Minister took his Leave, he call'd Jackson aside, and Said he hop'd he Rememberd he never Employ'd any of the People Call'd Methodists. This was Resolute in a Man who had a Wife and 4 Children, and only £20-a year, to a Gentleman who just made him a Present of 2 Guineas. Jackson assurd him that none of us were Methodists, but that I was the person he had engag'd to preach. I made Robertson's being Taken for a Methodist a Lasting Joke against [him].

We went to the Meeting House at the Hour of Eleven, the Entry to which was over a pretty Large Dunghill. Altho' the Congregation was Reinforc'd by 2 Officers of the Gray Dragoons, and by a Corporal and an officers Man, with Jackson's Man with his Head Bound up, with the D^r and Jackson and Coldstream and his Wife, they amounted only to 23. There were two Brother Scotchmen, Clothiers, who were there, who Invited us to Dinner. We repaird to them at one a clock, and after walking round their Garden, and Being much Delighted with two Swans Swimming in the Thames whom they had attach'd to them by kindness, we Sate Down to an excellent Citizenlike Dinner, and Drank some excellent Port-wine. Robertson and I bespoke a Piece of Parson's Gray Cloth of their Making, which they Sent to Scotland before us and which Turn'd out the best we ever had. We Divided it among our Friends. Before 5 a clock we mounted our Horses, by Orders of our Conductor, and Rode to Windsor Forrest; Where in Spite of the Warm Day before, we found the Frost hard enough to Bear our Horses. We Return'd without Going into Windsor. Next Day we went there time enough to See the Castle and all its Curiosities, and to Go Down to Eton. After which we Din'd at an Inn, and Rode back to Stains making a circuit round the Great Park. Much to our Satisfaction we found Dr Green waiting us, whom Jackson had appointed to meet us.

Jackson wish'd us to take a circuitous Ride, and see every place down the Thames to London. But as we were engag'd with a Party of Friends to Dine at Billingsgate on Fish of the Season, we took Leave of Mr Jackson, and left him to come at his Leisure, while we made the best of our Way Down the Thames, and Halted only at Richmond where Robertson had never been.

We arriv'd in time to Meet our Friends at the Gun, where Dr Dickson had provided a Choice Dinner of all the Varieties of Fish then in Season, at the Moderate Price of 25/– one Crown of which was paid for Smelts. We were a Company of 15 or 16, whose Names I can't exactly Remember; But when I say that there were Sir Dav^d Kinloch, James Veitch (Elliock), Sir Robert Keith, then only a Capt. in the Scotch Dutch, Robertson, Home &c. I need not say that we were Gay and Jovial. An Accident Contributed not a little to our Mirth. Charles Congalton who happen'd to sit next to Sir Dav^d Our Preses,[1] it was observ'd never Filld above a Thimblefull in his Glass, when being ask'd the Reason, Said he could [not] Drink any of their London Port, There was such a *Drawing togetherness* in it. Ring the Bell Charly, Said our Pr., and we [will] Learn if we can't Get a Bottle of Claret for you. The Bell was rung, The Claret came and was Pronounc'd very Good by the Bar^t and his Doctor. The whole Company soon Join'd in that Liquor without which no Scotch Gentleman in those Days could be exhilarated.[2] Bob Keith Sung all his Ludicrous Songs, and Repeated all his Comick Verses, and Gave us a foretaste of that Delightfull Company which he continu'd to be to the End of [his] Days. His Cousin Charles Dalrymple was only behind him, in Humorous Description, and naive Remark, as much only as he was in Age and the Habits of Company. Our Reckoning by this means however turnd out instead of 5/6 as Dickson had Suppos'd, to be 3 times that sum. The Bar^t and D^r were to set out in a few Days for France on their Way to Barege.

As I had been Introduc'd to the Duke of Argyle in the Autumn before in Scotland, I went sometimes to his evening parties which were very pleasant. He Let in Certain Friends every night about 7 a clock, when after Tea and Coffee there were parties at sixpenny Whist, his Grace never playing Higher. About 9 there was a Side Board of Cold Victuals and Wine, to which every Body resorted in their Turns. There was Seldom any Drinking, never indeed but when some of his Favourite

Young Men came in, such as Alex^{r} Ld Eglinton, Wm Lord Home &c., When the Old Gentleman would Rouse himself, and Call for Burgundy and Champagne, and prolong the Feast to a late Hour. In General the Company parted at Eleven. There could not be a more Rational Way of passing the evening, for the Duke had a Wide Range of Knowledge and was very open and Communicative.

The Right Honble Charles Townshend my Old Friend, had Married Lady Dalkeith the Duke of Buccleuch's Mother.—Home who was become Intimate with him, took me there one Morning, after having told him I was in Town and Intended to Call. He Rec'd [me] with Open Arms, and was perfectly familiar. But not a hint of having seen me before. He held the same Demeanour to Jack Campbell, Ld Stonefield, who had Married one of Ld Bute's Sisters—and in Spite of our Intimacy afterwards in Scotland, he never made the most Distant Allusion to any thing that had happen'd at Leyden. The Duke of B[uccleuch] and his Brother Campbell Scott, were in town for the Easter Holidays. Mr Scott was much Handsomer and more Foreward than the Duke, who was on a Table in this Room where there were some Books. The young Duke then not 12 years of Age, was turning over the Leaves of a Book. Come along Duke, Says Charles, I see what you would be at, Silent as you are, Shew the Gentleman that Dedication you are so Fond of. The [Duke] Slipt down the Book on the Table, and Blush'd to the Eyes, Retiring a Step or two from it. I took up the Book, and soon [Saw] it was Barclay the Schoolmaster's Latin Grammar, which he had Dedicated to his Patron. The Duke, Says I, The Duke need not be Asham'd of this Dedication, for the author of it is one of the best Schoolmasters and Gramarians of any in Scotland, and has brought the School at Dalkeith to its former Name and Lustre. This Reassurd the Young Man, and he Smil'd with some Satisfaction. Little did I think at that time, that I should live to See his Grace the Most Respected, and the Most Deservedly Popular of any Nobleman in Scotland. A Few Days after this, we Din'd with Mr T. and the Countess and one or two Gentlemen, but the Boys had Return'd to School.

The Clergy of Scotland Being under Apprehensions that the Window Tax would be extended to them, had Given me in charge to State our Case to some of the Ministers, and try to make an Impression in our Favour. Sir Gilbert Elliot Listen'd to me and was friendly. Marchmont pretended not to understand my Statement, and was Dry. But the only Man who really understood the Business, and seem'd ready to Enter into it with Zeal, was Jeremiah Dyson, who having been a Dissenter and 2 years at the University of Edin^{r}, and withall very acute, perfectly comprehended my Arg^{t} and was willing to assist in procuring an exemption. Without Robert Dundas, Then L⁴ advocate, nothing however Could be Done. I waited on him, and was Rec'd in his usual way, with Frankness and Familiarity Enough, but Did not think he Could Do any thing, But Deferr'd Saying much about it till some Future Day, when he would have some friends with me to Dinner, and talk over the affair. This Cold or rather Haughty Reception, added to some very Slighting, or Calumnious Sayings of his both about Robertson and me provok'd us not a little, and Reviv'd the Resentment we felt at his unhandsome Behaviour about the Tragedy of Douglas.

Our time Drew near for Returning, which we were to Do on Horse Back, and with that we set about furnishing ourselves with Horses. Home had his Piercy [in] Town, and Jˢ Adam (who was to be our Companion) had one also, so that Robertson and I were only to be provided, which we Did without Loss of time. We had some Inclination to be Introduc'd to Lord Bute, which John promis'd to Do, and for Robert Adam also, who Could Derive more Benefit from it than any of us. Robert had been 3 Years in Italy and with a first Rate Genius for his Profession, had Seen and Studied every thing, and was in the highest Esteem among forreign Artists. From the time of his Return viz. in Febʸ or March 1758 may be Dated a very Remarkable Emprovement in Building and Furnishing, and even Stone Ware in London and every part of England. As John put off the time of our Introduction to his Great Man, we Yielded to a Request of our Friend Sir David Kinloch to accompany him on a Jaunt he wish'd to make to Portsmouth. Home had Signified his Design to L⁴ Bute, who had agreed to his Absence for a few Days. And having Obtain a Letter from Sir Gilbert Elliot, then a L⁴ of Admiralty, to Lieut. Brett Clerk of the Cheque[1] at Portsmouth, we Set out, The Barᵗ and his Doctor in a Chaise, and we three on Horseback. As it was towards the end of April and the Weather Good, we had a very agreable Journey. We were much pleas'd with the Diversified Beauty of the Country tho' not a little Surpris'd with the Great Extent of uncultivated Heath which we went through. We View'd with much pleasure and exultation the Solid Foundation of the Naval Glory of Great Brittain in the amazing Extent and Richness of the Dockyards and Warehouses &c. and [in] the Grandeur of her Fleet in the Harbour and in the Downs. It appeard a New World to us, and our Wonder had not Ceas'd During all the four Days we Remain'd there. We had Good Mutton and Good Wine (Claret) at the Inn, and above all an additional Companion, Mʳ Richard Oswald, he who had so much Hand in the Peace of Paris long after, who was a Man of Great Knowledge and ready Conversation. There was a fine Fleet of 10 Ships of the Line in the Downs, with the Royal George at their Head all Ready for se[a], and one of our Great Objects was to Get on Board that Ship, which was always kept in the Highest Order for the admittance of Visitors. This Short Voyage was propos'd every night, but was put off Daily, as a Land Wind came on soon after Breakfast. As we were only to stay one Day Longer, Congalton and I in Despair, went in the Evening to Lieut. Brett, and Stated our Case to him. He said there was but one Remedy, which was for him to ask Sir Dav^d and us all to Breakfast Next Morning at 8, That his Dock Yard Sloop in which he could sail to America should be at hand and Ready at 9, and that we might Get to the Royal George not above 3 Miles off, before the Mackrell Breeze Sprung up.

This plan was accordingly put in Execution, But it Being half past 9 before we Got on Board, The Breeze Got up before we Reach'd the Fleet, and the Moment it arose, Fear and Sickness began to Operate on our Friends. Their Countenances Grew Pale, and the Poet Grew very vociferous for our Immediate Return. Our Pilot however held on his Course, and assurd them that there was not the Smallest Danger, and that the Moment they Set their feet in the Royal George their Sickness would Leave them. Congalton and I were quite Disconcerted and did not know what to do. Brett continued to assert that we might Board with the Greatest Ease, and without the Least Danger. But as we approach'd the Ship their Fears became so Noisy and so Unmanly, that Brett Yielded, and said it would be better, to sail round the Ship and Return Lest the Breeze should Increase. Dr Congalton and I were much Dissapointed, as this [was] probably the only opportunity we should have of seeing so fine a Ship again.

We behov'd to Yield however, and what was Remarkable, was that the moment we Set our Heads towards Land, their Sickness entirely abated, and they Got into Spirits. Robertson was the only one of them who had Thrown up his Breakfast. When we arriv'd near the Harbour we overtook the Ramilies a 90 Gun Ship Just entering the Port. Mr Brett proposd that we should go on Board her, when we should See her Rigging compleatly mand, a Sight that in some Degree would Compensate our not seeing the Royal George. Our Friends were Delighted with this proposal, and John Home exulted provokingly on the Superiority of the Sight we were so fortunatly Going to Have. We had no sooner Set foot on the Deck than [an] Officer came up to us Bawling, God preserve us, What has Brought the Presbytery of Edin^r here, for Damme If there is not Willy Robertson and Sandy Carlyle and John Home come on Board. This turnd out to be a Lieutenant Neilson, a Cousin of Robertson who knew us all, who Gave us a Hearty Welcome, and carried us to his Cabin and treated us with White Wine and Salt Beef.

The Remainder of this Day we past in seeing what we had omitted, particularly the Point after it was Dark, or rather towards Midnight, a Scene of Wonder and even Horror to the Civiliz'd. Next Day we took our Departure, and Sleeping a night by the way, as we had done Going Down, we arriv'd in London and prepar'd in Good Earnest to Set out on our Journey North. The Day was at last appointed for our Being Introduc'd to the Great Man, and we Resolv'd among ourselves, That if he Gave us an Invitation to Dine with him on an Early Day, we would Stay for it, tho' Contrary to our Plan.

John Home's Tragedy of Agis had been acted this Season with tolerably Good Success, for it Run the 9 Nights, and the Author made some hundreds by it. Garrick had Acted the Part of Lysander, as he Did a Year or two Later that of Emilius in the Siege of Aquileia, which I think superior in merit to Agis. I had undertaken to Review this Play for the British Magazine (Smollet's) but had been Indolent, and it now Cost me to Sit up all night to write it—and I was Oblig'd to Give it to the press Blotted and Interlin'd. But they are accustom'd to Decypher the Most Difficult hands.

The Day came when we were presented to Lord B. But our Reception was so Dry and Cold, that when he ask'd when we were to Go North, one of us said tomorrow. He Rec'd us Booted and Spurr'd, which in those Days, was a certain Signal for Going a Riding, and an Apology for not Desiring us to Sit down. We very soon took our Leave, and no sooner were we out of Hearing, Than Robert Adam who was with us, fell a Cursing and Swearing, What had he Been presented to all the Princes in Italy and France, and Most Graciously Rec'd, To come and be treated with such Distance and Pride by the Youngest Earl but one in all Scotland. They were better Friends afterwards, and Robert found him a Kind Patron when his Professional Merit was made known to him. When I was Riding with Home in Hyde Park a week before, trying the Horse I bought, we met his Lordship, to whom Home then Introduc'd me, and we rode together for half an Hour, when I had a very agreable chat with his Lordship. But he was a Different Man when he Rec'd Audience. To Dismiss the Subjᵗ how[ever] I believe he was a very Worthy and Virtuous Man, a Man of Taste and a Good Belles Lettres Scholar, and that he Train'd up the Prince in true Patriotick Principles and a Love of the Constitution, Tho' his own Mind was of the Tory Cast, with a Partiality to the Family of Stuart, of whom he believ'd he was Descended. But he prov'd himself unfit for the Station he had assum'd, Being not versatile Enough for a Prime Minister and tho' personally Brave, Yet void of that Political Firmness which is necessary to stand the Storms of State. The Nobility and Gentry of England had paid Court to him with such Abject Servility, when the accession of his Pupil drew near, and immediatly after it took place, That it was no wonder he should behave to them with Haughtiness and Disdain, and with a Spirit of Domination. As soon however as he was tried and Known, and the Dissappointed Hopes of the Courtiers had restor'd them to the exercise of their Manhood, he shew'd a wavering and uncertain Disposition, which Discover'd to them that he could be Overthrown. The misfortune of Great Men in such circumstances, is that they have few or no personal Friends on whose Counsels they Can Rely. There were two such about him who Enjoy'd his Confidence and Favour, Sir Harry Erskine and John Home. The first I believe was a truly Honest Man, but his Views were not Extensive, nor his Talents Great. The 2ᵈ had better Talents, but they were not at all adapted to Business. Besides Ambition and Pride to an high Degree, Lord B. had an Insatiable Vanity, which nothing could allay but Homes Incessant Flattery, which Being Ardent and Sincere and blind and Incessant Like that of a Passionate Lover, pleas'd the Jealous and Supercilious Mind of the Thane. He knew John to be a Man of Honour and his Friend, and tho' his Discernment pointed out the excess of John's Praise, Yet his Ardour and Sincerity made it all take place on a Temper and Character made accessible by Vanity. With respect to John himself, his Mind and Manners had always been the same. He flatter'd Lord Milton, and even Adam Ferguson and me, as much as he did Lord Bute in the Zenith of his Power. What Demonstrates the artlessness and purity of John[s] Mind, was that he never ask'd any thing for himself tho' he had the undisputed Ear of the Prime Minister. —Even those who Envied John for the place of Favour he held, exclaimd against the Chief for Doing so little for the Man of his Right Hand: and John might have starv'd on a Scanty Pension (for he was Requird to pay attendance in London for more than half the year,) Had not Ferguson and I taken advantage of a vacancy of an office in Scotland, and pressd Lord Milton to procure the Lord Conservators place[1] for him, which more than Doubled his Income. But tho' Home was Careless of himself, he was warm and active at all times for the Interest of his Friends, and serv'd a Greater Nº of People Effectually, than it had been in the Power of any private Man to do before, Some few of whom prov'd themselves not worthy of his Friendship.

We now were to Leave London and made all Suitable Preparations. And Finding that there was an Horse at Donaldsons at the Orange Tree Inn which the Owner wish'd to have Down to Edinᵣ we undertook to take him with us, and hird a Man to Ride him and carry our Baggage. As there were four of us, we found one Servant too Few to our Great Inconveniency. As the Adam's were a wonderfully Loving Family and their Youngest Brother James was Going Down with us, the Rest of the

Sisters and Brothers would accompany us as far as Uxbridge, (a very needless Ceremony some of us Thought) but since we were to be so Numerous my Sister thought of Joining the Party. We past a very Chearfull Evening in spite of the Melancholy Parting we had in View. We parted however, and made the Best of our Way to Oxford, Halting for an hour at Bulstrode, a seat of the Duke of Portlands, where we viewd the Park and the House and the Chappel, which pleasd us much especially the last, which [was] Ornamented in true Taste as a place of Worship. The Chappel which is still met with in Many Noblemen's Houses in England, was a Mark of the Residence of a Great Family which was striking and agreable. It was here that we Discoverd the truth of what I had often heard, That most of the Head Gardiners of English Noblemen were Scotch, for on Observing to this Man that his Pease seem'd late on the 4th of May, not being then fully in Bloom, and that I was Certain there were sundry places which I knew in Scotland, where they were farther advancd; He Answerd, that he was bred in [a] place, that I perhaps Did not know, that answerd this Description. This was Newhailles in my own Parish of Inveresk. This Man, whose Name I have forgot, if it was not Robertson, was not only Gardiner but Land Steward, and had the charge of the Whole Park and of the Estate around it. Such advantage was there in having been Taught in Writing and Arithmetick, and the Mensuration of Land, the Rudiments of which were Taught in many of the Country Schools in Scotland. This Man gave us a Note to the Gardiner at Blenheim who he told us was Our Countryman, and would furnish us with Notes to the Head Gardiners all the Way down.

We arriv'd at Oxford before Dinner and put up at the Angel Inn. Robertson and Adam who had never been their before had every thing to See; Home and I had been there before. John Douglas who knew we were coming, was passing Trials for his Degree of D.D. and that very Day, was in the Act of one of his Wall Lectures as they are Call'd for there is No Audience. At that University it seems the Trial is strict when one takes a Master's or Batchelors, but slack when you come to the Doctors Degree; and vice versa at Cambridge. However that be, we found Douglas sitting in a pulpit in one of their Chapells with not a Soul to hear him but 3 old beggar Women, who come to try if they might Get some Charity. On Seeing us 4 Enter the Chapel, he talk'd to us and wish'd us away, otherwise he would be obligd to Lecture. We would not Go away, we answerd, as we wanted a Specimen of Oxford Learning, on which he Read 2 or 3 verses out an Ep[istle] in the Greek Testament, and began to expound it in Latin. We listend for 5 Minutes, and then telling where we were to Dine, we left him to walk about. Douglas came to Dinner, and in the Evening, Messrs Foster and Vivian of Baliol

Carlyle, c. 1770 by David Martin

Mrs. Carlyle, c. 1770 by David Martin

Carlyle in Old Age by Archibald Skirving

College came to us, to ask us to Colation, to be Given us by that Society
Next Day. They were well inform'd and Liberal Minded Men, but from
them and their Conversation we Learn'd, that this [was] far from Applying to the Generality of the University. We staid all next Day, and
pass'd a very agreable Evening at Baliol College, where Several More
Fellows were assembled.

Next Morning we Set out Early for Woodstock where we Breakfasted
and went to See Blenheim, a Most Magnificent Park indeed. We
Narrowly Inspected the House and Chapel which tho' much Cried Down
by the Tory Wits of Queen Ann's Reign, appeard to us very Magnificent
and Worthy of the Donors and of the Occasion on which it was Given.[1]
Our Companion James Adam had seen all the Splendid Palaces of Italy,
and tho' he Did not say that Sir John Vanburgh[s] Design was Fault-
less, yet he said it ill deserv'd the aspersions Laid upon it, for he had
seen few Palaces, where there was More Movement as he Call'd it than in
Blenheim. The extent of the Park, and the Beauty of the water (now a
Sea almost, as I am told) Struck us very much.

From Blenheim we Made the best of our Way to Warwick, where as
we had been much Heated and were very Dusty, we threw off our Boots
and wash'd and Drest ourselves before we walkd out. John Home
would not put on his Boots again, but in clean Stockings and Shoes,
when he was looking at himself in the Glass and Prancing about the
Room, in a truly Poetical Style, he turn'd Short upon the Boot-Catch[2]
who had brought in our clean Boots, and finding the Fellow Staring at
him with Seeming Admiration, And am not I a pretty Fellow, Said
John? Ay says he, Sir, with half a Smile; And who Do you take me for
says John? If you Binna Jamy Dunlop the Scotch Pedlar, I Dinna know
wha you [are] but your ways are very like his. This Reply Confounded
our Friend not a little, and he lookt still more foolish than Robertson
when Jackson told at Staines, that the Dissenting Minister took him for
a Methodist.

Warwick we found to be a very pleasant old Town finely Situated
with a Handsome old Church. The Castle of Warwick, the Seat of the
Earl of that Name, with the Park was truly Magnificent, and the Priory
on the way to it, the Seat of Mr Wise, not unworthy of being viewd. We
Dind here, and was rather late in getting to Birmingham, where a
servant of Mr Garbetts Lay in wait for us at the Inn, and Conducted to
his House without Letting us Enter it. This Man of Singular Worth and
very uncommon Ability, with whom Robertson and I were intimatly
acquainted in Scotland,[3] had anxiously wish'd us to come his way, with
which we complied, not merely to See the Wonders of the Place, but to
Gratify him. Six or Seven Years before this, Dr Roebuck and he had

Establishd a vitriol work at Prestonpans, which succeeded well, and the profits of which Encourag'd them to Undertake the Grand Iron Works at Carron which had Commenc'd not long before. Garbet who was a Man of Sense and Judgment was much against that Great Undertaking, as Independent of the Profits of the vitriol works they had not £3000 of stock between them. But the ardent Mind of Roebuck Carried him away and he Yielded, Giving up to his Superior Genius for Great Undertakings the Dictates of Prudence and his own Sober Judgment. Roebuck having been Bred in the Medical School of Edin.ʳ had Science, and particularly the Skill of applying Chymistry to the useful arts.

Iron Works were but Recent in Scotland, and Roebuck had visited them all, and every Station where they could be Erected, and had found that Carron was by Far the Best; which if they Did not occupy Immediatly, some other company would, and they must Remain in the Back Ground forever. This Idea Dazzled and over-powerd the Judicious Mind of Garbett, which had been contented with the Limited Project of availing themselves of the Population of Musselburgh and Fisherow, and with the Aid of L.ᵈ Milton to whom I had introduc'd [him] to begin an Iron work on a Small Scale, on the Magdalen Burn, and Introducing the Manufactures of Birmingham at Fisherow. This was highly Gratifying to Milton, who would have lent his Credit, and Given the Labours of his then Active Mind, to bring it to Perfection.

Samuel Garbet was truly a very extraordinary Man. He had been an ordinary Worker in Brass at Birmingham, and had no Education farther than Writing and Accounts. But he was a Man of Great Accuteness of Genius and Extent of Understanding. He had been at first Distinguish'd from the common Workmen, by Inventing some Stamp for Shortening Labour. He was soon taken Notice of by a M.ʳ Hollis a Great Merchant in London, who Employed [him] as his Agent for purchasing Birmingham Goods. This Brought him into Notice and Rank among his Townsmen, and the more he was known the more he was Esteem'd. Let me observe once for all, That I have known no person but one more of such Strong and Lively Feelings, of such a Fair Candid and Honourable Heart, [and] of Such Quick and Ardent Conceptions, who still Retaind the Power of Cool and Deliberate Judgment Before Execution. I had been much in his way when he came 1.ˢᵗ to Prestonpans about the Year 51, or 52—and had Distinguish'd him and attracted his Notice. He knew all the Wise Methods of Managing Men, and was Sensible that he Could not expect to have the most faithfull Workmen unless he Consulted the Minister. To Obtain this aid he paid all due respect to my Father, and tho' of the Church of England regularly attended the Church; and indeed made himself agreable to the Whole Parish High and Low. Roebuck tho' a Scholar, and of an Inventive Genius, was Vain and Unconstant, and an Endless Projector. So that the Real executive and managing Power Lay in Garbett.

He Rec'd us with Open Hospitality, and we were soon Convinced we were Welcome by the Cordiality of his Wife and Daughter (afterwards Mrs Gascoign) who lodg'd the whole Company but me, who Being their Oldest Acquaintance, they took the Liberty to Send to a Friends House to Lodge. Hitherto they had liv'd in a very Moderate Style, but for his Scotch Friends Garbet had provided very Good Claret, and for the time we Staid, his Table was Excellent. Tho' at that time they had only one Maid and a Blind Lad as Servants. This last was a Wonder, for he Did all the work of a man, and even Brewed the Ale, [but] that of Serving at Table—and for that Garbet according to the Custom of the Place, where no Man was then asham'd of Inegality, made Patrick Dornay, who was then an Apprentice, Stand at our Backs and serve at Dinner. He afterwards Married the Maid who was the Mistresses Cousin, was Sent Down to Prestonpans as an overseer, and was at last taken in as a Partner. Such was the Primitive State of Birmingham and other Manufacturing Towns, and such Encouragement Did they then Give to Industry. Sed tandem Luxuria Incubuit.[1] Few Men have I ever known who United together more of the Prime Qualities of Head and Heart.

We past the Next [Day] after our arrival in visiting the Manufactures at Birmingham, tho' it was with Difficulty I could persuade our Poet to Stay, by Suggesting to him how uncivil his Sudden Departure would appear to our kind Landlord. I Got him however to Go through the Tedious Detail, till at last he Said, That it Seem'd there as if God had Created Man only for making Buttons. Next Morning after Breakfast Home Set out for Admiral Smith's his Old Friend, who Being a Natural Son of Sir Thos Littleton, had built himself a Good House in the village, close by Hagley the Seat of Ld Littleton. We who were left past the Day in Seeing what Remaind unseen at Birmingham, particularly the Baskerville Press, and Baskerville himself, who was a Great Curiosity. His House was a Quarter of a Mile from the Town, and in its way handsome and elegant.[2] What struck us most, was his First Kitchen, which was most compleatly furnish'd with every thing that could be wanted, kept as clean and Bright as if it had come Streight from the Shop, for it was us'd, and the fineness of that Kitchen was a Great point [in the] Family: For they Rec'd their Company, and there were we entertaind with Coffee and Chocolate. Baskerville was on hands with his Folio Bible at this Time, and Garbett insisted on Being allowd to Subscribe for Home and Robertson. Home's absence afflicted him, For he had seen and heard of the Tragedy of Douglas. Robertson hitherto had No Name; and the Printer Said Bluntly, that he would rather have one Subscription to his work of a Man Like Mr Home, Than an Hundred Ordinary Men. He Din'd with us that Day, and acquitted so well, that Robertson pronounc'd him a Man of Genius, while James Adam and I, thought him but a Prating Pedant.

On agreement with John Home we Set out for Ld Littleton's, and were to Take the Leasows, Shenstone's place[1] in our Way. Shenstone's was three or four miles short of Littletons. We call'd in there in our Way, and walkd over all the Grounds, which were finely laid out, and which it is Needless to Describe. The Want of Water was Obvious. But the ornaments, and Mottoes and Names of the Groves, were appropriate. Garbett was with us and we had [Seen] most of the place, before Shenstone was Drest, who was Going to Dine with Admiral Smith. We left one or two of [the] Principal Walks for him to Shew us. At the End of an High Walk from whence we saw far into Gloster and Shropshire, I met with what struck me most, That was an Emaciated Pale Young Woman evidently in the last Stage of a Consumption—She had a Most Interesting appearance with a Little Girl of 9 or 10 years old, who had led her there. Shenstone . . . and stood for some time Conversing with her till we went to the End of the Walk and Return'd. On some of us, taking an Interest in her appearance—He said she was a very sickly Neighbour, to whom he had lent a Key to his Walks as she Delighted in them, tho' now not able to use it much. The Most Beautifull Inscription he afterwards wrote to the Memory of Maria Dolman,[2] put me in mind of this young Woman. But if I remember Right she was not the Person. It is to me the most Elegant and Interesting of all Shenstone's Works.

We Set all out for Adm^l Smiths, and had Mr Shenstone to Ride with us. His appearance surpriz'd me, for he was a Large Heavy Fat Man, Dress'd in White Cloathes and Silver Lace, with his Gray Hairs tied behind and much Powderd. Which added to his Shyness and Reserve, was not at first prepossessing. His Reserve and Melancholy (for I could not call it Pride) abated as we rode along, and by the time we left him at the Admirals, he became Good Company, Garbett who knew him well, having Whisperd him, that tho' we had no Great Name, he would find us not common Men.

Lord Littleton's we found Superior to the Description we had heard of it, and the Day Being Favourable, the Prospect from the high Ground of more than 30 miles of Cultivated Country, Ending in the Celebrated Hill, the Wrekin, Delighted us much. On our Return to the Inn, where we expected but an Ordinary Repast, we found a pressing Invitation from the Admiral to Dine with [him] which we Could not Resist. Tho' a Good deal Disabled with the Gout he was kind and Hospitable, and

Rec'd Garbet who was Backward to Go, very Civilly. We Intended to have Rode Back to Birmingham in the evening, but in the afternoon there came on Such a Dreadfull Storm of Thunder accompanied with Incessant Rain, as Made the Admiral Insist on our Lodging all Night with him. With this we Complied, but as he had no more than 3 Spare Beds, James Adam and Garbett were to Go to the Inn. Finding an Interval of Fair Weather by 8 aclock, they Rode to Birmingham as Garbet was oblig'd to be home.

After Supper the Admiral made us a Spacious Bowl of Punch with his own Hand; a Composition on which he Piqued himself not a little, and for which John Home extol'd him to the Skies. This Nectar Circulated Fast, and with the usual Effect upon the Hearts of the Company of making them speak out. I[t] was on this Occasion that J. Home said to the Admiral, That knowing what he knew by Conversing with him at Leith, he was very much surpris'd, when he Recommended Bing to Mercy. You should have known John That I never could all my Life Bear the Idea of Being Accessary to Blood, and therefore I Joind in this Recommendation, tho' I knew that by Doing so, I should Run the Risk of never More Being Employ'd. This was a full Confirmation of what John Home had said at the Time of the Sea-Fight. This Fine Punch even unlock'd Shenstone's Breast, who had hitherto been shy and Reserv'd; for Besides Mixing freely in the Conversation he told Home apart, that it was not so agreable as he Thought to Live [in] Neighbourhood and Intimacy with Ld Littleton, For he had Defects which the Benevolence of his General Manners Conceald, which made him often wish That he had Liv'd at a hundred Miles Distance. When Home told me this I very easily Conceivd, That the Pride of a Patron, Joind to the Jealousy of a Rival Poet, must often produce Effects that might prove Intolerable.

We Return'd to Birmingham next Morning, and with the most affectionate Sense of the Kindness of our Landlord, and his Family, we Set out on our Journy North next Morning. I have forgot to mention that we had supt the Last night with Dr Roebuck, who tho a very cliver and Ingenious Man, was far behind our Friend in some of the Most Respectable Qualities.

We kept on thro' a Middle Road, by Litchfield, and Burton on Trent, where we could get no Drinkable Ale, Tho' we threw ourselves there on purpose; and Next Day Dining at Matlock, we were Delighted with the fine Ride we had, thro' a Vale similar but of more amenity, than any we had seen in the Highlands. We took the Bath too, which pleasd and Refresh'd us much, for the Day was Sultry. We went at night to Endsor Inn opposite Chatsworth the Duke of Devonshire's Fine House which we visited in the Morning, with much Admiration both of the Structure,

Ornaments and Situation. We ascended a Wild Moor, and Got to Sheffield to Dinner, where as we Declin'd visiting a Brother of Dr Roebucks on whom Garbet had Given us a Note of Credit, we Sent his Letter to him and went on. Next Day we saw Rockingham or Wentworth Castle in our Way, and became satisfi'd with Sights, So that we turnd no more off our Road till we came to Rippon where we could not resist the Desire of Visiting Studley Park, then a Great Object of Curiosity to all people from our Country, as it was then the Nearest Fine Place. Alnwick Castle had not then been Repaird and Beautified.

After we had left Sheffeild, where we might have Got Money, we Discover'd that we were like to Run Short. For Dr Robertson unlike his usual Prudence, had only put two Guineas in his Pocket Trusting to the full Purse of his Cousin J^s Adam, who had taken no more than he had Computed would pay the 4th Part of our Expense. Home and I had done the same. I was Treasurer, and at Leeds I believe Demanded a Contribution, when it was found that by Robertson[s] Deficiency, and our Purchasing some Goods at Birmingham with the Common Stock, I was sensible we would run out before we came to Newcastle. This Led us to Inferior Inns, which Cost us as Dear, for much In[f]erior Entertainment. We held out till we past Durham, which we Did by keeping to the west of that City and Saving 2 Miles, having made our Meal at   which Home knew to be a Good House. From hence we might have Got Early into Newcastle, had we not been Seduc'd by a Horse-Race we met with near Chester in the Street. This we could not Resist as some of us had never seen John Bull at his Favourite Amusement. There was a Great Crowd, and the M^rs and Miss Bulls Made a Favourite part of the Scene, the[ir] Equipages being Single and Double Horses, Sometimes triple, and many of them ill mounted, and yet all of them with a Keenness, Eagerness, Violence of Motion, and Loudness of Vociferation, that appear'd like Madness to us: For we thought them in extream Danger, by their Crossing and Jusling in all Directions at the full Gallop, and yet None of them Fell. Having [glutted] ourselves and tir'd our Horses with Diversion, we were oblig'd to halt at [an] Inn to Give our Horses a little Corn, for we had been 4 hours on Horseback, and we had 9 miles to Newcastle. Besides Corn to 5 Horses and a Bottle of Porter to our Man Anthony, I had Just 2 Shillings Remaining, but I could only spare one of them, for we had Turnpikes to pay, and so Call'd for a pint of port, which mixt with a Quart of Water made a Good Drink for each of us. Our Horses and their Riders, being both Jaded, it was ten aclock before we arriv'd at Newcastle. There we Got an Excellent Supper &c. and a Good Nights Sleep. I sent for Jack Widdrington when at Breakfast, who immediatly Gave us what Money we Wanted. And we who had been so

penurious for 3 Days became suddenly extravagant. Adam Bought a
£20-Horse, and the Rest of us what Trinkets we Thought we wanted,
Robertson for his Wife and Children at Gladsmuir and Home and I for
the Children at Polwarth Manse. As we Drew nearer home our Motion
became accelerated and our Conversation Dull. We had been in two
parties, which were form'd in about 5 or 6 Miles from London. For
having met with a Cow, with a Piece of old Flannel tied about one of her
Horns, pasturing in a very Wide Lane on the Road, Home and Robertson Made a Sudden Tack to the Left to be out of Reach of this Furious
Wild Beast. I Jeer'd them, and ask'd [of] what they were affraid? They
said a Mad Cow, Did I observe the Warning Given by Cloth on her
Horn. Yes says I, but that was only because her Horn was hurt, Did you
not see how Quiet she was when I past her? Adam took my Part, and the
Controversy Lasted all the way Down, when we had nothing to talk of.
There were so many Diverting Scenes Occur'd in the Course of our
Journey That we often Regreted Since that we had not Drawn a
Journal of it. Our Debates about triffles were Infinitely Amusing. Our
Man Anthony, was at once a Source of much Jangling and no Small
Amusement. He was never ready when we mounted and went slowly on,
but he was Generally half a Mile behind us; and we had to halt when we
wanted any thing. I had Got a Hickery Stick from Jackson, not worth
1/6, which I would have left at the 1ˢᵗ Stage, had not Home and Robert-
son Insisted on my [not] Doing it. But as I had less Baggage and an
Equal Right in Anthony and his Horse, and was Treasurer withal,
which they were affraid I would throw up, I carried my Point, and this
stick Being 5 feet long and sometimes by Lying across the Clokebag,
Entangled with Hedges, furnish'd him with a ready excuse. It was very
Warm Weather in May, and we Rode in the Hottest of the Day. We
seldom Got on Horseback before 10 aclock, for there was no Getting
Robertson and Home to Bed, and Jamy Adam could not get up, and
had besides a very Tedious Toilet. Our two Friends wanted Sometimes
to Go before us, But I would not pay the Bill, till James and Anthony
were both ready, and till then the Hostler would not Draw (or Lead out)
the Horses from the Stable. As I perceiv'd that Robertson and Home
were commenting on all my Actions, I on purpose with the Privacy of
James Adam, Did odd things on purpose to Astonish them. As for
Instance at the Inn near Studley, where we Breakfasted, having felt my
Long Hair Intolerably Warm about my Neck, I Cut off 5 or 6 Inches of a
Bit of Ragged Green Galloon,[1] that was Hanging Down from a chair . . .
in the Room, with which I tied my Hair Behind. This made a very
Motley Appearance, but when we come to Take Horse, in spite of the
Heat I appeard with my Great Coat, and had fasten'd the Cape of it

191

round my Head. In this Guise I Rode thro' the Town of Rippon, at the
end of which I Disengag'd myself from my Great Coat, and my friends
Saw the Reason of this Masquerade. Another Day between 12 and one,
Riding thro' very Close Hedges near Corn[h]ill, we were all like to Die of
Heat, and were able only to Walk our Horses. I fell behind, Pull'd my
Great Coat from Anthony, put it on, and came up with my Friends at a
hard Trot. They then thought that I had certainly Gone Mad. But they
Did not advert to it, that Chief Oppression of Heat is before the perspir-
ation. My Receipt had Reliev'd me, my fit of Phrenzy was off, and I
Reign'd in my Horse till they Came up to me. Soon after we left Cornill
we Separated. Home and I Stopt at Polwarth Manse for a Night, and
Robertson and Adam, went on by Longformacus to Gladsmuir, Robertson's abode. James Adam tho' not so Bold and Superior [an] Artist as
his Brother Robert, was a well Inform'd and Sensible Man, and furnish'd me with excellent Conversation, as we Generally Rode together.
Thus ended a Journey of 18 Days, which on the whole had prov'd most
amusing and Satisfactory.

We Got to our Respective abodes by the 22ᵈ of May, and were in time
for the Business Week of the Genl Assembly, of which Robertson and I
were both Members, and where we came in time to assist in sending Dr
Blair to the New Church, to which he had a Right, and of which a
Sentence of the Synod of Lothian and Tweeddale unjustly Depriv'd
him. This was the only Occasion on which he ever Spoke in the Genl
Assembly, which he Did Remarkably Well.

It was in the month of Augᵗ this Summer that Robertson and I passd
two Days at Minto with Sir Gilbert Elliot who was very open and communicative. About the Middle of Ocʳ I rode to Inveraray, Being Invited
by the Milton Family who always [were with] the Duke of Argyle, and
who Generally Remaind there, till near the End of the Year. I Got the
1ˢᵗ Night to my Friend Robin Bogle's at Shettlestone near Glasgow,
where I found him very happy with his Wife and Family. He was an
Honest Gentlemany Man, but had been very Dissipated before his
Marriage. From Glasgow, I went all night to Roseneath, where in a small
house near the Castle Liv'd my Friend Miss Jean Campbell of Carrick—
Living with her Mother who was a Sister of Genl John Campbell of
Mamore, afterwards Duke of Argyle and Father of the present Duke.
Next Day after passing Loch Long, I went over Argyle's Bowling Green,
Call'd so on account of the Roughness of the Road. As my Horses were
not Frosted¹ and the Ice was strong I had to walk about 6 miles. This
made me late in Getting to Sᵗ Catherine's Directly Opposite to Inver-
aray. I wish'd very much to Get across the Loch as [it] was but 6 in the
Evening, but the Mʳˢ of the House wishing to Detain me and my Servant

and Horses all night, pretended that the Boatmen were out of the way, and the Oars aseeking, and that I could not Get across that night. This vex'd me as it was a Miserable House to Sleep in. However I call'd for a Mutchkin[1] of Whisky, and prevaild with the Good Woman to taste it without Water. As she became so familiar as to ask where I was when I was at Home, I told her I was a Schoolfellow of Mackellumore,[2] and had some Letters, and was much Dissappointing at Not Crossing the Lake, as I had letters of Importance to Deliver to his Grace. She Star'd and said I was a Stalwart Carl[3] of such an Age. My Grisly undresst Hair favour'd this Deception. I added that If I could Cross the Loch, I Intended to Leave my Servant and Horses all night to her Care, to come round by the Head of the Loch in the Morning. But if [I] could not Cross, I must venture to Ride the nine miles round, Dark as it was. She took another Sip of the Whisky, and then left the Room. In Five Minutes she Return'd and told me that the Boatmen had appear'd, and were seeking for their Oars, and would be ready in a few Minutes. This was Good News to me, as I knew the Inn at Inveraray to be pretty Good, as I had been there 2 nights when I went to their Country in 1754 with Jamy Cheap of Saughie. I was very soon Summond to the Boat, and after Recommending my Man John McLaughlin to the Care of the Landlady, I bid her Farewell. We Got very Soon over, the night being calm and the Distance not much more than two miles.

I Did not Go that night to the Duke's House, as I knew I could not have a Bed there (as he had not yet Got into the Castle) but I went in the Morning and was very politely Rec'd not only by the Milton Family, but by the Duke and his two Cousins, The Present Duke and his Brother Lᵈ Frederick who were there. His Grace told me immediatly, That Miss Fletcher had made him expect my Visit, and that he was sorry he could not offer me Lodging, but that he would Hope to see me every Day to Breakfast Dinner and Supper.

It would be quite Superfluous to Say any thing here of the Character of Archᵈ Duke of Argyle, as the Charᵗ of that illustrious person, both as a Statesman and an Accomplish'd Gentleman and Scholar, is perfectly known. I had met him twice in London in his evening Parties and once at Brunstane; but I was told that he was a Great Humourist at Inveraray, and that you could neither Drink his Health, nor ask him how he Did, without Dissobliging. But this was exaggerated. To be sure he wav'd Ceremony very much, and took no trouble at Table, and would not Let himself be waited for, and came in when he pleas'd and Sate down on the Chair that was left, which was neither Head nor foot of the Table. But he Cur'd me of all Constraint the first Day, for in his first or 2ᵈ Glass of Wine he Drank my Health and welcom'd me to Inveraray, and hopd that as Long as I Staid which he wish'd to be all the Week at least, I would think myself at home. Tho' he Never Drank to me again, I was much more Gratified by his Directing much of his Conversation to me. His Colloquial Talent was very Remarkable for he never harangued or was Tedious, but Listen'd to you in your Turn. We Sate Down every Day 15 or 16 to Dinner, For Beside his two Cousins, and the Fletcher Family, There were always 7 or 8 Argyleshire Gentlemen, or Factors on the Estate at Dinner. The Duke had the Talent of Conversing with his Guests so as to Distinguish Men of Knowledge and Talents, without Neglecting those who valued themselves more on their Birth and their Rent Rolls, than on personal Merit. After the Ladies were withdrawn, and he had Drunk his Bottle of Claret, he Retird to an Easy Chair set hard by the Fire Place. Drawing a Black Silk Nightcap over his Eyes, he Slept or seemd to Sleep for an Hour and an half. In the Meantime Sandy McMillan who was Toast Master push'd about the Bottle, and a more Noisy or Regardless Company could hardly be. Milton Retird soon after the Ladies. And about 6 a clock, McMillan and the Gentlemen Drew off, for at that time Dinner was always Servd at 2 aclock, when the Ladies Return'd, and His Grace awoke and Calld for his Tea, which he made himself at a little Table apart from that of the Company. Tea Being over he played two Rubbers at 6 penny Whist as he Did in London. He had always some of the Ladies of his Party, while the Rest amus'd themselves at another Table. Supper was serv'd soon after nine, and there Being nobody left but those with whom he was familiar, he Drank another bottle of claret, and could not be Got to Go to Bed till one in the Morning. Jack Campbell of Stonefield who had lately Married his Niece Lady Grace Stuart, Came to us on the 2^d Day. I may add that the provisions for the Table were at Least Equal to the Conversation, for we had Sea and River Fish in Perfection, the Best Beef and Mutton and Fowls, and Wild Game and Venison of both kinds in abundance. The Wines too were excellent. I staid over Sunday, and preach'd to his Grace, who always attended the church at Inveraray. The Ladies told me that I had pleas'd his Grace, which Gratified me not a little, as without him no Preferment could be obtain'd in Scotland.* I may add here that when he Died in Spring 1762, It was found that he had mark'd my Name Down in his Private Note Book, For Principal of the College of Glasgow,

---

* The Duke had a Great Collection of Fine Stories, which he told so neatly and so frequently Repeated them without variation as to make one Believe That he had wrote them Down. He had been in the Battle of Sherriffmoor and was slightly wounded in his Foot, which made him always halt a little. He would have been [an] admirable Soldier, as he had every Talent and Qualification Necessary to arrive at the Height of that Profession, But his Brother John the Duke of Argyle having Gone before him with a Great and rising Reputation, he was advis'd to take the Line of a Statesman.

a Body in whose Prosperity he was Much Interested, as he had been Educated there, and had said to Andrew Fletcher Junior to whom he Shew'd the Note, That it would be very hard If he and I between us could not manage That troublesome Society. This Took no Effect, for the Duke Died a Year or two before Principal Campbell, when Lord Bute had all the Power. So that when the Vacancy Happen'd, in the end of 1761, or beginning of 62, Professor Leechman was preferd to it, who was the Friend and had been the Tutor of Mr Baron Mure.

I slept all the night at Levenside as I had promis'd to Stonefield, and Got home the 2d Day after.

In the End of this Year (1758), I was tempted by the Illiberal Outcry that was Raisd against the Minister Wm Pitt, on the Failure of Genl Bligh, on the affair of St Cas on the French Coast,[1] to Write the Pamphlet, *Plain Reasons For Removing The Right Honble Will Pitt, from his Majesty's Councils forever, by O. M. Haberdasher*, which was publish'd in London in the beginning of 1759, and had a Great Run. I had wrote it in the Ironical Stile of Dean Swift, like that about Burning the Tragedy of Douglas, and thought I had Succeeded Pretty Well. Besides Panegyrick on that Great Man, who had raisd us from a very Low State of Political Consequence, Not only in the eyes of all Europe, but in our opinion, To Make Rapid Progress to the Highest State of National Glory in which ever we had been, [it] Contain'd Likewise much Satyre against the Minister who had Reduc'd us so Low.

After I Return'd from Invoraray, I visited my Friend Mrs Wedderburn, whom to my Great Grief I found Low and Dejected. The Capt had been oblig'd to Join his Regiment in the West Indies in the Spring, where there was much Fighting, and she had not heard of him for some time. She was brought to Bed of a Daughter Early in Decr and Died of a Fever, universally Regreted at that time and never to be forgotten by those who were Intimately acquainted with her.

Thus Ended a Year of Greater Variety than any in my Life, For tho' I had been in London before and had Rode to Edinr likewise on Horseback Yet I had not till then seen such a variety of Characters, nor had I acquird such a Talent for Observation, nor possess'd a Line for Sounding the Depths of the Human Character, Commensurate to that purpose as I now had. On this Tour I had seen Great Variety of Characters, with many of whom Having been very Intimate, The Defect was in myself, If I had not been able to sound all the Depths and Shallows thro' which I pass'd.

[1759]

In this Year 1759 in the beginning of which I enjoy'd the Success of my Ironical Pamphlet In Defence of Willm Pitt afterwards Lord

Chatham, I was encouragd to take my pen again occasionally, when any thing should occur that suited it. Two or three years [after] this Period our Neighbourhood was Enrichd by Residence of a very Valueable Man, Lieut. Coll! Robert Campbell of Finab, a Man of the first Rate understanding and ability. He had been in the Duke Cumberlands War, and was Cap! of Grenadiers in the 42ᵈ Reg! But had been so much Disgusted with the Duke of Cumberland, and not having Good Health, he left the army I think with Majors Rank; and sometime thereafter having bought the Estate of Drumore, he came to Live there with his Family. As he had been at College with me, and in the same Class, and having had a Boyish Intimacy together, It was not Difficult to Renew my acquaintance, and to make it more Intimate. He was very Sociable, and Lik'd Golf, the sport in which I excell'd and took much pleasure. The Coll! had read very Little, but he had Taken a more Comprehensive View of Men and affairs Than almost any person I ever knew. Adam Ferguson and he had been very Intimate, and had a Mutual Regard for Each Other. This man, was truly a Great addition to our Society. He had been Member of Parliament for Argyleshire, and was Receiver Gen! of the Customs for Many Years before his Death. He left no Son but Lieut. Gen! Alex? Campbell of Monzie, The Heir of his Fathers Sagacity and Talents, with more experience in War.

There was Nothing very Material before the Gen! Assembly of this Year, unless it was an explanation and extension of the Act against Symoniacal practices which had become Necessary on account of some Recent Transactions. Dʳ Robertson had been translated to Edin! this Year but Did not yet take any particular Charge of the Affairs of the Church. Because not being yet Principal he could [not] be a Member of Assembly every Year as he afterwards was.

My Father had Gone to London in the Month of March to visit his Daughter Mʳˢ Dickson, and I had Rode with him to Berwick where . . .

He was very much pleasd and amusd at London, where Besides his Daughter and her Infant his first Grand child he had his Sisters Paterson and Lyon still alive which Gave him Great Satisfaction. As he had never been in London before he enjoyd it very much tho' he was now in his 70ᵗʰ [Year]. But Being fresh and vigorous and remarkably cheerfull he was a very Great Favourite with all his New Acquaintance. But as he would needs Ride Down in Midsummer, and had been unlucky in the purchase of a Horse, which was very hard Set;[1] and still more so in his Choice of a Companion, one of his Daughters Dissappointed Lovers, who paid no Regard to his Age in the Length of their Days Journey's, he was so much overheated, that as my Mother alleg'd the Fever never afterwards left him, which concluded his Life in the Year 1765 on the 8ᵗʰ of

March. A more kind and affectionate Parent and Relation, or more Benevolent Neighbour, or more Faithfull Pastor never existed.

It was near the end of Summer this Year That Charles Townshend and Lady Dalkeith with her Daughter Lady Franc[e]s Scott then about 8 Years of Age [came to Dalkeith] and Remain'd there, for 2 Months. As they had two publick Days in a Week according to the antient Mode of the Family, they Drew a Great Deal of Company to the House, and as I was Consider'd as Chaplain in ordinary to the Family, the Minister of Dalkeith for the time not [being] much in favour, I was very frequently There. Charles Townshend The 2ᵈ Son of Lord Townshend the Son of the Secretary of State in the Reign of Geo. 1ˢᵗ was lively and witty and eloquent to the last degree, and a Rising Statesman who aspir'd at the Highest Offices. As he and I had been at Leyden together, I became at this time very Intimate with him. A Project he concivd after he came here much Increasd this Intimacy. This was to offer himself a Candidate for the Seat in Parliament for the City of Edinʳ. The State of the City at that time, made it not Improbable that he might Succeed. A Mʳ Forrester a Counsellor at Law, of Irish Birth and Quite a Stranger here, had been Recommended by Baron Maule to the Duke of Argyle, to whom he was known and to Lord Milton. Forrester was by no means Popular in Edinʳ and Charles Townshend had Bewitch'd Lord Milton with his Seducing Tongue which made him more Sanguine in his Project. He Discoverd that I had much to Say with [the] Baron and his Lady, whom he Cajol'd and Flatter'd excessively. He took me for his Confidant and Adviser in this Business. I had many Conferences with him on the Subject and Endeavour'd to Convince him, that if he was not [Master] of his Wife's Uncle the Duke of Argyle, as he pretended to have his own Uncle the Duke of Newcastle, That he would never Succeed. For tho' Milton seem'd to Govern Argyle in most things, which was necessary for the support [of his] Credit as well as for the Duke's Ease, Yet there were points in which Milton could [not] Stir a Step without the Duke, and in my Opinion this was one of them. On this he fell into a Passion, and exclaim'd That I was so Crusty as never to be of his Opinion, and to Oppose him in everything. On this I laugh'd full in his Face, and took to my Hat, and said that If this was the way in which he Chose to treat his Friend and Adviser, It was time I were Gone for I could be of no use to him. He Calm'd on this and ask'd my Reason for thinking as I Did. I answer'd that the M. P. for the City of Edinʳ was of Great Consequence, as whoever held that, was sure of the Political Government of the country, and without it No Man would be of any Consequence; That his Lady's Being the Duke's Niece was against him, for as in Political Business No Regard was paid to Blood,

That very Circumstance was Hostile to his Design; For it was not to be Suppos'd that the Duke of Argyle, would allow a Young Nobleman from the South, who had made himself a Man of Importance in the North, by Having obtain'd the Guardianship of the Heir of one [of] our Greatest Families in his minority, to take the Capital of Scotland by a Coup De Main, and thereby undermine or Subvert his Political Interest, for without his Viceroyalty in Scotland His Grace was of no Importance in the State. I added that It was Impossible to Conceive That the Duke would be so Blind, as not to see that a Young Man of his Aspiring Temper and Superior Talents, would [not] think of making himself Member for Edin.ʳ merely to Shew his address in Political Canvassing to lay himself at the Feet of his Wife's Uncle. This with much more that I represented to him Seem'd to Open his Eyes, Yet he still went on, for he could not Desist from the Pleasure of the Courtship, tho' he had little Prospect of Success. He came at last to be Contented with the Glory of Driving Forrester off the Field, which was not Difficult to Do; For when Charles had the Freedom of the City presented to him, and a Dinner Given him on the Occasion, he Lessend the Candidate so much in their Eyes by his Fine Vein of Ridicule, that the Dislike of the Town Council was Increas'd to Aversion. But Charles while he effected one part of his Purpose, faild in another, for tho' he Drove away his Rival he Gain'd no Ground for himself. He was Imprudent and Loose Tongued Enough to Ridicule the Good Old King Geo. the 2.ᵈ, which tho' it was not unusual among Young Noblemen, and indeed Wits of all Ranks, yet could not be endur'd by the Citizens of Edin.ʳ, who Seeing their King Far off and Darkly, were Shock'd with the Fredoms that were us'd with him. Besides this Milton who had been Dazzld at first with Charles's Shining Talents, and Elegant Flattery, began to Grow Cold and Draw off. He had Sounded the Uncle and had found in him a Strong Jealousy of the Nephew Mix'd with some Contempt; The Effect of which Discovery was a Gradual Alienation of Milton, who had realy been enamourd of Charles, and perhaps Secretly thought that he could Manage him, if he had Success, with more absolute Sway, Than he Did the Duke of Argyle.

After Charles Return'd to England, he Did not for some time Desist, and I had much Correspondence with him on the Subject. Some of his Letters I have still, But I kept no Copies of my own, which I have since Regretted as they were Wrote with anxiety and Exertion.

The End of all was That Forrester Having Retreated from the Field, having No Friend but Baron Maule, and a Caveat Being Enter'd against Charles Townshend, The Good Town of Edin.ʳ were Glad to take an Insignificant Citizen for their Member[1] at that time. When I was in London in 1770, there was a Gentleman who prest me to pay a visit to

Lady Townshend his Mother, who having many Letters of Mine to her Son was Desirous to See me. But not chusing to be Introduc'd any where by That Gentleman, I missd the opportunity of Recovering my Letters which I have since understood are all Burnt, with all Charles's Correspondence.

While Mr Townshend was here we had him Chosen a Member of the Select Society in one Sitting against the Rules, that we might hear him Speak, which he accordingly Did at the Next Meeting, and was answer'd by Lord Elibank and Dr Dick, who were Superior to him in argument and knowledge of the Subject. Like a Meteor Charles Dazzled for a Moment, But the Brilliancy soon faded away, and left no very strong Impression, So that when he Return'd at the End of two months, he had Staid long enough here.

I must [not] forget however to Mention an anecdote or two of him which will explain his character more clearly. Nothing could excell the Liveliness of his Parts nor the Facility with which he made other people's thoughts his own in a Moment. I call'd on him one Morning at Dalkeith, when he Said I was come most apropos If not Engag'd: For that he was Going to ride to Edinr to make some Calls, and his Wife Being engag'd to Dine with the Duchess of Gordon, he would be very Glad of a small party in a Tavern. I agreed, and we rode to Edinr together. When we Drew near that city he beg'd me to ride on, and bespeak a Small Dinner at a Tavern, and Get a Friend or two If I could to Join us, as he must turn to the Left to Call on Some People who Liv'd in that Direction. I went to Town Directly, and Luckily Found Home and Ferguson in Kincaids Shop and Securd them; and Sent a Cadie to Robertson to ask him to meet us at the Cross Keys, soon after two a clock, who likewise came. During Dinner and for almost an Hour after Charles, who seem'd to be fatigued with his Morning Visits, Spoke not a Single Word, and we four went on with our own kind of Conversation without adverting to Mr Townshends absence. After he had Drank a Pint of Claret he seemd to awaken from his Reverie and then Silenc'd us all with a Torrent of Colloquial Eloquence, which was highly Entertaining, for he Gave us all our own Ideas over again, Embodied in the finest Language and Deliverd in the Most Impressive Manner. When he parted from us, my friends remark'd on his excellence in this Talent, in which Robertson agreed with them, without perhaps Being Conscious, That he was the Next able proficient in that Art.

It was in the 2d week of Augt when the School at Mussh was publickly examin'd, and when the Magistrates Gave what was calld the Solan Goose Feast.[1] I took this Opportunity of Inviting Mr Townshend to visit the School and to Dine with the Magistrates, as he was Tutor to his

199

Grace the Duke of Buccleugh, the Lord Superior of the Town. Mr Townshend sent them a fine Haunch of Venison, and Mr Cardonnell who was
Magistrate at this time and a Grandson of the Duke of Monmouth by
his Mother, Took Care to assemble a Brilliant Company of Men of
Letters to Meet Mr Townshend; among whom were Home and Robertson and Ferguson and Wm Wilkie. There was a Numerous Company and
the best Dinner they could make. Cardonnell in his anxiety to have the
Venison properly Roasted had Directed the Cook to put a Paste Round
it: But she not having Given it time enough It came up to the Table
half Raw, to the Great Dissappointment of the Company, but chiefly of
a Coll! Parr whose Serious Affliction made the Rest of the Company
quite Easy on the Occasion, For he literally weep'd and shed Bitter
Tears, and Whin'd out what an unfortunate Fellow he was, that the
only Haunch of Venison he had met with in Scotland, and the only one
he had any Chance of Seeing while here, should be Serv'd up Raw. This
Set the Whole table in a Roar of Laughter, and Reconcil'd them to their
Fates. After a little time The Coll! Recover'd from this Disaster, by the
use of the Gridiron to the venison, and having Got up his Spirits, with
half a Dozen Glasses of Good Claret, began to talk away with some
effect, for excepting his Effeminacy about venison, he was not a Bad
Fellow. He was unlucky however in one of his Topicks, for Wilkie
Having begun to Open, Parr addressing himself to him said something
Rude about the Professors of St Andrews, of which university Wilkie had
very Recently been Chosen a Member, and wishd they would keep their
Students and Professors within their Walls, for that his Corps had lately
Enlisted one of them, who was not only the most aukward Beast, but
the most unruly and Debauchd Rascal, who ever was a Redcoat. Wilkie
who was Indignant on this attack, and a very Great Master of Horseplay
Raillery, and in Scolding Fear'd neither Man nor Woman; Replied with
Witty and Successfull Tartness, which however Did not Silence the
Coll!—When the Company took Sides, and their Insued a Brawling Con-
versation which Lasted too Long. Mr Townshend had interpos'd with an
Intention to Support Wilkie against his Countryman,* but Wilkie Being
Heated, Mistook him, and after two or three Brushes on Each Side,
Silencd him, as he had Done the Coll!—and the Report afterwards went,
That Wilkie had compleatly foild the English Champion at his own
Weapons, Wit and Raillery. But this was a Mistake for Mr Townshend
had not the least Desire to enter the Lists with Wilkie, But whisper'd me
who sate next to him, that as Wilkie Grew Brutal he would put an End
to the Contest by making No Answer. A Silence ensued which Cardonnell one of the Best Toastmasters took advantage [of] and Giving us

* An Instance of Charles's Falsehood.

three Bumpers, in less than two Minutes, all Contest for Victory was at an End, and the Company united again. Townshend said to me afterwards, when he came to take his Carriage at My House, That he had never met with a Man who approach'd so near the two Extremes of a God and a Brute as Wilkie Did. Soon after this Mʳ Townshend and the Countess and her Daughter Lady Frances Scot, then about 8 years old, Set out for London. This was a very Cliver Child, whose Humour and Playfulness, Mʳ Townshend's Good Nature had to Encourage and Protect against Maternal Discipline Carried too Far. He Continued to protect and Instruct her, and frequently employd her as his amanuensis, as she has frequently told me since; and added that If he had not Died when she was only 16, he would have made her a Politician.

In the Middle of Sepʳ this Year, I went to Dumfries to visit my Friends as I usually Did and to accompany my Friend Dʳ Wight, who had come from Dublin to Dumfries, and forward to Musselburgh to visit me.* On our Journey to that Country, he told me that he was heartily tird of his situation as a Dissenting Clergyman, and of the Manner of Life in Dublin, which tho' Social and Convivial to the Last Degree, yet Led to nothing and gave him no heartfelt Satisfaction, There Being but a very few indeed with whom he could unite in truly Confidential Friendship. As I knew that the University of Glasgow, were Resolv'd to vacate Mʳ Ruats Professorship if he Remaind much longer abroad; and as I happend likewise to know that he would not Return During the Life of Lord Hope who was in a Slow Decline,[1] I formd the Plan of obtaining his Professorship which was that of History, and in the Gift of the Crown, for Dʳ Wight, and I set about to secure it Immediatly. This was Easyly Done, for I had access to his Grace the Duke of Queensberry not only by Writing to him myself but by Interesting John McKie

---

* While Wight was here we Sup'd one Night in Edinʳ with the Celebrated Dʳ Franklin, at Dʳ Robertson's House then at the Head of the Cowgate, where he had come at Whit. after his Being Translated to Edinʳ. Dʳ Franklin had his Son with him, and besides Wight and me there was David Hume and Dʳ Cullen and Adam Smith and two or 3 more. Wight and Franklin had met and Breakfasted together in the Inn at

without Learning one anothers Names, But they were more than half acquainted when they met here and Wight who could talk at Random on all Sciences without being very Deeply Skilld in any, took it into his Head, to be very Eloquent on Chymistry, a Course of which he had attended in Dublin, and Perceiving that he Diverted the Company, particularly Franklin who was a Silent Man, he kept it up with Cullen, then Proffʳ of that Science, who had imprudently Committed himself with him, for the greatest part of the Evening to the Infinite Diversion of the Company, who Took Great Delight in Seeing the Great Proffʳ Foild in his own Science, by a Novice. Franklins Son, was open and communicative, and pleas'd the Company better than his Father— and some of us observ'd indications of that Decided Difference of Opinion between Father and Son, which in the American War, alienated them altogether.

Ross in the Business with whom both Wight and I were Related, and also by Means of Sir Gilbert Elliot we could secure Lord Bute, while I thro' Ld Milton could Gain the Consent of the Duke of Argyle. I had favourable Answers from every Body, and had no Doubt of Getting the place if it was vacated.

Before I left Dumfries I was Witness to an Extraordinary Riot which took place there on Michaelmass, the Day of the Election of their Magistrates. Provost Bell had been two years Dead, and the Party which he had Establish'd in power, when he brought them over to their Natural Protector the Good Duke of Queensberry, Being Desirous to Preserve their Influence, Did not think they could Do better, than to Raise John Dickson that Provosts Nephew to be their chief Magistrate. As this Man was at Present Conveener¹ of the Trades who are powerfull in Dumfries, and was popular among them, he Thought his ambition would be Easily Gratifyed. But there were Sundry Objections to this Measure. And. Crosbie Adv., the Son of a Provost of that Name, who had been a Private Supporter of Provost Bell in Opposition to the Party of the Tories, thought this a proper time to attempt an Overturn of the present Magistrates and Managers, and put his own Friends in their Room; who would either be Directed by Crosbie's Maternal Uncle Ld Tinwald, then Justice Clerk and far advanc'd in years, or Gain the Credit and Advantage of Governing the Town under the Duke of Q. As Crosbie was a Cliver Fellow, and young and adventurous and a Good Inflammatory Speaker, he Soon Rais'd the Commons of the Town almost to a Pitch of Madness against Dickson. On the Day of Election which happen'd to be on Saturday they Rose in a tumultous Manner, and took possession of the Stair Leading up to the Townhall, and would not allow the Election to Proceed. They . . . But Supposing, That no Election could Take place, after the Day was elapsd, when 12 aclock struck, the[y] allow'd the Magistrates and Council to Depart. They come down separately and by Back ways to the George Inn, where Dr Wight and I were waiting to see the Issue of this Days Riot, John Dickson having Married a Sister of [Wights] for his 2^d Wife. We waited in [an] adjacent Room till the Election was over, and then Joind them for half an Hour, to Drink the Health of the New Provost. The Deputy Sherriff Kilpatrick had come down from his House 10 or 12 Miles off, with Several Country Gentlemen, but there Being no Soldiers in the Town, had not attempted to Disperse the Mob by any other means than Remonstrance. This affair Ended in a very expensive Lawsuit, and Dickson's Right to be Provost was Establish'd.

Wight was on his Return to Dublin, and I on mine Home. So I took Leave of my Friends on Monday, to take Leave of our Grand Father, who by that time had an assistant. On Tuesday Morn. Oc͟r 2ᵈ I Got to Moffat to Breakfast, where I knew John Home was, as he usually past 2 or 3 weeks every season at Moffat for some Dissagreable Symptoms &c. He Introduc'd [me] to Mᶜpherson in the Bowling Green &c. as I have narated in a Letter to the Highland Society.[1] He was Good looking, of a Large Size with very thick Legs, to Hide which he Generally wore Boots tho' not then the Fashion. He appeard to me Proud and Reserv'd and Shun'd Dining with us on Some Pretence. I knew him Intimatly afterwards.

The Duke of Argyle made his usual visit to Argyleshire in Oc͟r and stopt for a week or two at Brunstane, Lᵈ Milton's as he had seldom occupied his Lodging in the Abbey, Not Caring to be troubl'd with t[o]o many visitors from the City of Edin͟r—I was sent for to him and past a very agreable Day. He Rallied [me] on my Friend Char. Townshend's attempt to Steal the City of Edin͟r and said he was not a very Dutifull Nephew. His Grace knew perfectly my Intimacy with him, and so Did not push the Conversation.

It was after this that I was persuaded by Wᵐ Johnstone Adv., now Sir Wᵐ Pulteney, and Adam Ferguson, to write what was Call'd the Militia Pamphlet, under the Signature of a Freeholder of Airshire,[2] which I chose, because that was said to be the only Shire in Scotland, out of which there had not issued a Single Rebel in 1745—After an hours Conversation with the two Gentlemen I mention'd, I undertook to write the Pamphlett and finish'd it in a Fortnight, and Carried [it] to Johnstone who was highly pleas'd with it, and after Shewing it to Ferguson had it transcrib'd by his own Clerk and then Shewn to Robertson, who believ'd it to be of Johnstone's Writing as he had told him that the Author's Name was to be Conceald. Robertson was well pleas'd, tho' he took no Great Concern about those kind of writings and added a short paragraph in Page   which he laughingly alleged was the Cause of its Success. For Great and unexpected Success it Certainly had, for it hit the Tone of the Country at that time, who Being Irritated at the Line that was Drawn between Scotland and England with Respect to Militia, were very Desirous to have application made for it in the approaching Session of Parliament. The Parties here were so warm at this time, that it was Necessary [to] Conceal the Names of Authors, to which I had an Additional Motive from a Hint of Dʳ Cullen's, for supping one night with him Dʳ Wight Being only in company, after praising the Pamphlet, he added that he Did not know the Author, and was Glad of it, for that he who occasionally saw so many of the Superior Orders, could assure us that Those Pamphlets which were ascribed to Clergymen had raisd a Spirit of Envy and Jealousy of the Clergy, which it would not be Easy to stand. Ferguson had publish'd a very Superior Militia Pamphlet in London a year or two before, in which all the Genuine Principles of That kind of National Defence were clearly unfolded. As since the Days of the Faction about the Tragedy of Douglas, 3 or 4 of us were supposd to be the authors of all the Pamphlets which rais'd publick attention, we shelter'd ourselves in the Crowd, and it was a Good While before the Real Writers were found out.

Much Honour was Done to this Pamphlet, for the Honble Genl George, now Marquiss Townshend, had it Republish'd at London with a Preface of his own Writing, as a Provost Ferguson of Air had Done here. I had likewise a very Flattering Note from Sir Gil. Elliot, who mov'd for the Scotch Militia in the Next Session of Parliament, For he wrote me, that he had only spoken the Substance of my Pamphlet in the House, and had Got more praise for it from Friends, than for any Speech he had formerly made. But this Did not happen till Spring 1760, when a Bill Having been order'd and brought in was rejected. Robert Dundas then Ld Advocate Oppos'd it keenly, and it was said in Party Publications, That this Speech was the price paid for his Being Made President Immediatly after. But my Belief is, That as Political Principles were Form'd in the School of the Disciples and Followers of Sir R^t Walpole, whose ostensible Motive, if not his Governing one, was a Fear of the Family of Stuart, That Dundas sincerely thought, that arming Scotland was Dangerous, Tho' he rested his arg^t chiefly on a less unpopular Topick, viz. That a Militia would Ruin our Rising Manufactures.

[1760]

This Year was the Most Important of My Life, for before the End I was United with the Most Valuable Friend and Companion, that any Mortal ever possess'd. My Youth had been Spent in a Vain Pursuit; for my First Love, which I have mention'd as far back as the Year 1735, had kept Entire possession till 1753 by means of Coquettry and my Iresolution. She was of superior understanding as well as of Beauty. In this last she would have excell'd most women of her time, had she not been the worst Dancer in the world, which she could not be prevaild to Leave off, tho' her Envious Rivals Laughd and Rejoicd at her persevering Folly. Tho' she had a Bad voice and a Bad Ear, she was a Great M^{rs} of Conversation having both Wit and Humour, and with an Air of Haughty Prudery, had enough of Coquetry both to attract and Retain her Lovers, of which she had many. An Early Inclination she had to a Young Gentleman who was prevented from Marrying her, and was soon after killd at the Battle of Fontenoy, made her Difficult to please. I had never fairly put the Question to her till about the [Year] 1752, when she expressly refus'd me. This made me Lessen the Number of my Visits, and made her Restrain her Coquetry. Soon after another came in my way, whose Beauty and Attractions made me forget the Former, to whom tho' she was Inferior in Sense and even in Beauty, yet Being ten years younger and having Gaiety and Spirit, I became Deeply Enamour'd, and was in full belief that I had Gaind her affections, when I was inform'd that she had suddenly Given her Hand to a Young Man in every Respect, except in Birth perhaps, beneath her Notice. In both those Ladies I believe that vanity prevaild against affection. They could not think of Being Wife of a Minister. The first attempted after this to Ensnare me again. But I escap'd. To have Done with her, and to Justify me: two Gentlemen of my Friends, addrest her vehemently, Adam Ferguson, and Robert Keith the Ambassador. The First who pleasd her much, was rejected for the same Reason I was; he had been a Clergyman, and tho' in a more Lucrative profession now, It was not Higher. Her Rejection of the 2ᵈ I believe, was owing chiefly to Principle—Tho' he was 24 years older than her, his Rank was an [attraction] which Ballanc'd that; but she could not Bear the Idea of Quarrelling with his Daughters, some of whom were her Companions, and not much Younger than herself. At Last after having Rejected Rich and Poor, Young and Old, to the Number of Half a Score, She Gave her Hand at 45, to the worst temper'd and Most Foolish of all her Lovers, who had a Bare Competency and which added to her Fortune hardly made them Independent. They Led a Miserable Life and Parted; soon after which he Died, and she then Liv'd Respectably to an advanc'd Age.

I ow'd my Good Fortune to the Friendship of John Home who pointed out the Young Lady to me as a proper Object of Suit, without which I should never have attempted it on account of the Inequality of her age and mine, For she was then just past 17 when I was 38—I was well acquainted with her Sister and her as Children, and saw that they were very Remarkable; The Eldest Sarah for Beauty and Elegance accompanied with Good Sense and a Grave and Reserv'd Demeanour, the 2ᵈ for an Expressive and Lively Countenance with a Fine Bloom and Hair of a Dark Flaxen Colour. She had excellent parts, tho' uncultivated, and uncommon, and a striking Cheerfullness and Vivacity of Manner. After 9 Months Courtship, at First by Silent and imperceptible approaches, and for 3 months by a close tho' unwarlike Siege, I obtain her Heart and Hand, and no Man ever made a Happier Conquest. For with a Superior Understanding and Great Discernment for her Age she had an Ease and Propriety of Manners, which made her to be well Rec'd and indeed much Distinguishd in every Company. It is not Easy to [Convey] what Joy I felt, when I saw her so much approv'd of by my Closest and most Discerning Friends, such as Ferguson and Robertson, and Blair, and Bannatine, not merely by Words, but by the open, respectfull and Confidential Manner in which they Convers'd with her. Having Lost her Father and Mother, when her Sister was 5 years of Age and she only 2, The Father on Christmas Day 1744, and the Mother on the Same Festival in 1745, of the small Pox,—Each of their Trustees (for they were Coheirs of Heathpool in Northumberland Kirk Newton Parish, then only £180 pr ann.) Mr Collingwood of Unthank, Cousin German of their Mother, took the Eldest under his Care, and Mr Wm Home Minister of Polwarth, who had Married their Fathers Sister Mary Roddam, had the Charge of the Younger. By this Division Sarah the Eldest had Seemingly Many Advantages above her Sister, For she Liv'd with Superior People, who frequented and were indeed allied to the Best Families in their Country, attended the Best Schools in Newcastle, and was one Year in the first Boarding School in Edinr and accordingly turnd out an Elegant and well Bred Woman, Speaking perfectly Good English, without the Roughness peculiar to the [uncouth] Dialect; and was accordingly admir'd courted and respected wherever she went. Yet Mary the Younger with no advantage but that of Living with [an] aunt of Superior Understanding and Great Worth, tho' much uneducated, and Having only one Year of the Edinr Boarding School, soon had her mind enlarg'd and her Talents Emprov'd, by Some Instruction, and the Conversation of those who Frequented us, Insomuch that in not more than one Year after our Marriage, She appear'd not only without any seeming Defect in her Education, but like a person of high Endowments. Indeed the Quickness of her Parts, and the extent of her Understanding were Surprising, and her Talent both in speaking and writing, and in Delicacy of Taste, truly as admirable [as] any Woman I ever knew. Add to this that she was of a Noble and Generous [Heart], compassionate even to Weakness, and if her Friends were in Distress, totally forgetfull and negligent of her self. I Do not think it is possible I could Derive any Greater Satisfaction from any Circumstance in human Life than I Did from the High Approbation Given to my Choice, by the very Superior Men who were my Friends and Companions.

While I was Busy with this Important Change in my Domestick State, I was applied to by a Friend, to write a Satyrical Pamphlet in my Ironical Style, against the Opposers of the Scotch Militia Bill which had been Rejected in the preceding Session. Being too much Ingag'd to attempt any thing of that kind at the time, I proposd that it should [be] Entrusted to Adam Ferguson, Then Living at Inveresk, preparing his

Academical Lectures. My Friend answer'd that he was excellent at Serious Works, but could turn Nothing into Ridicule, as he had no Humour. I answer'd that he did not know [Ferguson] sufficiently, but advis'd him to Go and try him, as he would undertake nothing he was not able to execute. This happen'd about the Month of Aug.ᵗ, and Ferguson Having undertaken it, executed that Little Work Call'd Sister Peg, in the Stile of Dʳ Arbuthnot's John Bull,[1] as excited both Admiration and Animosity. The Real Author was Carefully Conceald, tho' it was Generally ascribd to me, as I had written two small pieces in the same Ironical Style. The Publick had no Doubt, but that it was the work of one out of four of us, if not the Joint Work of us all. The Secret was well kept by at Least ten or a Dozen Males and Females. This Pamphlet Occasion'd a very Ludicrous Scene, between Dav.ᵈ Hume and Dʳ Jardine who was in the Secret. David was a Great Blab, and could conceal Nothing that he thought for the Honour of his Friends, and therefore it had been agreed to tell him of none of our Productions, except Such as might have been publish'd at the Cross. He Sent for Jardine whom he first suspected of Being the Author, who Denying his Capacity for Such a Work, he fixt on me, never Dreaming of Ferguson, and when Jardine pretended Ignorance, or refusd to Gratify him, he told him that he had written it himself in an Idle Hour, and Desir'd Jardine to Mention him as the Author every where, that it might not fall on some of us who were not so able to Bear it. This I could not have believ'd, had not David himself wrote me a Letter to that Purpose, which I shall transcribe on the Margin.[2]

On the 14.ᵗʰ of Oc.ʳ was made the Important Change in my Situation, in John Home's House in Alisons Square,[3] when he was absent at Lord Eglinton's who had become a Favourite of the Earl of Bute's very much by John's Means. He was indeed a very able as well as an agreable Man, tho' his Education had been Sadly Neglected. We had Sundry Visits Next Day, and among the Foremost come, Sir Harry Erskin and Mʳ Alex.ʳ Wedderburn—I was not then much acquainted with the first, But as he was Older than me by Several Years, and Fanny Wedderburn, of whom he was then in full pursuit, was as much Older than my Young Wife, who was no more than 17 and 9 Months, while I was past 38, I Guess'd the Real Motive to this visit, as my friend Wedderburn Seldom Did any thing without a Reason, was to See how Such an Unequal Couple would Look, on the Day after their Marriage.

We Remaind in Edin.ʳ till Tuesday the 21.ˢᵗ of Oc.ʳ when Baron Grants Lady Came in her Coach to Carry us to Castlesteads, some necessary Repairs in the Manse not being Yet Finish'd. There I had the pleasure to find, that my Wife could acquit herself Equally well in all Companies, and had nothing to wish for in the Article of Behaviour. We went home on Sat. Morning and the Grants Follow'd us to Dinner and were met by the Cardonnells.

His Majesty Geo. 2.ᵈ Died on the 25.ᵗʰ of the Month which put the whole Nation in Mourning. John Home Came to Town for a night or two on his way to London with L.ᵈ Eglinton, when began his Greatness, for he really might have been said to have been the 2.ᵈ Man in the Kingdom while Bute Remaind in Power, which Influence he usd not for his own advancement to wealth or power, for he never ask'd any thing for himself, (and strange to tell, never was offer'd any thing by his Patron,) But for the Service of his Friends or of those, who by Flattery and application acquird the Title of Such, For he was Easily Deluded by Pretences, especially to Those of Romantick Valour. The Celebrated Coll! Johnstone afterwards Gov.ᵣ of Minorca, ow'd to him his being Restord to the Line of Preferment, of which the late King had Depriv'd him for his Insolent Behaviour to a Country Gentleman in the Playhouse—and Geo. Johnstone likewise.

Towards the End of Dec.ᵣ I went to Polwarth, and with M.ᵣ Home my wife's uncle and one of her Guardians, went to [Alnwick to meet] M.ᵣ Collingwood the other, with . . . For[re]ster the Attorney to Settle our Affairs—a trusty Fellow, and had already made a large Fortune, and what amusd me much, [taken the] Tone of a Discontented Patriot so strongly against the Ministry of his Grace . . . that they were Obligd in a Year or two, to Let him have a Share in the Management. The other Guardian Alex.ᵣ Collingwood of Unthank Esq.ᵣ the Cousin German of my Wife's Mother, was weak and vainGlorious, Proud of his Family and in all and above all of his Wife, who he oblig'd us to visit and whom we found very Handsome and very Cliver—too much so for the Squire. We Returnd by Lanton as we had come, where Liv'd Alex.ᵣ Davison and his wife, two Worthy People, who had acquir'd an Independent Estate by Farming, which had not been frequently Done at that time. Heathpool our Estate lies three miles from Lanton S.W. up Bewmont Water, and is [a] Beautifull Highland place. I had not been absent above 5 or 6 Days, and found my Wife at my Fathers where she was the Joy and Delight of the old Folks. At that time indeed she was Irresistable, for to Youth and Beauty, she added a cheerfull Frankness, and Cordiality in her Manner, which Joind with an agreable Elocution and Lively Wit, Attracted all who saw her. Which was not Relishd by my Old Flame, who in the midst of forc'd Praise, attempted a Species of Detraction, which was compleatly Foild by the Goodhumour'd Indifference, or rather Contempt with which it was Rec'd (This Young Lady of uncommon Parts and Understanding, but a Degree of vanity on account of triffling or Imaginary Qualities, Ended her Career at last in a very exemplary Manner as I have before Stated in p. 205.)

1761

Early in this Year my Wife's elder Sister Miss Rodham paid us a Visit, and Remaind with us till she was Married. She was a Beauti[ful] and Elegant Young Woman somewhat Taller than her Sister, and was a Finer Woman. But she was Grave and Reserv'd, and tho' she had Good Sense, and was perfectly hearty, she was not only Inferior to her Sister in point of Understanding, but in that Lively and Striking expression of feeling and Sentiment, which never fails to attract. They were knit together with the Most Sisterly Love—In which however the Younger Surpass'd, not having one Selfish Corner in her whole Soul, and being at all times willing to sacrifice her Life for those she Lov'd. This Young Lady soon attracted Our Friend Dr Adam Fergusons Warmest Addresses, to the [Ardour] of which she put an End as soon as he explaind himself. For with a Frankness and Dignity becoming her Character, she Assur'd him that had she not Inviolably engagd to Another Gentleman, she would not have Hastily Rejected his Addresses, as his Character and Manners were very agreable to her; and therefore pray'd him to Discontinue his Suit to her as she could not Listen to him on that Subject, but would be happy in his Friendship and the Continuance of a Society so pleasing to her. With this he Reluctantly Complied, But frequented our House as much as ever till she was Married.

The Gentleman she was engag'd to was John Erasmus Blackett Esqr the Youngest Brother of Sir Edward Blackett Bar^t of Matfen in N. Humberland, a Man of Large Fortune who Represented the Elder Branch of the Blackett Family, Then in Sir Walter Blackett C[al]verly, who was the Nephew of the Late Sir Wm Blackett of Newcastle. John E. Blackett was a very Handsome young Man of about 30, who had been bred at Liverpool with Sir Ellis Cunliffe and was now Settled Partner with Mr Alderman Simson, an Eminent Coal Dealer in Newcastle. John B. Call'd Erasmus after Erasmus Lewis, who was Secretary to Lord Oxford in Queen Ann's time, and an Intimate Friend of his Father John Blackett Esqr of [?Sockburn] in Yorkshire who never was Bart. having Died before his Uncle Sir Edward B. John E. was at this time a Capt and Paymaster in his Brothers Reg^t of N. Humberland Millitia, lately Rais'd, and Quarterd at Berwick since March or April 1760—As Miss Rodham was not of age till March, the Marriage was Delay'd till after that time, when she could Dispose of her Moiety of the Estate. As this Did not

209

make Miss Roddam . . . That Quieted a Suspicion, which some of her friends entertaind, that he meant to Draw off. But he came and visited us in the end of Jan.y when every Shadow of Doubt of his Fulfilling his Engag.t, was Dissipated. I was only affraid That a Man so imperfectly Educated as he had been, and of Ordinary Talents, could not long predominate in the Breast of a Young Lady, who had Sense and Sensibility[1] Enough, to Relish the Conversation of the High Minded and Enlighten'd Philosopher, who had enough of the World however to be Entitled to the Name of a Polite Philosopher.

I Return'd with M.r Blackett in the beginning of Feb.y to Berwick and Wooller where I met the Trustees, where our Estate was Let to Ralph Compton the 2.d [Son] of our Former Tenant for the usual Term, and Rose from £180 pr. ann. to £283.—Before we Parted M.r B. Settled with me that he would come to us in April, and compleat his Engagement.— He went on from Alnwick and I to the Roup at Wooller.

He came accordingly at the time appointed* from Berwick attended by a Brother Cap.t Edward Adams, whose Mother was a Collingwood, a Grand Aunt of the Young Ladies. They Come first to my House for a Day, and went to Edin.r where we follow'd them two Days after, when the Young Couple were Married by M.r Car of the English Chappel, as they were both Episcopalians. The Day after the Marriage Blackett Gave us a Handsome Dinner at Fortune's[2] for which he only Charg'd half a Crown a Head, and said he then never charg'd more for the best Dinner of two Courses and a Desert which he Could Set Down. M.r Ferguson D.d with us. Next day they came to Muss.h for two Days and then Departed for Newcastle thro' Berwick, where the Reg.t still was. There was one

---

* Miss Rodham had been for a Week before this, with her Great Friend Miss Susan Renton, afterwards the Lady of Sir Rob.t Murray, and I had met her at Haddington and brought her to my House 2 Days before the Gentlemen Came.

His Grace Arch.d Duke of Argyle Died Early in the Spring, as Suddenly almost, and at the same age of 77 as his Majesty Geo. 2.d had done in [Oc.r]—On this Occasion, Lord Bute wrote a very kind Letter to L.d Milton, the Friend and Subminister of Argyle, Lamenting his Loss, and assuring him, that there should be no Change in respect to him. Adam Ferguson was with Milton when he Rec'd this Letter, To whom he Gave it after Reading it, Saying is this Man Sincere. To which Ferguson, on Perusal: I have no Doubt that he was so, when he wrote it. Milton Declin'd Being longer employ'd; and it was well, For he soon fell into that Decline of Mental Powers, which lasted till his Death in 1766.

Lord Bute tried to make his Brother Stuart M.ckenzie succeed Milton—But he neither had Talents nor Inclination. Baron Mure who was a Man of Business, and of Sound Sense, was Employd while L.d Bute was in Power.

In this Year I lost my Grandfather and Grand Mother Robison, two very respectable People in their Day. He Died First at the Age of 86, and she who was half a year Younger than him, Gave way to Fate just 6 months after him.

thing very Remarkable of that Reg.t who tho' 600 Strong from all parts of the County, Yet lost not one Man, for one Year and four Months. So much for the Healthiness of Berwick.

My Youngest Sister Janet, a Beautifull Elegant and pleasing Young Woman, was Married at London, where she had Gone to be with her Sister, on Aug.t 30.th 1760, with Cap.t Tho.s Bell, a Nephew of Provost Bell's who had been Cap.t of [a] Trading Vessel in the Mediteranean, and Having been attackd by a Spanish Privateer, took her after a Short Engagement, and Got £1000, as his Share of the Prize. He was a very Sensible Cliver Man, much Esteem'd by his Companions, and had become an Insurance Broker.

On the 1.st of July this Year [1761] my Wife brought me a Daughter and my Sister gave a Son to Thomas Bell on the 6.th of the same Month. He was the 1.st of 8 Sons she had, 7 of which were Running,[1] of whom Carlyle, whom we took in 1782 at two years old is the youngest, who are all alive in Dec.r 1804; and 8 Daughters, all well Married, and have many children.

When my Wife was perfectly Recover'd I found myself under the Necessity of Carrying her to Newcastle to visit her Sister to whom she was most tenderly attach'd. M.r Blackett was then Living in Pilgrim St., a small but very pleasant House near the Gate. This was in the beginning of Oc.r when the Judges were in Town and a Great Crowd of Company. M.r Blacketts Brother Henry the Clergyman was then with him, who was an [Oxonian], a Good Scholar, and a very agreable Man of the World. We were visited by all their Friends in Newcastle and the Neighbourhood, and made many agreable acquaintance[s]. Sir Walter Blackett was one who liv'd in a Fine Old House Directly Opposite to M.r B.—He was a very Genteel Fine Looking Man turn'd of 40, who had not been happy with his Lady The Daughter (Natural) of his uncle Sir W.m Blackett, who had left him and [her] Heirs of his Estate, provided they Intermarried. He fulfilld the Will most Cordially, for he was in Love with his Cousin, but she Reluctantly, as she Did not care for him. By Report she was of Superior Understanding to him, for he was not a Man of Remarkable Parts, But Strong in Friendship, Liberality and Publick Spirit. And he had a Great Fortune not less than £20,000 with which he amply Gratified his own Disposition. He was Ostentatious, and fond of Popularity, which he Gain'd by his Publick Charities, but Liv'd to Lose it entirely. He was long Member from the Town of Newcastle, but never would ask any Favours of Ministers, while in the Mean[time] he brought in a Cliver Colleague, a M.r Ridley, who Got all the Favours from Ministers, Having both Sir Walters Interest and his own, by which the Credit of the former with his Townsmen was much Shaken.

Our Sister Mrs Blackett luckily prov'd a Great Favourite of Sir Walters, as his Cousin John Erasmus had been before, to whom he Gave the Payment of his Leadmines, which being very productive, was a place of Profit.

Mr Collingwood of Chirton was another valuable acquaintance. He was Recorder of the Town and a Lawyer of Great Ability, who had acquir'd the Family Estate, Tho' but the 2^d Brother, by means of the Dissipation of the Elder, who was Representative of an antient Family, and whose Son is Vice Admiral Collingwood The Husband of Mrs Blackett's Eldest Daughter. The Recorder had acquird Chirton by Marriage, For a Laird of Roddam, one [of] the 5 Families in the County who were Proprietors before the Conquest, Having been an attorney at Newcastle had purchas'd the Estate of Chirton, which he left to his two Daughters Mary and Elizabeth, one of whom Married a Mr Hilton Lawson, and the other Mr Collingwood, while the antient Manor of Roddam went by Entail to his Nephew Admiral Roddam. There were two houses at Chirton, only Divided from each other by a Road. By far the best was the Posession of Mary the Eldest Sister and her Husband Lawson, which had in the end of [the] 17th Century belong'd to Arch^d the 1st Duke of Argyle who had built or repaird it as a Convenient Place between London and Inveraray on his Journeys to and from the Capital. It was at this House that he Died on one of those Journeys. This House is now the Possession of Adam De Cardonnell Lawson Esqr which was left to his Mother Ann Hilton, by her Cousin Hilton Lawson; because if her Brother a Revd Mr Hylton had not Died, he would fallen Heir to that and several other Estates of Mr Lawsons. This Gentleman is the Son and Heir of my Old Friend Mansfield De Cardonnel formerly Mentiond, a Grandchild by his Mother of the Duke of Mon[mouth].

Those Families adopted our two wives as their Relations, as their Father was a Descendant of the Family of Roddam, and their Mother of that of Collingwood of Unthank, who was Related to Both. At this Period there were [not] many Conversible Gentlemen in Newcastle, which made one value Mr Collingwood the More, for the Men were in General very Ill Educated, while the Ladies who were Bred in the South, by their Appearance and Manners seem'd to be very unequally Yok'd. The clergy at the time were almost all underbred, There being only one Vicar in the Town, and the Rest only Curates or Lecturers. Sometimes a Neighbouring Clergyman of University Education, accepted of a Lectureship, for the sake of Living in Town in the Winter, tho' the Sallary's were no more than £100—Yet had it not been for the Ladies, the State of Society would have then been Dissagreable. For many years past it has been totally Different.

At a Grand Dancing Assembly our Ladies were Gratified as much as [they could] be, for Mrs Blackett had the Honour of Dancing with the Duke of Portland and her Sister with Viscount Torrington, and had the approbation of a [very Numerous] Company for their Genteel Appearance and Good Looks. His Grace had come Down to take Care of his Parliamentary Interest, Having Great Estates in the Northern Counties. He was oppos'd in Cumberland by Sir James Lowther, who after a ten years war, Drove the Beaten Duke with Infinite Loss of Money, out of the north. Lowther went off Conqueror, but more Detested than any man alive, as a Shameless Political Sharper, a Domestick Bashaw, and an Intolerable Tyrant over his Tenants and Dependants. John Home Cried him up as the Bravest and most Generous of Men; and he flatter'd and oblig'd John because he had the Ear of Ld Bute, whose Eldest Daughter, an amiable and Patient Woman, he had Married and Abus'd. Home prevaild with him to Prefer Geo. Johnstone the Govr of Florida, to Admiral Elliot for one of his Seats in Parliament, Tho' he was by no means the best man of the two. But what was still more flattering to John, In two Duels he was Involv'd in, (None of which however took place), he took him for his 2^d. John Cried him up for every Good Quality. Ferguson who had seen him often, said He thought him a very stupid man. Bob Home who Livd 9 Months in his House in London attending [his] Cousin Sir [Michael] Fleming, with whom he went to Groningen, thought him a Capricious and sometimes a Brutal Head of a Family. Robert Adam told me many stories of him which made me Conclude that he was truly a Madman, tho' too Rich to be confind.

As Mrs C. had never been in that Country before, we made Several Excursions in the Neighbourhood Such as to Tinmouth and Durham, and in Returning Home visited Roddam, tho' there was only There the Old Lady and her two Daughters. The Admiral who Succeeded his Elder Brother in a Few Years, built him self a Handsome House and Improv'd the place. He has had 3 wives but no Children.

[1762]

In the Beginning of 1762 was Instituted the Famous Club calld the Poker,[1] which lasted in Great Vigour Down to the year 1784. About the 3^d or 4th Meeting, we thought of Giving it a Name that would be of uncertain Meaning, and not be so Directly Offensive, as that of Militia Club, to the Enemies of that Institution. Adam Ferguson fell Luckily on the Name of Poker, which we perfectly understood, and was at the same time an Enigma to the Publick. This Club Consisted of all the Literati of

Edin.̲ and its Neighbourhood, most of whom had been Members of the Select Society except very few Indeed who adhered to the Enemies of Militia, together with a Great Many Country Gentlemen, who tho' not always Resident in Town yet were Zealous Friends to a Scotch Militia, and warm in their Resentment on its Being Refusd to us, and an Invidious Line Drawn between Scotland and England.

The Establishment was Frugal and Moderate, as that of all clubs for a Publick purpose ought to be. We met at our old Landlords of the Diversorium now near the Cross,¹ The Dinner on the Table soon after Two a clock at 1 sh. a Head, The Wine to be confind to Sherry and Claret, and the Reckoning to be Call'd at Six a clock. After the first 15 who were chosen by Nomination, the members were to be chosen by Ballot, two Black Balls to exclude the Candidate. There was to be a New Pr[eses] chosen at every meeting; Will.ᵐ Johnstone Esq.̲ now Sir W.ᵐ Pulteney was chosen Secretary to the Club with the Charge of publications that might be Thought necessary by him and two other Members with whom he was to Consult. In a Laughing Humour, Andrew Crosbie was chosen assassin, in case any officer of that Sort should be needed. But Dav.ᵈ Hume was added as his assessor, without whose assent [nothing should be done]; So that between plus and minus, there was likely to be no Bloodshed.

This Club continued to be in Great perfection for Six or Seven Years, because the expence was Moderate, while every Member was pleas'd with the Entertainment as well as the Company. During those Seven Years a very Con[s]tant Attendant has told me that he never observ'd even an Approach to Inebriety in any of the members. At the end of that Period, by means of an unlucky Quarell between one or two of the Members, and our Landlord who was an Absurd Fool, the club Left his House and went to Fortune's the Most Fashionable Tavern in Town, where the Dinners were more shewy but not Better, and the Wine only Dearer— But the Days expence soon came 3 times as much as the Ordinary Bill at Tho.ˢ Nicholsons, which made many of the Members (not the Least Conversible) Lessen the N.ᵒ of Days of attendance. And what was worse, as the Club had long Drawn the Attention of the Publick, many Members were admitted whose Minds were not Congenial with the old members. When this Change Seem'd to be in Danger of Essentially Hurting the Club a Few of us had Recourse to a plan for keeping the old Members together which was that of Establishing a New Club to be Call'd the Tuesday, to meet on that Day and Dine together, without Deserting the Poker. This Lasted for 2 years at Sommers's Tavern,² for we Did not Go to Nicholson's for fear of Giving Offence. In the Meantime the Poker Dwindled away by the Death or Desertion of many of the

Members, who had Lately been brought in, and then we broke up the Tuesday, and frequented the Poker. I found in the Hands of Ferguson a List of this Club taken in 1774, and wrote by Commissioner James Edgar, to which in other Hands were added the New Members as they were Elected.* I have seen no List previous to this; But from 1762 to 84 Sundry Members must have Died, two of whom I Remember viz. Dr Jardine and Ambassador Keith. Dr Gregory too might be added. But he Did not attend above once or twice. The amount of the Whole on this List is 66.

When James [Edgar] was in Paris with Sir Laur. Dundas his Cousin During the Flourishing State of this Club he was ask'd [by] D'Alembert to go with him to their Club of Literati at Paris, to which he answerd that he had no Curiosity to visit them as he had a Club at Edinr with whom he Din'd weekly, composd he believ'd of the ablest Men in Europe. Similar to this was a Saying of Princess Dashcoff, when Disputing with me one Day at Buxton, about the Superiority of Edinr as a Residence to most other Cities in Europe, when having alledg'd Sundry Particulars in which I thought we excell'd, none of which she would admit of. No, says she, but I know one article which you have not mention'd in which I must Give you the Precedency, which is, that of all the Sensible Men I have met with in my Travels thro' Europe yours at Edinr are the most Sensible. Let me add one Testimony more, that of the Honble Genl James Murray, Ld Elibanks Brother, a Man of Fashion and of the World. Being at the Cross (the Change) one Day just before

* **List of the Poker Club[1] in 1774 and Downwards to 1784 1. Lord Elibank 2. Dr Carlyle 3. Professor Ferguson 4. Mr John Fordyce 5. Mr John Home 6. Mr Geo. Dempster 7. Mr Js Ferguson Pitfour 8. Mr And. Crosbie 9. Mr Wm Johnstone Pulteney 10. Mr Wm Nairn Dunsinane 11. Mr David Hume 12. Mr James Edgar 13. Mr John Adam 14. Dr Robertson 15. Mr And. Stuart 16. Mr Adam Smith 17. Sir John Dalrymple 18. Dr Blair 19. Sir John Whiteford 20. Mr Baron Mure 21. Mr Dd Ross, Ld Ankerville 22. Dr Black, M.D. 23. Lord Elliock 24. Mr Baron Grant 25. Mr Isla Campbell Pr. 26. Mr Dundas of Dundas 27. Mr John Clerk Eld. . 28. L. Colll John Fletcher 29. Sir Js Stuart Coltness 30. Mr Home of Ninewells 31. Mr And. Grant 32. Colll Campbell Finab 33. Mansfeld Cardonnell Esqr 34. Mr A. Ferguson Craigdarroch 35. Mr Robert Chalmers 36. Mr Robt Cullen Adv. 37. Mr Geo. Brown Comr 38. Sir Adam Ferguson 39. Profr John Robison 40. Mr Wm Gordon 41. Mr Geo. Home W.S. 42. Ld Advocate H. Dundas 43. Capt John Elliot 44. Mr James Russel Surgeon 45. Mr Robt Keith Ambassador 46. Mr Wm Graham, Gartmore 47. Mr Al. Home Cl. of Session 48. The Earl of Glasgow 49. Mr Baron Norton 50. Mr Geo. Ferguson Ld Hermand 51. Sir John Halket Bart 52. His Grace the Duke of Buccleuch 53. The Earl of Glencairn 54. And. Fletcher Esqr Saltoun 55. Ld Mountstuart 56. Mr Baron Gordon 57. Mr Thos Dundas Ld Dundas 58. Mr Kennedy of Dun[ure] 59. Ld Binning 60. Mark Pringle Esqr Adv. 61. Mr Rutherford Egerton 62. Earl of Haddington 63. Mr Wm Muirhead 64. Mr Wm Millar Ld Glenlee 65. Marquis of Graham 66. Sir James Johnstone Bart.**

the Hour of Dinner which by that time was prolong'd to 3 aclock, he came up to me, and askd me If I had yet met with his Brother Elibank. I answerd no, was he Expecting him in Town that Day. Yes, said he, He promisd to come and Introduce me to the Poker. If that is all your Business, Replied I, and [you] will accept of me as your Introductor, I shall be Glad of the Honour, and Perhaps your Brother may come Late as he sometimes Does. He accepted, and the Club happen'd to be very well attended. When we broke up between 7 and 8 a clock, it Being Summer, and I was proceeding down Streets to take my Horse to Musselburgh, he come up with me, and exclaimd, Ah! Dr I never was so much Dissappointed in all my Life as at your Club, for I expected to Sit Silent and Listen to [a] Parcel of Pedants Descanting on Learn'd Subjects out of my Range of Knowledge, but instead of that, I have met with an Agreable, Polite and Lively Company of Gentlemen, in whose Conversation I have Join'd and Partook with the Greatest Delight. As Murray was a very Acute and Sensible Man, I took this as a very high Compliment to the Manners as well as the parts of our Club.

In April this Year Mrs C. went to Newcastle to attend her Sister who was to Ly in of her first child. I went with her to Lanton in N. Humberland and Return'd Home Mr B. having Met her there. I attended the Assembly of which I was a Member, for the 1st time out of my Course, when Dr Trail of Glasgow was Moderator.—He put upon me the 3 addresses which were sent up from this assembly, to the King, the Queen and the Princess Dowager of Wales on the Marriage of their Majesties, which were thought to be well compos'd, Especially that to his Majesty. This even met with the Approbation of the Commissioner tho' not pleas'd with me,[1] when on one of the Preceding Years, I had help'd to Raise bad Humour against him for Inviting Whitefield to Dine at his Table, and another Year he had entertaind [the design] of Dissolving the Assembly before the 2d Sunday. To be sure the Business before us was but slack, yet had we allow'd the precedent to take place, we should never have Recover'd that Sunday more.

On the last Day of this Assembly, I Learn'd to my Great Joy, that my Friend Dr Wm Wight was presented by the King to the vacant Chair of History at Glasgow. As he was my near Relation, his Advancement in which I had a chief hand was very pleasing, and as he was the most agreable of all men, his coming near me promis'd much Enjoyment.

Towards the end of June I was Earnestly Requested by Wm Johnstone Esqr now Pulteney, to Accompany his uncle Ld Elibank on some Jaunt, to take him from Home, as he had just Lost his Lady, and was in bad Spirits. I agreed on condition that he would take the Road which I wish'd to Go, which was to Newcastle to bring home Mrs Carlyle. This was agreed to and I went to him [in a] Day or two, and we set out on the 27ᵗʰ of June, and as he travelld with his own Horses, we Did not arrive there till the 29ᵗʰ to Dinner. My Fellow Traveller was Gloomy, and Lamented his Wife very much, who had been a Beauty in her Youth and was a Dutch Lady of Fortune, the Widow of Lᵈ North and Grey. He himself was now turn'd 60, and she was ten Years Older. She was a weak woman but very Observant of him, and seem'd proud of his Wit and fine Parts and had no uneasiness about his Infidelities, except as they affected his Prospects in a future World. She had a Large Jointure which he lost and which added to his affliction. But she had brought a Large Sum besides, and falling in with his humour of Saving, from being a very poor Lᵈ she had made him very Wealthy. When we Arriv'd at Newcle. he was at first overcome at the Sight of my Wife, who was well Acquainted with his Lady, but her Sympathy and the Gentle Manners of her Sister attracted his Notice. In this Tender State of Vexation Mingled with Grief and Penitence he met with a very Handsome young Lady [Miss Maria Feilding, a niece of Sir John Feildings][1], whose Manners Soften'd by his Recent Loss and melancholy Appearance so much Subdued him, [that] he fell suddenly in Love, and was ashamd and afflicted with his own Feelings, Falling into a kind of an Hysterical Fit. Mʳˢ C. told me afterwards, that she had made him Confess, which he said he Did, because he saw She had found him out. Hearing of some of his Friends, who were at Harogate, he left us on the 4ᵗʰ or 5ᵗʰ Day and went there; at this place, there was plenty of Gay Company and play, and every sort of amusement for an afflicted Widower, so that his Lordship soon forgot his Lady and her Jointure, and Maria Feilding, and all his cares and sorrow, and became the Gayest Man in the whole place before the Month of July Elaps'd.

As we were to Go Round by Dumfries to Visit my Sister Dickson who had fallen into a Decline, and was Drinking Goats Whey in the Neighbourhood, we propos'd to take the Road to Carlisle from Newcastle, and Mʳˢ C. not being very Strong, we Got Mʳ Blackett's Chaise for the 1ˢᵗ Days Journey. After you have Got 10 or 12 Miles West from Newcastle The Country becomes Dreary and Desolate, without a Single Interesting Object, But what employs the Curious Research of the Antiquarian, The Remains of that Roman Wall, which was Constructed to prevent the Inroads of the Barbarians on the Roman Province or the Defenceless Natives. The Wall in Many Parts is wonderfully Entire, and while it Demonstrates the Art and Industry of the Romans, brings full in our View the Peace and Security we now Enjoy, under a Government that unites the Interest and promotes the Common Prosperity of the Whole Island. We slept at Glenwilt a Paultry Place, and Got to Bramton early next Day, but had to Send to Carlisle for a chaise, as I Did not chuse to Carry Mr Blacketts any further. This place as is Noted in an account of Dr Wight, is Remarkable for the Birth of 3 persons in the Same Year or nearly so, who Got as high in their respective professions, as they possibly [could]: Dr Thomas, a Son of the Rector of the Parish, who came to be Bishop of Rochester, Mr Wallace, a Son of the Attorney, who arriv'd at the Dignity of Attorney Gen! and would have been Chancellor, had he Liv'd, and Dr Wm Wight the Son of the Dissenting Minister, who liv'd to be Proff^r of Divinity in Glasgow.

It was late in the Afternoon before the Chaise come from Carlisle for which I had Sent, so that we not only Breakfasted but Din'd here; when the Cheapness not Less than the Goodness of our Fare was Surprising; as 4/6 was the whole expence for M^rs C's Dinner and mine and Black[etts] Servant and 2 Horses, mine Having Gone on to Carlisle. The Environs of Carlisle are Beautifull, and Mrs C. was much pleas'd with them. The Road from thence to Dumfries is thro' a Level Country, but not very Interesting, the Country Being at that time unimprov'd and but thinly Inhabited. The approach to Dumfries on every side is pleasing. My Sister Dickson was Down at New-abbey, 10 M. below Dumfries on the W. Side of Nith, for the Sake of Goats Whey—We went Down Next Day, but found her far Gone in a Decline, a Disorder which had been so fatal to Our Family. She was well acquainted with M^rs C's Character before she Met her, which She Did with the Most Tender and Cheerfull Affection. Her Appearance she told [me] even Surpass'd all she had heard, and for the two Days they Remain'd together, There never was closer union of two Superior Minds, Soften'd by Tenderness and adorn'd with every Female Virtue. It was Difficult to part them, as they were Sure they would meet no more. Many confident promises were made however, To Lighten as much as possibly the Melancholy parting, which my Sister perform'd with such Angelic Gaiety, as [led] Mrs C. into the Belief that She thought herself in little Danger. I knew the Contrary. One thing she Did, which was to Confirm me in the Opinion, of what an excellent Mind it was to which I was united. But this needed no Confirmation. After this scene, Dumfries and the Company of our other Friends was Irksome, So we Made Haste to Meet my Mother who had taken the Road home from Penrith, Having been so long Absent from my Father. We found our Little Girl in Perfect Health.

It was this Year in Sepr That on the Death of Hyndman I succeeded him in the Place of Almoner to the King—an Office of No Great Emolument, but a Mark of Distinction, and very Convenient, as my Stipend was Small. For I kept my Resolution, to Defer a Prosecution for an Augmentation till my Patron was of Age.

I had Reason to expect this Office, not only by means of John Home now having much of Ld Bute's Ear, but from the Friendship of Sir G. Elliot and Sir Harry Erskine who were friends of Ld Bute. Charles Townshend too had made application at this time tho' he faild me before.

The Death of Hyndman was a Dissappointment to Robertson in the Management of the Church, which he had now in view. [By his Preference of Hyndman][1] he had provok'd Dick, who was a far better Man [and] who prov'd a very formidable and vigorous Opponent: For he Join'd the Wild or Highflying Party, and by Moderating their Councils, and Defending their Measures, as often as he Could, Made them More Embarrassing, than if they had been allow'd to follow their own Measures.

Hyndman was not a Right Man. We had Discover'd him at Glasgow where he had been admitted now and then to a Weekly Club we had at Mrs Dugalds opposite the Cross. . . .[2] Hyndman was a Cliver Fellow, a Good Preacher, and a Good Debater in Church Courts. Cuming had adopted him as his 2^d and had help'd to bring him from Collington to the West Church. Being unfortunate in his Family he had taken to Tippling and High Politicks. He finish'd his Constitution, and became Apopl[ectic]k. Cuming and he had Quarrell'd—and Robertson without adverting to his undone constitution. . . .[3]

It was about the end of this year That my Sister Bell and her two children William and Jessy come and paid a visit to my Father and Mother, and Remaind for some months. They occasionally staid with us. Mr Bell was Gone to the Havannah in a Cargo Ship full of Merchandise for that Market after it was Taken, with a Cargo not of Less Value than £40,000—Four or Five young Merchants such a[s] Robt Bogle of Dundonie, &c. were his Partners. But as their Ship was not the First that [arriv'd] and Ld Albemarle the Govr had laid a pretty high [duty], as was said, on those who had come first, Capt Bell was not allowd to Open Market for Several weeks or months after he arrivd, When the Market being Glutted his Sales were [not] Heavy, So that if he had not been Super-Cargo as well as Commander, he must have been a Loser. He Return'd Next Year, with an additional Cargo, and made a Better Hand of it.

1763

Besides my Sister and her Children, occasionally Miss Ann Collingwood my Wife's Cousin Staid a Good Deal with us. Her Brother Capt Gilfrid[4] had Got a Small Office on the Staff at Edin^r, and was taken ill of a Fever. She came down at 1ˢᵗ to Nurse him. He Recoverd, but being weak, my Wife had him for Country Air and New Milk to Restore him. He went well to his Duty in two or 3 weeks and she Remaind. She was then a handsome Lively Girl of 16 and was admir'd. Thoˢ Cheap Consul at Madeira My Friend come to Edinʳ in the beginning of the Year to visit his Friends and Look out for a Wife. After having been plied by two or 3, he at last fixt on Grace Stewart, a very pretty Girl, and Carried her. This pleasd his Sister well, who was always looking after Quality, for her Mother Lady Ann was a Sister of the Earl of Murray. This Courtship Occasion'd Several pleasant Meetings of Private Parties at Chrystals a Tavern in the Parish where Dʳ Robert Finlay, now possessor of Drumore, Display'd such Qualities as he had; for he was Master of one of the Feasts having Lost a Dinner and a Ball to the Consul's Sister. Ann Collingwood made a Good Figure in the Dance, but Grace Stewart Surpast her.

About the End of April my Sister and my Wife and [I paid] a Visit to our Friends in Glasgow, where we were most Cordially Rec'd by my old Friends, Mʳ Dreghorn, and Sundry other Merchants who were connected with Mʳ Bell in London, particularly Robin Bogle and the Dunlops. Dʳ Adam Smith and Dʳ Black as well as Dʳ Wight were now here, tho' the last had not yet Got into his House. We had many agreable Meetings with them, as well as with Our Mercantile Friends. It was there that I saw No. 45, when Just publishd by Wilkes[1]—of which Smith said on hearing it Read, Bravo, this Fellow will either be hang'd in Six Months, or he will Get Lord Bute Impeach'd. Supping with him in a Company of 22, when a Certain Young Peer was present, after a little while I whisper'd him, That I wonder'd they had set up this Man so high, as I thought him mighty Foolish. We know that perfectly Said he, but he is the only Lord at our College. To this Day There were not above 2 or 3 Gentlemen's Chaises in Glasgow, nor Hackney Coaches, nor Mens Servants to attend at Table. But they were not the worse Servd. Soon after we Return'd home in the beginning of May, my Sister and her Children Return'd to London, but took the way by Dumfries to visit their Friends there.

Dʳ Robertson was Moderator of the Assembly this Year, and Being Now Principal of the University of Edinʳ had it in his Power to be Member of Assembly every Year. He had Lost Hyndman, but he now adopted Dʳ John Drysdale,* who had married his Cousin, one of the Adams, a far

---

* Dʳ Drysdale was brought to Edinʳ by a Presentation, The Magistrates and Council having Resum'd that Right which had so long lain Dormant. During the Contest which was Violent, My Friend Dʳ Jardine Rode out to me, and Requested me to Draw up a Paper in their Defence which I Did on his Furnishing me with the Facts, and publish'd

Better Man in every Respect, for he had Good Talents for Business, tho'
his Invincible Modesty prevented his Speaking in Publick. He now
Manag'd the Highland Correspondence, and became extremely popular
in that Division of the Church. Robertson had now Dr Dick as his Stated
Oponent, who would have been very formidable had he not been tied up
by his own Principles, which were firm in support of Presentations, and
by his not having it in his Power to be a Member of Assembly more than
once in 4 or 5 Years on acc^t of the Strict Rotation observ'd by the Presbytery of Edin^r.

And. Crosbie the Advocate was Another Constant and Able Opponent
of Dr Robertson and his Friends, Tho' hamper'd a little by the Love of
Patronage. His Maternal Uncle, Ld Tinwald the Justice Cl. Being Dead,
who was his Patron, he wish'd to Gain Employment by pleasing the
Popular Side. Fairbairn the Minister of Dumbarton was another opponent, Brisk and foul mouth'd, who stuck at nothing, and was end[ow'd]
with a Rude Popular Eloquence. But he was a mere Hussar who had no
Steady Views to Direct him, and was a Member of every Assembly and
spoke in every Cause, but merely for Plunder, that is applause and
Dinners, for he Did not seem to care whither he Lost or Won. Robertson's Soothing Manner prevented his being hardmouthd with him.

Dr Robertson had for his assistants all the Moderate party in Edin^r
and the Neighbourhood, but many Clergymen annually from the most
Distant Synods and Presbyteries, who now that the Debates of the
Assembly were carried on with Freedom tho' still with Great Order
[prov'd] very Good Speakers and able Debaters. There were very few of
the Lay Elders of much consideration who oppos'd him; and Henry
Dundas (Ld Melville) who was in himself an Host, coming next Year to
our aid, [added greatly to our strength and made the Business fashion-
able, for till then],[1] many of the Superior Elders Deserted the Assembly.
Insomuch that I Remember one Year, That when a most important
Overture was Debated, There was neither one of the Judges, nor of the
Crown Lawyers in the Assembly.

In May this Year we had a Visit from the Blacketts who Did not stay
long. And I having an appointment with Dr Wight to go for a few weeks
to Harrogate, we set out in the Beginning of July, and in our way past

---

under the Title of *Faction Detected*. This I mention because, Mr Robertson the Procurator, ask'd me once if it was not of his Fathers Composing, for so it had been said to
him. But I told him the Fact, and at the same time Gave him the Reasons of Dissent
from a sentence of the Commission in 1751 or 1752 which had been originally Drawn by
Dr Robertson tho' Corrected and Enlarg'd by a Committee. I Don't know if Provost
Drummond and the Magistrates knew of the piece of Service I had Done them, but
They Never Thank'd Me for it.

some days at Newcastle, where Wight who was a Stranger made his usual empression as one of the most agreable Men they had ever seen. When we arrivd at the Dragon in Harrogate however Wights Vivacity was allarm'd at the shyness of the English who are backward to make up to Strangers till they have reconnoitr'd them awhile. Wight was much enragd at this, and threatend either to leave the place, or to Breakfast in a Private Room. I prevaild with him to have his Table set in the long Room, where our Demeanour Being observ'd by the Company we were soon Reliev'd from our aukward situation by an Invitation from 2 Ladies who had no man with them, to come to their Breakfast Table, according to the Custom of the place at this [time]. We found them very agreable and were envied for our Good Luck. When we enter'd the Dining Room at two a clock we were no longer Strangers and took our places according to the Custom of the House. There were 2 Tables in the Dining Room which held between 30 and 40 a Piece, and our Places were at the Bottom of that on the Right Hand, from whence we were Gradually to Rise to the Top of the Room, as the Company Chang'd, which was Daily.

Harrogate at this time was very pleasant for there was a Constant Succession of Good Company, and the best Entertainment of any Watering place in Brittain at the Least expence. The House we were at was not only Frequented by the Scotch at this time but was the Favourite House of the English Nobility and Gentry. Breakfast Cost Gentlemen only 2ᵈ apiece for their Muffins, as it was the fashion for Ladies to Furnish Tea and Sugar—Dinner 1 sh., Supper 6ᵈ, Chambers Nothing, Wine and other extraordinaries at the usual price, and as little as you please, Horses and Servants at a Reasonable Price. We had two Haunches of Venison twice a week During the Season. The Ladies Gave afternoons Tea and Coffee in their Turns, which coming butt once in 4 or 5 weeks amounted to a Triffle. The Estates of the People at our Table Did not amount to Less than £50 or £60,000 pr ann., among [whom] were several Members of Parliament, and they had not had the Precaution to Order one news paper among them all, tho' the time was Critical. But And. Millar the Celebrated Bookseller Supplied that Defect, for he had two papers sent to him by every post, so that all the Barᵗˢ and Great Squires, your Sir Thoˢ Claverings and Sir Harry Grays and Drumond of Blair Drumond, Depended upon and paid him Civil Accordingly. And yet when he appeard in the Morning in his old well m . . . . ed Suit of Cloathes, They Could not help Calling him Peter Pamphlet, [for] the . . . . Generous Patron of Scotch Authors with his City Wife and her Niece were Sufficiently Ridiculous when they came into Good Company. It was Observ'd however that she did not allow him to Go Down to the

Well with her in the Chariot in his Morning Dress. Tho' she ownd him at Dinner time as he had to pay the extraordinaries.

As Wight had never been in York, we went Down Early on a Sunday Morning when we heard that the Arch Bishop and the Judges were to be in the Cathedral. We had Dr Hunter M.D. who at that time frequented Harrogate for our Guide, but he was kept in such close Conversation that he mistook the road and led us two miles out of our Way, so that we had but just time to Breakfast before we went to Church; when the Service Being begun, we enterd The Quire where it was Crouded to the Door. Our Eyes were Delighted with a such a Magnificent Show. But our Ears were not so highly pleas'd, for no part of the Service seem'd to us to suit the Grandeur of the Scene. We were Invited to Dine with Mr Scott from Madeira, Thos Cheaps Partner, But Wight had Engag'd to Dine with the Honble Archdeacon Hamilton, whose Education he had Superintended for a Year at Glasgow, and with whom he was well acquainted in Ireland where his preferment Lay. His Beautifull Wife had elop[d] from him with a Sir [George] Warren, and he had Rec'd her again, and was Living privately at York till the Story became Stale. Wight extold her Beauty and her Penitence, and If I remember Right, they Continued to Live together and had Sons and Daughters. We pass'd the evening with Mr Scott, who had with him a large Party of Americans, Mr Allan Justice General of Pensylvania, and his two Sons and Daughters, fine young people Indeed, the Eldest of them not yet 20 years of Age. With them there was also a Mr Livingstone, and I think a Sister of his also. Mr Allan was a Man very Open and Communicative, and as he was of Scottish Extraction, His Grandfather Having fled from Stirlingshire, to escape the Cruel persecution of the Presbyterians, by Lauderdale and James 2.^d, he seem'd partial to us as clergymen from Scotland. He said he had Intended to have Gone as far as Edin.^r But found he should not have time at present, but was to Leave his Sons in England to Compleat their Education. He wish'd us to Stay all next Day, and come an hour in the forenoon, and examine his Lads, to Judge to what a Length young men could now be brought in America. This we Declin'd, but agreed to Dine next Day, and bring on Such Conversation as would enable us to Judge better of the Young Men than any Formal Examination.

There was a Circumstance that I shall never forget which past in one of our Conversations. Dr Wight and I had seen Dr Franklin at Edin.^r as I have formerly Related. We Mention'd this Philosopher to Mr Allan with the Respect we Thought due, and he answerd, Yes all you have said of him is true, and I could add more in his praise. But tho' I have now Got the better of him, he has Cost me more trouble since he came to Reside in our State than all mankind Besides, and I can assure you that he is a Man so turbulent and such a Plotter as to be able to embroill the 3 Kingdoms if he ever has an opportunity. Franklin was after this for several weeks in Edinͬ with D. H[u]me but I Did not see him Having been from Home on Some Jaunt. In 1769 or 70 I met him at an Invited Dinner in London, at John Stuarts the Provosts Son I think it was, where he was Silent and Inconversible. But this was after he had been refus'd the office of Post Master Genˡ of America, and had Got a severe Dressing from Wedderburn, then Sollͬ or Attorney Genˡ. We Returnd to Harrogate in the Evening, where Mͬ Scott and his Wife Join'd us next Day.

It was my Good Fortune at Dinner to Sit next Mͬ Ann a Roman Catholick Gentleman of Yorkshire who was very agreable and knew the whole Company. But it was our Misfortune to Lose our New Friends very fast, for at the End of a Fortnight I was at the Head of a Table above 30, and I Remember had to Divide a Haunch of Venison among 15 of them, without Getting any portion of Fat for myself—But what Signifies that, when you have an opportunity of Obliging your Friends, as Sir J. Dalrymple said to me one Day, when we had a Haunch at the Poker, flattering me for a Good Piece, for he was a Gourmand. But it was wonderfull to Observe how easily we united with our New Friends who took the places of the Deceast, for most of them were in Reality so to us. We fell in by accident with a very agreable Man, a Collˡ Roberts, who was a Lieut. Collˡ of the Royal Irish, and had been in that Country for 3 years, and had so Compleatly Caught the Brogue, That it was Impossible at first to think him an Englishman Born and Bred: Which he nevertheless was, and Nephew to Lord Egremont, Secͭ of State at the time. This Gentleman by ill luck had been Directed to the *Salutation Inn*, which was the Quakers House, of Excellent Entertainment but Indifferent Company. He took much to Wight and me, and we would fain have Drawn him to our House, but he would not for the world affront the Good people with whom he had liv'd a week. So we Compromisd the Matter, and went sometimes to Dine at his House, and he Returnd the Visit and came to Ours. He was truly a Man of Sense and of much Reading, and a Great Master of Conversation. He was the 1ˢᵗ whom I met with who struck out an Idea that has been follow'd Since; For talking much of Hume's and Robertson's Histories, he Said that Hume appear'd to him to be the Homer, and Robertson the Virgil of British Historians, a criticism, that has been of late Confirm'd by Dugald Stuarts Quotation.[1]

Our Friend Capͭ Fran. Lindsay was at the Granby, who Sometimes Dind with us, as we Did one Day with him, when we understood that Lᵈ Clive and his Train were to Dine there. He had arriv'd the evening before, of which Lindsay informd us, and we went in Due time to Dinner.

Clive was an ill looking man with the two Sides of his Face much unlike; one of them seeming Distorted as with the Palsy. When we enter'd the Long Room, he was Sitting at a Table in a window with a Great Many Papers before him, which he had Rec'd with that Days post. It was by those Dispatches that he had Learn'd his Jagire[1] was taken from him. Lindsay had watchd his countenance from the Moment he Got them, but could perceive no Change in the Muscles of his Face, which were well Suited to Bad News. But he must have known before this time what had happend. He Sate at some Distance from me on the opposite Side, but he seem'd to Converse with nobody During Dinner, and left the Table Immediatly after. There were half a Doz. people with him, among whom were his Favourite Secretaries both Jolly Fellows who Lov'd a Glass of Claret which Lindsay Recommended to them, and which was truly Good.

Tho§ Cheap my Friend from Madeira, who had been married at Inveresk with Grace Stewart, Came to Harrogate according to his promise to visit Lindsay and me. He came to the Dragon and Remain'd 4 Days with us. She was very handsome and Spirited and made a Great Impression. Robert Berry and his Beautifull wife were there at the same time, and it Could not be Doubted That she was the Finer Woman of the two. Yet our Fair Caledonian had so much Frankness and Spirit, and Danc'd so Exquisitely, that She Carried off all Hearts, Insomuch that there was a Sensible Degree of Regret and Gloominess in the Company, for a Quarter of an Hour at Least after she Left it.

Wight and I rode one Day to Hackfell, a place of the Aislybies a few Miles beyond Rippon, Thro' a most Delightfull Country, no part of which is finer than Ripley, Sir [John Ingilby's] place. Hackfell consists of a few Wooded Hills on both sides of a valley Terminating on a fine Village on the Banks of a Small River, Call'd Masham. There are fine walks cut thro' the woods, which make the place very Delightfull. Many such are now in Scotland since our Great Proprietors have found the Way to Lay open the Secret Beauties of their Romantick Domains to Strangers. Not being able to Reach Harrogate to Dinner we tried to Get Something at Gre[we]lthorpe the adjacent Village—But there was no Fire in the House, nor any thing indeed but very bad Oat Bread and some Ordinary Cheese. Rumaging in [the] amry[2] however I found at Last about 2 Lib. Weight of Cold-Roast Veal, which was a Great prize, especially now That 2 Gentlemen had Join'd us, an Hanoverian Nobleman and a D' Dod from London, not he of Infamous memory,[3] but another of perfect Good Character and very agreable Manners. We visited many fine places in the Neighbourhood, and particularly [Harewood] the Seat of Squire Lascelles Now Ld Harewood, where there is a very fine House Built by Robert Adam, and then not Inhabited. The

House might have had a Finer Site, had it been a Q.ʳ of a Mile more to the North, where there is a full view of one of the finest Vales in York-shire. Next year I visited this place again with my wife and the Black-ett's, and having been Rebukd by Sir David Dalrymple, for having omitted it before, (because I was Ignorant of its Curiosity) I went into the Village Church and saw the Monument of the chief Justice Gascoigne, a Native here, who had arrested Henry the 5.ᵗʰ when Prince of Wales for a Riot.

Harrogate abounded with half-pay Officers and Clergymen. The First are much the Same at all times, ill educated but well bred, and when you now and then meet with a Scholar such as Coll! Roberts, or my Old Friend whom I knew when Lieut. Ward at Muss.ʰ a little Stutter-ing Fellow, about the Year 1749, who had Read Polybius and Cæsar twice over, and who Rose to be a General, and Com.ʳ of the Cavalry in Ireland, you will find [him] as Intelligent as Agreable. Of the Clergy I had never seen so many together before, and between this and the Following Year, I was able to form a true Judgment of them. They are in General—I mean the lower Order—Divided into *Bucks* and *Prigs:* Of which the First, tho' inconceivable Ignorant, and Sometimes Indecent in their Morals, yet I held them to be most tolerable, because they were unassuming and had no other affectation, but that of Behaving them-selves Like Gentlemen. The other Division of them the *Prigs*, are truly Not to be indur'd, for they are but half Learn'd and Ignorant of the World, Narrow Minded pedantick and overbearing. Now and then you meet with a *Rara Avis*, who is accomplish'd and agreable, a Man of the World without Licenciousness, of Learning without Pedantry, and Pious without Sanctimony—but this is a *Rara Avis*.

This was the first time I had seen John Bull at any of his Watering Places: and I thought it not Difficult to account for his Resort to them. John is an Honest and Worthy Person as any in the World; But he is Seldom Happy at home. He has in his temper a shyness that Approaches to Timidity; and a Deference for the Opinion of his Servants that Over-awes him, and keeps him in constraint at home, while he is Led into unreasonable Expence. At his watering places, he is free from those Shackles. His Reserve is Overcome by the Frankness of those he meets; he is Master of his Servants, for he Carries only two with him, and the Man of £10,000 pr ann. can spend no more than the Man of £500—So that the Honest Man finds himself quite unfetter'd, and is ready to Shew his Kind and Sociable Disposition. He Descends from his Imaginary Dig-nity, by mixing with those who are Richer than himself, and soon shews you what he really is, viz. The very best Sort of Man in the World. The Late Wars [have] been very favourable to the Improving and Disclosing his character, for Instead of Going into France where he was flatterd Laughd at and Plunderd, he is now oblig'd to make all his Summer Excursions round his own Country where his Heart expands—and Being treated as he Deserves, Returns home for the Winter happy and much emprov'd.

At this Period everything was cheap and Good at Harrogate except Wine, which unless it was their claret which was every where Good and reasonable, was very Bad indeed. John Bull however has little Taste and does [not] much Care, for provided he Goes to bed Muzzy, whether it be with his own Native Drink Ale, or Sophisticated[1] Port, he is perfectly Contented.

As I Design'd to Convey Wight to Dumfries and Capt Lindsay was Going to Lochmabin to visit his Brother James the Minister we agreed to Set out together and made a very agreable Journey. Some part of the Road was Dreary after we past Sir Thos Robertson[s], which is a fine Place, and where there is an Inscription, fairly acknowledging That the Family Took its Rise from a Scotch Pedlar. When we approachd Appleby we were Delighted with the Appearance of the Country, which Being a Mixture of Hill and Dale, of Wood and Water, of Cultivated and Uncultivated is far more pleasing to the Eye and the Imagination, than those Rich plains which are Divided into Small Squares or Paralelograms, which Look like Bleachfields for Cottons on the Banks of the Clyde or Leven. At Penrith we Resolv'd to stop a Day to Rest our Horses, and to take the opportunity of Going to Visit the Lake of Keisack of which we had heard so much. Next Morning we took a Post chaise and Four and Drove thither over a Rough Road, thro' a Baren Country to the Village at the Distance of 18 Miles. We were unlucky for it prov'd a Rainy afternoon, So that we Could not Sail on the Lake and saw every thing to Great Dissadvantage. We Returnd to Penrith, where we had Good Entertainment and excellent Claret.

Next Morning we Set out Northwards, and separated from Capt Lindsay when we come to Longtown for he went to Lochmabin, and we took the Road to Dumfries, where after Staying a Few Days, I took the Road home by Moffat, and Wight went over to Ireland, once more to visit his Friends there. I found my wife and little Daughter in good Health with a fair prospect of another e'er long. My wife had Suppos'd that I had some Scorbutick Symptoms which had been Removd by Harrogate Waters. The Remainder of the Season passd on as usual—But I was not any more from home, except now and then in Edinr at the Poker Club, which ceas'd to meet by the 12th of August and re . . . . d on the 12th of Novr.

Luke Home our Aunt Home's youngest Son come to us to be at the

School, a year or two before and Remain'd 4 years—Their Daughter Betty come after and staid 2 or three years.

On the 1ˢᵗ Day of Decʳ this Year my wife brought me a 2ᵈ Daughter, which after trying [in] vain to Nurse she Gave to a very faithfull and trusty woman in Fisherow, who after Remaining one Quarter with us we allow'd to take the Child to her own House, where She Continued to Thrive to our entire Satisfaction.

1764

It was in Febʸ this Year I think That Mʳˢ C. being perfectly Recoverd she and I accompanied her Uncle and Aunt Mʳ and Mʳˢ Home to Glasgow to See their Son Walter, who was in Quarters there with his Regᵗ the 9ᵗʰ Foot. Dʳ Wight had by that time Got into his house in the College, and had Got [his] Yongest Sister to keep his house, who was Remarkably Handsome, had very Good parts with the Frank and Open Manner of the Dumfrisians. Her Brother Did not Dissapoint her turn for Social Entertainment, For he lov'd company, and the House was not without them almost any Day. Here we and our Friends were handsomly Entertain'd, as well as at Mʳˢ Drighorns where we Lodg'd, [and] at her Brothers Mʳ Bogle's who never Relax'd in his Attachment to me. Walter Home, then only a Lieut. whose Chum was a Mʳ Mainwaring a very agreable Man, had made himself very Respectable in Glasgow, to which he was well entitled, as much from his Superior Sense and Knowledge as for his Social Turn. John Home by one of his Benevolent Mistakes, had put him about James Stuart Lᵈ Bute's 2ᵈ Son, whom he was engag'd to attend Daily while he livd with Dʳ Robertson in Edinʳ.

At this Time Henry Dundas the most Strenuous Advocate for the Law of the Land respecting presentations, and the ablest and steadiest Friend to Dʳ Robertson and his Party that ever appeard in my time, became a Member of Assembly. He Constantly Attended the Assembly before and after he was Sollicitor Genᵗ. Tho when he Rose to be Lord Advocate and M. P. he was Sometimes Detain'd at London till after the meeting of Assembly. He was more than a Match for the Few Lawyers, who took the opposite Side and even for Crosbie who was playing a Game, and Dʳ Dick who was by far the Ablest Clergyman in opposition. I am not Certain whether Henry Dundas Did not excel more as a Barrister than he Did as a Judge in a Popular Assembly: In the first by his entering so warmly into the Interest of his Client, as totally to forget himself, and to adopt all the Feelings, Sentiments and Interests of his Employer. In the 2ᵈ by a Fair and Candid Statement of the Question, and followd it by Strong and Open Reasoning in Support of his Opinion. For a few Years at this period There was a Great Struggle in the General Ass. against the Measures Supported and Carried thro' by Robertson and his Friends, and we had to Combat the last exertions of the Party who had Supported Popular Calls. And it must be Confest that their efforts were vigorous. They Contriv'd to bring in Overtures from Year to Year, in which they propos'd to Consult the Country, in the Belief that the Result would be Such a General Opinion over the Kingdom, as would Oblige the Gen! Assembly, to Renew their Applications for the abolition of Patronage, or at Least for some more Lenient exercise of [it]. Those Endeavours were encouraged by a New Schism in the Church which was Laid by a Mr Baine Minister of Paisley, which in a few Years became a Numerous Body of New Seceders, Call'd the Presbytery of Relief, who had no fault to any thing but presentations. This Faction was Supported for Several Years, by a Strange Adventurer, a Mr Wm Alexander, the 2^d Son of the Provost of that Name, who of all the Men I have known, had the strongest propensity to Plotting, with the finest Talents for such a Business. As his attempts to speak in the Assembly were unsuccessfull and Drew nothing on him but Ridicule, he actually wrote to Dr Blair (I have Seen the Letter) offering him a Thousand pounds, if he could Teach him the art of Speaking in Publick.—As Blair was professor of Rhetorick and Belles Lettres he thought he was the most likely Person to Comply with his Request. But he had not observ'd that Dr Blair never spoke in Publick himself but from the Pulpit, from whence he might have Gather'd that the Knowledge of Rhetorick was Different from the Practice.

It was in this Year that Dr Drysdale was translated from Kirkliston to Edin^r after a long struggle with the Popular Body, the General Session of Edin^r, who with the Town Council had for many Years Elected all the Ministers.—The Magistrates and Council Reassum'd their Right [of Presentation] in this Case, and after much Litigation Establishd much for the Peace of the City. It was during this Litigation, That I wrote the Pamphlet, I think I mention'd before, entitled *Faction Detected*, which Wm Robertson the Procurator, thought was of his Fathers writing. This Pamphlet had so much Effect, that the Opposition employ'd their First Hand Dr Dick to write an Answer to it. And yet Neither the Provost, nor any of the Magistrates, nor Drysdale himself ever thank'd me for it. Dr Jardine who had requested this Service of me, perhaps never told his Father in Law Drummond, and I never ask'd him about it. Lindsay who was Restless, for whom John Home had obtain Lochmabin, now Got Kirkliston, and Lord Bute sent Dicky Brown to Lochmabin for which he had no thanks from the Neighbourhood, for tho' Lindsay[s] temper was not very Congruous to his Brethren and Neighbours yet he was a Gentleman, whereas the other was the Contrary and sometimes Derang'd.

In the end of Summer I went again with M^rs C to Harrogate, as her Health was not Good, and as the J[aunt] if not the waters might be Good for her. I Got an open chaise with two Horses—one before the other and the Servant on the first. As many of the Roads thro' which we went were not at all emprov'd, we found this an Excellent Way of Travelling. We visited our Friends in the Merse and in the North of England by the Way, and Staid some Days at Newcastle. As Mr Blackett and his Lady were Going soon to Rippon to visit his Mother, They agreed to come on for a week to Harrogate after which we would Return with them by York where M^rs C had never been.*

* The assizes were at Newcastle while we were there, and Alex^r Wedderburn was attending as a Counsellor. He had been there the preceding Year but had not a Cause. M^r   an old Counsellor who had left London and Settled at Leeds, had become acquainted with him, and had Discover'd the Superiority of his Talents. He Got him two or three Briefs this Circuit, and his appearances, were such as insur'd him of future success. This very Gentleman pointed out his First Lady to him with whom he Got £10,000. When the assizes were over he Din'd with us at Mr Blacketts, where his Talent for Conversation, not being Equal to that at the Bar, as it was Stiff and Pompous, he made not such an Impression on the Company as they Expected. The Appearance of Self-conceit always Disgusts the Ladies. He came to Harogate During the first Days of our Residence there; and Staid 2 nights, when M^rs C had some Difficulty to Get him a Partner.

It will not be Improper here to State, That on a future Occasion I had the Good Fortune for that time to Save a Man from the Gallows. There was a Man of the Name of Robertson who Livd near Belford, who was accus'd of having stolen a Heifer, and Killd it at his own House. The Heifer had belong'd to a Person Several Miles Distant from Belford, and was killd and skin'd before it was seen by any Body, But the Proof on its Marks and the Colour of the Skin, made it very like the one a missing. The Man had no Advocate, and being put on the Boards, was ask'd by the Judge (Yates) If he had any Defence to Make. He answer'd, That he was in use of Going annually to Dunse Fair, where he Generally bought a Beast or two for his own use, and this was one he had Got there. The Judge Sum'd up the evidence, and charg'd the Jury, Observing in his Conclusion that the only Defence the Man made, was That he bought the Heifer at Dunse Fair. Now it having been prov'd that this Heifer was of English Breed which could not be bought at Dunse, That Defence would Go for nothing. I was amaz'd at the Ignorance of the Judge and the Carelessness of the Grand Jury, and said to Coll! Dickson of Belford that the Judge had Gone Quite Wrong in his charge. He answer'd that Robertson was a Great Rascal and Deservd to be Hang'd. I answer'd that might be true, But that he ought not to Suffer for the Ignorance of the Judge or Jury, for he knew as well as I Did, That Cattle of Northumberland were to be bought at Dunse Fair, Nay that half the Cattle in Berwickshire were of that Breed, and that if he would not explain this to the Judge I would. I at last prevaild with him to Go Round and Whisper the Judge, who Calling in the Jury, Retracted what he had Said. He sent them out again, who after a Few Minutes Return'd and Gave in their verdict Not Guilty. I am affraid such Mistakes must frequently happen in England, in Spite of the Perfection of their Laws.

When we arriv'd at Harrogate the Dragon was not full; and the first Person we saw was the Late General Clerk, who tho' younger by at least a Year than me, I had known at College, and had sometimes met when I was last in London. This was a very Singular [Man] of a very Ingenious and Active Intellect, tho' he had Broke Short [his] Education by Entering at an Early Age into the Army, and having by Nature a [   ] and Copious Elocution, he threw out his Notions which were often New, with a force and Rapidity, which Stun'd you more than they Convinc'd. He applied his Warlike Ideas to Colloquial Intercourse, and attackd your Opinions, as he would do a Redubt or a Castle, not by sap[1] and mine, but by open Storm. I must Confess that of all the Men who had so much understanding, he was the Most Disagreable person to Converse, whom I ever knew. The worst of him was that he was not Contented with a Patient Hearing, or even the Common Marks of Assentation, such as yes, or Certainly or to be Sure, or Nodding the Head, as Charles Townshend, and Wm Robertson, and other Great Talkers were; you must Contradict him and wrangle with him or you had no peace. Elibank had something of the Same Humour, but he was better Bred. Clerk was truly the Greatest Siccatore[2] in the world. Like some of the Locusts, that Blast the vegetable World and Shrivle to Dust every thing that is Green, he was of the Caterpillar kind who have a particular Species of food, on which alone the[y] Fasten, and Leave the Rest untouch'd. I unluckily happen'd to be the only person of that Species at this time in the Dragon, whom he knew, and he fastnd on me like a Leech. M^rs C and I Breakfasted at a Table by our selves, not caring to Join with any Body, as we expected our Friends from Newcastle. In vain I hinted this to him as an excuse for not asking him to Breakfast. That he said he never Did as he wish'd to be Independent. On the 3^d Day however after our arrival, having been much taken with Mrs Carlyle's Manner of Conversing, and her not being alarm'd at his paradoxes, but only Laughing at them, he order'd his Tea Table to be set down close by Ours, and kept up a noisy palaver which attracted the attention of the whole Room, and had it not been for the Lady's entire possession of herself and her being a General Favourite of the Company who were there, might have Let Loose the Tongue of Scandal. He told me that he expected Adam Ferguson from Edin^r immediatly, who was to take the Two Brothers of Ld Greville, who was with Dr Robertson at Edinr. under his Care, and that he lookt every Day for his arrival. Ferguson had told me this before, and I now ardently wish'd for his Coming. In about 4 or 5 Days Ferguson Came, and most happily Reliev'd me from my Post of the Fatigue. For when every Body went a riding or walking in the forenoon, the 1st of which he Could not Do as he had no Horse, would you believe it, he patiently walk'd Backwards and forwards within sight of the Door, so that I could not possibly escape him, and was oblig'd to submit to my Destiny which was to walk and wrangle with him for 3 hours together. About the 4th Evening I had a little Relief by the arrival of 2 Gentlemen, whom as we met Driving to the Inn in Such a Carriage as mine, as we were walking on the Heath, Clerk having stopt and Spoken to them, return'd to me and said, That we were Now Lucky, for Those were Hands of the 1st Water. They were [John] Hall Esqr the Author of Crazy Tales, and the Famous Coll! Lee, commonly Call'd Savage Lee. As Clerk expected Ferguson, and Charles and Robert Greville, we had agreed to keep at the Foot of one of the Tables, that we might have them near us, and he Requested me to Remain in the same position, as the two newly arriv'd would be Glad to sit by us. I acquiesc'd and found the First a highly accomplishd and well bred Gentleman. Not so the 2d but might have been Endurd, had it not been for the perpetual Jarrings between Clerk and him, which if it had not been for the Mild and Courteous Manner of his Companion Hall, must have ended in a Quarrl. For the Moment after the Ladies Rose from Table which was very soon, The Two Soldiers fell a wrangling and Fighting like Pugilists, which made their Company very Dissagreable.

In a Day or two Ferguson arrivd, which Effectually took Clerk off me except at our Mealtime, which I could now endure as his Fire was Divided. Before Ferguson come, the House begun to be Crowded, and he was put into a very bad Lodging Room, near where the fidlers Slept and very Noisy. On the 3d Day he was Siez'd with a Fever, of which he was very Impatient, and said it was entirely owing to his Bad Room. I brought Mrs C to him who thought him very Feverish. I went to the Landlady to procure him a better Room and when Kilrington the M.D. from Rippon, who attended the House Daily, arriv'd before Dinner, I carried him to him, who prescrib'd nothing but Rest and Sack Whey.[1] After 2 Days more Kilrington who saw him twice a Day, told me to go to him, for he was better. I sat with him a few Minutes, and as [the Dinner] Bell rang I left him saying, I would send Clerk after Dinner. God forbid said he, in a voice of Despair, [Tomorrow perhaps] I may be able to Bear Mrs C for half an Hour, But not Clerk as you Regard my Life. This explosion left me no Room to Doubt what was the true Cause of his Fever. In two Days More he was able to Join us.

Soon after this There was a [Party] mad[e] out which amus'd us much. The Laird of McLeod with his Wife and Daughter (afterwards Lady Pringle), as we were their only acquaintance and they had arrivd after Dinner, Mrs C and I waited on them to Tea, in their Parlour, when they ask'd us [to a Concert] they were to have there an hour or two Later, which was to be private, but we might bring one or two of our Friends. We attended accordingly, and took Mess⁹ Hall and Lee and two Ladies with us. Miss M͏ᶜLeod was at this time in the prime of her Beauty, and a Few Months past sixteen: She was truly very Striking and attractive. When the Savage Saw her he seem'd astonish'd with her Beauty—When she Sang a Scottish Song he was Delighted—but when she finish'd with an Italian Song of the First Order, he was Ravished and fell into a silly amazement How a Young Lady from the Barbarous Coast of the Isle of Sky, Could possibly be such a Mistress of the Italian Musick and Italian Tongue. He Spake not another word all that night or next Morning, when he had several opportunities of Drinking Deeper in the Cyprian Goblet. But when he saw them preparing, to Leave us after Dinner, The Conquer'd Hero could not Stand the Mortifying Event but Retir'd from the Company and was Seen No More that night. The fit Lasted for Several Days, and he Bore the Raillery of Hall and Clerk, with a Meek-ness, which prov'd the Strength of his Passion. M͏ᶜLeod had only lookt in at Harro[g]ate, to Observe the State of Gaming there. But as he found Nothing Higher, than a Guinea Whist Table, he thought to Stay would be Losing time, and made the best of his Way to a Town about 40 miles [away], where there were Ra[c]es to begin Next Day.

M͏ʳˢ C never had been at any watering place before and considering that she was only 24, she Conducted herself with surprizing propriety, many Proofs of which I had to my Great Delight. One proof of it [was] the Great Joy that appear'd when she won the chief prize in a Lottery which was Drawn for the amusement of the company. There was another Lady from the South of popular Manners a M͏ʳˢ Mermill who had the Good Wishes of a few [to win] But our Party beat her both in Numbers and Sincere attachment.

Our Friends the Blacketts had now been for some Days at Rippon with his Mother, a Fine Hospitable [Old] Lady, The Daughter of M͏ʳ Wise of the Priory at Warwick. By a Message they Invited us to Dine there the next day, and Desird us to Bespeak their Lodging, as they were to come to Harrogate with us. This we accordingly Did and past a very Agreable Day with our Friends. She had a Fine Haunch of Venison for us from Studley Park, besides many other good things. Rippon is a Delightfull Vilage to Live at not merely on account of the Good pro-visions for the Table and a Beautifull Country as there is a Dean and Chapter and Generally Excellent Musicians. The Dean and Prebendary are well endowd and they and their Families furnish a Good Society. The Blacketts Return'd with us [to Harrogate], and Ferguson Being still there was a Great Favourite with Both. We past the time very pleasantly. On the Last Night Clerk and Hall ask'd me in the Evening to

Go to the Queens Head to see some of our acquaintance There, and to
Shun our own Ball. We went accordingly, and met with a Ball there of
which we tir'd, and that we might be Quiet, went to the Granby, where
there was no Ball and where there was excellent Claret. As Lee had
Refus'd to come abroad that Ev[en]ing, Hall was at Liberty and so
Taking Kilrington the Doctor with us as a 4ᵗʰ Hand we went there to
Sup, when Hall and Clerk fell a Debating so tediously and so warmly
about Lᵈ Bute's Character and Fitness for the Place of Minister that we
Did not return to the Dragon till six in the Morning. I was Diverted
to see how Clerk who Generally took part against Lᵈ Bute, that
night became his Zealous Friend, and not only Contended that his Being
a Scotchman was no Bar, but that his Talents were Equal to any high
Situation. Hall allow'd him Private Virtues but no Publick Ability.

This Conference was very tiresome and Lasted too late for me who
was to set out soon Next Morning. Ferguson's young Gentlemen were
not yet arrivd, and he Remaind a week Longer, without Being able to
Shake off his Dear Friend Clerk, who had procurd for him the Charge of
those Boys, and who through his Friendship to Lady Warwick, took a
Fatherly Charge of them.

Our Company Got to York before Dinner where we Staid most part
of next Day, and Got to Newcastle in Two Days and in a few Days more
arrived at home. Blackett's Horses were very Heavy and my Tandem
far out Run them. When we came home we found our Children in perfect
Health, which was a Great Delight to us, and prov'd the Fidelity of
Jenny's Nurse, with whom we had trusted them Both.

Ambassador Keith had Return'd home, and Having a handsome pension settled on him, he liv'd Handsomely for some time in Edinʳ and after
a while at Hermitage on Leith Links. He was a Man, tho' without wit and
Humour, yet of Good Sense and much Knowledge of the World. He had
been absent from Scotland for 22 Years, as Private Secretary to Marischal Lᵈ Stair, Envoy at Holland, and Ambassador at Vienna and Peters-
burgh. He complain'd that the Society of Edinʳ was alter'd much for the
Worse. Most of his old companions were Dead. The Scottish Lairds, Did
not now make it a Part of their Education to pass 2 years at Least
abroad, if they had but £300 pʳ ann., from whence they Return'd
polish'd in their Manners, and that portion of them who had Good
Sense, with their Minds Enlarg'd and their Manners Improv'd. They
found themselves now better Employ[ed] in Remaining at home and
Cultivating their Fields. But they were less Qualify'd for Conversation,
and could talk of nothing but of Dung and of Bullacks. The Lawyers had
Contented themselves with Studying Law at Home. The Medical Tribe,
had now the best School of Physick in Europe Establish'd at Edinʳ and a

Rising infirmary which promis'd the Students an ample Field of Practice, so that very few [of] that profession went now to Leyden or Paris. Keith Complain'd of the Dullness of the Society—In which he was confirm'd by his Son afterwards Sir Robt Murray Keith who had come down to Stay for 3 months, But Return'd by the End of one, not finding the State of Society to his Mind. The Ambassador had Recourse to our Order who had till lately never been thought Good Company, so that Finding Blair and Robertson and Jardine and mysel[f], to whom he afterwards added Ferguson, Good Company for him, he appointed us Ambassadors Chaplains, and Requird an attendance at Least once a week to Dine at his House, and was to Return our Visits when we ask'd him. He was soon Chosen a Member of the Poker Club which was Entirely to his Taste. Baron Mure and Lord Elliock were also much in this Society, especially the First, who Having been Intimate with Ld Bute During the 10 Years he Resided in Bute previous to 1745, was after Serving in Parl. for some years for Renfrewshire promoted to the place of Baron of Exchequer. When Milton's Infirmities made him Retire from Business, Baron Mure was the Man who was thought fit to Supply his Place, which accordingly happen'd, after Lord Bute's Brother who tried it for one Season, but finding his Being Sub-Minister not agreable to the Country and very Irksome to himself, he prudently Declin'd it, when Mure became the Confidential Man of Business, for which he was perfectly well qualified. For tho' his Manner was Blunt and unattractive, Yet as at the same time he was unassuming, of excellent understanding, and Great Ability for Business, he Continud to be much trusted and advis'd with as long as he liv'd. Elliock was an excellent Scholar and a Man of agreable Conversation, having many Curious [Anecdotes] in his Store, and to his other Fund, had the Good Fortune to be well acquainted with Frederick the Great of Prussia, when he Retir'd into Holland from his Fathers Tyranny, and visited him at Least once by Invitation after he came to the Throne.

This was the Year too when Dr John Gregory my Leyden Friend came to Settle in Edinr. Having found Aberdeen too narrow a Circle for him he had tried London for one year, but his manner was against his Being known there, which if he had once been, he would have kept his Ground. He had Return'd to Aberdeen and came a Widower to Edinr with 3 Sons and 3 Daughters; He soon came to be perfectly known here, and Got into very Good Business. Dr Rutherford Profft of the Practice of Physick beginning to Fail, and Being affraid of Cullen's becoming his Successor, whom he Held to be an Heretick, he readily Enter'd into a Compact with Gregory, whom he Esteem'd Orthodox in the Medical Faith, and Resign'd his class to him. In a Year or two That Dr Died, when Cullen and Gregory agreable to previous Settlement taught the 2 Classes on The Theory and Practice by Turns, changing every Session. I Got Gregory Elected into the Poker, but tho' very Desirous at First, yet he Did not avail himself of it, but Desisted after twice attending, affraid I Suppose of Disgusting Some of the Ladies he paid Court to, by falling in sometimes there with Dav.ᵈ H[u]me, whom they Did not know for the Innocent . . . Good Soul, which he really was.

Gregory had met with old Montagu at the Royal Society in London, who was fond of all Mathematicians, and had made himself master of his Mind. Montagu Introduc'd him to his Wife, a fine woman who was a Candidate for Glory in every Branch of Literature, but that of her Husband, and its Connections and Dependencies. She was a Faded Beauty, a Wit, a Critick, an Author of Some Fame, and a Friend and Coadjutor of Lord Littletons. She had some parts, and Knowledge, and might have been admir'd by the first Order of Minds had she not been Greedy of more praise than she was Entitled to. She come here for a fortnight from her Residence near Newcastle to visit Gregory, who took true [pains] to shew her off. But she Did not take here, for she Despis'd the Women, and Disgusted the Men with her Affectation. Old Edin.ʳ was not a Climate for the Success of Impostures. Lord Kaimes who was at first Catched with her Parnassian Coquetry said at Last, That he believ'd she had as much Learning as a well Educated College Lad here of 16. I could have forgiven her for her pretensions to Literary Fame, had she not loudly put in her claim, to the praise and true Devotion of the Heart which belongs to Genuine Feelings and Deeds in which she was Remarkably Deficient. We saw her Often in the Neighbourhood of Newcastle and in that Town, where There Being no Audience for Such an Actress as she was, Her Natural Character was Display'd, which was that of an active Manager of her Affairs, a crafty chaperon, and a keen pursuer of her Interest, not to be Outdone by the Sharpest Coal-Dealer on Tyne. But in this Capacity she was not Displeasing, for she was not acting a part.*

We had a Sight of the Celebrated Poet Gr[a]y at D.ʳ Gregory's, who passing thro' Edin.ʳ to the Highlands with my Friend Major Lyon for his Conductor, Six or Seven of us accordingly assembled to meet him and were Dissappointed.[1] But this Eminent Poet had not Justice done him for he was much worn out with his Journey, and by Retiring Soon after Supper, provd that he had been taken at a time when he was [not] fit to be shewn off.

* M.ʳ.ˢ Montagu was highly Delighted with Sister Peg which Ferguson had written and congratulated M.ʳ.ˢ C on having a Husband whose Conversation must be a Constant Source of Entertainment. She Did not advert to it, That in Domestick Life the Scene Did not always Ly in the Drawing Room.

1765

Early in March this Year I lost my Worthy Father at 75 years of age. He had been for some years Declining, and of late had Strong Symptoms, of a Dropsy, a Disease of worn out Constitutions. For tho' seemingly Robust and very active, he had been afflicted all his Life with Sundry Disorders of an Alarming Nature such as an Universal Rhumatism, Spasms in his Stomack and at regular hours every night for 3 months together &c. He Died with the utmost Calmness and [Resignation] and order'd all his affairs with a Prudence and foresight that was Surprising, amidst frequent Effusions of the most fervent Piety. Tho' long Expected I felt this a Severe Blow, as every Man of Common feelings must Do the Loss of a Respectable Parent. The Sincere Grief of his Parish, and the unaffected Regret of all who knew him, Rais'd pleasing Sensations in the Minds of his Family. I had withdrawn my Wife from this afflicting Scene, by Letting her Yield to the Importunity of her Sister, and Go to Newcastle in the beginning of March. This ascendant which her Sister had in her affections, accounted perfectly [for] our not Growing Rich as some of our free Judging Neighbours alledg'd we must certainly be Doing. For tho' our Income was tolerable, yet Those Frequent Visits to the South, not less than twice in a Year, left it only in our Power to pay our accounts at the end of the Year. As there were none of my Fathers Family now alive, but my Sister Bell who was the Youngest, and Sarah who was a Year or 2 older and unmarried, my Father had the Satisfaction That my Mother would be Independant, but advis'd her to come Close to me, which she Did by the Mart^s Term. Lord Prestongrange the Patron of the Parish, who was my Fathers Friend and old Companion at College, was Generous to my Mother by Giving her a Grant of the Glebe which was partly Sown, and a Considerable part of the vacant Stipend to which she was not entitled. The two Next Successors to my Father Died in four Years, So that his place was not well fill'd up, Nor the Regret of the Parishioners Lessen'd for his Loss, till Dr Joseph McCormick Succeeded in 1768 or 9.

I went to Newcastle before the End of April to bring my Wife home. On which or on some Such Occasion we brought with us Dr Gregory's two Daughters, Dolly and Ann, very fine Girls who were under 15, and had been staying with Mrs Montague. This Circumstance makes me believe that it must have been a year or two, as it must have been During Summer if they Resided with her.

In the General Assembly this Year There was a Strong push made to transmit an overture[1] to all the Presbyteries in the Church to Enquire into the Causes of Schism &c. from whence those in Opposition to Patronage believ'd there would come Such a Report, as would found and Justify a Fresh Application to the Legislature for their Abolition. It was thought best on our side, not Directly to oppose this Motion, but to [propose] a committee of assembly rather than agre to the Transmission, which was agreed to, and a Large Committee appointed, who strange to tell, in spite of all their Zeal, met only once and Did nothing tho' they had full powers, and made No Report to next Assembly.

It was in the Months of Aug.ᵗ and Sep.ᵗ this Year that D.ʳ Wight and I made our Tour round the North where neither of us had ever been, from whence we Deriv'd much amusement and satisfaction. We went on Horseback, by Queensferry, Perth, Dundee, Arbroath &c. We staid 4 Days and Nights at Aberdeen on acct. of D.ʳ Wights Horse having been Lam'd in Crossing the Ferry at Montrose. But we pass'd our time very agreably between the Houses of our Friends D.ʳˢ Campbell and Gerard. But as I wrote a Journal of this Tour Day by Day,[1] I must refer to that as Containing My Observations at the time.

When I Return'd (for Wight went to Dumfries, from Ed.ʳ) I found my Children well, but their Mother Recovering from a very Severe Rheum in her teeth owing to their Being Clean'd too much, which had Distress'd her Much.

A Fresh Call from Newcastle Carried M.ʳˢ Carlyle there again in the beginning of Nov.ʳ—I Did not Go with her, but went for her in the End of the Year, and Carried a Miss Wilkie with me from Ingrams and a Rev.ᵈ M.ʳ Forbes who married a Grand aunt of M.ʳˢ C.ˢ

1766

I have not mention'd some visits we had from our Friends at New.ᵗˡᵉ nor do I exactly [remember] the Dates of their Coming: But hitherto, they had not remain'd more than a week at a time. He soon tird and had always Business to Carry him back, not so his Lady, who lov'd our Society better than that at Newcastle. In April I made a Tour with Mary to Berwick, Lanton, and Fogo, for her Health and to visit our Friends. John Home was now always in London from Oc.ʳ till May, when L.ᵈ Bute parted with him for most part to come to the General Assembly, as Being L.ᵈ Conservator, he was now a constant Member, and tho' no Great Debater Gave us a Speech now and then.

In the Assembly this Year, there was the Last Grand Effort of our opponents to carry thro' their Schism Overture as it was Call'd, as it propos'd to make an Enquiry into the Causes and Growth of Schism. On

the Day before it came before the Assembly we had Din'd at Nicholson's. . . .¹ Before we parted, Jardine Told me that he had examin'd the
List of the Assembly with Care, and that we should Carry the Question;
That it would be nearly at Par till we Came as far on the Roll as Lochmabin, but that after that we should have it Hollow. I have mention'd
this on account of what happen'd next Day which was Friday the 29ᵗʰ.

There was a very long Debate so that the Vote was not calld till past
7 a clock. Jardine who had for some time complan'd of Breathlessness,
had seated himself on a High Bench near the East Door of the Assembly
House, There being at that time no Gallerys Erected. He had not half an
hour before, had a communication with some Ladies near him in the
Church Gallery, Who had sent him a Bottle of Wine of which he took
one Glass. The Calling of the Roll [began] and when it pass'd the Presbytery of Lochmabin, he Gave a Significant Look with his Eye, to me
who was sitting Below the Throne, as much as to Say, Now the Day's
our own. I had turn'd to the left to Whisper to John Home who was next
me the Sign I had Got. Before I could look round again Jardine had
tumbled from his Seat, and Being a Man of 6 F. 2 Inch, and of large
Bones, had born down all those on the two Benches below him, and
fallen to the Ground. He was Immediatly Carried out to the passage and
the Roll Calling stopt. Various Reports came from the Door, but [anx-
ious] to know the Truth, I Slipt behind the Moderators Chair and over
the Green Table, and with Difficulty made the Door, through a very
Crowded House. When I came there I found many people about him
Lying Stretch'd on the Pavement of the Passage, among the Rest his
Friend and mine James Russel the Surgeon. With some Difficulty I Got
near him, and whisper'd was it not a Faint? No No replied he, it is all
over. I Return'd to the House, and Resuming my place Gave out that
there were hopes of his Recovery. This Compos'd the House, and the
Calling of the Roll went on, when it was Carried to Reject the Overture
by a Great Majority. This was a Deadly Blow to the Enemies of Presentations, for they had Musterd all their Strength, and had been Strenuous
in Debate. Henry Dundas However, who had now come to our Aid, was
himself a Match for all their Lay Forces, as Robertson and a few Friends
were for all the Bands of Clergy—I was not a Member. A Party of us had
been engag'd to Dine with Mr Dundas, but could not now Go, as Dr Jardine was a Near Relation of his Lady: who was Deliver'd of her first
Child that night.

Robertson was much Dejected, as he had Good Reason. I immediatly
propos'd to him and J. Home to send for a post chaise and Carry them
out to Musselbrugh, which was Done directly, which Reliev'd us from all
troublesome company. This Death of Jardine was not only a breach in

our Society which we long felt, as John Jardine was one of the pleasantest of the Whole, who play'd Delight[ful]ly on the unbounded Curiosity
and Dupish Simplicity of Dav.ᵈ Hume, But was a Great Support to
Robertson and our Friends in the Management of Ecclesiastical affairs,
as he was the Son in Law of Provost Drummond and kept him Steady,
who had been bred in the Bosom of the High Flyers: and having had the
Management of the Burgh of Lochmabin for Charles Erskine of Tinwald
at 29 years of age, he acquir'd Early that Address and Dexterity in
managing Men, which could Easily be applied to Edin.ʳ Politicks, [tho']
they were on a much Greater Scale. In politicks he was artfull, in other
affairs quite trusty.

As Jardine however had ⅓. of the Deanery, Robertson availd himself
of the vacancy, to obtain it for Dʳ Drysdale, whose Wife was one of the
Adams, and Robertson[s] Cousin German. This attach'd Drysdale more
to him, and made him apply assiduously to the Correspondence with the
Distant Clergy, which open'd up to him a view of the Clerkship of the
Church which he afterwards Obtain'd.

I said that the Schism Overture which we Defeated was the last Blow
that was aim'd at Patronage, for whatever attempts were [afterwards
made were] feeble and ineffective. There still Remain'd however, in the
Assembly's Instructions to their Commission, an article which was a
Constant Reproach to the General Assembly, viz. That they should
watch for a convenient opportunity of applying to the King and Parliament, for Redress from the Grievance of Patronage. This was too much
at a time, when almost every Clerical Member of Assembly had been
Settled by a Presentation. This however was not left out, till Dʳ Robertson had Retir'd from the Conduct of our affairs, when in the Assembly
1784, I Got it propos'd by some of the Elders, when after Some Debate,
it was Carried to Leave it out by a Great Majority. Next Year there was
a Feeble Attempt, to Restore the article in the Instructions, But this
Did not even Raise a Debate, and we heard no more of it.

It was this year in the Month of Aug.ᵗ that Dʳ Robertson having Sollicited me strongly to be of a Party to the West Country with him and
the Hon.ᵇˡᵉ James Stewart Montague who was then attending the College
of Edin.ʳ and Liv'd in his House. I Could not set out one the same Day
with them, but Follow'd in the end of the Week and Got to Dʳ Wights at
Glasgow College on Sat. where I Remain'd all next Day, having got a
Little Cold. He had now been for some time in the House allotted to his
Office which tho' one of the old ones was Convenient, and had several
Apartments, so that he Could have Room for 2 or 3 Boarders. His
Youngest Sister had now been with him for more than a year, and they
Liv'd very Comfortably, which She tho' but just Turn'd of 20 Manag'd

very well. I Remain'd with them all Sunday, and Next Day Got to Caldwell (Baron Mure's) before Dinner. We went Next Day to L⁴ Glasgow where we were Joind by Mᴿ Oliphant, afterwards Postmaster, who with Baron Mure and Alexᴿ McMillan Esq. WS. were L⁴ Bute's Commissioners or Trustees, for the Management of his Estate. We had rode thro' a very Hilly Part of Renfrewshire to Kelburn, Lord Glasgows Seat Finely Situated on the Clyde almost opposite to Bute about 5 or 6 Miles Distant, where the Expanse of Water is Finely Broken by the two Islands of Cumbray, the 1ˢᵗ of which is not more than a Mile Distant, with the Channell for Ships Sailing up or Down the Clyde L[ying] between that Island and the Shore of Cunningham. We were very Late of Dining for that Period when the usual Hour was two a clock; But we sate long enough after Dinner to Loosen our Landlords Tongue, who Being in General a Reservd and Silent Man, partly thro' Modesty and partly thro' flat Spirits, yet after a long Repast Became not merely open and free, but truly Eloquent. Baron [Mure] who tho' a very Sensible Man was yet too Great a Friend of Lord Bute to hear Willᵐ Pitt extoll'd to the Skies, which Lord Glasgow had Casually Done; on which [Mure] made some tart Remarks. This Fird his Lordship, who Gave us a Panegyrick at Least on Mᴿ Pitts Character and Administration with as much force and energy and Eloquence, as that Great Man himself Could have done had he Dealt in Panegyrick. His Lordship was beginning to flag, and his Audience to Tire when Luckily we were Calld to Supper. Robertson whisper'd me in going to the Dining [Room] That his Powers had perfectly astonishd him. The Presence of the Ladies put an End to our Political Debate. We past Next Day with his Lordship, when we had such another Exhibition in the Evening. We agreed among ourselves, that had it not been for his Invincible Modesty, which Debar'd him from ever Entering the Drawing Room at Sᵗ James's, where he was Sure of a Good Reception, for he had been wounded at the Battle of Fontenoy, he might have [made] a very Conspicuous Appearance in the House of Lords. He was now the Lord High Commissioner to the Assembly, and was a great favourite with us not merely for his Obliging Manners, and Improv'd Entertainment at his Table, but for his attention to the Business of the House, and his Listening to and entering in to the Spirit of Every Debate. His Lordship Did not attend us to Bute, to which we saild next Day.

We Remaind Six Days on Bute and past our time very agreably. Alexᴿ McMillan was one of the best Landlords for a Large Company, for he was Loud and Joyfull, and made the Wine flow like Bachus himself. We past the Mornings which were not so long as now, for they extended only to 2 aclock when Dinner was on the Table, in Riding about the

Island which we found very Beautifull, tho' but little Cultivated; For Besides a Plantation around the House of Mountstuart, of very [fine] Trees, of a Square Mile, every little Cottage had a Dozen of Trees around. Lady Bute, while a Widow, had Got them planted in every Kailyard as their little [Gardens] are Call'd, and they make a pleasing Ornament. There is nothing like a Hill but on L⁴ Bannatyne's Estate on the N. East, where it is Seperated by a Narrow Straight Call'd the Kyle's of Bute. Rothsay, where Stand the Ruins of the Old Castle, which Gives a Ducal Title to the Prince of Wales, as it Did antiently to the Prince of Scotland, is a finely Situated Port and has thriven amazingly since that Period. We had to take an Early Dinner one Day, and Ride down there to be made free of the Burgh, which Cost us a hard Drink of new Claret. Mountstuart is truly a fine place with a charming View of the Islands and opposite Coast. The Soil every where Lies on Sea Shells, so that they have the Means of Emprovement at hand, and Being in Shape like the Convex of a Roman Shield, [wh]ere the Rain cannot Ly, seemd every where Capable of Tillage. What was done about Mountstuart and Rothsay, Gave Great Encouragement. We went to Kingarth Church on Sunday, where I lecturd¹ and Robertson Preacht. There are 3 parishes in the Island, in two of which the Minister must have the Erse Language.

Our Conversation at Table was Liberal and Lively, where there were so many Sensible Men, for Besides our company, there were several other very able men, particularly a Mr Dunlop a Son of the Greek Professors at Glasgow who was Remarkably Knowing and Goodhumourd. The Wine was excellent and flowd Freely. There was the best Cyprus I ever Saw, which had lain there since L⁴ Bute had left the Island in 1745—The Claret was of the Same Age, and excellent.

After we had been 4 Days there Robertson took me into a Window before Dinner and with some Solemnity propos'd to make a Motion to Shorten the Drinking If I would Second him, Because, Added he, tho' you and I may Go through it, I am averse to it on James Stuarts account. I answer'd that I should willingly Second whatever of that kind he should propose, but added that I was affraid it would not Do as our Toastmaster was very Dispotick, and besides might throw Ridicule upon us, as we were to Leave the Island the Day after the Next, and that we had not proposd any abridgement to the Repast till the old Claret was all Done, The Last of which we had Drank Yesterday. Well, Well, replied the Doctor, Be it so then and Let us end as we began.

We left the Island on the Day we proposd, I in a Boat for Port-Glasgow with the Post-Master Oliphant, as we Could not Join the Rest, to pass two Days more at L⁴ Glasgow's (Kelburn) on their Return, as they had promisd. We Got very Rapidly to Port-Glasgow in the Custom

House Yacht, and to Glasgow on horseback Early in the Evening: Where he visited his Friends, and I Remaind with mine at the College that night and all next Day. I was Moderator of the Synod this Year, Webster having made it Fashionable for Even the Moderators of that Court, to Give handsome Suppers, It cost me 5 Guineas. But there being very few who Could afford Such Expensive Repasts, and Having Gone thro' 6 or 7 of us, This Entertainment Ceas'd, and the Moderators of the Synods, were Contented with Small Committees, and Meagre Suppers as they had been heretofore, and Webster of Course absented from them.

In Dec.ʳ this Year* we made another Journey to Newcastle Mʳˢ C being absolutely necessary to her Sister, when she lay in or was at all ill. Blackett was but a Dull Man, and his Cousin Sir Walter B. no better tho' Rich, Magnificent and Generous. The Company about them, were not very agreable. Some of their Bucks had humour, but they were illiterate and Noisy. Two or 3 of their Clergy Could be endur'd, for they playd well at Cards and were not Pedantick Prigs; John Withrington was then almost the only Man who had any Literature. Mʳ Moyse a clergyman was now Master of the Grammar School, and Being Able and Diligent in his profession, Soon made a Great Change on the Young Natives of Newcastle, Insomuch that soon after There issued from it several Distinguishd Characters, Such as Mʳ Chambers, a Judge I think in India, or a Professor of Law at Oxford, and the two Scotts, Sir Wᵐ and his younger Brother the Chancellor of England. Dʳ Akenside was also a Native of that Town, and had Studied Physick in Edinʳ in the Years 1744, and 45. As he was of Low Descent, his Father Being a Butcher, he Stole thro' his Native Town in[c]og. as often as he had occasion to pass, and never acknowledg'd his Relation to it.

[1767]

The next Year 1767, nothing Remarkable Happen'd for Several Months. In the Month [of Aug.ᵗ], Mʳˢ C not being very well, we went in our open chaise to visit our Friend Mʳ Alex.ʳ [Glen] at Galashiells with our Friend Dʳ Wight. I had been there before, But Mʳˢ C never had, and was much Delighted with the amenity of the place, as well as the kindness and Hospitality of our Landlord, who was not yet Married. We Visited Melrose abbey to Gratify Mʳˢ C—The Fine Pastoral Stream of Gala falls into the Tweed a mile below the Church and village, from whence 4 miles Down the River Stands the Famous Abbey of Melrose,

* It was this Year I think that we brought the two Misses Gregory from Newcastle, in the Neighbourhood of which they had been staying for some time with Mʳˢ Montagu.

The exquisite Beauty of whose Ruins, is well supported by the Romantick Scenery around it. About a week before we visited Galashiells and Melrose, a water Spout had fallen into the Mountain Stream Slitterick, which Joins the River Teviot at Hawick, which occasion'd a Great Alarm there, had Broken down a Bridge which Joind the Town to a Street where the Church Stands, had Ruin'd a Mill on the Rivulet, and Drown'd one of the Millers, and Threatned the whole Town with Inundation. But as it had come Down in the Night, it abated Early in the Forenoon.

This Phenomenon so uncommon in this Country excited our Curiosity, and we Resolvd to proceed to Hawick to See the effects of it. Mr Glen Gladly accompanied us; Wight and he Being Great Companions.

We Set out in the Morning after an Early Breakfast that we might Reach Hawick some time before Dinner. We had Given notice to Laurie the Minister there that we would Dine with him and stay all night, which Information was necessary as there were so many of us; Altho' the Fashion of Men's Sleeping in the Same Bed together was not yet at an End. After we pass'd the Tweed near Selkirk where the Delightfull Streams of Ettrick and Yarrow fall into it from the fine Pastoral Valleys or Glens which Run nearly Parallell to each other to the Summit of the Country, The Scenery was by No Means Interesting. Selkirk was then a very paultry Town, and the Fields around it very poorly Cultivated, tho' now there is a very Different Face on Both. Hawick is Beautifully Situated, and tho' but an ill Built Town, very much Resembles the Famous City of Bath in its Situation, Being a Close Warm Looking Nest in the Midst of Surrounding Hills, all but the Openings made to the South and North of the Town, by the Beautifull River Tiviot which Runs within a Quarter of a Mile of it and whose clear untroubled Stream, except when Great Rains Descend, Glides Gently by, and Like a Mirror Reflects the adjacent Pastoral Scenery. We visited the Devastations made by Slitterick, which falls from the Mountain in a Tremendous Torrent, into Teviot which was quite unmovd, as the Two Channels Lay at Right Angles from each other.

We past the Day very pleasantly with Laurie and his Wife, who was an old Acquaintance of Mrs Cs when they Livd at Langton, the next Parish to Polwarth where she pass'd her Infant Years. Wight Rallied Laurie not a little for his Having Delay'd Calling the People to Prayers, on the Morning of the Inundation, till he saw from his Garden the Flood a little abating and then Continuing so long in Prayer (for a full Hour) when it had Fallen so much that a Man on Horseback could pass below the Mill, which the Good People ascrib'd to the Fervency of their Pastor, [and] would have Continued to Believe in the Efficacy of his Prayer, had not the Surviving Miller assurd them that the Inundation had Fallen 6 Inches before the Church Bell Rang. Laurie was perfectly Pleas'd with so much address Being ascrib'd to him, tho' he lost a little in the Article of Interest in Heaven, which was Imputed to him.

Laurie was an uncommon Character. Dr John Armstrong and he were at College together and one year During the Vacation they Joind a Band of Gipsies who in those Days much Infested the Border. This Expedition which Surely took place, as Armstrong inform'd me in London, Furnishd [Laurie] with a fine Field for Fiction and Rhodomontade, which was so closely United to the Ground work which might be true, that it was imposible to Discompound them. After Armstrong had Settled in London for some time, Laurie went to visit him about 1739, or 40. On that he founded Many Marvellous Stories of his Intimacy [with Secretaries] of State and Courtiers, with whom he pretended he had been quite Familiar. When he alledg'd that he had been quite at his Ease with the Chancellor and the Speaker of the House of Commons at that Time, and could Call on them at any Hour, and Remain to Dinner or Supper without Being Invited, we us'd to Call to him, Halt there Laurie; if you Don't know the Boundary between Truth and Falsehood, you should Draw the Line between what is probable and what is not so. Like a Snowball we Gatherd as we Roll'd along, he fix'd himself upon us for the Rest of the Journey.

We Set out in the Morning after Breakfast, That we might [reach] Langholm 22. Miles off, in time for Dinner, and travell'd over a Beautifull Pastoral Country 11 miles to the Top of the Ridge, beyond which the Waters run South, whereas before that their course is North and East. The Road had been finish'd some time before, and was so perfectly Good and well-laid out, that in my open Chaise I could keep at the Trott both Down and up the whole way. The first place we past was the Seat of Dr Langlands M.D., a very pleasing place about a mile above Hawick on the Teviot. Of late it was in the Possession of Lord Napier and much Improv'd by him, and is now bought up at £12000 by James Anderson Esqr a younger Brother of St Germains. In a mile or two farther we Reach'd the First [House] of the Family of Buccleuch, the Castle of Branxome, which an Ancestor of that Family exchang'd. When we Got to the Top of the Ridge we stop'd to Feed our Horses at a Rural Inn kept by a Curious Fellow, Call'd Rob. Achison, with whom we had not conversd many Minutes, when we Discover'd the Cause of his Being Reduc'd from the Condition of an opulent Farmer, to that of the keeper of a mere halting place to Divide a Long Stage. Robert had been a Border Rake or Buck of the first Head in his younger Days, and to Wit and Humour of which he had abundance, he added a sufficient Portion of Address and Impudence, which he Cover'd with an Air of Careless Indifference. He had Eloquence enough however to Make us both Eat and Drink in his House, for the first of which he was but ill provided. But he Soon made us understand by the Scurrility which he pourd out against those who had past his House, without Calling for Something besides Corn for the Horses, How we should be treated for the Entertainment of the Next who came. So we took a sorry Repast with Robert, and Drank of his Liquors.

The Slope from this to Langholm is just Eleven Miles, and the Road Excellent. The Country was exceedingly Picturesque tho then without Trees, and Full of Sheep, which as the young Duke of B. and his [Dutchess] were Daily expected, had been taught to Line the Road thro' which they were to pass, That they might see wherein the Riches of the Land Consisted. As it was now in the beginning of Augt the Fields had a fine variegated cloak of verdure, For as the Fearns, or Brackens as they are Call'd here [were] now in Perfection, and of a Different Shade from the Grass, They look'd like a Large Curtain or Mantle of Green Silk Damask.

We arriv'd in the Evening at Langholm, where the Village is Situated at the Confluence of the Two Streams of Ewes and Wauchope with the Esk, which from thence flows, after Being almost Doubld by the Liddale, thro Delightfull [Scenery] to the Solway Firth, which with it makes the Western Boundary between England and Scotland.

It was t[o]o late to attempt to See the Castle, so we Sent Immediatly for John Dickie the Minister who was an old Batchelor, and who had such a mixture of odd Qualities in his Composition, such as Priggism and Pedantry, with the affectation of Being a Finished Gentleman: very Sanctimonious in his Manners, with a Desire of Being thought free and Liberal in his Sentiments: Not without a Portion of Knowledge, But more proud of it than Dr Bently or Purdie the Schoolmaster. As M^{rs} C had never seen him before, she was highly Diverted with him; and having in a moment Discover'd all his weaknesses, she met them in so Caressing and encouraging a manner, that he would have lept over the House to Serve her—and before he left us at 12 to Go home, he became her Sworn Knight Errant. To make her Conquest Compleat over the Little Man, she would not let him Go, till a Horse was Got ready for an Hostler to Conduct him thro' the Water. Laurie and Glen thought this Carrying Coquetry too Far; but Wight and I knew better, for she was of that [turn of mind] That if any thing had befallen the little Man, as he had Got enough of Wine, and had no better Seat than a Clue[1] on a Horse, she would never have forgiven herself. With all his Imperfections he was Good Natur'd and Social, which after a Banquet never faild to appear. He had a young Mare which he wish'd to Sell, and was Going to Send to be Sold at Hawick or Jedburgh, When Hearing there was to be a Fair at Carlisle next Day, and that we were Deliberating about Going or not, when somebody happend to say that Carlisle was the best place, and that we would all go there; M^rs C immediatly said, I will Consent to Go, if you will be so Good as [accompany us]. The Honest Soul instantly yielded, and we all Resolv'd to Go, now amounting to 5 Gentlemen and a Lady, with only one Servant.

We Set out next Morning and had a very agreable Ride down the River Esk for 7 or 8 Miles, thro' a Valley finely Cover'd with young Plantations. We Stopt at Longtown—where there is a fine Bridge over the Esk, which has Sav'd Many a Life which [was] annually Lost in passing over Dangerous Fords of the River a mile or two Lower Down; and Crossing some Sands in the Channel of the Frith of Solway, where the Traveller was frequently overtaken by the Rapidity of the Tide, we arriv'd at Carlisle before Dinner and found the Town as much Crowded as curious Travellers could wish as there was not only a Great Fair holding on this Day, but the Judges were in Town, and a Set of Players to Entertain the Company. The Kings Arms was so much Crowded that we were obligd to Resort to the large Dining Room which was Crowded like a Coffee House. But as the Company Consisting chiefly of Country Lads and Lasses, were all to Disperse in the evening, we were able to Secure Beds, which was the chief point in View.

After Strolling about the Town a while, I attempted to go into the Court house, which was so much crowded and so Hot, that I only remaind a few minutes in the outskirts, where I heard my Friend Wedderburn pleading as well as he could under a Severe Hoarseness. We Returnd to the Inn, where we found Govr Johnstone, and John Scotland Minister of Westerkirk with our Friends. Johnstone was employ'd in canvassing the Citizens, and Scotland had come with a Dumfermline Friend, on purpose to see Mr Wedderburn. The Govr told us of the Players, and we all set out Immediatly to try for Places, but it was so much Crowded that we were Dissappointed and obligd to Return. Laurie however Remaind after the Rest, when he had a Quarrel with a very Drunken Squire of the Name of Dacres, who had Insulted him with foul Language, which Laurie Return'd with a Blow, forgetting That he was now in a Country, where a Breach of the Peace, is much more Dangerous. Dacres attempted to have him Committed, but Laurie Made his Escape and Johnstone having Interfer'd and said it was only a Drukken Scotch parson, who had been Riotous, and was Ignorant of English Laws, who had broken the Peace, he Got Dacres pacify'd, and we heard no more of it.

The Govr had promis'd to Sup with us, and I proposd Sending to M^r

Wedderburn, but Scotland Said it was Needless, as he had seen him, and found him preparing to Go to Bed as he was very Hoarse. I wrote him a Note however telling him That M^rs C, Wight and I were there and that Govr Johnstone had promis'd to Sup with us, and that I would Infallibly cure his Hoarseness before tomorrow Morning. His answer was That he would be with us in half an Hour. He was as Good as his Word, but was very Hoarse. The Supper was Good enough, but the Liquors were execrable. The Wine and Porter were not Drinkable—We then made a Bowl of [the worst] Punch I ever Tasted. Wedderburn Said if we would mix it with a Bottle of the Bad Porter it would be emprov'd. We Did as he Directed, and to our Surprise it became Drinkable; and we were a Jolly Company. The Counsellor Did not forget the Receipt to Cure his Hoarseness. This was nothing more than some Castile Soap, Shaven into a Spoon, and mixd with some White Wine or Water so that it could be Swallow'd. This he took and Return'd to us at nine next Morning, perfectly Cur'd and as Sound as a Bell.

Dicky having Sold his Mare, we Return'd by the Road we came, and passing one night at Hawick, and one at Galashiels, arriv'd at home with Wight next [night] and found all well. It is remarkable that I Remember very exactly most of the Circumstances on Going from home even on a Long Journey, but that in Returning I can Seldom find any trace of them in my Memory, and all Seems a Blank. Is this owing to the Imagination being fully occupied with the thoughts of home which is always agreable? Or is it owing to the Eagerness and Curiosity, with which one begins a Journey, and the rising Hopes of New pleasures or amusements, and the Drowsy and unactive State of the Imagination as you Return?

The Young Duke and Dutchess of Buccleuch, were expected at this time to arrive in Scotland, to take possession of their Fine Estate, in the South, and their Palace at Dalkeith as their Chief Residence. They were Eagerly expected over all the Country where we had been, Great Part of which from Tweedside to the Borders of Cumberland, was the property of that Noble Family. There had been a Long Minority, for this Duke's Grand Father had Died in 1752, and his Son Ld Dalkeith 2 years before him. The Family had been kind to their Tenants, and the hopes of the Country were high That this New Possessor of so large a Property, might Inherit the Good temper and Benevolence of his Progenitors. I may anticipate what was at first only Guess'd but came soon to be known, that he Surpassd them all, as Much in Justice and Humanity, as he Did in Superiority of understanding and good sense.

The Duke and Dutchess, with Lady Frances Scot the Duke's Sister, arriv'd at Dalkeith in the Beginning of Sepr where his Grace had never been before; Being witheld by Charles Townshend his Father in Law, Lest he should become too Fond of Scotland. This Stratagem was Defeated by the Duke's Sagacity. For he Discoverd on his Journey through his own Great Estate, from the Mark'd Attention of the People, That he would be a much Greater [Man] in this Country, and would have a much more extensive range for his Benevolence, than he could possibly have in the South where his own Estates were Small, and where there was such a Number of more Opulant Lords, his Rivals in all the Attributes of true Nobility.*

Between their arrival at Dalkeith, and his Grace's Birthday the 13th of Sepr The Right Honble Charles Townshend Died after an illness of a few Days, of an Inflamation in his Bowels. This event Oblig'd them to Postpone the Celebration of the Birthday, when they were to have had an Entertainment for all their Friends. This Sudden Death affected the Duke and his Sister very Differently. She who had been bred up under him from the 4th or 5 year of her Age, and had found in him an Enlightend Instructor and a kind Protector, felt all the Grief which a Dutifull Child feels for an Indulgent Parent. But the Duke who had been very little at home during Mr Townshends Marriage with his Mother, and whose more Ripend Discernment had probably Disclos'd to him his Father in Laws Defects, as well as his shining Qualities, was much less affected on this Melancholy Occasion, and was heard to Say a few Days after the News, That tho' He Sincerely Regreted Mr Ts premature Death, yet to him it was attended with the Consalation that it left him at Liberty to chuse his own [Line] of Life, For had Mr Td Surviv'd, he might have been Drawn into the Vortex of Politicks much against his Will.

---

* In order to make the Duke and Dutchess feel more Impressively the attachment of their Vassals and Tenants in the South, I wrote a Copy of Verses on the Birthday [of the Duke] which I had Copied in another Hand, and Sent on the morning of that Day. It was some time before they could Guess that I was the Author, and one of their Tenants had for a while the Credit of it. I had by Good Luck truly predicted by way of advice What Her Grace became—But no predictions could then Reach the extent of her Merit. The verses were Sent to the Scotch Magazine, where Dr Gregory Read them, and Suspected me for the Author. When I next saw him, he ask'd me, and I own'd them, when he Said they were very Good, too Good for the Subject, for they would never act up to the Strain of praise in that Poem. Do you know them Dr? No, answer'd he, but Mrs Montagu Does, and She says, That tho' very Good Young People, They have no Energy of Character, and will remain Obscure and Insignificant. Mrs Montagus Line then is too short my Good Dr, you may trust me, to measure their Depth, and you will Live to See that her Discernment on this Occasion has faild her. Gregory with many Good Qualities, had so much of the Apothecary about him, that he did not think much of any Body who was not Likely to frequent his Shop. He knew that Smith would Recommend Both Cullen and Black, to be their Physician in ordinary rather than him.

Such was the Soundness of this Young Nobleman's Mind at an Early Age, from whence a Discerning Observer might predict the Excellence of that Character which Gradually Evolv'd on his Admiring Country Men.

In two or three weeks the Day came when they were to see Company, and when they assembled by Cards about 50 Ladies and Gentlemen of their Friends and the Neighbourhood, of whom few indeed were Ladies, as they were hardly yet acquainted with any Body. The Fare was Sumptuous, but the Company was formal and Dull. Adam Smith their only Familiar at Table, was but ill qualifi'd to promote the Jollity of a Birthday, and Their Graces were quite unexperienc'd. The Duke indeed had been more than two years in France and 4 months in London since he Came home. But he was Backward at that time to set himself Forward, and Shew'd a Coldness and Reserve which often in our Superiors [is] thought to be Pride. Had it not been for Alex.ᵗ McMillan W.S. and myself, the Meeting would have been very Dull, and might have been Dissolv'd without even Drinking the Health of the Day. After that Health, and a few more Toasts had Gone round and the Ladies had Mov'd, and McMillan and his Companions at a Bye Table had Got into the Circle, we Got into Spirits that better Suited the occasion. The Dutchess at that time was extremely Beautifull. Her Features were regular, her Complexion Good, her Black Eyes of an Impressive Lustre, and her Mouth when she Spoke uncomonly Gracefull. The Expression of her Countenance was that of Good Sense and Serenity. She had been bred in too private a way, which made her shy and backward, and it was some time before she acquir'd Ease in Company, which at last enabl'd her to Display that Superiority of Understanding which Led all the Female Virtues in its Train, accompanied with the Love of Mirth and all the Graces of Colloquial Intercourse. Her Person was light, tho' above [the] Rank of Women, but active and Elegant.

Smith Remain'd with them for two months, and then Return'd to Kirkcaldy to his Mother and his Studies. I have often thought Since that If they had brought Down a Man of more Address than he was, How much sooner their first appearance might have been; their own Good Sense and Discernment, enabled them sooner to Draw round them as familiars, a better Set of people of their own chusing, than Could have been pick'd out for them by the assistance of an Aid De Camp, or Led Comptain.[1]

By means of an Establish'd Custom of their Predecessors, they had two publick Days in the Week, when every Body who pleas'd come to Dine with them. But that on Thursday, was soon Cut off, and Saturday was their only publick Day. But [it] would have been far better, If that Day had been also abolish'd, and if in place of that, they had taken to

Invited Companies, which might have been well assorted, and might have prevented all that Dullness and even Ennui, which overclouded large Companies little Acquainted, and Seldom Capable of Making a Company of a Score tolerably Agreable. I must aver however without pretending to uncommon Discernment, that I soon Discover'd in Both, that Superior Understanding and that uncommon Degree of Humanity, as well as the Highest Sense of Probity and Virtue, which have made them a Blessing and Honour to their Country for Many Years Past. For the Duke's uncommon Abilities, as well as his Publick Spirit, became e'er long as Conspicuous, In the exercise of those honourable Offices of Trust, which fell on him unsought, as his unassuming and familiar Manners made him appear a Compleat Gentleman in all the Intercourse of Private Life. The Family tho' Rich and Great had long been in a state of Obscurity, through Want of Talents, and Long Minorities. In this Duke was Reviv'd the Character which Sir James Melville gave his Renownd Predecessor in Q. Mary's Reign: Walter Scot of Buccleugh, Wise and True, Stout and Modest.

No two Characters I ever have known, are so free of Defects as that Noble Pair, while Each in their Departments, Displaid Such Talents and Virtues as made their Numerous Descendants not only happy in themselves, but also traind them up in the Habitual Disposition, to become Blessings to all their own Connexions to the latest Posterity.

The Duke's Sister Lady Frances, tho' far from Handsome, or in any respect attractive in her Person, tho' then only 17, Shew'd the opening of that Character which she has since so fully Display'd as Lady Douglas. She had Taste and Knowledge in the Belles Lettres, a pleasant vein of Ridicule without the Least Grane of Malignity, for she like her Brother was the very Milk of Human kindness. As I had been Intimately Acquainted with Charles Townshend her Father in Law, who protected her from Domestick Tyranny, and had even opend her Mind by his Instructions, She took readily to me, and I soon became Intimate with her, and kept up a Correspondence with her both in Prose and Verse which Conduc'd to our Amusement. The Prosperity and Happiness of Ld Douglasses Family, which Consisted of 3 Sons and one Daughter, which she Increasd by 3 Sons and 3 Daughters, Demonstrate the Excellence of her Domestick Character. It was Remarkable that she was the First Female Descendent of the Dutchess of Monmouth and Buccleuch, who was Married.

I had been Moderator of the Synod in Novr 1766, and open'd the Synod in May 1767 with a Sermon which was Printed. The Window Tax was now levied[1] which Gave a Serious Allarm to the Clergy; There was a Standing Committee of Assembly which had hitherto Done Nothing

Effectual. As I had been the Champion for Resisting Payment of the Tax I was oblig'd to Bestir myself very much about it. And as Dʳ Robertson was of opinion we ought to Submit to it, I had uphill work with it.

1768

Towards the End of Jany this Year it was, That Mʳˢ C and I accompanied her aunt and uncle to Visit their Son Walter Home, Then a Lieut. in the 7ᵗʰ Regᵗ and lying at Glasgow. Walter had a Chum of the Name of Mainwairing, a very agreable young Man. As Dʳ Wight was now fully Establish'd in Glasgow, and had one of his Sisters for his Housekeeper, he was very Hospitable and Popular, and we met Daily there several of the Professors, who were able Men, and had agreable Conversation, Such as Alexʳ Stevenson D.M. and John Millar. This last had even begun to Distinguish himself by his Democratical Principles, and that Sceptical Philosophy, which young Noblemen and Gentlemen of Legislative Rank carried into the world with them, From his Law class, and many years afterwards, particularly at the Period of the French Revolution, Displayd with Popular Zeal, to the no Small Danger of Perversion to all those under their Influence. I had a Hint of this from Dʳ Wight, before 1782, when he Died, who added that Tho' some Sound Heads, might find antidotes to this Poison before they went into the World, and See in the British Constitution all that is Valuable in a Democracy without its Defects and Faults, Yet as it was Connected with Lax Principles in Religion, There might be not a few of such a Contexture of Understanding as Could not be Cur'd. Millar Liv'd to the End of the Century.*

* I met with a Strong Proof of what is Containd in this Paragraph Respecting Professor Millar, a long time afterwards, when Dining with Robert Colt Esqʳ then Residing at Inveresk. I Don't exactly remember the year, but I think it was before the war of 1798. There was Nobody with Mʳ Colt but a Brother in Law of his, when we were Joind by the late Sir Hew Dalrymple of North Berwick who had Din'd in Edinʳ. After consenting to Stay all night, Sir Hew Said, Colt was not you a Student of Law for two Years with Millar at Glasgow. Yes I was, answer'd Mʳ Colt. Then Replied Sir Hew, I find I am Right, and as my Hew has been 4 years at Sᵗ Andrews, and seems now Desirous of following the Law, I have been advisd to Send him to Millar, and have come to Consult you about [it]. We'll Talk about that Coolly tomorrow Morning Sir Hew, in the mean time Give me your Toast. I knew well the Meaning of this Reserve, and a few Days afterwards meeting Mʳ Colt, Well said I, Did you Settle your Friend Sir Hew's Mind about Sending his Son to Glasgow. Yes, answer'd he, and you'l hear no more of that Project. This Mʳ Colt, was an able and a worthy Man, but he was Shy and Reserv'd, and Died unknow[n] but to a few in the Year 1797. He had overcome Many Disadvantages of his Education, for he had been Sent to a Jacobite Seminary of one Elphinstone at Kensington, where his Body was Starv'd, and his Mind also, That in

Lieut. Walter Home, before the end of the American War was Major of the 42ᵈ Regᵗ, was an able Man and an Excellent Officer. He was the Ablest of all the Family, except Robert the Clergyman, altho' his 3ᵈ Brother Roddam the Admiral got to a Higher Rank. By means of my old Connexions at Glasgow, and Dʳ Wights Freinds, we were feasted and every way well entertain'd there. Nothing Could Surpass the Satisfaction, Mʳ and Mʳˢ Home had in Seeing their Son so well Receivd in the Best Society in Glasgow. In Those Days The Members of the University, excepting a very Few Indeed, were the only People of Liberal Conversation in that City.

Dʳˢ Blair and Robertson were at London this Year During the time of the Assembly. The 1ˢᵗ to visit London for the first and only time in his Life; The 2ᵈ to Transact with his Bookseller for his History of Charles the 5ᵗʰ Emperor of Germany and the King of Spain, and to Enjoy the Fame of his former Publication. Dʳ Robertson was Introduc'd to the first company in London, as all the People of Fashion both Male and Female, were eager to See the Historian of Queen Mary, who had Given them so Much Pleasure. He Did not Dissappoint their Expectation, for tho' he Spoke Broad Scotch, in point of pronunciation and accent or Tone, his was the Language of Literature and Taste, and of an Enlighten'd and Liberal Mind. Dʳ Blair exhibited in a Much Narrower Circle, For Nothing of his Having been yet Publish'd but his Dissertation on Ossian, he had rais'd but little Curiosity, and excepting the Family of Northumberland, a Son of which Lᵈ Algernon Peircy had been 3 years under his Roof at the University, he hardly was known to any of the English Nobility or Gentry, and Depended chiefly for his Entertainment there, on Such Literary People as he had seen at Edinʳ or was Introducd to by Dʳ Blair of Westminster, or James Mᶜpherson the Translator of Ossian.

Blair had taken Charge of Lord Glasgow The Kings Commissioner During the General Assembly, who tho he was a very able Man, had so much Distrust in himself, that he could not compose his own Speeches. This Service was Laid upon me: and I had much pleasure in the close Communication which this Gave me with his Lordship, as it open'd to me a Near View of uncommon Talents and exalted Mind, of the Service

---

the little Food it Got there was a Mixture of Poison. Dʳ Blair Prebendary of Westminster, Having some Alliance with his Family Sent or Went in his Carriage for him every Sat. [Morning], where he remaind till Monday, and in those two Days made up for the Loss he had Sustain'd in the preceding part of the week. When he Return'd to Edinʳ to College he had hardly a word of Latin, and was oblig'd to work hard with a Private Tutor. At Glasgow to be sure he Learn'd Publick Law, but took in Poison with it, which he had strength of Understanding to expel, as well as to overcome many other Disadvantages.[1]

of which the World was in Great Measure Depriv'd, by the most Insuperable Diffidence and Modesty.

I was a Member of the Assembly this Year, in which there was little Business of any Consequence. Henry Dundas, who was now well known there, Took an attentive charge of it, and Lean'd on me as his best clerical assistant.

In July this Year I went a Jaunt to Fife with M^rs C to my Cousin Thom^s Hendersons at   in Fife. He had a very Large Farm and was a Great Emprover on an extensive Scale. He was a Well Educated young Man of Good Breeding and Taste. After Staying some Days with him we went to Perth, by Lesly and Loch Leven, and Return'd by John Adams House of Blair, with whom we were Intimate. This Jaunt in an Open Chaise Delighted my Wife.

In Augt we Met M^r and Mrs Blackett at Wollerhaughhead, and pass'd some Days very agreably, Returning by Fogo to visit our Uncle and Aunt.

1769

The Window Tax alarm'd the Clergy more and more, and as I had been the Great Champion in Maintaining on every occasion that the Scottish Clergy by our Law ought to be exempted from this Tax, on the Same Grounds, on which they are exempted from paying the Land Tax for their Glebes, while one of our Meetings were Deliberating What was to be Done, I told them that as I Intended to be in London in the Spring on private Business, I would very Gladly Accept of any Commission they would Give me, to State our Claim to the Kings Ministers and particularly to the Lords of the Treasury, and at least to prepare the way for an application for Exemption to the Parliament in the following Year in Case it Should be found expedient. Robertson who had thought it more advisable to pay rather than Resist any Longer, was Surpris'd into Consent with this Sudden Proposal of mine, and frankly agreed to it. Tho' he told me privately that it would not have Success. The Truth was that M^rs Cs [Health] was so Indifferent that I became uneasy, and wish'd to try Bath, and to visit London where she never had been on our Way. The Clergy were highly pleasd with my offer of Service, without any expence, and I was accordingly Commissiond in Due form by the Committee on the Window Tax, to carry on this Affair. We prepard for our Journey, and set out about the Middle of February. We had the Good Fortune to Get Martin The Portrait Painter, and Bob Scott a Young Physician, as our companions on our Journey. This made it very pleasant, as Martin was a Man of uncommon Talents for Conversation. We Stopt for two Days with the Blacketts at Newcastle, and then went on by Huntington and after that to Cambridge. As I had not been there when I was formerly in London, I was Desirous to see that Famous University. And Besides had Got a Warm Exhortation from my Friend Dr Robertson, to Deviate a Little from the Straight Line, and Go by Hockwell where there were the finest Eels in all England. We took that place in our way, and arriv'd long enough before Dinner to have our Eels Drest in various ways. But tho' the Pitch Cock'd[1] had been so highly Recommended by our Friend we thought nothing of them, and M^rs C Could not Taste them. So that we had all to Dine on some very Indifferent Mutton Broth which had been Order'd for her. I Resolv'd after this never to Turn off the Road by the Advice of Epicures.

We Got in to Cambridge in the Dark, but Remaind all next forenoon, and saw all the Public Buildings, some of which are very fine Particularly Kings College Chapel. As none of us had any Acquaintance there that we knew of, we were not induc'd to stay any longer, and so made the best of our way to London.

We arriv'd in London on Feby 11th 1769 and took up our Residence with my Brother and Sister Bell who then Liv'd in Aldermanbury, but had a Country House Down at Merton in Surry, where their Children out of the Nurses Arms Resided all the Year, and where they went themselves in Summer, as he could Be in town every Day, and Return Easily to Dinner, Being only 9 Miles and a Q^r from London and the Road excellent. We went Down there to visit them in a Day or two, and found them as fine Healthy Children as could be seen. They had 5 already all of whom my Sister had Nurs'd, the eldest W^m who had been in Scotland in 1763, was now at School at Fourtree Hill some Miles North of London. Charles Hope now Ld Justice Clerk in Scotland was there also, his Mothers Father Being Lord of the Manor there. Merton was a very agreable place. The House had been originally Built by Ld Eglinton, and soon after Forsaken and Sold. It was too large for Bell, but he had it cheap. There was a large Garden of 3 acres, Divided into three parts, and planted with the best Fruit trees, on which when I afterwards saw it in the Season, I said there were more Peaches and Apricots than Grew then in Midlothian. For I well Remember that [there were very few] till we had Hot Houses here, which had then only had a beginning by Ld Chief Baron Ord at the Dean, and Baron Stuart Moncrieffe, and were not in Great Numbers till 1780.

About the 3^d night after we came, we went with the Bells to the Scotch Dancing Assembly, which Then met in the Kings Arms Tavern in Cheapside, when we met many of our acquaintance, and were Introduc'd to several others with whom we were not before acquainted. I was Glad to find from them all that Mr Bell was in high esteem among them as a Man of Business, Not only for his Integrity but his Aptitude for Business. My Sister was much admir'd as a fine Woman, and no less for the Elegance and Propriety of her Manners, Than for her handsome Face and Fair Person. Bell had the Good Luck to be call'd Honest Thom Bell, In Distinction to another who frequented Loyds Coffee House, who was not in so much Favour, and was Besides a very Hot Wilkite. After a few Days more we were Invited to a fine Subscription Dinner at the London Tavern, where there was a Company of about 50 Ladies and Gentlemen. The Dinner was sumptuous, but I was not much Delighted with the Conversation. The Men especially were vulgar and uneducated, and most of the English among them violent Wilkites, and Gave Toasts of the Party kind, which Shew'd their Breeding, where the Majority were Scotch. It was with Some Difficulty, that I could Get Honest Thom to treat their bad manners with Ridicule and Contempt, rather than with Rage and Resentment.

We Dind on the Sunday following at Merton, where 3 or 4 Scotch Gentlemen follow'd us. This was the Case every Sunday at Merton, and the Road Being fine, with Lamps on every part of the Road, They Did not much mind how long they staid.

Having now been near a week in London It was thought That I should Give a Commencement to the Business, which I had undertaken. I therefore applied myself to making the necessary Calls on Dr Gordon of the Temple a Scotch Sollicitor at Law, and the Lord Advocate for Scotland, and whoever else I thought might be of use. I had Drawn a Short Memorial on the Business, which Dr Gordon approv'd but wishd it to be left with him for Corrections, and Additions. This I Did, But was Surpris'd to find that when he returnd it Several Weeks after, as fit to be Sent to the Press, that There [was] hardly any change on it at all. But I was still more surpris'd when Calling on Ld Advocate (James Montgomery Esqr) and Opening the Affair to him, to hear him answer That he wish'd me Success with all his Heart, but could Give me no Aid. For he added, That when the clergy were lately in 4 years arrears, The Payment of which would have Greatly Distrest them, Dr Robertson had come to him in Edin^r and had strongly Interceded with him to Get that arrear excus'd and he would answer for the Punctual Payment of the Clergy in Future. He had accordingly on this Promise applied to the Duke of Grafton then first Minister and obtaind what the D^r had ask'd on the Condition promis'd. In this state of things, it was impossible that he could assist me as Ld Advocate. But that as a private Gentleman, he would do all he could, That was to Introduce me to the Minister, to

speak of me as I Deserv'd, and to say that he thought the Petition I
brought very Reasonable, and agreable to the Law of Scotland. All this
he punctually Fulfill'd for he was an Honourable Man.

The Church of Scotland had been at all times very meanly provided,
and even when they were Serving their Country with the Utmost
Fidelity and Zeal, at the time of the Restoration,[1] and ever afterwards
Supporting that Part of the Aristocracy, which resisted the encroach-
ments of the Crown and Maintaind the Liberties of the People, even
then their most Moderate Requests to be Rais'd above Poverty were
denied. After the Union of the Crowns, and even after that of the
Legislatures, They have on every application for Redress, been Scurvily
Treated. The History of our Country Bears the Strongest Testimony, of
their Loyalty to the King, while they warmly oppos'd every apearance
of Arbitrary Power, even to Persecution and Death. They were Cajol'd
and Flatter'd by the Aristocracy when they wanted their Aid, but never
Reliev'd till Cromwell Consider'd their Poverty and Relievd them for
the time. Yet after Presbytery was finally settled at the Revolution, the
Clergy were allow'd almost to Starve, till down in our own time in the
Year 1790 A Generous and Wise Man[2] was rais'd to the Presidents Chair,
who Being also President of that Court when it sits as a Committee of
Parliament for the Augmentation of Ministers Stipends, with the Con-
currence of his Brethren has Redress'd this Grievance and enabled the
Clergy and their Families, to survive such Years of Dearth as the 1799
and 1800, which but for that Relief must have Reduc'd them to Ruin.
This happend by Good Luck while the Land Estates in Scotland were
Doubled and Tripled in their Rents, otherwise it could not have been
Done without a Clamorous Opposition.

It is Observable that no Country has ever been more tranquill, except the triffling insurrections of 1715 and 1745, Than Scotland has been,
since the Revolution in 1688, a Period of 117 years, while at the same
time the Country has been Prosperous, with an Increase of Agriculture
Trade and Manufactures, as well as all the Ornamental Arts of Life to a
Degree unexampled in any Age and Country. How far the Steady
Loyalty to the Crown and Attachment to the Constitution, together
with the unwearied Diligence of the Clergy in Teaching a Rational
Religion, may have Contributed to this Prosperity, Cannot be exactly
Ascertain'd; But Surely Enough [appears] to Entitle them to the high
Respect of the State and to Justice from their Country in a Decent
Support to them, and to their Families: and if possible to a Permanent
Security, like that of the Church of England, by Giving the Clergy a title
to vote on their Livings for the Member of Parliament of the County,
which would at once Raise their Respect, and by making them Members

of the State, would forever Secure their Interest in it, and firmly Cement and Strengthen the Whole.

Before I began my Operations Relative to the Window Tax, I witness'd something Memorable. It Being Much the Fashion to Go on a Sunday evening to a Chappel of the Magdalen asylum,[1] we went there on the 2d Sunday we were in London, and had Difficulty to Get Tolerable Seats for my Sister and Wife, the Crowd of Gentile People was so Great. The Preacher was Dr Dodd, a Man afterwards too well known. The unfortunate Young Women, were in a Lattic'd Gallery, Where you Could only see those who chose to be Seen. The Preachers Text was from [Matt. 5. 28], If a Man Look on a Woman to Lust after her &c. The Text itself was Shocking, and the Sermon was composd with the Least possible Delicacy, and was a Shocking Insult on a Sincere Penitent, and Fuel for the Warm Passions of the Hypocrite. The Fellow was handsome and Deliverd his Discourse Remarkably well for a Reader. When he had finishd there were unceasing Whispers of Applause, which I could not help Contradicting Aloud, and Condemning the Whole Institution as well as the Exhibition of the Preacher, as Contra Bonos Mores, and a Disgrace to a Christian City.

On the Day after this, I went to the House of Peers and heard Sir Fletcher Norton's Pleading on the Douglas [Cause],[2] on the Side of Douglas, but in a manner Inferior to what I expected from his Fame. But this was not a Question of Law but of Fact. I Din'd and Sup'd that Day, with Coll! Dow, who had translated well the History of Industan, and wrote tolerably well the Tragedy of Zingis. As Js Mcpherson the Translator of Ossian and he liv'd together and as his play in point of Diction and Manners had Some Resemblance to the Poems of Ossian, there were not a few who ascrib'd the Tragedy to Mcpherson. But such People Did not know, that Could Mcpherson have Claim'd it, he was not the Man to Relinquish Either the Credit or Profits which might arise from it; For the Tragedy Ran its nine nights. Dow was a Scotch Adventurer who had been bred at the School of Dunbar, his Father Being in the Customs there, and had Run away from his apprenticeship at Eymouth and found his way to the E. Indies, where having a Turn for Languages which had been foster'd by his Education he soon became such a Master of the Native Tongue as to accellerate his preferment in the Army, for he Soon had the Command of a Regiment of Seopoys. He was a Sensible and knowing Man, of very agreable Manners and of a Mild and Gentle Disposition. As he was telling us that night, that when he had the Charge of the Great Mogul with two Regts under his Command at Delhi, he was tempted to Dethrone the Monarch and Mount the Throne in his Stead, which he Said he Could Easily have Done. When I ask'd him what prevented him from Yielding to the Temptation, he Gave me this Memorable Answer, That it was, Reflecting on What his Old School Fellows at Dunbar would think of him, for Being Guilty of Such an Action. His Company were D.r John Douglas and Garrick, The two M.cphersons, John Home, and Dav.d Hume who Joind us in the Evening. I have before I believe Given Some Acct. of them all, but Rob.t M.cpherson the Chaplain, whom I had not known till now. Tho' not a Man of Genius, he was a Man of Good Sense, of a Firm and Manly Mind, and of much Worth and Honour. He was a Younger Brother of M.cpherson of Banchors, a Man near the Head of the clan in point of Birth, but not of a Large Fortune. He had been Bred at Aberdeen for the Church, but before he past trials as a Probationer, he had been offer'd pay in his Reg.t of Highlanders by Simon Fraser and had accepted. But when the Reg.t Rendevouz'd at Greenock, he was told with Many Fair [Speeches] That the Captains Commissions, were all Dispos'd of much against the Coll.s Will, But that he might have a Lieut.cy, or the Chaplainry, if he lik'd it Better. M.cpherson Chose the Last and took Orders immediatly from the Presbytery of Lochcarron, where he Return'd for ten Days. He soon made himself acceptable to the superiors as well as to the Men, and after they Landed in Nova Scotia, on every Skirmish or Battle, it was Observ'd that he always put himself on a Line with the Officers at the Head of the Reg.t. He was Invited to the Mess of the Field Officers where he Continued. On hearing this from Gen.l Murray, I ask'd him if it was true. He said it was. How came you to be so Foolish? He answer'd, that Being a Grown Man, while many of the Lieut.s and Ensigns were but Boys, as well as some of the Privates, and that they lookt to him for example as well as precept, he had thought his Duty to advance with them, but That he had Discontinued the Practice after the 3.d time of Danger, as he found they were perfectly Steady. Dining with him and Gen.l James Murray and one or two more at the British[1] one Day, I put him on telling the Story of the Mutiny at Quebec when he had the Command after the Death of Wolfe. He told us that the first thing he had Done, was to Send to Enquire If Mac had taken advantage of the Leave he had Given him to Sail for Brittain the Day before, for If he had not Saild there would have been no Mutiny. But he was Gone, and I had to do the best I could without him, and so he went on. Not Being Certain if this anecdote might not have been much exaggerated according to the usual stile of the *Windy Murrays*, as they were styl'd by *Jock at the Horn*, I ask'd Mac when the Company parted, how much of this was true. He answer'd that tho' the Gen.l had exceeded a Little in his compliments to him, That it was so far true that he Being the only Highland chaplain there, he of Fraser's Reg.t having Gone home, he had so much to Say with Both of them, That he could have persuaded them to Stand by their officers, and the Gen!—In which if those two Reg^{ts} had Joind, they would have prevented the Mutiny.

One Anecdote more of this Worthy Man, and I shall have Done with him. In one of the Winters in which he was at Quebec, he had provided himself in a Wooden House, which he had furnish'd well, and in which he had a tolerable Soldiers Library. While he was Dining one Day with the Mess, his House took Fire and was Burnt to the Ground. Next Morning the 2 Serjeant Majors of the 2 Reg^{ts} of Highlanders, came to him, and Lamenting the Great Loss he had Sustaind, told him that the Lads, out of their Great Love and Respect for him, had Collected a Purse of 400 Guineas, which they beg'd him to accept of. He was movd with their Generosity—and By and Bye Answer'd, That he was never so much Gratified in his Life as by their Offer as a Mark of Kindness and Respect, of which he would think himself entirely unworthy, If he could Rob them of the Fruits of their Wise and Prudent Frugality; and added that by Good Fortune he had no need of the exertions of their Generosity. The Annals of Private Men I have often Thought, as Instructive and Worthy of Being Recorded as those of their Superiors.

Having formerly Given some Account of James M^{c}pherson and Garrick I shall Say nothing more of them here, But that in their several ways, They were very Good Company. Garrick was always Playsome, Good humour'd, and willing to Display. James was Sensible, Shrewd and Sarcastic. Dow went a Second time to India, and after some time Died there.

By this time I had Discover'd that I should have no Need to Go to Bath, as M^{rs} C had Fallen with Child, which left me sufficient time to wait even for the very slow method of Transacting Treasury Business, which made me sometimes Repent that I had undertaken it. I had found Sir Gilbert Elliot at last, who both encourag'd and assisted me. I had also met Mr Wedderburn, who was not then in the Line of Doing me much Service. Mr Grey Cooper, who had been brought forward by the Honble Charles Townshend, and was then a Secretary of the Treasury, frankly Gave me his Services. But the only Person, (except Sir G. Elliot) who understood me perfectly was Mr Jerimiah Dyson. He had been two years in Edin^r University, at the same time with Aikenside and Monckly, and had a perfect Idea of the Constitution of the Church of Scotland, and the Nature and State of the Livings of the Clergy. Of him I expected and obtaind much Aid. Broderip Secretary to the Duke of Grafton, on whom I frequently Call'd, Gave me Good Words but little Aid.

On the 23ᵈ of this Month, I went with John Home to his first night of the Tragedy of the Fatal Discovery, which went off better than we expected. This was and is to my Taste the 2ᵈ Best of Home's Tragedies. Garrick had been Justly allarm'd at the Jealousy and Dislike which prevaild at that time against Lᵈ Bute and the Scotch, and had advisd him to change the Title of Rivine¹ into That of The Fatal Discovery, and had provided a Student of Oxford who had appear'd at the Rehearsals as the Author, and wishd Home of all things to Remain Conceald till the Play had its Run. But John whose Vanity was too sanguine, to admit of Fear or Caution, and whose Appetite for Praise Rebelld against the Counsel that would Deprive him for a moment of his Fame, too Soon Discover'd the Secret, and tho' the Play Surviv'd its nine nights, yet the House evidently Slacken'd, after the Town heard that John was the Author. Home however in his Way, ascrib'd this to the attention of the Publick, and especially of the Scotch, being Draw[n] off by the Douglas Cause, which was Decided in the House of Lords on the 29ᵗʰ, forgetting that this took up only one night, and that any Slackness Deriv'd from that Could not affect other nights.

To finish my Account of this Play, I shall add here, That Garrick still continu'd to perform it on the Most Convenient lines. Mʳˢ C and J. Home and I Dind with Mʳ A. Wedderburn at his House in Lincoln's Inn Fields, and went to the Fatal Discovery with him and his Lady, and his Brother Collᴵ David Wedderburn, when we were all perfectly well pleas'd. We Return'd with them to Supper, Wedderburn having Continued Cordial and Open all that Day. His Brother was always So.

We became acquainted with my Wife[s] uncle and aunt, Mʳ Laurie and Mʳˢ Mary Reed, Brother and Sister of her Mother by another Wife. Mʳ Reed was a Mahogony Merchant in Hatton Wall, a very Worthy and Honourable Man, and his Sister whom I had seen once or twice before in Berwick, was a Handsome and Elegant Woman, tho' now turn'd of 30, with as much Good Sense and Breeding as any person we met with. Mʳ Reed was not Rich, but between an Estate of £250 which he had near Alnwick, and his Business, he Livd in a very Respectable Manner. Their Mode of Living was quite Regulated, for They saw Company only 2 Days in the week, on Thursday to Dinner, when you met a few Friends, chiefly from N. Humberland, and here if you pleas'd you might play Cards and Stay the Evening. On Sunday Evening they Likewise saw their Friends to Tea and Supper, But they were too oldfashiond, to play Cards, which was very Convenient for me. The Uncle and Aunt were Proud of their Niece, as they found her in point of Conversation and Manners, at least Equal to any of their Guests; and the Niece was Proud of her uncle and aunt, as in him she found as Honest a Man as

Mr Bell, and in her a Woman who for Beauty and Elegance Could Cope
with my Sister, who was not Surpassd by Anybody in the City. Here I
met with many old acquaintance, and made some New ones, such as Sir
Evan Nepean and his Lady, Then only in their Courtship, and A. Collingwood a cliver Attorney, Said to be Nearly Related to the Family of
Unthank, indeed a Natural Son of my Wife[s] Grand Father. To this
very agreable place we Resorted often, and when I came next year
alone, I availd myself of it especially on Sunday nights.

I was also much indebted to my Hospitable Friend Dr Blair of Westminster, at whose House I met with sundry people, whose acquaintance
I cultivated. On the 26th of this month I met him at Court, after having
attended Service in the Chapell Royal, and in the Chaplains Seat, and
was by him Introduc'd in the Drawing Room, to Ld Bathurst, then very
old but extremely agreable, Dr Barton Dean of Bristol, Rector of S^t
Andrew Holburn &c. and to Dr Tucker Dean of Gloucester, very excellent People whose acquaintance I very much valued.

On the 27th I attended the House of Peers on the Decision of the
Douglas Cause. The Duke of B[uccleuch] had promisd to Carry me Down
to the House, but as I was Going into Grovenor Square to Meet him at
10 aclock, I met the Duke of Montagu, who was coming from his House,
and took me into his Chariot, Saying that the Duke of B. was not yet
Ready. He put me in by the Side of the Throne, where I found two or 3
of my Friends, among them Thos Bell. The Business Did not begin till
Eleven, and from that time I stood with now and then a Lean on the
Edge of a Deal Board till nine in the Evening, without any Refreshment
but a Small Roll, and 2 Oranges. The Heat of the House was chiefly
Oppressive, and Ld Sandwich's Speech, which tho' Learned and able,
yet Being 3 hours long was very Untolerable. The Duke of Bedford Spak
Low, but not half an Hour. The Chancellor and Ld Mansfield united on
the Side of Douglas. Each of them Spoke above an Hour. Andrew
Stuart, whom I saw in the House Sitting on the left side of the Throne,
seem'd to be much affected at a Part of Ld Cambdens Speech, in which
he Reflected on him, and immediatly left the House. From whence I
concluded that he was in Despair of Success. Ld Mansfield overcome with
Heat, was about to Faint in the Middle of his Speech, and was oblig'd to
Stop. The Side Doors were Immediatly Thrown Open, and the Chancellor rushing out, Returnd soon with a Servant who followd him with a
Bottle and Glasses. Ld Mansfield Drank two Glasses of the Wine, and
after some time Reviv'd and proceeded in his Speech. We who had no
wine, were nearly as much Recruited by the Fresh Air, which rush'd in
at the open Door, as his L^dship by the Wine. About 9 the Business ended
in Favour of Douglas, There Being only 5 Peers on 'tother side. I was

well pleas'd with that Decision, as I had Favour'd that Side; Professor Ferguson and I Being the only two of our Set of People who favourd Douglas, Chiefly on the Opinion, That if the Proof of Filiation on his Part was not sustain'd, the whole System of Evidence in Such Cases would be overturn'd, and a Door be Open'd for endless Disputes about Succession. I had ask'd the Duke of B. Some Days before the Decision how it would Go; he Said That if the Law Lords Dissagreed there was no saying how it would Go, because the Peers however Imperfectly prepar'd to Judge, would Follow the Judge [they] most respected. But if they united, the Case would be Determind by their Opinion, it being [customary] in their House, to Support the Law Lords in all Judicial Cases.

After the Decision, I persuaded My Friends, as there was no Coach to be had, not to attempt Rushing in to any of the Neighbouring Taverns, but to follow me, to the Crown and Anchor in the Strand, where we arriv'd, Thoˢ Bell, Alderman Chrichton, Robert Bogle Junʳ and I, in time enough to Get into a Snug Room, where we wrote some Letters for Scotland, the Post then not Departing till twelve, and after a Good Supper, Bell and I Got home to Aldermanbury by one a clock, where our Wives were waiting, tho' not uninform'd of the Event, as I had Dispatch'd a Porter with a note to them immediatly on our arrival in the Tavern.

The Rejoicings in Scotland were very Great on this Occasion, and were outragious, altho' the Douglas Family had been long in obscurity, Yet The Hamiltons had for a long Period lost their Popularity. The attachment which all their Acquaintance had to Baron Mure, who was the Original Author of this Suit, and to And. Stuart who Carri'd it on, Sway'd their Minds very much their way. They were Men of uncommonly Good Sense and Probity.

Mrˢ Pulteney Being Still Living, we had a Fine Dinner at Bath House, after which Mrˢ C and I paid an evening visit to Mrˢ Montagu.* On this first Mission to London I was much oblig'd to Sir Alexʳ Gilmour, who was a Friend of the Duke of Graftons; he knew every Body, and

* Pulteney at this time, had fallen much under the influence of General Robert Clerk, whom I have mentioned before. I happened to ask him when he had seen Clerk; he answered he saw him every day, and as he had not been there yet he might probably pay his visit before 10 o'clock, and then enlarged for some time on his great ability. Clerk had subdued Pulteney by persuading him that there was not a Man in England fit to be Chancellor of the Exchequer, but himself. Mrˢ Pulteney's good sense however defeated the effect of this influence. Pulteney was unfortunate in not taking for his private secretary and confidential friend Dʳ John Douglas, who had stood in that relation to the late Lord Bath, and was one of the ablest men in England. But on Pulteney's succession, he found himself neglected and drew off. Clerk came at 10, as Pulteney had foretold, and I saw how the land lay.[1]

Introduc'd me to every Body. One Day he Carried me to the Arch.ᴾ of
Canterbury, Cornwallis, who Rec'd me Graciously. In short I calld on all
the Scotch Noblemen and Members of Parliament, Many of whom I
Saw, and left Memorials at every House where I Call'd. Lᵈ Frederick
Campbell was particularly Obliging. At this time I Dind one Day with
Sir A. Gilmour on a Sunday after having been at Court. Gen! Graham
and Pulteney and Coll! Riccart Hepburn Dind there. In the Conversation
there, I found to my Surprise [Graham] talking Strongly against admin-
istration, for not advising the King to Yield to the Popular Cry. Gilmour
oppos'd him with Violence, and I Drew an inference which provd true,
That he had been tampering with her Majesty, and using Political Free-
doms, which were not long afterwards the Cause of his Disgrace.
Graham was a Shrewd and Sensible Man, but the Qˢ Favour and his
Prosperity, had made him Arrogant and Presumptuous, and he blew
himself up. Not long after this time he lost his office near the Queen, and
Retir'd into Obscurity in Scotland for the Rest of his Days.

My Conexion with Physicians, made me a Member of two of their
Clubs which I seldom Miss'd. One of them was at the Horn Tavern in
Fleet Sᵗ, where they had laid before them Original Papers Relating to
thir own Science and had publish'd a vol. or 2 of Essays which were well
Rec'd. Armstrong who took no share in the Business, Generally arrivd
when I Did about 8 a clock, and as they had a Great Deference for him,
and as he was Whimsical, They Delay'd bespeaking Supper till he came,
and then laid that Duty on him. He in complaisance wishd to turn it
over on me as the Greatest, or rather the only Stranger, for I was admitted *speciali gratia*, but I Declin'd the office. The Conversation was
Lively and agreable, and we parted always at 12. There was another
Club held on the alternate Thursday at the Queens head in Pauls church
yard, which was not confin'd to Physicians, but included Men of other
Professions. Strange the Engraver was one, a very Sensible, Ingenious,
and Modest Man.

*In the Course of my Operations about the Window Tax, I had fre-
quently Short Interviews with Lord Mansfield. One Day he sent for me
to Breakfast, when I had a long Conversation with him on Various Subjects. Amongst others he talk'd of Hume's and Robertsons History's,
and said that tho' they had pleas'd and Instructed him much, and tho'
he Could point out few or no Faults in them, Yet when he was Reading
their Books, he Did not think he was Reading English. Could I account
to him, how that happen'd? I answer'd that the Same Objection had not
occurd to me, who was a Scotchman Bred as well as born, but that I had

* All that follows on this page, is an anticipation, and Did not happen till Febʸ
1770.

a Solution to it, which I would Submit to his Lordship. It was That to every Man Bred in Scotland, The English Language was in some respects a Foreign Tongue,[1] the precise Value and Force of whose Words and Phrases he Did not Understand, and therefore was Continually Endeavouring to Mend his Expressions, by additional Epithets, or Circumlocutions, which made his writing appear both stiff and Redundant. With this Solution his Ldship appear'd entirely satisfied.

By this time his Lordship perfectly understood the Nature of our claim to Exemption from the Window Tax, and promis'd me his aid and suggested some New Arguments in our Favour. On Taking Leave, I said to his Lordship, I said to him, that as this was his Opinion, If his Lordship would only be so Good as Repeat it to the Duke of Grafton, My Business would be Done, and I should ask no more. . . . *

I made a very valuable acquaintance in the Bishop of London R. Terrick, Having been introducd to him by his Son in Law Dr Anthony Hamilton, whom I had met at Dr Pitcairns. I found the Bishop to be a truly Excellent Man, of a Liberal Mind and Excellent Good Temper. He took to me, and was very Cordial in Wishing Success to my Application. And was very friendly in Recommending it and me to his Brethren on the Bench. He never Refusd me Admittance, and I Dind frequently with him this year and the Next. He was then Consider'd as having the Sole Episcopal Jurisdiction over the Church of England in America. He was So Obliging to my Requests, That he ordain'd at my Desire two Scotch Probationers, who having little Chance of Obtaining Settlements here, were Glad to try their Fortunes in a New World. As I was unwilling to forfeit my Credit with this Good Man, I had not Recommended them, but with perfect assurance of their Good Characters. The First who I think he had sent to Bermudas, he Gave me thanks for, when I saw him a Year after, as he told me he had fully answerd the Character I had Given him. He[2] was a Famous Good Preacher and the best Reader of Prayers I ever heard. Being Dean of the Chappel Royal he Read the Communion Service Every Sunday. Tho' our Residence was at my Sisters in Alderman[bur]y, as I had occasion frequently to Dine late in the west end of the Town, I Lodg'd in New Bond Street with my Aunt— and Resorted often at Supper to Rt Adams whose Sisters were very agreable, and where we had the freshest news from the House of Commons, of which he was a Member, and which he told us in the most agreable manner, and with very Lively Comments.

My Good Aunt Patersons Husband, a Cousin of Sir Hew Paterson took Care to have us visit his Sons Widow Mrs Seton the Heiress of

* This anecdote is told too Soon, for it Did not happen till the Month of Jany 17[70]. [*Infra*, p. 272.]

Toach, whose first Husband, was Sir Hew's Son who had Died without Issue. There we Din'd one Day with a large Company Mostly Scots, among whom were Mrs Wauchinshaw, who had a place at Court, tho' she was Sister of the Lady who was said to be Mistress to Prince Charles, the Pretenders Son, and Dav^d Hume, by that time underSecretary of State. The Conversation was Lively and Agreable, But we were much amus'd, with Observing How much the Thoughts and Conversation, of all those in the least Connected, was taken up with every Triffling Circumstance that Related [to the Court]. This kind of Tittle Tattle, suited Dr John Blair of all Men, who had been a Tutor to the Kings Brother the Duke of York, and now occasionally assisted Dr Barton as Clerk of the Closet to the Princess Dowager of Wales. [It] was truly amusing to observe how much David H's strong and capacious mind, was fill'd with Infantine Anecdotes of Nurses and Children. Mr Seton was the Son of a Mr Smith, who had been Settled at Boulogne a Wine Merchant, was a Great Jacobite, and had come to Scotland in the time of the Rebellion 1745. Poor Mrs Seton who[se] 1st Husband Paterson, was by his Mother a Nephew of the Earl of Mar's, Had fallen a Sacrifice to that Prejudice, For Seton possess'd no other charm. I call her a Sacrifice, because his Bad usage Shorten'd her Days. She was a very amiable Woman. His Future History is well known.

At this time we had a Dinner from Dr Garthshore, whose Wife the Heiress of Riscow in Galloway, was my Cousin. Besides Drs Blair and Dickson there were Several Dissenting Parsons, Such as Drs Price and Kippis, and Alexander, who were very bad company indeed, For they were Fiery Republicans and Wilkites, and very Pedantick, Petulant, and Peremptory. Blair and I however, with the Help of Dickson, kept them very well Down. Garthshore himself acted the part of umpire, with a Leaning to their Side, as they had an ascendent over many of his Patients.

John Home who was very Obliging to us, when I was at Liberty, in the Middle of April, went with M^rs C and me to see Hampton Court and Windsor. After we had seen the 1st we went and Shew'd M^rs C Garrick[s] Villa in Hampton Town, which she was highly pleas'd with. The Family had not yet Return'd to the Country. We went all night to Windsor. In the Morning we Call'd on Dr Douglas and his Lady, a Grand Daughter of Sir Geo. Rooke of Q. Ann's Reign, Then in Residence and he Engag'd us to Dine with him. We went to Church and heard him Preach an Excellent Sermon tho' ill Deliver'd. His Conversation was always Instructive and agreable. He had a Greater N^o of Anecdotes, and told them more Correctly than any Man I ever knew. In Going thro' his Library, which was pretty full of Books, he Selected one small Elegant French Novel, and Gave it as a Keepsake to Mrs Carlyle, which [She and] I were much pleas'd with as a Token of Regard.

We had past one Day with Mrs Montagu by Invitation, which Did [not] please us much as the Conversation was all preconceiv'd and Resembled the Rehearsal of a Comedy, more than the True and unaffected Dialogue, which Conveys the unaffected and unstudied Sentiments of the Heart. What a Pity it was that she Could not help Acting, and the woman would [have] been Respectable, Had she not been so passionatly Desirous of Respect. For she had Good Parts, and must have had many allurements when she was Young and Beautifull.

John Home [went] with us to See Sion House, the Inside of which had been Most Beautifully Adorn'd by Robert Adam. We Dind with Mr and Mrs Barry, who had been Old Friends of John's, and Barry had been his Military Companion [at] Falkirk, and escap'd with him from Doun Castle. John was much attachd to him and he Deserv'd it. There Dind with us Macp[herson and] Blair besides Home. Our Stay in London Drew to a close, and Having Obtain'd all I expected from the Treasurery, which was encouragement to Apply to Parliament next year, I made haste to Shew Mrs Carlyle what she had not Seen. We went to Greenwich in the Morning, and the same Day, Dind again with Mr and Mrs Seton and Sup'd with my Old Friend Lady Lindores. I sate to Martin for the large Picture that went next year into the exhibition. This was for the 3d time. Another Sitting in Jany thereafter Did the [Business.] We went to the opera with my Sister. We Staid for our last Fortnight at my Aunts, as my Business at the Treasury, Made it more Convenient, and my Wife had to make all her Farewell Visits. She had not seen Garrick who was at last to play for 3 nights. With Difficulty, and Bribery we Got Places. But Mrs C fell sick and we were Oblig'd to Leave it in the Middle. We went to See Westminster Abbey, and Dind with our kind Friends the Blairs who had Engagd us. My Sister Being now Gone to Merton with her Children, we took aunt and pass'd a Day there. On the Last Day we went into the City and took Leave and Dind at Uncle Reeds. Mr Home had Got a Partner, a Young Man of the Name of Douglas Going to Berwick. This Lad Being Fantastick and Vain, because he had an Uncle who was under Door Keeper to the House of Commons, Diverted us much. To Enjoy him, Home and I took him Stage about. My Wife was Delighted with him in the Inns, but she Did not chuse him to Go in the Chaise with her, as she was at this time apt to be Sick. We Dind on the Last Day the 25th of [April] at the Brands Head with some Friends, and Set out on our Journey North at 5 in the Evening.

My Wife's Condition made us Resolve to Travel Slow, tho we were to halt some time at Newcastle. We had agreed for my Wife's Amusement and our own to take the Middle Road, and Go down by Northampton and Nottingham where we had never been, and were much amus'd with the Beauty of the Country, and the Variety of its Scenery. When we Came to Nottingham however, as the Road was Rough which Did not suit M^rs C present Condition, and the Houses and Horses inferior, [we thought] That it would be better to Turn into the East Road again, and make the best of our way to Doncaster. When we Drew near that place M^rs C found out that we had Chang'd our Route and was well pleas'd. We had come by Mansfield, and Welbeck (the Duke of Portlands) and the Duke of Norfolks, places well worth seeing. The Road Goes thro' the Trunk of a Famous Oak tree.[1] The Woods in that part of the Forest of Nottingham are very Fine, and the Oaks are Remarkably Large. We arriv'd at Walls End, a very Delightfull Village about 4 Miles below Newcastle on the Road to Shiells, where Mr Black[ett] had a very agreable House for the Summer. There were other two Gentlemen's Houses of Good Fortune in the village, with a Church and a Parsonage House. Next Day the 1st of May was so very warm, that I with Difficulty was able to walk Down to the Church in the Bottom of the Village not more than 200 Yards Distant. Mary Home, a Cousin German of M^rs Bs and my Wife was residing here at this time and had been for Several Months at Newcastle. This was the Young Lady whom John Home Married, who was then a Pretty Lively Girl, and Reckond very like Queen Charlotte. She unfortunatly had bad Health, which Continud even to this Day: For She is now 67, and is still very Frail: Tho' better than She has been for Several Years. It was in Some Respects an unlucky Marriage for she had no Children—Ld Haddington [how]ever Said She was a very Good Wife for a Poet. And Lady Milton, Having ask'd me What made John Marry Such a Sickly Girl, I answerd that I suppos'd, it was because he was in Love with her. She Replied, No, No, it was because She was in Love with him.

We Staid for 8 or 10 Days and visited all the Neighbours, who were all very agreable, even the Clergyman's Wife, who was a little Lightsome. But as her Head run much on Fine Cloaths which she Could not purchase to please her, but only Could Imitate in the most Tawdry Manner, She was rather Amusing to Mrs B. who had a Good Deal of Humour, More than her Sister, who had a Sharper Wit and more Discernment. The Husband was a very Good Sort of Man, and very Worthy of his Office, But oppress'd with Family Cares. Mr Potter I think was an Oxonian.

We Did not fail to visit our Good Friend Mr Collingwood of Chirton and his Lady Mary Roddam, of both of whom my Wife was a Favourite. We went Down together to Berwickshire in the Middle of May, where we Remaind some Days at Fogo Manse, The Revd Mr Wm Home's, where Leaving John with his bride we came on to Muss.^h about the 27.th of May near the End of the General Assembly.

I had been persuaded to buy a Young Horse from a Farmer near Mr Home's an awkward enough Beast, but only 4 years old, which if he Did not Do for a Riding Horse might be turnd to the Plough: For I had at the preceding Mart.^s Enter'd on a Farm of 100 acres of the Duke of B[uccleughs]. On the Sale Morning after I came home, I unfortunately Mounted this Beast, who Run away with me in my Green before the Door, and was in Danger of throwing me on the Railing that was put up to Defend a Young Hedge. To Shun this I threw myself off on the opposite Side in Sight of my Wife and Children. I was much Stun'd and could not Get up immediatly, but luckily before She could Reach the Place I had Rais'd myself to my Breach; otherwise I Did not know what might have befallen her in the Condition She was in. No harm however Happen'd to her, and the New Surgeon who had come in our Absence, a John Steward or Stewart, a North-humbrian, an apprentice of Sandy Woods, was sent for to Bleed me. I would not be bled However, till I had made my Report on the Window Lights ready for the Genl Assembly, which was to be Dissolv'd on Monday, Lest I should not be able to write after Being Bled, or not to attend the Assembly on Monday. But it so happen'd that I was little Dissabled by my Fall, and Could even preach next Day.

On Monday I went to Edin.^r and Render'd an Account of my Mission at the Bar of the Genl Assembly. I Rec'd the Thanks of the Genl Assembly for my Care and Diligence in the Management of this Business, and at the same Time was appointed by the Assembly Their Commissioner with full powers to apply to next Session of Parliament for an Exemption from the Window Tax, to be at the same time under the Direction of a Committee of assembly, which was Reviv'd with additions. This first Success made me very popular among the Clergy; of whom one half at least Lookt upon me with an ill Eye, after the affair of the Tragedy of Douglas. There is no Doubt That Exemption from that Tax was a very Great Object to the Clergy, whose Stipends were in Genl very Small; and besides was opposing in the Beginning any Design there might be to Lay Still Heavier Burdens on the Clergy, who having only Stipends out of the Tithes allotted together with Small Glebes and a Suitable Manse and offices, free of all Taxes or Publick Burdens, would have been quite undone, had they been oblig'd to pay all that has since been laid on Houses and Windows. For as much use as the Clergy were at the Reformation, and for as much as they Contributed to the Revolution, and to preserve the Peace and Promote the prosperity of the

Country Since that Period, The Aristocracy of Scotland have always [been] Backward to mend [the] Situation of the Clergy, which had it not been for the Manly System of the President (Isla Campbell) must have fallen into Distress and Contempt. As it is, Their Stipends keep no pace with the Rising Prosperity of the Country, and they are Degraded in their Rank, by the Increasing Wealth of the Inferior Orders. Had the Nobility and Gentry of Scotland Enlargement of Mind and Extensive Views, They would now for the Security of the Constitution, Ingraft the Clergy into the State, as they have always been in England, and by Imparting all the Privileges of Freeholders except that of being M.P.s on their Livings, They would attach them, still more than ever to their Country. They would widen the Basis of the Constitution, which is Far too Narrow, without Lessening their own Importance in the Smallest Degree. For there Could be no Combination of the Clergy against their Heritors; on the Contrary, They would be universally Dispos'd to unite with their Heritors if they behav'd well to them in all Political Business. But I know very Few People capable of thinking in this Train, and far less of acting on So Large and Liberal a Plan. In the Mean time, on account of Many unfortunate Circumstances, One of which is that Patrons, Now that by help of the Moderate Interest as it is Call'd, There is No Opposition to their Presentations, Have restor'd to them that Right they so Long Claim'd, and for most part Given them the Man they like Best, That is to say, the Least Capable and commonly the Least Worthy, of all the Probationers in their Neighbourhood. The unfitness of one of the Professors of Divinity,[1] and the Influence he has in Providing for Young Men of his own Fanatical Cast, Increases this Evil not a Little, and accelerates the Degradation of the Clergy. His Cousin Sir James H. Blair, never Repented so much of any thing as the Placing him in that Chair, as he soon Discover'd the Disadvantage to the Church that might [arise] from his Being put in that Situation. It is a pity that a Man so Irreproachable in his Life and Manners, and even Distinguish'd for his Candour and Fairness, Should be So Weak. But he Does more Harm than if he were an Intriguing Hypocrite.

When we Return'd from the South we were Happy to find our two Fine Girls in such Good Health. But my Mother and unmarried Sister Sarah had liv'd for some time close by us, and saw them twice every Day. Sarah the eldest was now 8 years of Age, and had Display'd Great Sweetness of temper with an uncommon Degree of Sagacity; Jenny the 2^d was now 6, and was Gay and Lively and engaging to the Last Degree. They were both Handsom, in their Several kinds, The First like me and My Family, the 2^d like their Mother. They already had made a Great proficiency in writing and arithmetick, and were Remarkable Good

Dancers. At this time They Betray'd no Symptom of that Fatal Disease which Rob'd me of them, unless it might have been predicted from their Extream Sensibilities of Taste and Affection which they already Displayd. It was the Will of Heaven that I should lose them too Soon—But to Reflect on their Promising Qualities ever since, has been the Delight of Many a Watchfull Night and Melancholy Day. I Lost them Before they had Given me any Emotions but those of Joy and Hope.

On the 25th of Sepr this year, Mrs C was Deliver'd of her 3d Daughter Mary Rodham, and Recoverd very well. But the Child was unhealthy from her Birth, and Gave her Mother the Greatest Anxiety. She continud to Live till June 1773; when she was Reliev'd from a Life of Constant Pain. In Novr 11th that year She Had her Son Willm who was very Healthy and promising Till within 6 or 8 weeks of his Death when he was siez'd with a Peripneumony, which left such a Weakness on his Lungs as soon clos'd his Days.

During the Summer 1769, After I had Given the Clergy Such Hopes of Being Reliev'd from the Window Tax, They Set about a Subscription (the Funds of the Church being quite Inadequate at any time, and then very Low) for Defraying the Expence of their Commissioner and of processing an Act of Parliament. Nearly two thirds of the Clergy had subscrib'd to this Fund, For a Sum of about £400 was subscrib'd, if I Remember Right, by Subscriptions from One Guinea, to 5 shillings, and put into the Hands of Dr George Wishart Then Principal Clerk of the Church.

Mrs C Having perfectly Recover'd of her late Inlying, I prepar'd to Go to London to follow out the Object of my Commission. And Lest I should be too late I set out in such time as to arrive at London on the 21st of Decr. I had a Major Paul as my Companion in the chaise, and tho' we took five Days to it, The Expence in Those Days was No More Than £10: 8: 3. As my Business Lay Entirely in the West End of the Town, I took up my Lodging in New Bond St and Engag'd the other Apartment for John Home who was to be there in a Fortnight. But I immediatly Took Niel   a trusty Servant who had been with him last year, and Could Serve us both Now, as I Requir'd but very little personal Service. The very Day after I came to London, I had wrote a Paper sign'd *Nestor* in Support of the Duke of Grafton who was then in a Tottering State. This Paper which appear'd on the 23d of Decr Drew the attention of Ld Elibank and other Scotch Gentlemen, who attended the British Coffee House, which Convinc'd me that I might Continue my Political Labours as they were acceptable to Administration. At this time, I Did not know that the Duke of Grafton was so Near Going out. But Soon after I Discover'd it by an accident. On one of the Mornings which I pass'd with

Ld Mansfield, after he had Signified his Entire Approbation of my measures to Obtain an Exemption for the Clergy of Scotland, I took the Liberty of Saying to him in Going Down stairs, That his Lordships Opinion was so Clear in our Favour, That I had Nothing to Wish, but that he would be so Good as to say So to the Duke of Grafton. His Answer Surpriz'd me and open'd my Eyes. It was, I can't Speak with the Duke of Grafton. I'm not acquainted with his Grace. I never convers'd with him but once, which was when he came a Short While ago from the King to offer me the Seals. I can't talk with the Duke of Grafton. So Good Morning D^r—Let me See you again, when you are farther advanc'd. I went Instantly with this Anecdote to My Friend Mrs Anderson at the British, and we Concluded almost Instantly without Plodding, That the change of the Ministry was right at hand. When I Saw her next Day, She told me that She had Seen her Brother Dr Douglas, who was struck with my anecdote, and combining with it some things which he had observ'd, concluded That the Fall of the Duke of Grafton was at hand. Which prov'd true.

This accordingly took place not long after, when Charles York the 2^d Son of the Chancellor Hardwick having been Wheedled over to Accept of the Seals, and being upbraided Severely for having Broken his Engagements with his Party, put himself to Death that very night, which was consider'd a Publick loss as he was a Man of Parts and Probity. Pratt was appointed Chancellor and Lord North became Minister. I was in the House of Commons, the First night that he took his place as Premier. He had not intended to Disclose it that night, But a Provoking Speech of Coll! Barré's oblig'd him to own it. Which he Did with a Great Deal of Wild Humour. Barré was a cliver Man and a Good Speaker, but very hard Mouth'd. I was the first person at the British after the Division. And telling Mrs Anderson the Heads of North's Speech, and the Firmness and wit with which he took his place as First Minister, she concluded with me That he would Maintain it long. Ld North was very agreable and as a Private Gentleman as Worthy as he was Witty. But having unluckily Got into the American War, brought the Nation into an Incredible Sum of Debt, and in the End lost the whole American Colonies. He profess'd himself Ignorant of War, but Said he would appoint the Most Reputable Genl^s and Admirals, and furnish them with troops and money. But he was weak enough to Send the Howe's[1] tho' of a Party opposite to him, who seemd to act rather against the Minister than the Americans. They were chang'd for other Commanders: But the Feeble Conduct of the Howe's, had Given the Americans time to become Warlike, and they finally prevaild. North maintain'd his Ground for no less than 12 years thro' this Disgracefull War, and then was Oblig'd to

Give Way that a Peace might be Establish'd. This at first was thought necessary to Great Brittain. But Lord North's attempt to make a Coalition with his former Opponents Having Faild, and Charles Fox['s] Scheme of Governing the Nation by an aristocracy with the Aid of his India Bill Being Discover'd and Defeated, made way for Mr Pitts first administration in 1784, which soon Restor'd National Credit, and promis'd the Greatest Prosperity to the British Empire, had it not been Interrupted by the French Revolution in 1789 and the Subsequent most Dangerous War of 1798. It was Discover'd Early in this Period, that the Revolt and final Disjunction of our American Colonies, was no loss to Great Brittain Either in Respect of Commerce or War. I have been Led to this Long Digression by Lord North's Having become Premier in the beginning of the Year 1770.

[1][Altho' the discharge of my Commission required attention and activity, yet the Lords of the Treasury having frequently referred me for an answer to a distant day I took the opportunity of making frequent excursions to places where I had not been.

One of the first of them was to Bath with John Home to pay a visit to his betrothed Mary Home whom he married in the end of Summer; he had sent her to Bath to improve her health for she was very delicate. We set out together and went by the Common road, and arrived on the second day to dinner.

Miss Home had taken a small house at Bath where she lived with a Miss Pye a companion of hers and a friend of Mrs Blacketts. They lived very comfortably, and we dined with them that day. Bath is beautifully built and situated in a vale surrounded with small hills cultivated to the top, and being built of fine Polished Stone, in warm weather is intollerably hot; but when we were there in the beginning of March, it was excessively cold. The only thing about it not agreeable to the eye is the dirty Ditch of a river which runs through it.

On the Morning after we arrived we met Lord Galloway in the Pump Room, who having had a family quarrel had retired to Bath with one of his daughters. The first question he asked me was, if I had yet seen our cousin Sandy Goldie? I answered no but that I intended to call on him that very day. (His wife was a Sister of Patrick Herons.) Do said his Lordship, but dont tell his story while you are here for he is reckoned one of the Cleverest Fellows in this City, for being too unreasonable to sign receipts for above a £1000 the produce of the reversion of his Estate, he makes a very good livelihood at the Rooms by betting on the Whist Players for he does not play—Lord Galloway engaged us to dine with him the next day—we went to the rooms at night and to a Ball where I was astonished to find so many old acquaintance.

We had called on Goldie who engaged us to dine with him the day after we were to dine with Galloway.

At Lord Galloways we met with Dr Gusthard M D who had charge of Miss Homes health. He was the Son of a Mr Gusthard Minister of Edin^r and being of good ability and a winning address had come into very good business. Lord Galloway tho' quite illiterate by means of the negligence of his Trustees or tutors was a clever man of much natural ability and master of the common topics of conversation. We dined next day at Alex^r Goldies where we had the pleasure of his Lordships company—In our Landlord we discovered nothing but an uncommon rapidity of speech and an entertaining flow of imagination, which perhaps we would not have observed if we had not known that he had been cognosced[1] at Edin^r and deprived of the management of his Estate.

Next day we made a party to Bristol Hot wells and added to our Company a Miss Scott of Newcastle a very pleasing young woman who afterwards married an eminent Lawyer there and another Lady whose name I have forgot who was a good deal older than the rest, but was very pleasant and had £30000 by which means she became the wife of one of the Hathorns.

This place Bristol appeard to me dull and disagreeable and the Hot wells not much better. Next day we dined at Dr Gusthards and on the day after set out on our return to London; we resolved to go by Salisbury Plain and Stonehenge as neither of us had ever been there, both of which raised our wonder and astonishment especially Stonehenge, but as we were not antiquarians, we could not form any conjecture about it. We got to London next day before dinner]

A Comparison of Two Eminent Characters Attempted after the Manner of Plutarch

A Comparison of Two Eminent Characters Attempted after the Manner of Plutarch[1]

Doctors Hew Blair and Wm Robertson in their Characters, Pursuits and Fortunes, were in Many Things alike, and in some very Dissimilar.

In their Descent from Antient Scottish Families, and in their Relation to Clergymen, They were Equal, some of Blairs Ancestors having been Distinguish'd Men of that Order, and Robertsons Father a very Respectable Minister first at Borthwick and afterwards in Edinburgh.

As their Births so their Education was similar, the one Being at the High School of Edin^{r} and the other at that of Dalkeith, Then in the Greatest Reputation of any School in the Country. In their Boyish Days, Blair was the Most Distinguish'd of the two, For in Robertson there appear'd not then, any Symptoms of his Future Fame. Robertson was bred in all the Strictness of an Ecclesiastical Family at That Period, having been Denied the Amusements of the Theatre and other Publick places, which favour'd his Recluse and Studious Bent. Blair was bred with Less Austerity, but not being of an Opulent House any more than the other, and confin'd mostly to the City, they were equally unacquainted with those . . . Sports and Amusements, which not only Envigorate the Body, and Give Ease and Grace to its Motions, but at the same time Enlarge the Sphere, and excite the Activity of Mental Operations.

To have been a Domestick Tutor, was not thought to be an Emprovement of personal Character in this Country, when the Pride of the Aristocracy in those Days, was thought to Induce Habits of Servility in their Dependants. Robertson in this Respect was the most Fortunate, for he never Serv'd in that Capacity, Whereas Blair attended the Honble Simon Fraser of Lovat for one Season, in the Highlands, which to a Man of his Observation, prov'd a School of Instruction, where his Conduct had been highly praiseworthy, if we may Judge from the markd attachment of his pupil Genl Fraser, which ended only with his Life.

Blair coming within one Year after he was ordaind to Edin^{r} was soon Distinguishd as a First Rate Preacher, while Robertson Remaind for 8 years in Obscurity in the Country, his Pulpit Talents in which he excelld Being only observ'd by a Few of the Neighbouring Gentry and Clergy: By whom, it was thought, that had he Devoted himself to this species of composition he might have even Surpass'd his Rival, as he could accommodate himself more to Common Life and Ordinary Manners, than the other has Done.

In Marriage, an Article of Great Importance to Literary Men, as it frequently Rules over their Fame and Fortune, They were Equally and Remarkably Fortunate. They Both Married Early Clergymens Daughters and Each his Cousin German. Nothing could be better Suited to Each other than the Qualities of the Parties. Robertson who was in himself Equal to Every Domestick Arrangement, and was never push'd about any thing, was Lucky Enough to find a Wife (Mary Nisbet) of a Mild and Equal temper, tho' of Good Sense, and of Talents quite Suited to Domestick Œconomy, whose Mind had no Strong Features, and aspird only at Being her Husbands Humble Scholar and Admirer. Not so his Competitor in Letters, who Being of an Infantine Disposition, needed a Mate of a Superior and Decisive Mind, on which he could Rely for advice, in all his Doubts and Perplexities, which Occurd almost every Hour. In his Matrimonial Choice he was Most Fortunate, for his Cousin (Catherine Bannatyne) was a Person of a Masculine Understanding, of a Cheerfull Temper and Amiable Manners.

In Respect of Posterity their Fortune was quite Unequal, for of 6 Children Born to Robertson 5 are still Living, 3 of whom are Sons,[1] all of them filling up Respectfully their Several Stations in Life, which are higher than their Early Expectations. But Blair and his Wife had only two children, a Boy who Died in Early Infancy, and a Girl who Liv'd to be a Woman, whose premature Death Dissappointed their Sanguine Expectations, and afforded them a Dolefull Subject for the exercise of their Christian patience and magnanimity.

In Domestick Enjoyments Those two Rival Friends were nearly Equal. For tho' Robertson had a Temper that was never Rufld and Blair was Easily Mov'd, yet like the Coruscations in a Fine Sky, his Emotion tended only to make it more Delightfull. At no time Did Blair betray any Sentiment that was unsuitable to his Profession, Tho' he was perfectly Open and Unreserv'd. But Robertsons Great Love of Dissertation not only made him appear tedious to his Friends[2] but now and then Ensnar'd him into more free Communications with Young People than were proper, and raisd in them a False Idea of the Laxity of his Principles. As for Instance, when he us'd to expatiate on the Folly of Publick Men who Did not make Sure of something Good for themselves in the First place, while they were Serving their Country. Such Notions amaz'd the Youths, whose Bosoms were warm with Patriotism, who expected from him a Splendid Display of a high standard of Publick Virtue, While in the mean time those unguarded Speeches [were] only meant to Shew That the Principal was a Man of the World.

Both of those Eminent Men having applied themselves Early, Each to his particular Line of Study in which they persever'd, were Less Masters of General Learning, than might have been Expected considering the Extent of their Capacities. Neither of them were skilld in Mathematicks or any of the Sciences Connected with them. In the Moral and Metaphysical Sciences, Blair was more an adept than his Rival. With respect to Taste, it was uncertain which excell'd. For Robertson compensated his Less extensive knowledge of Poetry and Belles Lettres, By a Natural Delicacy of Taste, which made Nearly as Trusty a Guide in those Matters as was to be found in Blairs Maturity of Judgment. When Both agreed the Oracle was Certain.

They were Each in their Several Departments much Resorted to by young Authors, and they were Equally Sound in their Judgments and Fair in their Advices. If they were ever wrong it was by Means of a Snare which has Entangled the Greatest of Men, Flattery and Adulation. In one Respect Blair was more fortunate than Robertson, for he made no Personal Enemies. Whereas the Principal partly owing to his Temper, and partly owing to his Habits in the Management of a Party in the Church was apt to Raise False Hopes, which Failing Begat a Suspicion, however Unjust, of Duplicity, and in some Instances, Created an Irreconcileable Hatred.

As the Leader of a party in the Management of Ecclesiastical Affairs, Robertson stands unrivald for ability and Success. As at the Head of Learning in the first University of Scotland for Importance, the Conduct of the Principal was highly Meritorious: and his Influence with the unlearnd Body, who have the Nomination of Professors, for the whole Period of 30 Years was invariably Impartial, and highly Successfull for the Advancement of Learning, and the prosperity and Glory of the City, and the Honour of its Magistrates, as Patrons of one of the Most Illustrious Schools in Europe for the whole Circle of Learning, and all Arts and Sciences Usefull and Ornamental.

With Respect to Political [Talent], Tho' neither of them had any part to Act but in Conversation alone, from whence any Influence can be ascrib'd to them, It must be allow'd that Blair had the advantage for steadiness and uniformity, and for never bringing on himself any Reproach for the Desertion of Friends: Whereas the Versatility of Robertson in this article open'd the Mouths of some against him, who thought they could accuse him not merely of Fickleness, but of Ingratitude. It may perhaps Serve with some as a Sufficient Apology for this Change of

Side, to Say That The Historian of Mary, of Charles the 5th and of America, had an Indefeasable Title to think and Talk as he pleas'd, without Being Restrain'd by any Party Attachment. But the Leaders of Conversation should not forget that their Words are Mark'd, and that [it] is sometimes better to be accounted Weak, Than Unstable and Inconsistant, for which the best Motives are seldom ascrib'd.

Till Robertson Retir'd from Church Business in 1780, or 81 and his Change of Political Creed in 1783, Blair had never appear'd in any Respect as a Publick Character. But after this he was not averse to be Considered as a Person of some Importance even in Affairs, and Dr Adam Ferguson whom of late the Patrons had advis'd with, Having fallen into Bad Health, They now Resorted occasionally to him for Advice, which he Gave with Impartiality. And as he affected no Superiority and Did not Dictate, They were pleasd with his Counsel, and he was pleasd with Being Consulted.

With Respect to the Works They have Publish'd, They may be Consider'd as nearer Equality, in Classical Elegance and Celebrity, than is commonly Imagind. Robertson's Histories, tho' composd with the Nicest Selection and the Soundest Judgment, and the purest Style, and undoubtedly are among the First Rate Productions of the Historick Muse, are nevertheless Compilations from Antient Records and Annals, and are not works of Original Genius, any more than Dr Blairs Lectures on Rhetorick and Belles Lettres, in which he was bound to Lay before his Students a Compleat Compendium of the Science he profess'd to Teach. But his Sermons are a work of Original Genius,[1] which Reaching the Highest Degree of Perfection, must therefore Stand in the Foremost Rank of Ingenious and Inventive Composition. What has been Said of Robertson's Works, must be understood with the Exception of his Preliminary Book of the History of Charles the 5th which is fully Entitled to all the Merit of a Work of Original Genius, and had he wrote Nothing Else, was Sufficient to Establish his Fame as a First Rate Writer.

When Robertson Died in 1793, Blair Betray'd no Wish for the Principality, and even Disclaimd all views on it to his Friends and yet he must Surelly have Entertaind Hopes that it would be offerd him: For when it was Given to another, he was not only Dissappointed but Irritated far Beyond the usual Pitch of his Temper. A few such Instances of Partial Favour in the Patrons, and of their Turning a Deaf Ear to the Publick Voice, which Call'd without variation for the Advancement of Dr Blair, will soon Sap the Foundations of their University, and make their unfinish'd walls[2] be Deserted. Had Blair been appointed to that Dignity, Tho' not possessed of a Leading Mind like Robertson, yet would he have filld the Station with Distinction, For he had a Fair and Impartial Mind, and was Steady in his Political Views; whilst Robertson was warpd by the Spirit of Party, and so much Dazzled by the Splendor of the French Revolution, That even his Sagacity was Impos'd on, and he Could not Listen to the Ravings of Burke as he Call'd them, which in Spite of the High Enthusiastick Strain of Eloquence in which they are Involv'd, Have prov'd almost Literal Predictions, and have Entitled their Author to be Call'd *The Prophet of Nations*.

In one Important Point Those two Eminent Men seem to have been perfectly Equal viz. in Diligence and Industry and unwearied application in the Several Paths of Literature the pursuit of which they had Chosen.

In the Ordinary Intercourse of Society, There is no Doubt That Robertson Display'd The Strongest and Most Leading Mind, and Blair the most attractive and amiable Disposition. In the Eye of the World the First was more Respectable on the whole, But the Second possess'd a Purer Mind, and approach'd nearer to Moral Perfection.

Both of those Celebrated Men Have Done honour to their Country and the Age in which they Liv'd, with this Distinction, That Robertson's Elegant, Clear and Judicious Page, which Instructs the Scholar and Politician not only in the Succession of Events, but in the Character of Nations, and of the Great Men, who in different Periods have Sway'd their Fate, and it may be fairly predicted That his works will Rise in Fame Thro' the Different Ages which they are to pass, like those of the Great Authors of Antiquity, which raise admiration in proportion to the Distance of the Times in which they flourished. While Blairs Sermons will continue to warm and enlighten the Enraptur'd Nations as long as a System of Rational Religion and Pure Morality holds its place in the Mind of Cultivated Men. Both of them shed a Glory on their Native Land, and add to the Laurels of that Church from the Bosom of which they Sprung.

Dr Blair was three Years older than Dr Robertson and out Livd him Seven Years, The 1st having Given Way to Fate in 1793, and the 2^d in the End of 1800.

It may not be Improper to Add That those two Illustrious Men Liv'd in perfect Concord and the Daily Interchange of Friendly Offices During the 32 Years in which they were Members of the University of Edin^r. Nor was this in that Period an uncommon Exertion of Amity: For the Whole Circle of Men, of Learned and Ingenious Men, who had Sprung up together at this time, [was notable] for the unbroken Union which prevaild in it. There were Circumstances Relating to the Capital at this time which contributed much to this Fraternal Concord; Such as the small Size of the City, tho' Containing a Great population, and the Social and Hospitable Manners which then prevaild. It was peculiar to this City and to this Period, That [one] could arrive from the Country in the Afternoon, and be almost Certain of assembling Such Men as David Hume, and Adam Smith, and Blair, and Robertson and John Home and Ad. Ferguson &c. &c. in a Tavern by 7 aclock which was the Hour of Supper in those Days and the chief time of convivial entertainment, till about the Year 1760—Those Circumstances Conduc'd not a little to that Harmony, which Then Reign'd among an Order of Men, said proverbially to be of Irritable Minds.

The Club they Instituted in 1762 Call'd the Militia or the Poker Club, not only Included the Literati, But many Noblemen and Gentlemen of Fortune and of the Liberal Professions, who mixd together with all the Freedom of Convivial Meetings once a week During 6 months in the Year; which contributed much to Strengthen the Bond of Union among them. Altho' the Great Object of those meetings was National, of which they never lost sight, They had also Happy Effects on Private Character by Forming and polishing the Manners which are Suitable to Civilis'd Society. For they Banish'd Pedantry from the Conversation of Scholars, and exalted the Ideas and Enlarg'd the Views of the Gentry: and Created in the several Orders a New Interest in each other, which had not Taken place before in this Country.

It is a Phenomenon not a little Rare and Memorable That two such Men as Blair and Robertson should have appeard on the Scottish Literary Sphere at the same Moment, so much alike in their Talents, Tho' Dissimilar in their Pursuits, and that they should have finish'd their Illustrious Career with Such Equality of Fame and Fortune, and left behind them such a Shining Track to Guide the Future Candidates for Literary Fame.

Explanatory Notes

Page 4.   (1) *very Narrow Circumstances, till . . . 1732:* the average clerical income early in the century was £40; paid in kind; in 1749 the General Assembly was informed that although 340 livings ranged from £70 to £100, 600 were between £24 and £60, 'the pay of a land waiter or the lowest excise officer' (H. G. Graham, *The Social Life of Scotland in the Eighteenth Century*, 1950 edn., pp. 282, 361–2). For Carlyle's own stipend, see *supra*, p. xix.

(2) *Heritors:* landed proprietors responsible for the upkeep of the parish church.

(3) *the South Sea:* the ruinous financial scheme for trade with the Spanish colonies which crashed in 1720.

(4) *an accomplishment . . . very Rare:* on the efforts of the Scots to speak English with propriety, and Sheridan's ludicrous attempt to assist them in an Irish brogue, see Graham, op. cit., pp. 118–21; cf. Carlyle on Robertson, p. 253.

Page 5.   (1) *afterwards:* p. 107.

(2) *their Shipping was reduc'd, &c.:* but sea trade with London was to increase greatly (cf. H. Hamilton, *An Economic History of Scotland in the Eighteenth Century*, 1963, p. 214).

(3) *the Witty Epitaph . . . Last:* 'Here continueth to rot The Body of Francis Chartrés, Who with an Inflexible Constancy . . . Persisted, In spite of Age and Infirmities, In the Practice of Every Human Vice . . .' (Pope, 'Epistle to Bathurst', 1. 20, note; Twickenham edn., III. ii. 85–6).

Page 6.   (1) *the Rebellion:* the Jacobite rising of 1715.

(2) *Close . . . Lawn Market:* narrow entry; between the High Street and the Castle.

Page 7.   (1) *the Witches Bill:* the abolition of the act against witchcraft in 1736 (see Graham, op. cit., pp. 487–9).

(2) *the Gen! Assembly:* the annual representative meeting of the Church of Scotland.

Page 8.   (1) *Lib.:* pound.

(2) *Enthusiast:* 'one who claims special revelation', has 'a vain confidence of divine favour or communication' (Johnson, *Dictionary*).

Page 10.   *the Reason:* i.e. that given in the text, pp. 10–11.

Page 11.   *Police:* government, civilisation. For a fine 'character' of Drummore, see Ramsay of Ochtertyre, *Scotland and Scotsmen in the Eighteenth Century*, 1888, i. 94–100. Many of Carlyle's *dramatis personae* appear also in Ramsay.

Page 12. (1) *Mess:* Master (of Arts); equivalent to English 'Reverend'.
  (2) *Principal Paper:* document in its original form.
  (3) *a Scotch pint:* equivalent to *c.* 3 English pints.

Page 13. (1) *Grieve:* bailiff, farm manager.
  (2) *Hoddan Grey Coat:* made of homespun cloth of undyed white and black wool.

Page 14. *Righteous overmuch:* Eccles. vii. 16.

Page 15. *Peat-pot:* hole from which peats have been dug; cf. Kelly, *Proverbs* (1721), 'Out of the Peat-Pot into the Mire'.

Page 16. *Val:* English name for Laeffelt in Flanders, where Cumberland fought in 1747.

Page 17. *The Academy at Woolwich:* established in 1741.

Page 18. *Tolbooth Church in Edin*.*:* by Parliament Close and the Tolbooth or town jail.

Page 20. (1) *Land Market:* (surviving as Lawnmarket) where agricultural produce was sold.
  (2) *Dyers Tree:* cf. Scott's account of this event, *The Heart of Midlothian*, ch. vii: 'Why do you trifle away time in making a gallows?—that dyester's pole is good enough for the homicide'.

Page 21. (1) *Lecture:* exposition of a passage of scripture in lieu of reading it; a seventeenth-century practice abandoned in the nineteenth century. See W. D. Maxwell, *A History of Worship in the Church of Scotland*, 1955.
  (2) *Argathelian and Squadrone:* apparently the party which welcomed the influence of the Dukes of Argyll (*Argathelia*), and the independents.
  (3) *Highflying and Moderate Clergy:* the main ecclesiastical parties: the first evangelical, 'orthodox' Calvinist, rhetorical, the second liberal in theology and calmly moralistic in preaching. See James Kinsley, *The Poems and Songs of Robert Burns* (1968), iii. 1045–6.

Page 22. *Regents:* formerly senior academic teachers in Arts; replaced in the eighteenth century by a professoriate.

Page 24 (1) *Virrall:* ferrule, metal band.
  (2) This paragraph is drawn (with slight modifications) from a verso note by Carlyle, and replaces the paragraph 'I pass'd . . . Epistolary Stile' (*infra*, p. 26) which he dated wrongly.

Page 25. (1) *penny weddings:* at which the cost of entertainment was met by the guests.
  (2) *papers in the Spectator:* (1711–2), nos. 67, 334, 376, 466.

Page 26. (1) *W.S.:* Writer to the Signet, Scotch solicitor.
  (2) *one of them . . . lasting Effects:* 'the younger . . . was born for my perdition, for from the moment I saw her, I loved her with a constancy of adoration which was not surpassed by that of Petrarch for his Laura' (Carlyle's *Recollections*, quoted in Burton's edn., p. 57).

Page 28. *Lady Dick . . . said:* I follow Carlyle's verso note, which sorts out a confused report of her witticism in the main text.

Page 29. (1) *Dull and Tedious in his Lectures:* cf. p. 44.
  (2) *Curling:* played on the ice with hemispherical stones weighing upwards of 40 lbs. Cf. Kinsley, *Poems of Burns* (1968), iii. 1074.

Page 30. (1) *Lucky:* familiar name for an ale-wife.
  (2) *the Proverb . . . off:* not traced.

Explanatory Notes

Page 31. *S! Peters mark on the Shoulders:* on each side of the pectoral fin; supposedly made by the saint's finger and thumb when he caught the fish (Matt. xvii. 27).

Page 32. *100 Lib. Scots:* £8. 6s. 8d. sterling; at this time double the wage of a ploughman who had free bed and board.

Page 33. (1) *Castle Cary . . . Wall:* near Falkirk; a main station on the Antonine Wall.

(2) *the Abbey:* i.e. Holyrood.

(3) I have omitted matter repeated here in the manuscript from the annal for 1739.

Page 36. *Cambuslang Work:* see Index of Books, s. n. Robe, John.

Page 38. (1) *the Virginia Trade:* mainly in tobacco, re-exported to London, France and the Netherlands; up to the American War, Scotland's largest import and export. See Hamilton, op. cit., ch. ix.

(2) *Incle:* linen tape. See Hamilton, op. cit., p. 267.

Page 40. (1) *Drams:* small draughts of spirits.

(2) This note appears here in the manuscript on a facing verso, and is not in Carlyle's hand. I have followed the later autograph version (MS vi. 209–10).

Page 41. *Preferr'd a Satyr to Hyperion:* Shakespeare, *Hamlet*, I. ii. 140.

Page 45. (1) *a W.S.: supra*, p. 26, note.

(2) *Continue to flourish in . . . Air:* Richard Oswald bought Lord Cathcart's estate of Auchencruive, St. Quivox, in 1764, and continued Cathcart's agricultural improvements.

Page 46. *Mareschal Saxe:* (1696–1750), at this time humiliating the Duke of Cumberland in Flanders. In 1744 he assembled an (abortive) expedition at Dunkirk on behalf of Prince Charles Edward.

Page 47. (1) *a Probationer:* a student minister, licensed but not ordained.

(2) *Christianity not founded on Argument:* see Index of Books.

(3) *Fat and unwieldy:* phrases following are deleted in the manuscript.

Page 50. *the System:* i.e. of Calvinist theology.

Page 51. (1) *the Bony Lass of Livingstone:* quoted in part by Burns in his manuscript notes on Scotch songs; and published in a bawdy version in *The Merry Muses of Caledonia* just before Carlyle wrote this (Kinsley, *Poems and Songs of Burns*, no. 653).

(2) *Mrs D.:* unidentified; perhaps the 'Married Lady' of the Limekiln family of Carlyle mentioned above (p. 37).

Page 52. *the Tragedy of Cato:* by Addison (1713).

Page 54. *old Style:* according to the Julian calendar. The Gregorian calendar, in which the year began on 1 January instead of 25 March, was adopted in 1751 (24 Geo. II. c. 23).

Page 55. (1) *Rack-Punch:* made with the oriental spirit *arak*.

(2) *the Dog-Kennell:* 'old Castle of Cadzow' (note on MS), the scene of Sir Walter Scott's ballad (*Minstrelsy*, ed. T. Henderson, 1931, pp. 689–98). On the 'Romantick Gardens' at Barncluith (Baron's Cleugh), see Dorothy Wordsworth's *Journals*, ed. E. de Selincourt (1941), i. 230–1.

Page 56. *Sederunts:* sessions.

Page 57. *Shealing:* orig. 'sheil', shepherd's hut of turf on summer pasture.

Page 58. *favour'd the Pretenders Cause:* for Drummond's evidence against Stewart, see *State Trials*, xviii. 962.

Page 59. (1) *the British or Forrests Coffee House:* see p. 96. The British was in Cockspur Street, off the Strand, frequented by Scotsmen; Forrest's was in Charing Cross, opposite the Mews Gate.

(2) *Potterow Port:* looking south over Lady Nicolson's Park.

Page 60. (1) *Land Mercat: supra,* p. 20, note.

(2) *the Colt Bridge:* on the Water of Leith at Murrayfield, to the west of the city.

(3) *the Luckenbooths:* 'lock-up shops', a row in the High Street north of St. Giles' Kirk, selling mainly jewelry and silver; demolished in 1817.

Page 61. *a Passage in Livy . . . expos'd: Ab Urbe Condita,* V. xl *et seq.*

Page 63. *one of the weakest parts of the City:* on the north side. Leith Wynd ran from the west end of the Canongate towards Leith, over what is now Waverley Station.

Page 64. (1) *George Street:* north of and parallel to Princes Street; built in the 1780s. The Long Dykes (formerly the Lang Gaitt) was an old country road.

(2) *Land Market: supra,* p. 20, note.

Page 65. (1) *thro' the Abbey . . . Jocks Lodge:* through the Abbey Close and south of the Palace, and out of the King's Park to the east. Jock's Lodge was then a village.

(2) *Lucky Vents Court Yard: supra,* p. 30.

Page 66. (1) *Skull Caps:* made of iron and fitting close.

(2) *Creels on Horseback:* deep wicker baskets slung on each side of a horse.

(3) *a Coal Pit:* if abandoned, probably *c.* 100 feet deep.

Page 67. (1) *Burgundy . . . never Tasted:* introduced into England after the Restoration.

(2) *Broad Sword and Target:* the two-handed Highland sword, with a blade nearly 4 feet long; and the round shield.

Page 72. (1) *shots:* pieces of ground cropped rotationally. A *Rigg* was a strip of ploughed land; a *Rigg Length,* a measure of land *c.* 15 feet wide and *c.* 200 yards long (a length allowing plough-horses proper rest).

(2) *Dauphiston:* Dolphingston.

Page 73. *Merse:* flat marsh; Berwickshire.

Page 75. *Drawers Head:* top of a chest of drawers.

Page 76. *Nᵒ——:* left blank in manuscript.

Page 77. *Merse: supra,* p. 73, note.

Page 78. *Mask:* infuse, brew.

Page 80. *Far Less . . . Sacrament:* but he was a Roman Catholic. Carlyle himself, however, was liberal in such matters—receiving communion in the Church of England, and defending the Test Act before the General Assembly (1791) as having paradoxically 'enlarged and confirmed the principles of toleration' (Hill Burton's edn., 1910, pp. 580–1).

Page 81. (1) *Narrated in Home's Hist.: Works,* ed. Henry Mackenzie (1822), iii. 84.

(2) *fallen Down:* sailed to.

Page 82. *Kit's:* tubs made of hooped staves.

Page 83. (1) *the Oaths:* of allegiance, and of abjuration (1701).

(2) *Suspended:* as it was in times of crisis—nine times between 1688 and the Forty-Five.

Page 84. (1) *Lestoff:* Lowestoft.

Explanatory Notes

(2) *Schout: schuyt*, Dutch flat-bottomed river-boat.

(3) *Bombcase: boompjes*, small trees that lined the canal.

(4) *the Scotch Dyke:* Schotse Dijk, popular name for part of the Schiedamse Dijk, and site of the Schotse Kerk.

(5) *Doit Boat:* apparently a ferry across the (now vanished) Leuven Haven; *duit*, eighth part of a *stuiver* (p. 85, note), and current in Scotland (*doit*) until the early eighteenth century.

Page 85.   *Stivers: stuivers*, roughly equivalent to English pennies.

Page 86.   (1) *Exemption . . . Student:* students enjoyed freedom from toll duties, from government dues on wine and beer, and from duties on books and clothes (D. van Arkel in *Geschiedboek*, Leiden Student Corps (1950); cf. G. D. J. Schotel, *The Academy of Leiden*, Haarlem 1875, pp. 272–3).

(2) *Bukkam: bokking*, red herrings.

Page 88.   *he Confesses . . . audience:* Dugald Stewart who, in his 'Account of . . . Robertson' (1796), records his 'exertions to amuse and inform' strangers; but then 'I enjoyed his society less than when I saw him in the circle of his intimates, or in the bosom of his family' (Hill Burton).

Page 92.   *Batsons:* a coffee-house in Cornhill, frequented by physicians.

Page 93.   *The Poker Club: infra*, pp. 213–6.

Page 96.   (1) *the British . . . Daily: supra*, p. 59, note.

(2) *a Ridotta:* or *ridotto*, an assembly for music and dancing, introduced in England in 1722 at the Opera House in the Haymarket.

Page 99.   (1) *Tears of Scotland:* sent by Smollett to Carlyle in 1747 as 'a Ballad set to Musick . . . a Performance very well received at London, as I hope it will be in your Country' (*Letters*, ed. L. M. Knapp, 1970, p. 5).

(2) *Ansons Voyage:* round the world (1739–44); account ed. Glyndwr Williams, Oxford English Memoirs and Travels (to appear in 1974).

Page 100.   (1) *vapouring:* pretentious, high-flown.

(2) *Goat Whey Quarters:* resorts where this popular health drink could be taken; superseded by watering-places in the latter half of the century.

(3) *the Wager:* one of Anson's ships.

(4) *Cazique:* (Sp. *cacique*) native chief in W. Indies.

Page 101.   *excellent in their way:* Hannah Pritchard (1711–68); Kitty Clive (1711–85), protégée of Cibber and friend of Horace Walpole; the Irish actor-dramatist Charles Macklin (*c.* 1697–1797).

Page 104.   (1) *Ormiston . . . Gladsmuir . . . Athelstaneford:* about 3 miles south, 4 miles south-east, and 9 miles east of Prestonpans. Carlyle's move to Inveresk took him only a few miles further west.

(2) *an obscure Distant Place . . . Study:* on the east coast 36 miles from Edinburgh with, in Carlyle's time, well under 1,000 people.

Page 105.   *Drumlanerick:* Drumlanrig Castle in Durisdeer parish, Upper Nithsdale; 17 miles north-west of Dumfries.

Page 107.   (1) *the Defects they saw in me:* including, says Carlyle in his *Recollections*, frequent dancing, wearing his hat 'agee', and one day galloping through the Links between one and two o'clock.

(2) *a Seceder of the Strictest Sect:* a member of one of the schismatic 'societies' formed by the secession from the Kirk in 1737 over the

287

Explanatory Notes

issue of patronage, and making up the 'Associate Synod'. They proved too much even for George Whitefield, and—progressively—for each other. See Graham, op. cit., pp. 372 ff.

(3) *out of . . . Sucklings &c.:* Ps. viii. 2; Matt. xxi. 16.

(4) *Stairhead:* here the top of a staircase built against the front wall of a two-storey cottage.

(5) *The Reign of Enthusiasm:* the time of the Covenanting fanatics. Cf. *supra,* p. 8, note.

Page 108. (1) *the South Sea: supra,* p. 4, note.

(2) *anasarga:* dropsy.

Page 110. (1) *twopenny:* ale originally sold at 2*d.* a Scots pint (3 imperial pints).

(2) *Doubted:* suspected, thought (Scots; O.F. *douter,* to fear).

Page 111. *Burgh of Regality:* a borough under the jurisdiction of a lord of regality, whose power was almost co-extensive with the Crown's in civil and criminal matters; abolished by the Heritable Jurisdictions Act (1747).

Page 112. (1) *Birth:* berth, job.

(2) *Adam De Cardonnell:* Carlyle is confused. Three French Protestant brothers, Adam, Philip, and Peter, were adherents of Charles II, the first being appointed collector of customs at Southampton. His son (also Adam; d. 1719) was secretary to Marlborough, father to Lady Talbot, and the *uncle* of Carlyle's friend Mansfeldt. Smollett's Matthew Bramble takes tea with Mansfeldt and Carlyle at Mussel-burgh on 18 July (*Humphry Clinker,* ed. L. M. Knapp, 1966, pp. 216–7).

(3) *Descended from the Usurper . . . Royal Line:* Edmund Waller's mother was aunt to John Hampden, 'the zealot of rebellion' (Johnson, *Lives of the Poets*); Hampden was cousin to both Waller and Oliver Cromwell.

Page 113. *Loretto:* beyond the east gate of medieval Musselburgh, the site of a chapel and hermitage dedicated to Our Lady of Loreto, associated with miracles, and destroyed at the Reformation.

Page 114. *the Mirror:* (1679–80), published by Creech for a number of young lawyers and eventually edited by Henry Mackenzie. No. 83 is an 'Enquiry into the causes of the scarcity of *humorous* writers in *Scotland*'.

Page 116. *a General Augmentation . . . Money: supra,* p. 4, note. *800 Merks:* £533. 6*s.* 8*d.* Scots, £44. 7*s.* 6*d.* sterling. *Chalder:* a variable dry measure; about 100 bushels of grain. Among the arguments against augmentation were Marchmont's fear of clerical lust for the 'means of luxury and extravagance', and Auchinleck's cant about a poor church being a pure church. It was not till 1810 that the minimum stipend was raised to £150. See H. G. Graham, op. cit., pp. 361–2.

Page 117. *the Case of St Ninians:* 'the settlement of Mr Thomson . . . occupied the General Assembly from 1767 to 1776' (Hill Burton).

Page 118. (1) *he fail'd:* Garrick 'did not think it well adapted to the stage and declined bringing it on, much to the mortification of its author' (Mackenzie, Home's *Works,* 1822, i. 35), who wrote these verses on Shakespeare's monument in Westminster Abbey:

Image of Shakespeare! To this place I come
To ease my bursting bosom at thy tomb;

[For] day and night revolving still thy page,
I hoped, like thee, to shake the British stage;
But cold neglect is now my only mead,
And heavy falls it on so proud a head. . . .

See *infra*, p. 175.

(2) *a letter to Smollet:* cf. Smollett, *Letters*, ed. L. M. Knapp (1970), pp. 10, 11.

(3) *escap'd . . . from the Castle of Down:* Doune Castle in Perthshire, where they were imprisoned after the Battle of Falkirk (1745). Barrow broke his leg in the escape on ropes made of bed-sheets (Mackenzie, op. cit., i. 5–6).

(4) *Collins the Poet . . . Intimate:* Collins's 'Beautiful *Ode* on the *Superstitions in the Highlands* lay long among Mr. Home's papers unknown to him till Dr. Carlyle found it and gave it to the Royal Society of Edinburgh. I filled up at the desire of Mr. Tytler a chasm that had somehow been made in it' (Mackenzie, *Anecdotes and Egotisms*, ed. H. W. Thompson, 1927, p. 166).

(5) *Marchmont . . . Ignorantly Extoll'd by Pope:* Pope met Marchmont late (in 1740, when he succeeded to the title) and thought sufficiently of him to make him one of his executors; see *Epilogue to the Satires*, ii. 130; *One Thousand Seven Hundred and Forty*, l. 79; and *Verses on a Grotto* (1740), ll. 9–12.

Lo th' *Ægerian* Grott,
Where, nobly-pensive, St. John sate and thought;
Where *British* Sighs from dying Wyndham stole,
And the bright Flame was shot thro' Marchmont's Soul.

Page 119. (1) *Gil Morrice: The Oxford Book of Ballads*, ed. James Kinsley, no. 41; described by Thomas Gray as 'divine'. The success of *Douglas* brought the ballad into fashion.

(2) *with the Same Bad Success as Formerly:* pp. 118, 157, 173.

(3) *Mr Home . . . Sword Drawn: Works*, 1822, iii. 72: '. . . idolized by the Jacobites, and beloved by some of the best Whigs, who regretted that this accomplished gentleman, the model of ancient simplicity, manliness, and honour, should sacrifice himself to a visionary idea of the independence of Scotland.'

Page 120. (1) *the Popular Sermon:* preached to the people of the parish. The other *trials* of a probationer were undergone before the presbytery.

(2) *assoilzi'd:* absolved; a decision should be taken in the panel's favour.

(3) *the System: supra*, p. 50, note.

Page 121. *the High Flying Party: supra*, p. 21, note.

Page 122. (1) *all his excesses were pardon'd:* Dr Bonum Magnum had his own canny defence. When homeward bound and inebriate one morning early, he was asked, 'Eh, doctor, what would the auld wives o' the Tolbooth say if they saw ye noo?', and replied, 'Tut, man, they wouldna believe their een'.

(2) *Mountaineer:* properly, Covenanter in the time of persecution, 1670–88.

Page 123. *the New Town . . . plan'd out:* James Craig's plan was approved in April 1767.

Page 124. (1) *Mortcloths:* palls for covering coffins on the way to the grave, usually hired out by the Kirk Session for a fee.

(2) *comparative Trial:* demonstration by candidates before a committee.

Page 125.   *their Restoration . . . Ann:* the Presbyterian system was re-established and lay patronage abolished in 1690 (*Acts of the Parliaments of Scotland*, 1820–75, ix. 133, 196). Patronage was restored in 1712 (*Statutes of the Realm*, 1822, ix. 680–1).

Page 128.   *Polwarth is a slave: Epilogue to the Satires*, ii. 130. Cf. *supra*, p. 118, note.

Page 131.   *Juvenile Poems:* some of Carlyle's poems are among his papers in the National Library of Scotland.

Page 132.   (1) *The Parish of Inveresk . . . Regularly:* these events are recorded twice in the manuscript, on ff. 111 and 118; I have followed the second, more coherent version.

(2) *His 2ᵈ Lady . . . Quiet Woman:* on Marchmont's surrender to the charms of this daughter of a bankrupt linen-draper, which 'had fatigued every eye but that of his Lordship', see David Hume's letter to James Oswald, 29 January 1748 (*Letters*, ed. J. Y. T. Greig, 1932, i. 110).

(3) *Lord Register:* till 1707 chief clerk of the Parliament of Scotland and Privy Council; keeper of the registers and archives till 1806; still president at the election of representative peers (*Scot. Nat. Dict.*).

Page 133.   (1) *Roderick Random:* (1748), chs. xxxi–xxxiii.

(2) *H. Clinker: supra*, p. 112, note. Smollett pays tribute to Carlyle's humour, conversation, and friendship (ed. cit., pp. 216–7, 233).

(3) *He went west . . . all night:* written on a facing verso in another hand (presumably from Carlyle's dictation or autograph note), expanding a short deleted sentence in the main text (f. 113).

Page 134.   (1) *an Elegant . . . acct.:* like Xenophon's eyewitness account in the *Anabasis* of Cyrus's expedition against Artaxerxes.

(2) *the Famous Cocoa Tree Club:* in Queen Anne's time a Tory rendezvous in Pall Mall; later a Jacobite centre in St. James's Street.

(3) *Southboards:* 'sooth-bourds', repartees.

Page 135.   (1) *the Talent of Mimickry beyond all Mankind:* 'He was particularly successful with . . . Robertson, whose character he once endangered in a tavern by indecorous toasts, songs, and speeches, given with such a resemblance of the original, that a party on the other side of the partition . . . [believed] they had caught the reverend historian unawares' (Cockburn, *Memorials*, 1946 edn., p. 92).

(2) *Nicholson's:* a carriers' inn at the lower end of the West Bow kept by Thomas Nicolson (see *infra*, p. 156). For the Poker Club, see pp. 213–6.

Page 136.   *the Wild Beast in the Gevaudon:* which turned out (1764) to be a large wolf. Horace Walpole viewed its carcass at Versailles (*Paris Journals*, 1 October 1765).

Page 137.   (1) *Milton:* cf. Ramsay of Ochtertyre, op. cit., i. 86–90.

(2) *the Squadrone Party: supra*, p. 21.

Page 138.   (1) *One of them . . . History:* Hume's *Letters*, ed. J. Y. T. Greig (1932), i. 158–60 and 196.

(2) *Baron Montesquieu:* prob. an error for Holbach (E. C. Mossner, *Life of David Hume*, 1954, p. 498), though this conjecture is based on the insertion of 'Holbach' in the next paragraph, where Carlyle left a blank.

Explanatory Notes

Page 140.   (1) *Militia and the Poker: infra*, pp. 213–6.

(2) *Inventions of Macpherson:* for Hume's part in 'the Ossianic affair' see Mossner, op. cit., pp. 414–20.

Page 141.   (1) *Cadies:* 'a very useful Black-guard, who attends the Coffee-Houses and publick Places to go of Errands; and though they are wretches, that in Rags lye upon the Stairs, and in the Streets at Night, yet are they often considerably trusted' (E. Burt, *Letters from the North of Scotland*, 1754, i. 26).

(2) *the Select Society:* founded by Allan Ramsay the portrait painter in 1754, and in 1755 renamed the Society for Encouraging Art, Science, and Industry. 'It has grown', Hume wrote to Ramsay, 'to be a national concern . . . all the world are ambitious of a place amongst us' (*Letters*, i. 219).

Page 142.   (1) *the Duke . . . Disadvantages:* Buccleuch, however, acknowledged 'every advantage that could be expected from the society of such a man . . . a friend whom I loved and respected, not only for his great talents, but for every private virtue' (*Peerage of Scotland*, 1813 edn., i. 258).

(2) *64 or 65:* an error for April 1776 (Home's *Works*, 1822, i. 168–82).

Page 143.   *the expedition . . . Sinclair:* for Hume, who was St. Clair's secretary, 'a Romantick Adventure' against the French in Canada reduced to a farcical 'Descent on the Coast of Brittany' (Mossner, op. cit., pp. 187–204).

Page 144.   (1) *Robertson and Blair:* cf. Carlyle's 'Comparison', pp. 277–82.

(2) *Finlayson . . . Hill:* see Index of Books.

Page 147.   *till Harry grew up:* this note is confusing. 'Harry' is Henry Dundas, later Viscount Melville; 'his Sons having Charge of Ecclesiastical Affairs' refers to Robertson's son William, procurator of the Kirk; and 'his Cousin John Adam' is William Adam, who was returned to Parliament in 1774 and 1782–3 and negotiated the Fox–North coalition during Shelburne's administration.

Page 148.   (1) *Window Tax:* imposed at rates governed by the number of windows in a house in 1696, frequently reimposed, and replaced by house tax in 1851.

(2) *Cady: supra*, p. 141, note.

(3) *Dispers'd:* put into circulation, sent out.

(4) *Sist:* (Lat. *sistere*), stay, suspension.

(5) *Walkers:* probably Charles Walker's tavern in Writers' Court, on the north side of the High Street near the Royal Exchange.

Page 149.   (1) *Kind encouragers of young Men of Merit:* indeed——but in 'improving' the poems of Burns, Blair turned out to be a blundering nuisance.

(2) *Exertion:* display, expression. Cf. Elinor's 'exertion of spirits' in Jane Austen, *Sense and Sensibility* (Oxford English Novels, 1970, p. 112).

(3) *the Select Society: supra*, p. 141, note.

Page 150.   (1) *Strong Buchan:* the dialect of the north-east.

(2) *The Fair Penitent:* by Nicholas Rowe (1703).

Page 151.   (1) *Napping:* the clipped imitation of 'fine' English. Cf. Ramsay of Ochtertyre: 'It was alleged of a relation of mine, then a young woman of fashion, that her language kept pace with her dress. When going to a ball . . . in a *manteau* and petticoat, she knapped English insufferably' (op. cit., ii. 543–4).

(2) *I have Given . . . before: supra*, pp. 120–1.

291

Explanatory Notes

Page 152. (1) *Merse:* flat marsh; Berwickshire.

(2) *Wooller Haugh Head:* a mile south-east of Wooler, Northumberland.

Page 153. (1) *Atra Cura:* the phrase is Horace's (*Odes*, III. i. 40, III. xiv. 13, IV. xi. 35); the application (*cura* = (a) trouble; (b) a source of concern . . . mistress) is perhaps Carlyle's.

(2) *come Down:* i.e. in spate.

Page 154. *Rumers:* large drinking-glasses (Du. *romer*).

Page 155. *the Bow:* the West Bow running from the Lawnmarket south to the Grassmarket; probably the earliest entrance to the city.

Page 156. *James Adam . . .:* the paragraph which follows in the manuscript is elaborated *infra*, p. 189; I have omitted it here.

Page 157. (1) *Nigg in Ross shire:* on the north side of the Cromarty Firth. This paragraph is omitted in Hill Burton's edition, apparently for decorum's sake.

(2) *assoilzied:* absolved, got off.

(3) *In Oct. 1756:* I have brought this paragraph forward to MS f. 133 from f. 135.

(4) *Digges . . . Debar'd:* 'It has generally been considered that he was the natural son of the Hon. Elizabeth West, who in 1724 married Thomas Digges, Esq., of Chilham Castle. . . . But . . . the report very likely arose from his mother's relatives not wishing to be connected with an actor' (Dibdin; quoted in Burton, 1910 edn.).

Page 158. (1) *The Town . . . Judgment:* Mackenzie had 'a perfect recollection of the strong sensation which Douglas excited', rehearsals attended by 'the chief arbiters of taste', striking passages copied and recited, and the tears 'which the tender part of the drama drew forth unsparingly' (Home's *Works*, 1822, i. 37–8; citing Carlyle).

(2) *The High Flying Set: supra*, p. 21, note. A fuller account of the 'clerical contest' is given by Mackenzie, op. cit., i. 39–50.

(3) *Griskins:* loin chops.

Page 159. *David Hume . . . Crying it up . . . Century:* Hume hailed Home as a true disciple of Sophocles and Racine; 'I hope in time he will vindicate the English stage from the reproach of barbarism' (*Letters*, ed. Greig, 1932, i. 204; cf. i. 215–6).

Page 160. (1) *Confest he had done:* White, says Mackenzie, got a 'mitigated sentence' after an apology and admission 'that he attended the representation only *once*, and endeavoured to conceal himself in a corner, to avoid giving offence' (op. cit., i. 44).

(2) *Libel:* (*libelli accusatorii*), formal indictment before an (ecclesiastical) court. Carlyle was accused of keeping company with actors 'who by their profession . . . are of bad fame', of the 'disorderly' possession of a box at the theatre (turning 'some gentlemen out of it in a forcible manner'), and of witnessing a play which profaned the name of God 'by mock prayers and tremendous oaths' (excerpts in Hill Burton's edn., pp. 335–6).

Page 162. *Lachité:* (F. *lâcheté*) cowardice, meanness.

Page 164. *still Maintains . . . Language:* exaggerated; but *Douglas* ran to more than a dozen editions before 1800, and about 20 more in the nineteenth century.

Page 165. *Fratricide:* Sir Francis was shot by his younger brother Archibald (1795), who was declared insane.

Explanatory Notes

Page 166.   *Some time . . . Intimates:* I have brought this note back (MS f. 140) from f. 134ᵛ.

Page 167.   *the House of Gosford:* in the MS there follows (f. 142) a paragraph on Wedderburn which I omit; it is repeated on f. 187 (*infra*, p. 195).

Page 168.   *on that Hand:* in the manuscript the rest of the page (f. 142) and the top of the next have been torn away (*c.* 12 lines lost).

Page 170.   *the British: supra*, p. 59, note.

Page 172.   *Forrests Coffee House: supra*, p. 59, note.

Page 174.   (1) *Living . . . Rise:* echoing Pope, *An Essay on Man*, i. 14 (hunting metaphor).

        (2) *a Diversion peculiar to Scotland:* but played in medieval England. Carlyle was prominent in the golfing fraternity of Musselburgh.

        (3) *Land of Cakes:* popular name for Scotland, where oatcakes were part of the staple rural fare. Cf. Kinsley, *Poems and Songs of Burns* (1968), iii. 1321.

Page 175.   *her former state: supra*, pp. 95–6.

Page 176.   *Factor:* estate steward.

Page 178.   (1) *Preses:* president (Lat. *praeses*).

        (2) *that Liquor . . . exhilarated:* until 1780, when it became subject to duty. Port was before 1780 drunk only by the gouty (Ramsay of Ochtertyre, op. cit., ii. 81); cf. John Home's epigram:

> Firm and erect the Caledonian stood,
> Old was his mutton, and his claret good;
> 'Let him drink port,' an English statesman cried——
> He drank the poison, and his spirit died

        (*Works*, 1822, i. 164). David Hume bequeathed to Home 'ten dozen of my old Claret at his Choice; and one single Bottle of that other Liquor called Port' (Mossner, *Life of Hume*, 1954, p. 599). ——Since claret figures quite largely in Carlyle's manuscript, it should be said that 'if the old claret was very cheap, it had little strength' (Ramsay of Ochtertyre, op. cit., ii. 80).

Page 180.   *Clerk of the Cheque:* title of controllers in the royal ports and dock-yards.

Page 183.   *Lord Conservator:* Conservator of Scots Privileges at the staple of Campveere, superintendent of trade between Scotland and the Netherlands; appointed by Parliament. The salary was £300 (Home's *Works*, 1822, i. 59).

Page 185.   (1) *the Occasion . . . Given:* by the queen and Parliament after the victory at Blenheim (1704); designed by Vanbrugh and completed in 1724.

        (2) *Boot-Catch:* servant who pulled off guests' boots.

        (3) *This Man . . . Scotland:* Samuel Garbett cooperated with Dr John Roebuck in setting up a sulphuric acid works in Birmingham (1746); another at Prestonpans (1749) to supply the growing linen industry (there was a bleach-field at Ormiston); and the great Carron iron-works near Falkirk, central in the industrial development of Scotland (1759). See Hamilton, op. cit., pp. 140–1, 193 ff.

Page 187.   (1) *Sed tandem Luxuria Incubuit:* luxury has however overshadowed us; adapting Juvenal, *Sat.* vi. 292.

        (2) *His House . . . elegant:* gutted in riots (1791).

Page 188.   (1) *Shenstone's place:* at Halesowen, 7 miles from Birmingham. In 1745 he 'began to point his prospects, to diversify his surface, to entangle his walks, and to wind his waters, which he did with such judgement and such fancy as made his little domain the envy of the great and the admiration of the skilful' (Johnson, *Lives of the Poets*, 1905, iii. 350 ff.)

(2) *Maria Dolman:* Shenstone's cousin, who died of smallpox at 21. The inscription reminded Landor of Petrarch: ' . . . heu quanto minus est cum reliquis versari, quam tui meminisse'.

Page 191.   *Galloon:* (F. *galon*) narrow silk ribbon or braid used for trimming.

Page 192.   *Frosted:* protected against slipping by the insertion of 'frost-nails' at the back of the shoes.

Page 193.   (1) *Mutchkin:* ¼ pint Scots, *c.* ¾ imperial pint.

(2) *Mackellumore:* MacCailein, the Gaelic patronymic of the Duke of Argyll, chief of the Campbells (cf. Sir Walter Scott's 'MacCallum More').

(3) *Carl:* old fellow.

Page 195.   *the Failure . . . Coast:* a diversionary attack on the French coast in 1758 was led by General Thomas Blighe (then 73); St. Malo could not be besieged, and the army had to re-embark at St. Cas with severe losses. Blighe retired to Ireland under censure.

Page 196.   *hard Set:* obstinate. Cf. Scott, *The Heart of Midlothian*, ch. xiii, 'It's a hard-set willyard beast this o'mine'.

Page 198.   *their Member:* the lord provost, the Rt. Hon. George Lind (Hill Burton).

Page 199.   *the Solan Goose Feast:* the solan goose (*sula bassana*) or gannet breeds on the Bass Rock in the Firth of Forth, *c.* 20 miles from Musselburgh.

Page 201.   *Lord Hope . . . Slow Decline:* Charles, 1st son of the 2nd Earl of Hopetoun, voyaged to the W. Indies for his health and died at Portsmouth on his return in 1766. Apparently William Roet, professor of ecclesiastical history (1752), accompanied him.

Page 202.   *Conveener:* president of a trades union.

Page 203.   (1) *in a Letter . . . Society:* Carlyle was shown some Ossianic fragments, and was 'perfectly astonished at the poetical genius displayed in them'.

(2) *the Militia Pamphlet: The Question relating to a Scots Militia Considered.* The militia was revived in England in 1757; the politicians were reluctant to restore it in the lately rebellious north.

Page 207.   (1) *Sister Peg:* see Index of Books. John Arbuthnot's *History of John Bull* was published at Edinburgh in 1712.

(2) *a Letter . . . Margin:* not transcribed; but see Hume's *Letters*, 1932, i. 341–2.

(3) *Alisons Square:* between Potterrow and Nicholson Square.

Page 210.   (1) *Sense and Sensibility:* see Claire Lamont's introduction to Jane Austen's novel of this name, Oxford English Novels (1970).

(2) *Fortune's:* the most fashionable tavern of the day, where Boswell saw 'a genteel, profligate society who live like a distinct nation in Edinburgh' (*Boswell in Search of a Wife 1766–1769*, ed. F. Brady and F. A. Pottle, 1957, p. 125).

Page 211.   *Running:* successive.

Page 213.   *the Poker:* being an instrument for stirring up the flame of resentment on the militia issue.

Explanatory Notes

Page 214.   (1) *the Cross:* the Mercat Cross in the High Street.

                (2) *Sommers's Tavern:* in the High Street opposite the Guard House (*Book of the Old Edinburgh Club*, v. 173).

Page 215.   *List of the Poker Club:* more than half of these (including Carlyle) were to subscribe to Burns' *Poems* in 1787. At the end of the manuscript is a 'List of the Young Poker, which with a Mixture of the Old Members was tried to be Establish'd about the year 1786 or 87, and met 4 or 5 Times, but was Dropt on account of Non attendance, on the Part of the Young Members'. The 'Old Members' were only Carlyle, Blair, Black, Campbell, Edgar, and Home.

Page 216.   *the Commissioner . . . not pleas'd with me:* Charles, 9th Lord Cathcart (1721–76), lord high commissioner to the Assembly 1755–63.

Page 217.   *Miss Maria . . . Feildings:* this is salvaged from Carlyle's cancelled first account of the episode (f. 207).

Page 219.   (1) *By . . . Hyndman:* this phrase originally followed 'a far better Man' *infra* (MS f. 209).

                (2) *opposite the Cross:* in the manuscript there follows a passage I have taken back to p. 40, *supra*, footnote, 'There met . . . Tale Bearers'.

                (3) *constitution . . .:* left blank by Carlyle; 'had taken him as his second' is added in another hand (f. 210).

                (4) *Gilfrid:* prob. Wilfred, brother of the Admiral, baptised in 1749. *G* often replaces *W* in latinized forms of English Christian names.

Page 220.   *No. 45 . . . Wilkes:* in the *North Briton*, no. 45 (23 April 1763) Wilkes attacked part of the speech from the throne as 'the most abandoned instance of ministerial effrontery ever attempted to be imposed on mankind'; was illegally committed to the Tower and had his papers seized; and won £1,000 damages.

Page 221.   *added . . . till then:* inserted in the manuscript in another hand.

Page 224.   *Quotation:* perh. an error for *Dissertation* (on Robertson, 1796).

Page 225.   (1) *Jagire:* the assignment of the produce of a district, as an annuity; *c.* £25,000 a year bestowed on Clive by the Nawab in 1757, disallowed by the E. India Company in 1763, and finally restricted (as a compromise) to one decade.

                (2) *amry:* aumbry, pantry.

                (3) *he of Infamous memory: infra*, p. 258 and note.

Page 227.   *Sophisticated:* adulterated.

Page 231.   (1) *sap:* covered trench dug in attacking a fortress.

                (2) *Siccatore:* bore (Ital. *seccatore*).

Page 232.   *Sack Whey:* made with dry white wine (*vin sec*).

Page 236.   *We . . . were Dissappointed:* Gray had spent a day and a half visiting the Castle, Holyrood, and Arthur's Seat, seeing 'that most picturesque (at a distance) & nastiest (when near) of all capital Cities' (*Letters*, ed. Toynbee and Whibley, 1935, ii. 888). The date was September 1765, not 1764.

Page 237.   *overture:* in the Church of Scotland, a call for legislation or executive action, transmitted from presbytery to synod or General Assembly.

Page 238.   *a Journal . . . Day:* a transcript is in Nat. Lib. Scot. MS 3732.

Page 239.   *at Nicholson's:* Carlyle here (f. 223) repeats an earlier anecdote on Cullen (*supra*, p. 135, 'I was witness . . .').

Page 242.   *lecturd: supra*, p. 21, note.

Page 246.   *Clue:* ball of yarn.

Explanatory Notes

Page 250.   *Led Comptain:* apparently (a) mere tame calculator (cf. Burke's contemptuous reference to 'the age of . . . æconomists, and calculators'). But see *supra*, p. 142, note, Buccleuch on Smith.

Page 251.   *Window Tax . . . levied: supra*, p. 148, note.

Page 253.   *one Elphinstone . . . Disadvantages:* Col. Alexander Ferguson wrote a eulogy of Elphinstone on Carlyle's manuscript (f. 237ᵛ).

Page 255.   *Pitch Cock'd:* spitchcocked eels; cut into bits and fried with breadcrumbs and herbs.

Page 257.   (1) *Restoration:* possibly an error for *Reformation*; cf. the similar passage *infra*, pp. 269–70.

            (2) *A Generous and Wise Man:* Sir Ilay Campbell; cf. p. 270.

Page 258.   (1) *the Magdalen asylum:* or 'Magdalen House'. Horace Walpole reacted differently to a similar performance by Dodd in 1760 (cf. Boswell, *Life of Johnson*, ed. Hill and Powell, 1934, iii. 139).

            (2) *the Douglas Cause:* the most celebrated civil trial of the day (1762–9) on 'that great principle of law——filiation' (Boswell). Archibald, Duke of Douglas, died in 1761, and the title was claimed by the survivor of twins born in Paris to the Duke's sister Lady Jane Douglas when she was fifty. The claim was disputed on behalf of the Duke of Hamilton; it was argued that the twins were spurious. The Court of Session found for Hamilton; its decision was reversed by the Lords on appeal.

Page 259.   *the British: supra*, p. 59, note.

Page 261.   *Rivine:* the name of the heroine, taken from *Ossian*.

Page 263.   *Pulteney . . . land lay:* written on a facing verso (f. 247) in another hand.

Page 265.   (1) *a Foreign Tongue:* cf. David Craig, *Scottish Literature and the Scottish People 1660–1830* (1961), ch. viii. *et passim*.

            (2) *He:* i.e. Terrick.

Page 268.   *a Famous Oak tree:* not the 'major oak'; probably the Greendale Oak at Welbeck (see R. Pococke, *Travels through England* (1750), Camden Soc., 1888, p. 73; Thoroton's *History of Nottinghamshire*, ed. J. Throsby, 1797, iii. 360).

Page 270.   *one of the Professors of Divinity:* Prof. J. S. McEwen has identified him for me as Dr Andrew Hunter of the Tron Church (1786), professor of divinity at Edinburgh (1779) and moderator of the General Assembly (1792). Sir James Hunter Blair was powerful in city affairs in the 1770s and provost (1784). Prof. McEwen draws attention to one of Kay's *Portraits*, 'The Modern Hercules destroying the Hydra of Fanaticism': Hercules is Carlyle, and one of the hydra-heads is Hunter's.

Page 272.   *the Howe's:* Admiral Richard Howe (1726–99), who defended the American coast against the French in 1778, and his brother William (1729–1814) who succeeded Gage as commander-in-chief in America in 1775.

Page 273.   The remaining paragraphs of the manuscript are not in Carlyle's hand, and were presumably dictated.

Page 274.   *cognosced:* investigated.

Page 277.   *after the Manner of Plutarch:* Hume thought of writing brief lives in the manner of Plutarch in the 1760s (Mossner, *Life of Hume*, 1954, p. 398).

Page 278.   (1) *3 . . . Sons:* William, who became a law lord (see Index of Persons); James, who served under Cornwallis and became a general; and David, who raised the first Malay regiment in Ceylon.

           (2) *tedious to his Friends:* Carlyle had perhaps too much of Robertson. Henry Mackenzie says that Robertson 'spoke, as became him, a good deal; but there was nothing assuming or authoritative in . . . his discourse. He took every opportunity of calling on his hearers for their share of the dialogue . . .' (Home's *Works*, 1822, i. 55–6).

Page 280.   (1) *a work of Original Genius:* Burns places Blair 'at the head of what may be called fine writing', but records his vanity and occasional neglect; 'in my opinion, Dr Blair is merely an astonishing proof of what industry and application can do' (Edinburgh Commonplace Book, 1787).

           (2) *their unfinish'd walls:* the foundation-stone of Adam's building (now the 'Old College') was laid in 1789, but funds came in slowly and the design was never quite completed.

Index of Persons

Akenside; clerk to House of Commons (1748–62); M.P. for Isle of Wight (1762–8) and Weymouth (1768–74); learned in parliamentary process, 'the Jesuit of the House': 179–80, 260

EDGAR, JAMES, commissioner of customs: 17, 37, 215

EGLINTON. *See* Montgomery

ELCHIES. *See* Grant, Patrick

ELCHO, DAVID (1721–87), Lord; son of 4th Earl of Wemyss; colonel in Prince Charles's 1st troop of horse guards; escaped at Culloden and attainted; d. in Paris: 74

ELDON. *See* Scott, John

ELIBANK. *See* Murray, Patrick

EL(L)IOCK. *See* Veitch

EL(L)IOTT, GEORGE AUGUSTUS (1717–90), Lord Heathfield (1787); 7th son of Sir Gilbert Eliott, 3rd bart. of Stobs; army engineer; major (1749), lieut. col. (1754); col. of 1st light horse in Germany (1759–61); maj. general (1759); governor of Gibraltar (1775) and its defender in siege of 1779–82: 97–8

ELLIOT(T), SIR GILBERT (1722–77), of Minto, 3rd bart. (1766); entered parliament (1754); treasurer of navy (1770); song-writer and brother to Lady Jean Elliott, author of *The Flowers of the Forest*: 22, 119, 125, 126, 128, 149, 151, 157, 161, 171, 179, 180, 192, 202, 204, 219, 260

ELLIOTT, THOMAS, W.S.: 9

ELPHINSTONE, JAMES (1721–1809), schoolmaster and author of translation of Martial with 'too much folly for madness, I think, and too much madness for folly' (Johnson): 252–3

ERSKINE, SIR HENRY (HARRY) (d. 1765), 5th bart. of Alva and Cambuskenneth; lieut. general; M.P. for Ayr (1749) and Anstruther (1754–65); married sister of Alexander Wedderburn (*q.v.*); reputed author of *Garb of Old Gaul*: 183, 207, 219

ERSKINE, JAMES (1679–1754), Lord Grange; 2nd son of 10th Earl of Mar; lord justice-clerk (1710–14); Calvinistic rigorist and libertine: 4, 5, 6–9, 21, 30–2

ERSKINE, RACHEL (née Chiesly), Lady Grange; kidnapped in Edinburgh (1732), imprisoned on St. Kilda 7 years; d. Skye (May 1745): 6, 7–8, 9

FAIRBAIRN, REVD. JOHN (1723–73), minister of Dumbarton (1757): 221

FALL, JENNY; daughter of James Fall of Dunbar; married Sir John Anstruther (1750): 45

FERGUSON, REVD. ADAM (1723–1816), LL.D.; born Logierait, Perthshire; chaplain, Black Watch (1745–54); succeeded Hume as librarian to Society of Advocates (1757); professor of natural philosophy at Edinburgh (1759–64) and of moral philosophy (1764–74, 1776–85); secretary to North's American commission (1778–9); author of *An Essay on the History of Civil Society* (1766), *Institutes of Moral Philosophy* (1772), *History of the Roman Republic* (1782), *Principles of Moral and Political Science* (1792): 25, 45, 93, 141, 142–4, 146, 157, 158, 165, 166–7, 172–3, 183, 196, 199, 200, 203, 204, 205, 206–7, 209, 210, 213, 215, 231, 232, 233, 234, 235, 263, 280, 282

FINLAY, REVD. ROBERT (*c.* 1710–82), D.D., of Drummore; (minister of Inch (Stranraer; 1739); inherited (1761) fortune made by brother David in India: 88, 220

FITZROY, AUGUSTUS HENRY (1735–1811), 3rd Duke of Grafton; secretary of state under Rockingham (1765); Pitt's 1st lord of treasury (1766–70): 265, 272

FLETCHER, ANDREW (1692–1766), Lord Milton; nephew of the 'Patriot' of the same name; advocate (1717); lord of session (1724) and justiciary (1726); lord justice-clerk (1735–48): 119, 131–2, 137, 157, 159, 161–2, 166–7, 183, 186, 192, 194, 197, 198, 202, 203, 210, 235

Index of Persons

Common Sense school; author of *An Inquiry into the Human Mind on the Principles of Common Sense* (1764) and *Essays* on the intellectual (1785) and active (1788) powers of man: 25

ROBERTS, COL., Royal Irish; nephew of Lord Egremont: 224, 226

ROBERTSON, ARCHIBALD, 'The Gospel': 110

ROBERTSON, GEORGE; condemned smuggler: 18

ROBERTSON, REVD. WILLIAM (1721–93), D.D.; historian and leader of the Presbyterian Moderates; minister of Gladsmuir (1743) and Lady Yester's Edinburgh (1758); author of *The History of Scotland* in the reigns of Mary and James VI (1759), *The History of . . . Charles V* (1769), and *The History of America* (1777); principal of Edinburgh University (1762–92); moderator of Gen. Assembly (1763): 24, 25, 29, 33, 34, 45, 58, 62, 65, 66–70, 88, 95, 104, 110, 113, 117, 119, 124–6, 130, 131, 134, 135, 139, 141, 143, 144–9, 156, 157, 159, 162, 163, 164, 168–9, 170–1, 172, 173, 174–5, 176–8, 180–92, 196, 199, 200, 201, 203, 206, 215, 219, 220–1, 224, 228, 229, 231, 235, 239, 240, 241, 242, 252, 253, 254, 255, 256, 277–82

ROBERTSON, WILLIAM (1753–1835); son of prec.; advocate (1775); procurator of the Kirk (1779); judge (Lord Robertson; 1805–26): 145, 147, 221, 229

ROBISON, REVD. ALEXANDER (d. 1761), minister of Tinwald, Dumfriesshire (1697); C's grandfather: 12, 14–15, 16, 21–2, 26, 27, 33, 103, 114, 202–3, 210

RODDAM. *See* Carlyle, Mary

ROEBUCK, JOHN (1718–94), M.D. (Leiden 1742), F.R.S.; Sheffield consultant chemist; collaborator with Garbett; friend of Hume and patron of James Watt: 185–6, 187, 189, 190

ROSS, WILLIAM (1712–54); Master of Ross; 14th and last Lord Ross (1754): 125, 126–7, 157

RUDDIMAN, THOMAS (1674–1757),

classical scholar; schoolmaster of Laurencekirk (*c.* 1695); librarian and press reader in Edinburgh (1700), and printer (1715); librarian to Society of Advocates (1730–52); editor of Gavin Douglas's *Eneados* (1710), Buchanan's *Opera Omnia* (1715), Livy (1751); author of standard *Rudiments of the Latin Tongue* (1714): 25

SCOTT, LIEUT. ALEXANDER: 63

SCOTT, LADY FRANCES (b. 1750); sister of 3rd Duke of Buccleuch; married Archibald Lord Douglas (1783); C's correspondent: 197, 201, 248, 251

SCOTT, HENRY (1746–1812), 3rd Duke of Buccleuch; 2nd son of Francis Earl of Dalkeith (1721–50) and Lady Caroline Campbell (see *infra*, Townshend); married Elizabeth (born 1743) daughter of Duke of Montagu (May 1767); C's patron; pupil of Adam Smith; agricultural improver and promoter of industry: 97, 142, 150, 179, 200, 215, 246, 248–51, 262, 263, 269

SCOTT, JOHN (1751–1838); 1st Earl of Eldon (1799); lord chancellor (1801–6 and 1807–27): 243

SCOTT, WALTER, of Harden: 39, 43

SCOTT, WILLIAM (1745–1836), Lord Stowell (1821) D.C.L.; judge; M.P. for Oxford University (1801–21); distinguished in maritime law: 243

SECKER, MOST REVD. THOMAS (1693–1768), M.D., D.C.L.; rector of St. James' Westminster (1733–50); bishop of Bristol (1735) and Oxford (1737); archbishop of Canterbury (1758): 102

SELKIRK. *See* Hamilton, Dunbar

SELLAR, WILLIAM: 45, 51, 52, 55, 79–80

SETON, ARCHIBALD (d. 1818), Jacobite; administrator in India: 266, 267

SHAFTESBURY. *See* Cooper

SHENSTONE, WILLIAM (1714–63), poet; 'his whole philosophy consisted in living against his will in retirement and in a place which his taste

STEWART, REVD. MATTHEW (1717–85), D.D., F.R.S.; pupil of Robert Simson and McLaurin; minister of Roseneath, Dunoon (1744–7); professor of mathematics at Edinburgh (1747–75); father of Dugald Stewart: 42

STONEFIELD. *See* Campbell, John

STOWELL. *See* Scott, William

STRANGE, SIR ROBERT (1721–92); Orcadian; premier line engraver; Jacobite, out in 1745; knighted 1787: 264

STUART. *See also* Stewart

STUART, ANDREW (d. 1801); 2nd son of Archibald Stuart of Torrance; writer to the signet; guardian of Duke of Hamilton and principal lawyer on that side in Douglas Cause; in France 1762: 138, 215, 262, 263

STUART, JAMES ARCHIBALD (1747–1818); 2nd son of 3rd Earl of Bute and Mary Wortley Montague; M.P. for Rothesay (1768), Bute (1774, 1784, 1806), &c.; succeeded to his mother's estates (1794), taking name of Wortley; succeeded uncle James Stuart Mackenzie (1800) taking name of Mackenzie of Rosehaugh (1803): 135, 240, 242

SUTTIE, SIR GEORGE; lieut. col. and M.P. for E. Lothian: 137–8

TERRICK, RT. REVD. RICHARD (1710–77), D.D.; preacher at the Rolls Chapel (1736–57); canon of Windsor (1742–9) and St. Paul's (1749); bishop of Peterborough (1757) and London (1764): 265

THOM, REVD. WILLIAM (1710–90); minister of Govan (1748–90); a notable eccentric and wit: 52

THOMSON, JAMES (1700–48), native of Roxburghshire; poet; author of *The Seasons* (1726–30), *Liberty* (1735–6), and several plays: 101

TOWNSHEND, CHARLES (1725–67); son of 3rd Viscount Townshend; M.P. for Gt. Yarmouth (1747), Saltash (1754), Harwich (1761); secretary at war (1761); reputed brilliant 'by always doing the opposite of what was expected of him and of what, for that matter, was sensible' (Steven Watson); married widow of Earl of Dalkeith (1755); (*see* Scott, Henry): 86, 87–8, 93–4, 134, 142, 179, 197–201, 203, 219, 231, 249, 251, 260

TULLIDELPH, REVD. THOMAS (d. 1777); professor of divinity, St. Mary's College, St. Andrews (1734); principal (1747–77); 'excelled in close reasoning, and in reconciling dark passages of Scripture', 'one of the ablest . . . speakers of the Moderate side' (Ramsay of Ochtertyre): 129–30, 136

VEITCH, JAMES (1712–93), Lord Eliock; advocate (1738); sheriff-depute for Peeblesshire (1747); M.P. for Dumfriesshire (1755–60); judge (1761); correspondent of Frederick the Great: 156, 170, 178, 215, 235

VIOLETTI, EVA MARIA (1724–1822); Viennese dancer at the Haymarket; married David Garrick (1746): 95, 102, 174–5

WALKINSHAW, KATHERINE; 3rd daughter of John Walkinshaw of Barronfield and Camlachie, Glasgow, a Jacobite agent, and Catherine, daughter of the Jacobite Sir Hugh Paterson of Bannockburn; sister of Prince Charles Edward's mistress Clementina; housekeeper to the mother of George III: 266

WALLACE, GEORGE (d. ?1805); advocate (1754); commissary of Edinburgh (1792); son of Robert Wallace (*q.v.*); author of *A System of the Principles of the Law of Scotland* (1760) and works on ancient Scotch peerages: 161

WALLACE, REVD. ROBERT (1697–1771), D.D.; assistant to Prof. James Gregory the mathematician (1720); minister of New Greyfriars (1733) and New North Church (1738), Edinburgh; moderator of Gen. Assembly (1743); author of *A Dissertation on*

Index of Books

Aristotle, *Poetics*: 22

Baillie, Robert (1559–1662), *Letters and Journals 1637–62* (1775): 6

Barclay, James (rector of Dalkeith school), *Rudiments of the Latin Tongue* (1758): 179

Blackmore, Sir Richard, *Prince Arthur. An Heroick Poem* (1695): 51

Boston, Thomas (minister of Ettrick), *Human Nature in its Fourfold State* (1720; over 20 editions in 50 years): 140

Christianity not founded on Argument; and the True Principle of Gospel-Evidence Assigned [by Henry Dodwell] (1741; answered by Doddridge and many others): 47

Collins, Anthony, *A Discourse of the Grounds and Reasons of the Christian Religion* (1724): 108

Doddridge, Philip (1702–51), *Some Remarkable Passages in the Life of . . . Colonel James Gardiner* (1747): 10

Dodwell. *See* Christianity

Ferguson, Adam, *The History of the Proceedings in the Case of Margaret, 'Sister Peg'* (1761); *An Essay on the History of Civil Society* (1766); *History of the Roman Republic* (1783), transl. into French (1784–91) and German (1784–6): 207, 236

Finlayson, James, *Life of Hugh Blair* (prefixed to Blair's *Sermons*, 1777): 144, 146

Grotius, Hugo, *De Veritate Religionis Christianae* (1627; transl. 1653 and reptd. into the 19th cent.): 36–7

Gurnall, William, *The Christian in Compleat Armour; or, A Treatise on the Saint's War against the Devil* (3 vols; 1655, 1658, 1662): 10

He(i)neccius, Johann (1681–1741), on logic: 22

Hill, John, *Account of . . . Hugh Blair* (1807): 144

Hume, David, *History of England, from the Invasion of Julius Caesar to the Revolution in 1688* (6 vols.; 1754–62); *Philosophical Essays concerning Human Understanding* (1748; later known as *Enquiry . . . Understanding*): 224, 264

Hutcheson, Francis, *An Essay on the Nature and Conduct of the Passions and Affections* (1728): 52

Locke, John, *An Essay concerning Human Understanding* (1690, 1700): 22

Longinus, *On the Sublime* (transl. into French by Boileau, 1674; into English by Welsted, 1712): 22

Molière, Jean Baptiste, *Le Médecin malgré lui* (1666): 22

Peden, Alexander (d. 1686; Covenanter and prophetical preacher), *The Lord's Trumpet sounding an Alarm against Scotland* (1739) and *Life and Prophecies* (by Patrick Walker; frequently reptd. till late 19th cent.): 46

Pictet, Bénédict (Swiss theologian), *Theologia Christiana* (last rev. edn., 1734): 29

Puf(f)endorf, Samuel von (1632–94), writer on jurisprudence; C's reference is prob. to *De Habitu Religionis Christianae* (transl. 1698): 25

Robe, James, *A Short Narrative of the*

317